Robert Roc
The Bea...

Revolver: How the Beatles Re-Imagined Rock 'n' Roll
(2012 – *Backbeat*)

Winner of the 2013 ARSC Award for Excellence -
Rock and Roll Research

"Of the literally thousands of books out there about The Beatles, this one stands head and shoulders above the usual fare. *Revolver: How The Beatles Re-Imagined Rock 'N' Roll* is one of the more original takes on this band I have had the pleasure to read. My hat is off to you Mr. Rodriguez for telling this portion of The Beatles' story in a very compelling manner."
Greg Barbrick – *Blinded by Sound*

"Of the umpteen books written and published about the Beatles in 2012, this will undoubtedly hold as one of the best. It's well-written, well-researched, and presented to us by an author with a sense of authority that makes you eager to read—and listen to—what he has to say."
Jedd Beaudoin – *Popmatters*

"For fans like me who have long held the belief that *Revolver* is the finest album the Beatles made, Rodriguez's book is essential….If Rodriguez wanted me to appreciate *Revolver* even more (which I didn't think was possible), he certainly did his job."
Daniel S. Levine – *The Celebrity Cafe*

"Just when you may have thought the world didn't need another Beatles book, he has delivered a focused, compelling, and impeccably researched volume that emphasizes the artistry in their 1966 classic."
The Other Chad – *Blogcritics*

"Rodriguez crafts a complete and compelling portrait of one of Rock's key years…. In an era when books seem to escape the editor's desk with any number of embarrassing factual errors intact, *Revolver: How The Beatles Re-Imagined Rock 'N' Roll* is a true rarity. This is an impeccably researched work. The writer doesn't let a single question about some of Rock's greatest music go unaddressed."
Mike Segretto – *Psychobabble*

"Speaking of superior work, that's what we have here from Rodriguez…I feel safe in saying his volume on *Revolver* is a major contender for Beatles book of 2012."
Bill King – *Beatlefan*

Fab Four FAQ 2.0: The Beatles' Solo Years, 1970-1980

(2010 – Backbeat)

"A hugely enjoyable, fresh and well researched 500 page book. I loved it."
—Craig Smith, *British Beatles Fan Club*

"Fab Four FAQ 2.0 is a true work of pop scholarship."
—*Schlockmania.com*

"…full of original observations, provocative positions, and humor…"
—*Hellbomb*

"I love it…great tidbits of info, and I learn something new with each page"
—Bart Shore, *Time Warp Radio*

"Fab Four FAQ 2.0 is a must-own"
—Terry Ott, *The Pop Culture Connection*

"… a fascinating book that filled in more blank spaces than I could ever cover
here…a tremendous addition to my collection…"
—Barry Rudolph, *The Music Connection*

"You could easily pick the book up and start reading any page without feeling lost,
and you'll get tons of interesting information in minutes"
—BeatleLinks: *The Beatles Internet Resource Guide*

"There will never be an end to the Beatles' story or probably ways to tell it. *Fab
Four FAQ* and *Fab Four FAQ 2.0* find an interesting way amidst all the old ones.
And that's a great reason why these very enjoyable books are welcome additions."
—Steve Marinucci, *Beatles Examiner*

"A unique perspective of the aftermath of the break-up of the Beatles. Robert offers
a thorough analysis not only of the individual band members' recordings but of the
events that shaped their lives and careers through the tumultuous '70s. A complete
overview of the rumors, the scandals, the triumphs and the music that followed the
end of the best band ever."
—Dennis Mitchell, *Breakfast with the Beatles*

Fab Four FAQ: Everything Left to Know about the Beatles...and More!

(with Stuart Shea; 2007 – Hal Leonard)

"I LOVE this book...Definitely one of the better books out there."
— Chris Carter, host of the nationally syndicated *Breakfast With The Beatles*

"Enthusiasts will thoroughly enjoy this extremely well-researched book."
— Keith Badman, author of *The Beatles Off The Record 1 & 2*

"Gets the grand prize for packing in more obscure and arcane information than any of the dozen books I've read on the Beatles—combined."
Barry Rudolph, recording engineer (Mick Jagger, Ringo Starr, Keith Moon, et al.)

"More than 'just another Beatles book,' this one you can pick up, thumb through, and every stop is interesting." — Eric C. Shoaf, *Vintage Guitar magazine*

"The kind of book you pick up to skim through, but you end up getting sucked in, and before you know it, half an hour has passed." — *Goldmine*

"Finds fresh angles, insightful observations, and delightful Beatlebits...all presented in a delightful writing style that makes me declare — dare I shout it? — 'yeah, yeah yeah!'" — Lou Carlozo, *Chicago Tribune*

"Any book that can teach you this much about something you already know a lot about is a very good book." — Ari Spool, *Seattle Stranger*

"If you thought you knew the Beatles, this book will make you think again."
Glen Boyd, *Blogcritics*

"Shea and Rodriguez have certainly added to the large body of discourse on the Fabs and done it on the whole very well."
—Terry Ott, *Boomer Media Review*

"Brilliant!"
—*ReviewScout.co.*

"Having the information neatly organized in a very well written, thoroughly researched book makes this an enjoyable read, as well as a handy reference tool. Fans who appreciate more serious study should take particular interest in the authors' selections of notable performances by each Beatle on his respective instruments, and the skillful way they articulate their positions. The authors' obsessive attention to detail elevates *Fab Four FAQ* to more than just another book on a ubiquitous subject."
— *Ugly Things magazine*

Solo in the 70s
John, Paul, George,
Ringo: 1970-1980

Robert Rodriguez

Parading Press
Chicago, Illinois

To
Mal, Kathie and Jackie:
fellows travelers who departed too soon

Table of Contents

BEATLES

*Stoking the fires of Fabness past and present was **Capitol/Apple,** who wasted no opportunity in 1974 to commemorate the 10th anniversary of their collective US arrival while tying it to their current individual releases.*

ZIPPED UP MY MOUTH 'CAUSE I WAS STARTING TO DROOL: AN INTRODUCTION

*Could any Beatle fan have known at the time
how good they had it in 1974?*

The year began with Ringo—yes, Ringo—riding high in the US singles charts, giving Paul's Wings a run for their money with the success of his self-titled career re-boot. (His two earlier long players, the genre exercises *Sentimental Journey* and *Beaucoups of Blues*—a pop standard and country-themed collection, respectively—apparently didn't count, at least by the time of his second Atlantic release.) Though he had taken the longest to get his solo act together—as a musical artist, at least—he found himself unexpectedly the right man at the right time with the right product. (The timing was impeccable, though—it must be said—the near-full reunion on Ringo's "I'm The Greatest" was a selling point that was hard to beat.)

The previous year, George, who'd been sidelined for nearly two years in the wake of his *All Things Must Pass/ Concert for Bangladesh* efforts, bounced back with a chart-topping album and single: *Living in the Material World* and "Give Me Love." 1974 saw him, like John, going through a personal downward spiral with the break-up of his marriage and an appetite for blotting out the pain with hard partying. But also like John, he recognized the healing and revitalizing powers of work. As if a triple-record debut followed by a global charity event wasn't enough to demonstrate his ambition, George announced the formation of a new record label, to be followed by a full-scale North American tour by years' end. *Dark Horse* would be an extravaganza unlike any other attempted before in rock, fusing Western and Eastern music onstage—whether audiences were ready for it or not.

John began the year likewise battling some demons. His much-touted togetherness with Yoko had come to a sudden estrangement, while at the same time his commercial fortunes had fallen into decline. (*Mind Games*—the album and single—had been outperformed in the charts by Ringo's latest, released nearly simultaneously.) Beneath his personal and professional travails was the overhanging prospect of losing legal residency in the United States. The battle against forces within the Nixon Administration was entering its third year, with—like the Phil Spector oldies project—little to show for all the court time and legal costs incurred thus far.

As for Paul, he may have had the longest way to go in terms of public redemption. Universally derided by critics and fans alike as the guy who broke up the Beatles, he followed that by putting his non-musician wife in his new band, drawing further scorn. But he soldiered on with a determination that would not be defeated by the naysayers by doing what he did best, cranking out a series of accomplished singles (and patchy albums) before his professionalism and artistry were at last equaled in late 1973 with *Band on the Run*.

It was against this backdrop that Capitol/EMI geared up for a major promotional push of Beatles back catalog, hanging their efforts on the tenth anniversary of the group's American debut on Ed Sullivan's stage. A prevailing wave of fifties/early sixties nostalgia happened to be sweeping the country around that time, and the record company was fully prepared to capitalize on it (pun not intended) by pushing their goods—past and present—in a way that suggested the four ex-bandmates were only a project away from resuming business as usual, with graphics rejoining them as a single entity in a way that they hadn't quite done yet themselves.

For all the wishing and hoping going on within their fandom—the four of them—John, Paul, George and Ringo, were in fact far more socially and professionally close as the year began than they'd been at any time since making their self-titled Apple debut album. While encumbered by various visa issues that kept them from coming and going out of America as they might have liked (owing to the drug-related convictions John, Paul and George all had in common), they also never wasted an opportunity in 1974 to share each other's company, schedule allowing.

One reason might have been the healing that time provided, as bitterness stirred by Paul's December 1970 legal action against the other three faded away. Another reason—a very big reason—was the end of the contract between Apple and ABKCO. With Allen Klein no longer representing three of them, a major obstacle to their resuming a creative partnership had been removed. (To his credit, Paul was quick to move on without shoving the warranted "I told yer so" in their faces.

But there was undoubtedly another factor facilitating the possibility of their working together again. Though a certain segment of the population will forever remain convinced that John's taking up with Yoko Ono was what drove the most successful popular musical act of the sixties apart (as if, but for that, their career would have gone on indefinitely with the Beatles churning out one game-changer after another), life is far more nuanced and complex than that. That's a discussion for another day, but what does seem on its face much more truthful: that when John and Yoko were together, their all-consuming relationship left no room for any other undertaking or partnership. (John Lennon was an all-or-nothing kind of guy, anyway: once committed to a cause, he threw himself in completely.)

With Yoko no longer a day-to-day force in John's life, the door was now open to renewing ties to three others who, at the end of the day, weren't Beatles to each other but friends: sharing a brotherhood understood only by each other. This opportunity happened to come along at a time in their lives when most adults, having established families and careers by this age, begin looking back to the people who meant so much during their formative years.

And so it was that John and Paul began hanging out, as proximity allowed. Ringo, who'd scarcely been out of contact with any of his former bandmates, shared a sort of college roommate existence with John that year, living in a house together in Santa Monica. George, tied up with his own business dealings, remained somewhat distant: wasting few opportunities to verbally dig at Paul McCartney when given a chance, but, at other times, refreshingly candid about the idea of doing something with the other three ("I'm ready for the Beatles to reform and kick down some doors," he told a radio interviewer in 1974.)

All four were spending more and more time in America that year, thus making the opportunity for being in the same room at the same time much more likely. But first, there were their own career juggernauts to keep stoking. Paul found himself in the unique position of enjoying critical and commercial acclaim at last (with *Band on the Run*) while Wings was on blocks, undergoing the process of rebuilding after the departures of guitarist Henry McCullough and drummer Denny Seiwell. Ringo was keen to strike again while the fire was hot and—with John's help—began crafting a follow-up, *Goodnight Vienna*.

George, who'd been so hands-on when it came to Ringo's career, sat this one out, given all on his plate that year. In his own typically generous manner, he put the start-up of his label first, producing a film (*Little Malcolm*) and getting his artist roster (Ravi Shankar and Friends; Splinter) ready to launch before tending to his own project. As for John, no longer convinced of his own commercial potency, he sought redemption by working with others. With his Phil Spector-produced oldies project on indefinite hold, he took on collaborative duties for Harry Nilsson; chiefly as producer, but also as spiritual guide. The two hit a rough patch on the wrong end of some Brandy Alexanders in

A Celebration

Four decades after Mark Lapidos conceived of providing a focal point for fans to celebrate the Beatles' lives and music, The Fest for Beatles Fans (formerly known as Beatlefest) is still going strong. It all began in 1974, after Mark personally received John Lennon's blessing.

March, at The Troubadour Club, but bounced back through art. Though *Pussy Cats* proved a tough sell to record buyers, it did point the way to what would become John's own renewal: a collection of soul-baring confessionals, this time (unlike with *Plastic Ono Band*) presented with a listener-friendly commercial sheen.

So it was by the autumn of the Beatles' tenth anniversary year that fans were witness to a season of riches: new records from John, Paul, George and Ringo all on the charts. John recouped his lost mojo with *Walls and Bridges*, a chart-topping album that spawned a number one single: "Whatever Gets You Thru The Night." (The first out of the Beatle gate with side projects, he was last at achieving this particular benchmark. The co-starring role of one Elton John during his hottest commercial year certainly didn't hurt.)

Hot on his heels was Paul. With Wings now reconstituted, they entered the charts with "Junior's Farm" / "Sally G," a tough rocker backed by a country and western ballad that underscored their versatility. Paul's Apple Records swan song, the single peaked at number three in the states. Ringo followed soon after with a hit single John himself had suggested, arranged and played on: a remake of The Platters' "Only You." It came from *Goodnight Vienna*, his last Apple release (save the best-of collection, *Blast From Your Past*) and like Ringo, it too spawned three hit singles: "No No Song" and the title track followed (though none matched the stellar successes of the earlier album).

Arriving last and with the biggest splash was George, with Ravi Shankar and Billy Preston in tow. The *Dark Horse* tour—under different circumstances—could have been something that would have sealed his status as the ex-Beatle at the top of the food chain. But for many reasons, it proved a misfire: George's being in a dark, dark place chief among them. His annoyance at fans showing up expecting the old George, sitting impatiently through the World Music extravaganza before them when they simply came to rock, showed through all too often. (Then too, there was that fried voice...)

Still, for a year that began by offering Beatle fans much nostalgia for past glories, it drew to a close with plenty to celebrate in the present: hit records from all four, plus the chance to actually see one of them live in concert. Add to this: two albums that year by the Beatles' heirs Badfinger (albeit on Warner Brothers, not Apple; the latter—*Wish You Were Here*—representing their finest hour); a proxy Wings album, *McGear*—from Paul's brother, produced by Paul and featuring members of Wings, and two films from Ringo, *That'll Be The Day* and *Son of Dracula* (one his finest cinematic outing; the second, not so much).

There was also John's heightened visibility, whether assisting Harry Nilsson in the studio or Elton John; the latter collaborations resulted in #1 hits for each man. By year's end, there'd been weeks of a media blitz featuring the return of the old John on radio and TV: relaxed, funny and bereft of any hectoring causes that tended to alienate the fan base. Less than a year away from an unprecedented disappearing act that would see him out of the recording business indefinitely, it was hard to escape him, even in the least likely of settings. (John showed up to chat with Howard Cosell on *Monday Night Football*, of all places, in December; their meeting would carry chilling resonance six years later.)

One last benchmark must be added to the year in review: on December 19, George and Paul were filmed at New York's Plaza Hotel—the same locale where they'd been besieged a decade before at the dawn of American Beatlemania—signing papers for the group's official, legal dissolution. At Disney World in Florida ten days later, John's signature on the docs made it all official. (Ringo had signed in England earlier.) With the dissolution of their formal ties, could this act have conversely freed them to work together again, of their own volition?

As we know, it didn't: the last best chance they'd had in five years to resume musical relations came and went. With John's return to the Dakota and subsequent announcement that he was taking time away to raise his child, the second half of the seventies proceeded along, seeing Ringo's commercial fortunes recede, George rebound with his two strongest back-to-back releases in years and Paul go from strength-to-strength, culminating in his receiving an award from the folks at Guinness in 1979 as the "all-time best-selling songwriter and recording artist" in history. The window would not re-open again until late 1980, when each ex-Beatle, including the newly-unretired John Lennon, told Ringo that they would work on his new album.

1970 through 1980 represented years that saw unexpected triumphs and tragedies among the former Beatles. Years in the making, their announced break-up in 1970 came to most fans as a shock, though far less of the truly epic one that the world first learned of on a cold December night ten years on. Between those two dark milestones lay a decade as eventful as the one that had made them stars in the first place, though far less chronicled.

It unfolded like an unmapped road: there'd really been no precedent for a pop act to go their separate ways and for each member go on to successes on their own. But then again, there was no precedent for the Beatles: a group comprised of four distinct personalities and talents that, as a whole, seemed to heighten each other's strengths while canceling each other's weaknesses. The legions that loved them worldwide seemed to understand this intuitively: might the ceaseless clamor for a reunion by the public throughout the decade been less out of nostalgia for an enjoyable part of their youth than it was an astute desire by fans to see the four musicians operating under optimum conditions once more?

The answer to this sort of hypothetical might depend on which end of the decade it was being asked. In 1970, fans might have had their expectations most heightened for the two "top tier" Beatles, but as reality played out, these expectations were confounded. No one would have dared believe that Ringo would become the ex-Beatle to chart two number one singles from the same album, a feat none of the others duplicated (while living). The "Quiet One" made the biggest splash in the marketplace upon arrival, with a three-album set and hit single that topped charts round the world—an achievement no one would've expected not to come from John or Paul first. But it would prove to be an accomplishment that was far easier to achieve than it was to sustain.

Though the first to assert his independence from the group he'd started as a teen, John Lennon found it difficult to truly focus on a recording career. He was an artist of self-expression, spread over an array of media, and though a self-professed singles junkie, his own fortunes in this area were only as successful as his undivided commitment with each one. But he alone among the ex-Beatles was facing a battle few entertainers ever shared: the full force of the US government to dislodge him from the land he'd hoped to make his home. That his output was inconsistent, untill he finally made the decision to walk away entirely, is understood within the context of what weighed upon him. That his solo output has endured as well as it has, given the short period he actively recorded, speaks well of his talents.

Though the Beatle most committed to keeping the machinery running during their lifetime, Paul had the most difficulty eliciting respect from the public once that act folded. Factual truth aside, it was he who bore the brunt of disfavor in terms of blame for the group's split. (His *McCartney* emancipation announcement, coupled with legal action against the other three by 1970's end, assured this; nowadays, with memories of these events long faded, it's Yoko who gets held liable.) His wildly uneven recorded output seemed to reveal a clothes-less emperor: for every "Maybe I'm Amazed" or "Uncle Albert/ Admiral Halsey," there were far too many "Mary Had A Little Lamb"s or "Mumbo"s to get him the due his talents warranted. As if blame for the break-up wasn't enough, some wondered if the prime mover behind the creation of *Sgt. Pepper* or *Abbey Road* really *was* dead.

But Paul's commitment to reclaiming past glories within the arena best-suited to him was indomitable. Through force of will, he made his photographer wife a musician: a full-time partner and bandmate occupying the space John Lennon once did in his life. A supporting cast was drafted, and in time, he was able to regain his place in the musical world, within a spotlight he didn't need to share with three other distinct personas. But for all the success, which included a triumphant world tour that showed everyone that there were second acts in life (literally), it was not the same as what he'd once had. The Beatles never had to answer critics with a "Silly Love Songs."

Solo in the 70s explores new avenues within the study of their first post-split decade, begun with *Fab Four FAQ 2.0*. Just as there are numerous volumes out there exploring one facet or another of The Beatles' story throughout the sixties as a whole, their post-union history is equally compelling, offering rich areas for understanding their lives and work: what shaped the end product and influenced artistic decisions made or not made. This volume expands the lens to cover other players in their story, as well as the reverberations of what they did in the sixties and how it lived on, competing for bandwidth alongside their individual efforts.

At this distance, understanding the context within which they created becomes harder to grasp—even if you were there. Terrestrial radio doesn't place things in their original settings: you are as likely to hear "Imagine" on the radio today alongside "Hurt So Good" as you are "Tales of Brave Ulysses." That setting tells you nothing about what the record meant when it was new, nor is that radio's job. Still, it's how most people experience this music in their daily lives. But for the truly curious wondering how it all came into being, books like this are made.

Much of what's presented here comes in the familiar form of free-standing chapters that invite you to begin the journey wherever your interests pull you in. But beyond this, I've put together a day-by-day timeline, giving a true real-time context for what went on in their lives— and everyone's—in the rock world. I hope you will find it valuable for the insight it offers into how the decade unfolded, and exactly what the lay of the musical landscape looked like when their post-Beatles music was new.

Robert Rodriguez
Summer 2013
Revolverbook.com

1964 - 1974

LENNON/ONO
with The Plastic Ono Band

INSTANT KARMA!
B/w Who has seen the wind?
Produced by Phil Spector
Ritten, Recorded, Remixed 27th Jan 1970

APPLE RECORDS   APPLES 1003

The near-simultaneous arrival of "Instant Karma" in stores so soon after it was written and recorded was an achievement John touted proudly. Only in the download era could he have reached his goal any faster.

CHAPTER 1

HUNG ON THE TELLY:
A SELECTION OF PROMO FILMS -
PART ONE

As with so much else, the Beatles—collectively and individually—
also contributed to the evolution and development of the rock
music video. As detailed in my *Revolver* book, promotional
films designed to serve as a substitute for personal television appearances
with each single release were something that the group was quite
pioneering with: maintaining high production values informed by the
style that their feature films and behind-the-camera talents involved.

This recognition of the value of visual art carried over into the solo
years, though with a decided lack of consistency. John, who'd been
busy making films with Yoko since their first partnering up, had initially
compulsively documented nearly every waking moment, leaving a
wealth of personal footage for future chroniclers. But his habits were
capricious: while 1968 and 1969 yielded a mountain of footage, 1970
saw little of his musical life captured—a real shame, considering the
landmark status of *Plastic Ono Band*. The following year's *Imagine*
project would make up for it, but afterward, his engagement with
getting his work life on camera became sporadic, typically limited to
singles promos and little else.

George—the future film producer—might have been expected to
have shown an interest. But not until four years and three studio albums
into their break-up did he produce promo films of any kind. Thereafter,
it was feast-or-famine with him; for some projects, like *Thirty-Three
& 1/3*, he went all out. For others, like *Extra Texture*, he couldn't be
bothered. His attitude was echoed by Ringo, who ran hot and cold in
the video department: early singles, yes; later projects, all or nothing.

Paul at least took the time to represent his newest releases nearly
always with some kind of visual documentation/promotional tool. At
times, he would even revert to Beatle habit and create more than one
promo for the same song (e.g. "Mary Had A Little Lamb"). While some
of the efforts issued under his name (or Wings) are laughably crude by
even Beatle standards, other times he really went all out to turn in an
effort that stood the test of time.

1

Here is part one of an overview of the films they produced; some of which have circulated widely, others not so much.

"INSTANT KARMA" (1970)

While the familiar *Top of the Pops* "performances" (the "knitting" and the "cue card" clips, so-designated by fans for Yoko's on-camera activity) have become an established part of John's video record (issued to the public on the various home video compilations), the first publicly aired clip has all but vanished. It was a seemingly randomly assembled montage, providing nothing more than arbitrary visual accompaniment to John's "insta-single."

The black-and-white footage included film shot at Apple throughout 1968 and 1969 (a smiling Paul McCartney is seen at one point), as well as portions of *Apotheosis 2*—the John & Yoko hot air balloon art film, showing the caped duo in the snow-struck Suffolk countryside. Other visuals include John in a suit for the December 1969 *Man of the Decade* British TV documentary; John in a clown's nose from "The World of John and Yoko" (also a British TV documentary from December 1969) and the apparently-not-completely-disgraced "Magic Alex" Mardas. This promo was screened on *Top of the Pops* on February 5, 1970.

On February 11, John and an entourage that included his *Live Peace In Toronto* band (save Clapton), plus Mal Evans and Irish photographer and future rock journalist, B.P. Fallon, traipsed down to the studio home of *Top of the Pops* to film a pair of actual performance clips. With John on piano and sporting a none-too-subtle set of headphone monitors; Klaus and drummer Alan White on their usual instruments and Yoko (serving as an onstage focal point around which all activity was staged), the ensemble mimed along to the record. One wonders, with two separate performances captured (that included a distinct variance in the camera work and a change of clothing), why the musical approach changed: the clip broadcast on February 12 is purely the record, while the second one aired one week later features a heavily-echoed live vocal atop the backing.

Further distinctions: in the February 12 broadcast, John is wearing a black turtleneck; Yoko is blindfolded and knitting; the stage includes two "bassists": Klaus, plus Fallon (in floppy hat and furry vest) ludicrously miming along in a manner seen regularly on US television at the time from Danny Partridge; Mal is playing tambourine and Apple's "House Hippie" Richard Dilello can be seen (if you watch carefully) snapping away. The direction focuses mostly on John's face throughout.

In the February 19 clip, John is now wearing a denim jacket, with a "People For Peace" armband. While Yoko still wears her turtleneck (and blind fold), she's now holding up cards, reading variously "Smile," "Peace" and "Hope." (As the mic she's seen intoning into throughout is apparently not live, she was spared the indignity of being gagged.) Fallon, now hatless, is behind John at the start, but mounts the stage to play an instrument better suited to his skill set: Mal's tambourine. Overall, this edit captures much more of the ambiance, with frequent shots of White's stellar work and the studio dancers.

Both performance promos are terrifically engaging, providing suitably dynamic visuals to a powerful song.

"SENTIMENTAL JOURNEY" (1970)

With the UK release of Ringo's first solo album pending, on March 15, he filmed a promo for the title track—a song *not* considered for single release. Directed by John Gilbert and produced by Neil Aspinall (who'd been previously tasked with compiling the "Something" promo), it was shot at London's Talk of the Town club. The performance featured a live vocal over a mono backing track, coming off like an extension of *Magical Mystery Tour*'s "Your Mother Should Know" finale: an old time staging of a cabaret act, bearing no connection whatsoever to anything going on in the musical world inhabited by Mr. Starkey's peers in 1970.

Ringo appears much as he does on the album's back cover (albeit sporting the suit jacket he was last seen wearing on the *Abbey Road* cover), with the addition of a pink bow tie. For visual interest, he's flanked by white-clad dancers, segregated by gender; meanwhile, a huge backdrop depicting Liverpool's Empress Pub looms behind the club's orchestra. Patrons at tables ring the stage, and—adding a final touch of eye candy—a platform drops near the song's end, bearing Apple artist Doris Troy, Madeline Bell and Marsha Hunt, all on backing vocals.

Though such an array of spectacle might have overwhelmed a lesser talent, the manifest Starr charm manages to shine through. In the end, the success of the effort depends in large part on how endearing one finds him. In America, it screened—fittingly enough—on The *Ed Sullivan Show*; in Britain, David Frost.

"MAYBE I'M AMAZED" (1970)

One day before the McCartney album's US release, this promotional clip aired on *The Ed Sullivan Show*. It was directed by Charlie Jenkins, who'd worked on *Yellow Submarine* ("Special Sequences") and who would, in 1972, direct Cat Stevens' "Moonshadow" animated video. Produced by the McCartneys, the film for this non-single track was, in its way, the audio-visual equivalent of Paul's self-interview broadside: a statement evoking the pleasures of home and family who were now the focus of his life and work. Rather than performance or recording footage, it was a slide show: an array of pictures very much echoing the images of Paul, Linda, Heather and Mary gracing the McCartney inner gatefold.

Paul would one day become much more ambitious with the creation of the promotional visual accompaniments to his recordings, but this one, with its complete lack of pretension, was a perfect representation of the parent album.

"IT DON'T COME EASY" (1971)

Though Ringo had two albums under his belt by the time this single was issued, as the real start of his post-Beatles career, much was riding on its success. This may have informed the decision to produce two separate promo films for this tune, a gift from George to jump-start the drummer's brand.

The first was one assembled by Ringo himself: a sort of found object montage, with some footage going back as far as late 1967 and the *Candy* film. The bulk of the clips look like home movies: shots of pets, Ringo's backyard (at Sunny Heights) and visual non-sequiturs (such as Ringo playing an undersized drum kit with ping-pong paddles). Some nodding penguin statuary serves as a running motif. This version, since issued on the *Photograph* compilation on the DVD reel, was broadcast on *Top of the Pops* on April 22.

One week later, the second "It Don't Come Easy" clip aired on the same show. This one—known as the "snow" video—was shot in Norway, while Ringo was on location to take part in Cilla Black's *Cilla in Scandinavia* television special. It's not a terribly ambitious affair, consisting of shots of Ringo alternately playing a piano while wearing mittens and cavorting (ineptly on skis ala *Help!*'s "Ticket To Ride" sequence) in the snow. Probably for the reason that there wasn't much to it did this promo make it to the airwaves via *Top of the Pops* two days after it was filmed.

"BACK OFF BOOGALOO" (1972)

As contrasted with his previous video efforts, the promo for Ringo's second rock single seemed to have been produced with a great detail more care. It was directed by one Tom Taylor and shot at John's Tittenhurst Park estate during the time Ringo performed frequent house-sitting duties (he would buy it from John in September 1973).

A recurring motif connected with this release is the Frankenstein monster imagery, played for laughs. It adorns the picture sleeve (where the creature is represented by a rubber-masked individual, clutching a cigar), while ads proclaimed "Another monster from Apple." Then there is this video, which starred a hirsute Ringo (who could easily pass for a Wolfman, as-is), strolling the grounds, apparently in search of his monster.

Ringo's "monsterous" second rock single showed his musical partnership with George intact. The song was widely regarded as a slap at Paul, something Ringo always denied.

The latter stays hiding, watching him from a safe distance, until Ringo can take it no more: he spots the monster and runs to him, arms outstretched; the two joyously embrace. The remainder of the film depicts them together happily walking the grounds and taking tea. (King Kong makes a cameo appearance.)

Exactly who played the towering co-lead has been a matter of considerable conjecture. There's been the suggestion that it was Harry Nilsson, who was certainly tall ("I said Jesus..."). If true, it could explain the monster theme, as the Apple film *Son of Dracula* (then titled *Count Downe*) was in pre-production at the time. But this

5

doesn't appear likely: first, a close-up of the monster's face about midway through makes it look as though someone considerably older than Harry was playing him. More importantly, if it was him, then he displayed significantly more charisma and acting chops in this promo than he would in the feature film the two made together.

"Back Off Boogaloo" aired on *Top of the Pops* on April 6.

"HELEN WHEELS," "MAMUNIA" and "BAND ON THE RUN" (1973-4, 1978)

By this time in Paul's post-Beatles career, he'd enjoyed a steady run of chart and touring successes, none of which earned him the esteem he drew so effortlessly as a Beatle. Facing down the potentially catastrophic loss of 40% of Wings this year, he rebounded, not only staying on track commercially but at last drawing the laurels he so clearly craved. *Band on the Run* restored his fortunes and placed him atop the ex-Beatle heap of highest public acclaim, a position he'd more or less retain at least through the end of the decade.

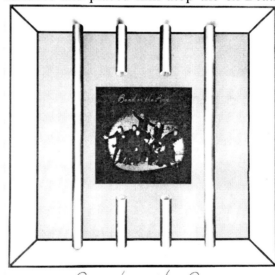

The first taste of what he, Linda and Denny had created in Lagos arrived with the "Helen Wheels" single. This jaunty rocker was issued in advance of the album, though in America, its stand-alone status was denied when Capitol insisted it be added to *Band on the Run*. Released in the fall of 1973, the single was promoted with a video far more visually engaging than what he's turned in for "Mary Had A Little

Band on the Run
is
Paul McCartney and Wings
NEW LP OUT NOW

Recorded after setbacks that could've crippled a lesser act (the departures of their drummer and lead guitarist on the eve of the sessions), Band on the Run put Paul back into the public's (and critic's) good graces. In America, it yielded three hit singles – an accomplishment bettered chart-wise only by Ringo's concurrent release.

6

Lamb," "Hi Hi Hi" / "C Moon" or "My Love," all of which had been straight performance clips.

This one, while remaining very much of its time, showed a marked forward movement in getting past what had been more or less perfunctory efforts. To begin with, it reunited Paul with director Michael Lindsay-Hogg for the first time since the *Let It Be* film. Now one can make the case that what they came up with in this instance hardly matched the timeless artistic heights of the work he'd done in the sixties; not just with the Beatles' "Paperback Writer" / "Rain" and "Hey Jude" / "Revolution" promos, but also his work with the Rolling Stones, The Who, et al. But as an encapsulation of mullets and wide lapels, it's hard to beat.

One thing for certain the short underscores is that the sound you hear was produced by the trio alone: they are shown at their respective instruments, and in Paul's case: drums, bass and guitar. Though he's sometimes given credit for being a better hand behind the kit than he actually is, Paul did a decent job on the album as a whole, even impressing Keith Moon, who assumed it was some talented unknown. Beyond the shots of them performing, there is a recurring sequence of the McCartneys and Denny on the road, with Paul behind the wheel (naturally).

It raises an interesting aside about their attitude toward their own history. In the driving sequences, Linda is seen wearing a fur collar on her jacket. To be sure, her animal rights activism hadn't yet kicked in as fully as it one day would, but one or both of the McCartneys must have found the fashion of cruelty embarrassing. By the time of the 2007 *McCartney Years* DVD set, the "Helen Wheels" clip had been altered and rendered retroactively PC: an unsubtle digital effect rendered the offending garment sufficiently furless (while drawing attention to itself). Though Linda had moved on to the next level of existence by the time this was made public, her legacy of good works was thus preserved.

One of the least familiar cuts on the *Band on the Run* album was the side two opener. "Mamunia," an acoustic number augmented with deft synthesizer touches, was never a part of Paul's live set list, nor did it ever garner much in the way of airplay. And yet, one suspects it was a tune that Paul once harbored greater ambitions for. To begin with, it was initially coupled with "Jet" when first released in the US (on January 28, 1974). This changed on February 19—one day after its issue in the UK—when the B-side was switched to "Let Me Roll It," matching the overseas issue.

One doesn't stop the presses casually. Though double A-side singles

The first pressing of "Jet" in the US featured "Mamunia" on the flip but consideration of the song for A-side status caused Paul to pull the plug and switch it out for "Let Me Roll It." The latter tune has been a concert staple for years; "Mamunia" has not.

were hardly unknown in Paul's world, it would appear that "Mamunia" was under serious consideration as a separate A-side release and he may not have wished for it to stay buried beneath "Jet." Also suggesting this was the fact that he commissioned a promo film for it: something he hadn't done for "Jet"—a song he had resisted issuing as a single at all until his hand was forced by radio stations (that had begun airing their own edited versions) and Capitol's Al Coury. (Technically, that's not completely true: apparently a perfunctory clip was assembled quickly by MPL, basically a slide show set to the song—one that depicted only Paul, Linda and the lyrics, omitting Denny completely—and vanished after airing.)

The "Mamunia" promo was almost entirely animated and did not feature likenesses of Paul or any Wings members at all. Instead, it was a fairly literal interpretation of the lyrics, produced as though for a children's after school special. Only at the very end does a live figure appear: clad in a yellow rain slicker, he's missing his frontmost teeth (pretty much establishing he's English)—while not readily identifiable as anyone connected with McCartney. Credit for the direction of this clip goes to one "Jim Quick." Whoever he was, he was not available as of the 1990s, when the Wings/McCartney *Club Sandwich* fanzine attempted to track him down for a follow-up.

"Band on the Run" was another reluctant single issue from Paul. When album sales momentum stirred by "Jet" began to dissipate, the title track was then released. Only then did what was critically regarded as Paul's finest post-Beatles hour catch fire, topping the album charts for four weeks (on three separate occasions) between April and June, the last time coinciding with "Band on the Run" hitting number one on the US singles chart. What made this traction impressive was the lack of any concerted promotional push: there were no live appearances during this time, and what's come to be called the "official" video for the song did not exist. Yet.

In 1974, Michael Coulson was an English university student, in his final year at the Hornsey College of Art. For a senior project, he was moved to create an animated film telling the story of the Beatles in graphic form, set to the instrumental opening of "Band on the Run." (It was his mentor at the school who persuaded him to go ahead and use the entire song.) For imagery, a former school librarian granted Coulson access to years of pop culture magazines, which—greatly influenced by the aforementioned Charlie Jenkins' work in *Yellow Submarine* (specifically, the "Eleanor Rigby" sequence)—he then animated, following an easily discerned chronological pattern.

It would take Coulson two years of painstaking work to complete his film. The results are mightily impressive and wholly worthy of his influences, which also included equally Richard Lester and Terry Gilliam. That said, don't look for anything remotely concerning Wings or a band on the run. His film is strictly a Beatles affair, and a damned good one. It was nominated for—and received—a Gold Star Award in 1978 at the Movie Maker Young Filmmakers competition. As for Coulson, he went on to a career in film that included producing videos for a number of other artists; most notably, Peter Gabriel.

"PHOTOGRAPH" (1973)

Until resurfacing not long ago on YouTube (and then vanishing again), the promo film for Ringo's first number-one single was something of a unicorn—believed by many to have existed, but remaining unseen by most and longed for by all. Happily, this recent sighting will be enough to convince the doubters that it's no will o' the wisp: what now remains is for this elusive clip to get some sort of official sanction for release, perhaps as a bonus for a remaster upgrade of the *Ringo* album.

It was filmed at Tittenhurst, which Ringo took ownership of that year. While it's nothing that should be regarded as great visual art, it fascinates due to its lack of familiarity, as well as the fact that it captured Ringo at a time where he was just re-establishing himself as a musical force, after spending the first several years of the decade working in film. From 1974 onward, he'd be a near-constant presence in public; not so much at the time this film was shot.

The promo began, depicting Ringo in a throne-like chair in the garden. Unlike other efforts he'd filmed to this point, Ringo *did* at least suggest that he was singing the song, but covered his mouth while doing so. The usual visual incongruities followed, including a picture frame containing a live woman; a gorilla and other animals; motor-powered furniture; Ringo shooting a (toy) sub-machine gun and—most bizarrely—a shot of a Ziggy Stardust-era David Bowie.

It was produced by the late Michael Hurlls, in cooperation with *Top of the Pops*, which broadcast it—one time only—on November 1: a couple of weeks after the single was issued in Britain.

ONE HAND CLAPPING and "JUNIOR'S FARM" (1974)

With Wings once again re-constituted with the 1974 additions of Jimmy McCulloch and Geoff Britton, Paul had been chomping at the bit to get his group on the road again. *Band on the Run* had come and gone without a supporting tour as he spent the year rebuilding, helping out his brother on the *McGear* album, doing a few tracks in Nashville, and laying down some Linda compositions (that would sit unreleased until after she died). Paul had also spent time hanging around with John, as if angling for an opening to resume their songwriting partnership. This never happened, of course, but it came awfully close.

Back in London in August, the band assembled at EMI's home-like Abbey Road recording facility, doing a little recording and much rehearsing: all of which was documented on film for a project dubbed *One Hand Clapping*. Directed by David Litchfield (whose credits did not include directing; he was mostly a camera operator and effect technician), the film ran fifty-five minutes long and was intended for television, probably in advance of their next tour. Seemingly, Paul had learned his lesson from the universally-panned *James Paul McCartney* special approach over a year earlier. This time out, he would give fans what they really wanted to see. (Although— inexplicably—he throws in a performance of the hoary 1926 standard, "Baby Face." It's as if the man simply couldn't help himself).

Essentially, the film presented the band at work, with very little in the way of departing from the script. Songs are performed; played back; commented upon. Clearly, Macca wanted the public to get to know the band, for each is afforded a brief vignette. (Britton, the karate pro, is seen performing a few moves; in some shots, he's garbed in martial arts attire while behind the kit.) Songs offered were a mix of *Band on the*

Run tracks: the title song; "Jet"; "Bluebird"; and an odd clip of Paul singing a live vocal to "Nineteen Hundred and Eighty-Five" over the original backing; plus newer songs like the concert pounder "Soily," as well as past singles like "Live and Let Die" (shown with full orchestra) and "C Moon." No Beatles songs were attempted, although the band did take a fair stab at Bo Donaldson and the Heywood's current hit, "Billy Don't Be A Hero."

Of interest to fans are the odds and ends strewn throughout, like "Suicide," a song going back to the *McCartney* album, where a snippet of it was heard at the end of "Hot As Sun/Glasses." "Let's Love," his composition for Peggy Lee from that same year, was also performed, as was a throwaway called "I'll Give You A Ring," later issued on the B-side to 1982's "Take It Away."

Exactly why the film never aired is not known, only surmised. Speculation is that Litchfield, using the same filming method that Tony Palmer had on *200 Motels* (video-shoot-to-film transfer) wasn't quite as adept and the results simply looked sub-par for a broadcast. When the work was finally given a release in 2010 as part of the *Band on the Run* deluxe remaster package, it was revealed as eminently watchable while falling short of what one would expect to see for a production on this level. Aside from a short film on Britton's karate career (*Open Hand*), Litchfield never directed again.

The "Junior's Farm" rehearsal sequence, shot at EMI's Abbey Road facility, was sent out to serve as a promo at the time, airing in France and Australia, apparently. But the more enduring take was the glossy one shot for *Top of the Pops*, broadcast on November 21. It remains the definitive visual documentation of Wings with Geoff Britton on drums; it was later issued as part of the *McCartney Years* DVD set.

"ONLY YOU" (1974)

With Ringo now a hot commodity in the wake of his eponymous album's success (*three* hit singles, two of them number ones), EMI was prepared to offer up a good-sized budget for a proper video for the first single from the follow-up album: none of the previously acceptable montages would do. The shoot took place on November 14 in Los Angeles: at considerable expense, a helicopter was hired to lower an 800-pound flying saucer model in from the sky, big enough to hold the Starr. It's shown "flying" past the Hollywood sign, establishing without a doubt the locale. The saucer then lands atop the landmark Capitol

The Day the Earth Stood Still motif tied to Ringo's Goodnight Vienna album manifested itself in the packaging, ad campaign and promo film; not in the music itself.

Records tower on Vine, near Yucca; on the rooftop, Harry Nilsson, lounging in a folding chair, awaits.

Wearing his Klaatu space suit and a pair of starred sunglasses (as was Harry), Ringo crooned the tune, as Harry read a copy of the trade journal, *Radio and Records* (it bears Ringo's photo on the cover, as well as the headline, "Elton Knocked Unconscious in Greensboro"). He disrupts his smoking and reading to periodically emote into the microphone dangling before him. Ringo does a creditable job of miming, even when wearing an arrow-through-the-head comic embellishment during the song's spoken word bridge.

The film continued in this lighthearted vein, finally ending with an overhead shot revealing not only the two friends swaying to the fade-out, but also a thirty-foot "Gort" and similarly-sized Ringo-as-Klaatu atop the tower. (The giant Ringo replica had been repurposed from statuary purchased from a car dealership.) The promo and *Goodnight Vienna* TV commercial, shot the same day, were directed by the acclaimed producer and director Stanley Dorfman. He was still with the BBC at the time, and had already enjoyed an eventful career, working with artists ranging from Dusty Springfield and Bobbie Gentry to—in one of rock's most fabled vignettes—Lulu's TV show on the night when Jimi Hendrix went off the reservation with an impromptu tribute to Cream (deftly managing to avoid an on-air duet with the show's host).

The TV spot—which exists in three different running times—opened with Ringo (still as Klaatu) amidst a marching band, parading as it were (literally). He gets inside the landed space craft, which ascends into the smoggy Los Angeles sky, depositing him atop the Capitol tower, where he's last seen waving to fans below. The voice over features John and Ringo ("Is that Ringo Starr advertising his new album *Goodnight Vienna* on Apple Records and tapes?" "It certainly is, John!"). The favor would be returned with Ringo contributing likewise to John's *Walls and Bridges* TV spot—an ad ("Listen to this television commercial") that relied on musical excerpts and the album's unique packaging to get its point across. All in all, a fine time in history to be a Beatles fan.

"WHATEVER GETS YOU THRU THE NIGHT" and "#9 DREAM" (1974)

There have been at least a pair of officially sanctioned John Lennon video compilations made available since the advent of home video: *The John Lennon Collection* and *Lennon Legend*. Where promos did not exist to represent a handful of hit singles, Yoko—as guardian of Lennon estate—commissioned new films, put together under her direction. When serving to fill some gaps, this can be useful: songs that lacked contemporaneous video representation (like "Power to the People" and "Happy Xmas," for instance), benefited by their inclusion within these compilations.

Where things can get warped is when revisionism takes the place of fulfilling an accurate representation of artistic intent. Since John is no longer around to speak for himself, we must look to what he did do in his lifetime to see for ourselves how he intended his work to be presented. In the case of the two singles released from 1974's *Walls and Bridges*, what now exists as part of the visual record represents a serious divergence from the choices he made when he was alive.

It's not a coincidence that the most egregious whitewashing of history occurred on the one album of original material John made completely apart from Yoko: one that not only went to number one, but also spawned a chart-topping single—a feat that not even *Imagine* accomplished. While the couple was separated during this time, John completed *two* albums (this plus *Rock 'N' Roll*); produced a Harry Nilsson album (*Pussy Cats*); recorded with Ringo ("Goodnight Vienna"—which he wrote—plus "Only You") and Mick Jagger ("Too Many Cooks"—which he also produced); recorded with Elton John and David Bowie (both "Lucy in the Sky with Diamonds" and "Fame" topped the US charts). He also renewed personal ties with Paul and George, and appeared frequently on radio and TV. If this was a "Lost Weekend," everyone's should be so productive.

Listen To
This Dream.

#9 DREAM. b/w What You Got

from

John Lennon's
Walls and Bridges
SW-3411

Walls and Bridges' arrival was coordinated with his novel "Listen to this..." campaign, which took the form of buttons, bumper stickers, billboards and practically anything else you can think of.

On November 15 (the day after Ringo's LA shoot), John was filmed walking around New York City—in Central Park; at the Beacon Theater (where the show *Sgt. Pepper's Lonely Hearts Club Band on the Road* had just opened)—at Tiffany & Company jewelers—for the express purpose of getting footage for the two promos. Wearing a long black coat, platform shoes and a floppy hat (with a feather), John looked more at ease and relaxed than he had in years: playing for the camera, interacting with fans, posing with one of the stars of the stage show. Whatever else he may have been going through, he appeared to be having the time of his life.

A promo for "Whatever Gets You Thru The Night" was assembled quickly (well, the single *was* already out), edited at a local college facility. Other footage was set aside to be used later for "#9 Dream"; *Top of the Pops* ran it on February 27, 1975—but, per prevailing BBC practice—did not archive it. Still more footage, literally left on the cutting room floor, was scooped up by a student: years later, it was put up at auction and bought (for over $50,000) by Yoko, who used it to construct a video for "Mind Games."

The latter-day videos now in circulation for these two songs in no way represent John's design at the time. Instead, they come off like valentines from John to Yoko: the first being part night scenes of New York City (looking much like some kind of alternate *Saturday Night Live* opening), and part animation of John's drawings, covering all years of their marriage. The second one even more boldly re-writes history: not only is it loaded with plenty of "John loves Yoko" shots, but also had the cheek to insert shots of Yoko calling John (from the *Imagine* long-form video) over the part of the song where *May Pang* says his name.

By design, it is by these films that future generations will know John's work. Only those that take the time to do the research will ever know the falsity of these representations.

"DARK HORSE" and "DING DONG DING DONG" (1974)

Last out of the gate when it came to producing music videos for his work was George. The first ex-Beatle to score a number one single, he therefore may have felt he didn't need to. For such a late starter, he was a quick learner: though the first of the two he produced for the *Dark Horse* album was purely a performance video, the second featured a concept and a big dose of humor. *Dark Horse*—the label, album and tour—was a burdensome undertaking, plagued by delays and the strain it put on its creator's vocal chords; the defining characteristic in the minds of most observers.

In truth, he'd simply put too big a burden on himself to carry through in too short a time. Typical of the way the year was going was the fact that the album itself the tour was ostensibly built around did not arrive in stores until the tour was three-quarters over. In a professional atmosphere, all the promotional pieces would have been in place before he ever even landed on US soil. Instead, even the relatively simple task of creating a straightforward music video for his new single would have to be done on the fly.

For two days—October 30 and 31—George and his entourage prepared for the grueling road show with a regimen of rehearsals at A&M Studios in Los Angeles. It

To roll out the "Dark Horse" single – tied to the album and tour of the same name - George produced a quick-and-dirty music video that few people saw at the time.

was while there that the "Dark Horse" promo was shot. (George would write in the *I Me Mine* book that the song was recorded "live" during rehearsals.) The clip depicts the band on a crowded stage, in performance mode. Oddly, the existing print in circulation does not feature the entire song, but a shortened version that begins with the third verse, followed by two choruses. Surely a better print exists than what has been making the rounds, which is very dark. For all the half-hearted effort that went into producing it, the only record of its having aired took place in France in 1977.

Following the end of the tour a week before Boxing Day and George's return to England, the promo for the next single, "Ding Dong Ding Dong," was shot at Friar Park. This one displayed much more effort, as well as a theme: riffing off the song's incessant "Ring out the old /Ring in the new" sentiments, it featured George revisiting the past several times, in the form of costuming himself as his earlier incarnations: leather-jacketed Hamburg; collarless suit Beatle circa 1963 (although the Rickenbacker he's seen playing didn't come along until the following year); *Sgt. Pepper*, and thereafter, as the modern solo George, in three separate attires; four, if one counts his nude-but-for-boots middle 8th interlude.

Pattie Boyd wrote in her 2007 memoir, *Wonderful Tonight* (or *Wonderful Today*, depending on which side of the Atlantic you are on) that upon discovering Maureen Starkey locked in a bedroom with her husband at Friar Park, her worst fears were confirmed. In a fury, she then went outside, where she lowered George's "Om" flag from atop the pole and replaced it with a Jolly Roger. In the "Ding Dong" promo, a skull-and-crossbones flag is sure enough shown being lowered, with an "Om" taking its place. The public could not have had any clue what it all meant at the time, but with Olivia Arias now living at the estate, George may have indeed been ringing in the new.

"STAND BY ME" and "SLIPPIN' AND SLIDIN" (1975)

Still fully energized despite the separation and his ongoing immigration battle, John scratched a major item off his to-do list with the completion of his oldies project in October 1974. Left in limbo since Phil Spector had absconded with the "John Dean" tapes, their recovery in the wake of John's *Walls and Bridges* triumph gave him the motivation to finish off the project before moving on to his next originals release, provisionally titled *Between The Lines*, with possibly some work with Paul in New Orleans before. This did not happen.

Still, until the *Rock 'n' Roll* project again went sideways upon release (after Morris Levy attempted to steal a march on him with the Adam VIII edition), John was fully prepared to give the album a proper launch. Two singles had been penciled in for release from the album: covers of Ben E. King's 1961 hit, "Stand By Me," and "Slippin' and Slidin'"—recorded by both Little Richard *and* Buddy Holly. John produced promos for each, and would perform both numbers, along with "Imagine," at the *A Salute to Sir Lew Grade* taping in April. Sadly, the proposed release of the latter song would be canceled, though not before promo copies (backing it with "Ain't That A Shame") were pressed.

Still, the films are a joy to watch. Backed by BOMF—"Band of Motherfuckers" (alternately known as Dog Soldier)—John led the ensemble through spirited performances, recorded at the familiar stomping grounds of the Record Plant East on March 18. In truth, these two films consisted of live vocals over the instrumental track

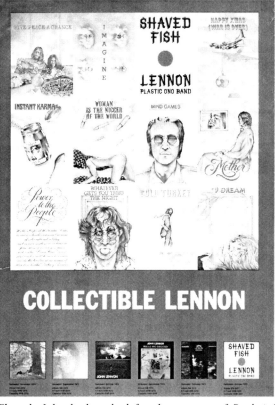

COLLECTIBLE LENNON

Though John had pushed for the success of Rock 'n' Roll's (near) two singles at every opportunity in 1975, the album was left wholly unrepresented on the all-original Shaved Fish collection released later that year.

(which the musicians then mimed to). In their way, the last promos John would ever produce mirrored the "Instant Karma" films at the start of his solo career: both feature him wearing monitor headphones as he listens to the studio backing.

What draw our interest are his ad libs. In "Stand By Me," John issued a call out to Julian, with whom he'd spent Christmas break with in Disney World a few months before. He also offered greetings to "all the folks in England"; it's hard not to conclude that he was at least a *little* homesick. In the second video (wherein he was now wearing his headphones atop his cap), he ended the performance with a weary "..and I've been doing this for one hundred years..." Was it a clue to his fatigue at being under contract for over a dozen years at this point?

The clips aired on BBC2's *The Old Grey Whistle Test* on April 18 (the same day the Lew Grade performances were taped; John's last time before an audience). The broadcast also included an interview with DJ Bob Harris, filmed at The Dakota.

Paul and Linda leaving court, February 1971. One would have thought that, with the public seeing him as the instigator of the Beatles' dissolution, Paul would've kept a lower public profile – but no. The other three did stay away, submitting responses through the legal counsel.

CHAPTER 2

WE BELIEVE THAT WE CAN'T BE WRONG: THE EX-BEATLES IN COURT

P aul's lawsuit to dissolve the Beatles' partnership at the end of 1970 represented but the opening salvo in an entire decade's worth of courtroom wrangling among the ex-Fabs. Individually and collectively, the former bandmates entered into what their parodic counterparts the Rutles described—quite accurately—as a "golden era for lawyers." This description proved to be no exaggeration, with charges and counter-suits ranging from copyright infringement and breach of contract to unauthorized releases and even tax evasion dogging the former bandmates and those coming into their orbit. Here are the most noteworthy battles.

Note: Ringo would escape the decade largely unscathed from any litigious bouts, but in the years to come, would become the unhappy player in a pair of high profile lawsuits: first, a 1981 palimony suit; later, with efforts to block the release of an album recorded while his alcoholism was in full swing. Since both cases fall outside the parameters of this book, they will be discussed another day.

(Years given are for when litigation began – not ended.)

ATV MUSIC VS. PAUL AND LINDA MCCARTNEY – 1971

John often went out of his way to extol the virtues of his bride as a worthy replacement for his estranged songwriting partner. Upon their coupling up in 1968, Yoko's influence (if not to say direct input) on John's writing became manifest. Though "Lennon-Ono" credits began popping up as early as 1971's "God Save Us" benefit single, not until he issued a track of universal appeal ("Happy Xmas") was Yoko's contribution questioned, at least as far as their music publisher was concerned. While the matter was settled relatively quickly in America, the crediting dispute delayed release of the holiday tune in England for an entire year.

(John would later express his regret at not properly crediting his missus on "Imagine," his best-loved solo composition, which after all, expressed a litany of fanciful possibilities after the fashion of Yoko's own "instructions" in *Grapefruit*. He blamed his innate chauvinism for the omission.)

But Yoko, at least, had been a classically trained musician and well-documented free verse writer for years prior to marrying one half of the sixties' most celebrated songwriting team—adding her to the credit line was *plausible*. For the former Linda Eastman, whose musical renown heretofore was limited to *proximity* to musicians—lots of them, as it happened—the sudden co-crediting of her on hit material posed a problem.

When "Another Day" was issued in early 1971 bearing a "Mr. and Mrs. Paul McCartney" songwriting credit, the alarm was sounded at ATV, the new owners of the Northern Songs catalog. (Had due diligence been performed, Grade and company would no doubt have been even less pleased to discover that the song existed as far back as January 1969, when debuted in rough form during the *Let It Be* sessions; had it been finished and the Beatles taken it up, it would have emerged as "Lennon-McCartney" product. This surely would've begged the question: "Exactly when did this songwriting partnership commence?")

Since the McCartneys never released anything remotely as deliberately experimental as *Two Virgins* or even *Live Peace In Toronto*, one could rightly assume that commercial success was always their goal. As such, the conjoining of a rank amateur with an established tunesmith guaranteed that eyebrows would be raised at ATV. Since Linda was not contractually bound to the entertainment conglomerate, they could not claim ownership of her 50% of the royalties.

The McCartneys, for their part, had been somewhat defensively chatting up their partnership to the press, as if competing for validity alongside the much higher profile John and Yoko axis. Isolated in their Scottish farm and embracing all things organic, they described their bucolic lifestyle with a narrative that could be encapsulated by: "We write our songs together in bed, man. Groovy—far out!"

Inherent smugness aside, Sir Lew Grade and his board would have none of it. With Linda *not* under publishing contract to Grade's corporation, losing half the earnings on a Top Five record was no small deal—it smacked of chicanery by the former Beatle who, after all, might've had his reasons for sticking it to ATV. After *Ram* appeared with *six* co-writing credits, Sir Lew filed suit, asserting that the McCartneys were defrauding ATV for the purpose of enriching their bank account. (With Paul's royalties flowing unreachably into Apple's financial black hole, Linda's earnings—not under ATV's control—were all he could actually touch for some years.)

Bracing himself for another nasty legal battle, Paul actually took the effort to back up his claims of Linda as England's newest hit-maker by "strapping her to the piano bench" (his words) until she composed a song on her own. Whether or not that song was worthy of the McCartney name is in the ear of the beholder; only in 1977—years after the matter had been settled—did the recording of "Seaside Woman" finally escape the Macca vault for a public airing.

The stalemate was settled and the suit withdrawn only after the McCartneys agreed to produce a one-hour television extravaganza entitled *James Paul McCartney* for ATV. This time, Linda was not co-billed, though she did receive plenty of airtime—not always as a musician. Though she would continue contributing vocals and instrumental support to albums issued under both Wings and her husband's byline, the co-writing credits ceased after 1973's "Live and Let Die" single release (although reissues of material previously credited to "McCartney-McCartney" eventually reverted to one Macca).

BRIGHT TUNES VS. GEORGE HARRISON - 1971

As the recipient of the most notorious copyright infringement lawsuit(s) in rock history, one can understand George's bile, as expressed in his 1973 "Sue Me, Sue You Blues": "Bring your lawyer and I'll bring mine / Get together and we can have a bad time." That the aggressive pursuit for monetary damages came over a spiritual tune expressing devotion to the Almighty was an incongruity seemingly lost on everyone.

The courtroom proceedings pitted one set of musical experts against another, included behind-the-scenes jockeying by Allen Klein, and ultimately led to George paying a fine before taking ownership of the song he was found to have accidentally boosted. With the whole complicated mess dragging out for years, here is an attempt to summarize the salient points.

In late 1970 —just a year after enjoying his first and only Beatle A-side—"My Sweet Lord" became George Harrison's debut solo single. Despite his own misgivings about issuing the song in this fashion (being perhaps mindful of Billy Preston's concurrent cover version), popular demand from radio stations forced his hand. While Paul hadn't yet released a solo seven-inch disc outside the Fabs, John had by this time placed a raft of Plastic Ono Band singles into the Top Forty. Both men must have been truly stunned to watch their junior partner unleash a monster upon the world, scoring the first ex-Beatle number one.

With the accolades came some unwanted attention from the publishers of the 1963 Chiffons hit, "He's So Fine." The comically named Bright

The Story Behind "This Song"

PRODUCED BY GEORGE HARRISON 1976

Five years ago, suit was filed against George Harrison and Harrisongs Music, Inc. by the estate of songwriter Ronald Mack and Bright Tunes publishing. The suit alleged that George Harrison's 1970 composition "My Sweet Lord" infringed on the copyright of Mack's "He's So Fine," recorded in 1963 by the Chiffons. In February of 1976, the case went to court before Federal Judge Richard Owen. Over three days of testimony and cross-examination, both sides attempted to prove the musical derivation of "My Sweet Lord." Both plaintiff and defendant solicited the opinions of musicologists and music experts from various fields. At one point in the proceedings, huge charts were introduced, on which were inscribed the 3-note pattern Harrison was alleged to have plagiarized. In the confused discussion which followed, differences arose as to whether or not the 3-note sequence constituted a "song." "That ain't no song," testified gospel music expert David Butler, "that's a riff!" On August 31, 1976, Judge Owen ruled against Harrison, finding "My Sweet Lord" and "He's So Fine" "virtually identical," but adding that Harrison had unknowingly lifted the riff, owing to an "unconscious" familiarity with the chord pattern in question.

"The whole thing made me sort of paranoid," Harrison explained. "I got to thinking, what if every time you sat down to write a song, you had to pass your music by some expert or into a computer, to make sure you weren't copying someone else's notes. It's all a joke, really. Basically, songs are written to entertain and that's all there is to it. That's where it's at."

Promo copies of the "This Song" single arrived in a sleeve that summed up the case against George, and why it didn't matter.

Tunes recognized that, beneath the layers of orchestration, "Hare Krishnas," and "Hallelujahs," there lurked a passing resemblance to one of their own holdings. (The actual songwriter had been a 25 year-old amateur named Ronnie Mack, who had pounded doors relentlessly before finding a taker for his compositions. Tragically, he was diagnosed with Hodgkin's disease soon after and was literally on his deathbed in the hospital when awarded a gold record for the hit.)

Just as "My Sweet Lord" had completed its ninth week of ten in *Billboard*'s Top Ten (four of those weeks lodged at number one), Bright Tunes filed suit against George, Apple, Harrisongs, and every other connected party they could serve. As it happened, Bright Tunes was in financial disarray at the time—that an ex-Beatle had apparently appropriated their property to score a mega-hit must've seemed (fittingly enough) like a godsend.

Through Allen Klein, George offered to buy Bright Tunes. Had the proposition been accepted, it would undoubtedly have spared George much grief, as well as public embarrassment. But instead, Bright's owner, Seymour Barash, wanted George to turn over the copyright of "My Sweet Lord" to *him* (with George to retain half the monies generated). The counter-offer was spurned, Bright Tunes went into receivership, and that's where things lay for the next five years.

In February 1976, George found himself in the witness box in a New York City courtroom, giving an extended explanation into the origins of "My Sweet Lord." By the end of the proceedings, several facts revealed themselves. First, the court ruled that the two songs were musically indistinguishable, with common note progressions and the presence of an uncommon "grace note," akin to a fingerprint. "Motif A" and "motif B" were shown to overlap between the songs, but the grace note proved key.

Second, while George had come up with the germ of the composition himself, the musical ideas had been fleshed out by Delaney Bramlett, Billy Preston and the various musicians accompanying Delaney and Bonnie during their late 1969 tour, when the soon-to-be ex-Fab had introduced the bare bones of the song during a jam. In fact, the "smoking gun" of the case—the errant grace note—occurs in Billy's recording and *not* George's. He *did* come up with the original concept and *did* write the final lyrics, but many hands shaped the tune itself.

As sole attributed author on the song, George lay himself open to take the financial hit. Had he issued "My Sweet Lord" as a joint composition, perhaps some of the "blame" might have been spread around. (Absorbing ideas from others during the journey a song makes from idea to recording remains a touchy subject. The Rolling Stones are a perfect example of a band that might have properly shared co-writing credits—but didn't. The issue was a sore point with bassist Bill Wyman, who conceived the signature riff to "Jumping Jack Flash," while guitarist Mick Taylor rightfully pointed out that "Time Waits For No One," among other tunes, was his baby. Both songs are credited Jagger-Richards.)

The most stunning revelation concerned Allen Klein. By the time the case had come to trial, he was no longer representing three-quarters of the band formerly known as the Beatles. Instead, he was embroiled in litigation of his own against his former clients (see below) and further, had "flipped." Armed with intimate knowledge of the sales of "My Sweet Lord" and thus how much revenue the song had generated, he secretly made an offer to buy Bright Tunes, not for George but for ABKCO. By controlling the copyright of "He's So Fine," Klein was also taking over the lawsuit and now suing George himself.

With the latter's offer still on the table before the trial started and another from Klein, Barash and company correctly divined that Klein almost certainly knew how the case would end and therefore what Bright Tune's stock would be worth. But the parties could not agree on a final price before proceedings resumed.

On August 31, 1976, the court ruled that George was guilty of "subconscious plagiarism." Familiar with "He's So Fine," the court asserted that he inwardly had to have known that the combination of notes and chords that he put together would work, though on a conscious level George did *not* realize what he was replicating. With copyright infringement thus determined, a complicated formula set the damages at $1.5 million, based on the song's earnings (calculating its single and sheet music sales, as well as commercial value to both *All Things Must Pass* and *The Best of George Harrison*).

However, the sale of Bright Tunes to Klein between the trial and the damages phase of the litigation threw the proceedings into disarray. To sum up what took well into the 1980s to settle: George successfully amended his pleading to assert that Klein's meddling in the case had unnecessarily muddied the waters. The judge agreed, and George himself was able to take ownership of "He's So Fine" by paying Klein the purchase price—the latter would not profit by his shady dealings.

Rock's rich tapestry is replete with borrowed musical ideas and "tributes." Far stronger cases for plagiarism can certainly be made against other songs, but the worldwide success of "My Sweet Lord" made it a target. The affair didn't seem to damage George's reputation too badly in the short run: he rebounded that year with a strong album, *Thirty-Three & 1/3*, which included his own defiant take on the case: "This Song."

But others wouldn't let go so easily. In their 1977 Beatle parody issue, *National Lampoon* magazine savaged George by featuring an "unreleased" album he'd recorded, *Lifting Material From The World*. The cover art sported George in court being sworn in, fingers crossed, while the album itself was claimed to contain such Harrisongs as "My Sweet Lullaby of Broadway" and "My Sweet Beethoven's 9th Symphony."

In his 1980 *Playboy* interview, John, no stranger to copyright infringement himself, claimed that George knew exactly what he was doing. "Maybe he thought God would just sort of let him off."

APPLE CORPS VS. ABKCO – 1973

The management contract between Allen Klein and Apple (as embodied by Messrs. Lennon, Harrison, and Starkey) ran from August 1969 until March 31 1973. Not long after it expired, Klein filed suit against his former clients, perhaps out of habit. The opening salvo came in June 1973, when Klein, as embodied by ABKCO, filed suit against John for over half a million dollars, claiming payment due on unpaid loans. (In fact, John, George, and Ringo had been remarkably casual about using Apple's resources as a personal piggy bank.) In September, an out-of-court deal was struck, with Ringo purchasing Tittenhurst Park, John's sprawling Ascot estate that had served as the site of the final Beatles photo shoot. The home had been sitting neglected in the two years since the Lennons had moved to New York, though portions of Ringo's T. Rex film, *Born To Boogie*, were filmed there, as was his promo film for "Back Off Boogaloo."

Come November, Klein's three ex-Fab clients filed suit against ABKCO, charging misrepresentation. Klein countersued for $19 million, claiming unpaid commissions, fees, and expenses. For good measure, he filed a separate suit against Paul McCartney, who he didn't even represent, claiming damages of $34 million. This last filing was laughed out of court.

At the time of the litigation, Klein had trouble brewing with the IRS, stemming from some under-the-counter dealings he and promoter Pete Bennett had been engaged in. (See "The United States vs. Allen Klein" below) So it probably came as a rare bit of good news in January 1977 that with all the accusations flying on both sides, an agreement to end the standoff could be brokered by an outside (though not disinterested) party: Yoko Ono.

For three straight days at New York's Plaza Hotel, the Lennons, Klein, and a coterie of attorneys conferenced without letup. Acting as envoy was Yoko, who shuttled back and forth between the warring factions in a manner described by Klein as "Kissinger-like." Indeed, for a woman not terribly renowned for qualities of tact and self-effacement, she drew high praise from Klein himself, a man not known for generosity with compliments.

"That woman is extraordinary," he marveled to reporters. "There was no way that she was going to quit until everything had been straightened out." Summoning her most disarming diplomatic skills, Yoko finessed a deal that saw ABKCO pay Apple $800,000 and Apple in turn settle with Klein for $4.2 million. The deal was sealed over a pleasant dinner, each side walking away with no further repercussions.

The wheeling and dealing revealed a heretofore hidden skill set from Yoko—that of a tough minded businesswoman. Perhaps it was traits inherited from her father—a highly successful Tokyo banker—that finally asserted themselves, but in any event, it marked the beginning of Yoko's takeover of the Lennons utterly mismanaged finances. While John stayed home and— per his aggressively asserted narrative, at least—baked bread, cleaned the litter box, and looked after Sean— Yoko rebuilt the family fortune much in the same adroit manner as Priscilla Presley did after Elvis' death.

Others were less impressed, notably Linda McCartney. "It is true that she settled with Klein…but it wasn't her money, really. Each Beatle gave a share, Paul included, and he never wanted that man as manager in the first place." Indeed.

BIG SEVEN MUSIC VS. JOHN LENNON - 1973

In the summer of 1969, John drew upon a couple of wellsprings to compose one of his stronger contributions to the *Abbey Road* album. The phrase "come together" was taken directly from the slogan acid avatar Timothy Leary hoped would propel him to the California governorship in 1970: "Come together: join the party." When hanging out with the politically awakened Beatle in Montreal during his Bed-In for Peace, Leary asked if the tunesmith would like to compose a campaign song for him.

While that task, like Leary's run, ended up a non-starter, the phrase did not. Drawing from his beloved Chuck Berry songbook, John wedded the words to a melody that was a throwback to the Fabs' Hamburg repertoire. As if to underscore the homage, he borrowed (only altering slightly) a line from Berry's "You Can't Catch Me" to open the song.

The inherent resemblance between "Come Together" and any number of Berry tunes did not escape Paul's ever-alert ears. He gently steered John to less litigious waters by slowing the tempo, adding an electric piano lick that John described as "swampy," and generally shaping an arrangement that John himself would declare "independent of Chuck Berry or anyone else on Earth."

He was sorely mistaken on that last point, for the song's popularity drew notice. Morris Levy was the head of Roulette Records, as well as the owner of Big Seven Music, which owned the publishing to the Berry catalog. Unmoved by the "tribute," he demanded a Beatle-size cut of the royalties generated by the song. (Interestingly, he did not hold the song's credited co-author, Paul McCartney, accountable. All parties acknowledged that, crediting aside, it was *John's* song.)

Bedeviled by any number of legal assaults, John was quick to assume responsibility for the "theft." (John would jam with Chuck Berry himself on the *Mike Douglas Show* in February 1972; one wonders whether or not the pending lawsuit came up during their small talk.)

Big Seven could have asked that Chuck's name be added to the songwriting credits, creating the first Lennon-McCartney-Berry song (not counting "I Saw Her Standing There"—in spirit, anyway). Precedent existed; in 1964, when it was noted that the Beach Boys' "Surfin' U.S.A." bore more than a little resemblance to Chuck's "Sweet Little Sixteen," the credit was altered accordingly. Instead, a settlement was reached out of court: on his *next* album release, John would have to record *three* Big Seven tunes to atone for his borrowing. With royalties thus generated, plus the possibility of another artist covering John's cover, the potential financial windfall could more than make up for any allegedly lost revenue.

The plan dovetailed nicely with a notion that had been germinating in John's head at least as far back as the *Let It Be* sessions: to record an album of beloved oldies. This gave John a suitable vehicle to fulfill his obligations and end any further litigation, while simultaneously recharging his creative batteries before tackling any new originals. With Phil Spector on board as producer, what could go wrong?

JOHN LENNON VS. MORRIS LEVY - 1975

What *could* go wrong, *did* go wrong. The *Rock 'N' Roll* sessions, as the project was eventually dubbed, started out as a chance to recapture

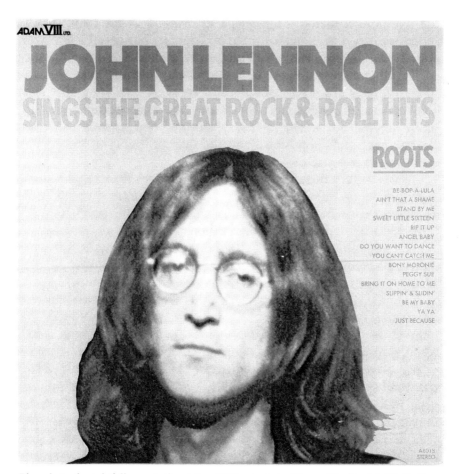

ADAM VIII LTD.

JOHN LENNON
SINGS THE GREAT ROCK & ROLL HITS

ROOTS

BE-BOP-A-LULA
AIN'T THAT A SHAME
STAND BY ME
SWEET LITTLE SIXTEEN
RIP IT UP
ANGEL BABY
DO YOU WANT TO DANCE
YOU CAN'T CATCH ME
BONY MORONIE
PEGGY SUE
BRING IT ON HOME TO ME
SLIPPIN' & SLIDIN'
BE MY BABY
YA YA
JUST BECAUSE

A8015
STEREO

Though Apple rightfully went after Adam-VIII's pirated edition of the Rock 'n' Roll album
– Roots - its shoddy sound and cut-rate design made it far less of a sales threat than they
suggested, TV and radio campaign notwithstanding.

the raw vitality of John's musical roots, but soon degraded into a Hamburg-like, surreal, drunken free-for-all. From the onset, the ex-Fab was intent on playing the role of singer, deliberately abdicating *artiste* responsibilities to Spector. The latter was only too happy to take full control—a position thwarted by John's tight rein in their previous collaborations.

But in trying to reclaim his glory days of a decade earlier, Spector overreached himself. Well past the point of operating within the realm of reality, the producer attempted to employ the recording methods of the early sixties, bringing in nearly thirty musicians to replicate his Wall of Sound, playing live. This being 1973 and Los Angeles, a certain lack of discipline, shall we say, permeated the proceedings. With Spector spending hours perfecting details that only he could hear, much tedium for those unoccupied was lifted through illicit refreshments, with no one hitting the bottle harder than John.

Depressed at his marital situation; the critical slam he took for the *Some Time in New York City* album and the lackluster reception for the newly-released *Mind Games*; being upstaged in the charts by his former *drummer*, fercrissake; and his ongoing legal battle to avoid deportation, John was ready and willing to completely annihilate himself in booze. His lead was soon met by Spector himself, whose increasingly bizarre behavior portended an even grimmer descent into madness years later.

As detailed in *Fab Four FAQ 2.0*, the whole project finally imploded with a climax culminating in gunplay and stolen master tapes. The upshot of this turn of events was that for the first time since the *Let It Be* sessions, John was forced to walk away from a project that was dead in the water. As winter turned to spring, John began composing a new batch of tunes with a mind to record a new album. Just as the *Walls and Bridges* sessions began in July 1974, the *Rock 'N' Roll* tapes were recovered—after Capitol was forced to pay Spector $90,000 for them.

Unwilling to lose his mojo by returning to the oldies project, John soldiered on with *Walls and Bridges*, not immediately realizing that he was breaking the terms of the 1973 agreement by not including the three required Big Seven tunes on his "next" album. (He did include a snippet of one, "Ya Ya," in the form of an album-closing father and son vignette, but it's altogether likely that Levy regarded this as a thinly-veiled "up yours.")

Levy demanded an explanation and in October, the two met at New York's Club Cavallero so that Lennon could bring him up to speed on the Spector situation and how the oldies album had been momentarily shelved. Both wishing to avoid further courtroom battles, Lennon offered to flesh out what he'd started in L.A. with the same crew he used on *Walls and Bridges* in order to fulfill his commitment. Levy, in turn, provided facilities at his upstate New York farm for the musicians to rehearse. Upon listening to the Spector tapes, Lennon was mortified to realize that much of it was, in his opinion, unreleasable. The performances were sub-par; the instrumental backing frequently out of tune. Though the mandatory three Big Seven tunes were already cut, John recognized that some would need to be replaced. Visiting Mick Jagger at his Long Island home, the two brainstormed over potential material to complete the project.

The balance of the album was knocked out in less than a week, in striking contrast to the Spector sessions. John and Levy met up following the completion and as a good faith gesture, the former presented the latter with a 7-1/2-ips reel dub of the album's rough mixes. The import of the action became the subject of their next court battle, with Levy asserting that the delivery of the tape constituted John's tacit approval for Adam VIII, Levy's television-marketed record label, to issue the album as a mail order product. Indeed, the notion of retailing a record in that fashion while bypassing the traditional outlets caught John's fancy, being the TV junkie that he was. But to suggest that John gave the go-ahead without at least informing Capitol, Apple's distributor, assumes pure foolishness on John's part, a disingenuous defense by Levy, or both.

Levy claimed that he and John had entered into an "oral contract" back at their Club Cavallero meeting in October, authorizing Adam VIII's release of the project (which Levy dubbed *Roots*— two years before the Alex Haley television blockbuster). Lennon not only denied this, but as his lawyer Harold Seider pointed out, he was hardly at liberty to negotiate deals outside the purview of EMI, to whom he was contractually bound. Through Seider, Levy was informed that he proceeded with the release at his own risk.

Ever the gambler, Levy pressed on, utilizing the sonically inferior tape that John had given him. To be sure, his iteration added a pair of lesser tracks absent from the Apple issue: "Angel Baby" and "Be My Baby." But the remarkably ill-conceived Adam VIII package featured a grainy cover shot of John taken by Ethan Russell during the *Let It Be* sessions— *six* years earlier. Capitol's fury was manifest; having spent $90,000 to recover the masters to the ill-starred project, they could hardly stand by and see their investment tarnished for $4.98 a pop (of which they stood to earn a pitiful twenty-three cents per unit, owing to Levy's creative accounting).

As far as they were concerned, EMI had *every* right to distribute *Rock 'N' Roll* (on the Apple label) just like any other John Lennon release. Their plans called for an elaborate gatefold presentation of the record, designed with input from John's Hamburg friend Jurgen Vollmer, who had shot the 1961 image that graced the cover. But the packaging, along with an ambitious marketing campaign, was unceremoniously scrapped in order to rush the record into retail outlets before *Roots* could gain a foothold with the public.

Roots was first advertised publicly on television on February 8, 1975, a day after Capitol began shipping *Rock 'N' Roll*. Less than 1,300 copies of the Adam VIII release were sold before distribution ceased, creating an instant collector's item. (John himself ordered several copies and noted that the delivery took three weeks.) But the dueling releases drew both sides into legal battle, each claiming legitimate grievances. In Levy's mind, Lennon's releasing only two of the three required Big Seven songs constituted a breach of the 1973 settlement. But to EMI, Apple, and Lennon himself, the unauthorized issue of the tapes caused monetary damages, cutting into the sales of *their* product while damaging Lennon's reputation by offering such shoddy goods, both in sound quality and packaging. A suit and countersuit were filed in short order.

In 1973, a fifties nostalgia boom swept across America, sparked in no small part by the film *American Graffiti*. (Yes, it was set in 1962, but director George Lucas populated the film's soundtrack with songs going back as far as 1953.) The television series *Happy Days* debuted in January 1974, capitalizing on the film's success; the show, in turn, sent Bill Haley's "Rock Around The Clock" back onto the *Billboard* charts. But while capitalizing on that particular fad might have been a good idea in 1973-1974, by 1975 the revival had played out. *Rock 'N' Roll* proved to be John's slowest seller since *Some Time In New York City*, despite the presence of the radio-friendly "Stand By Me." This ironically proved to be a plus—in calculating damages for breaking the 1973 agreement, sales estimates for the current release proved lower than that of a typical John Lennon album, resulting in a ruling of $6,795 to be paid to Big Seven.

Lennon's charges against Levy were threefold: the unauthorized Adam VIII issue suppressed sales of *Rock 'N' Roll*, stirring confusion in the marketplace. Second, a $4.98 price tag when the industry norm was $6.98 caused EMI to lower their price by a dollar, further lowering their profits. Lastly, the substandard aesthetics of the presentation were asserted to have injured Lennon's reputation as an artist. While the first two charges were relatively easy to litigate, the last was a somewhat nebulous proposition, especially given that the artist in question had already let it all hang out on an album cover.

Indeed, William Schurtman, Levy's lawyer, tried to make this very point before the jury. His artless attempt at displaying *Two Virgins* resulted in the judge ordering a mistrial. (Schurtman also tried bullying John on the stand. Making light of his cleaned up appearance—in contrast to his myriad hirsute incarnations through the years—the attorney suggested that Lennon was purposely attempting to influence the jury with freshly shorn locks. Retorted John: "Nonsense. I cut it every 18 months.")

During the retrial, which dispensed with a jury altogether, the court found that while there was no sinister attempt at fraud by Levy, he was certainly no innocent in the industry and had to have known that the "oral contract" he claimed wasn't worth the breath it took to bespeak it. Ultimately, he was ordered to pay nearly $85,000 in damages to Lennon, EMI, and Apple.

Though conceived as a respite from more demanding artistic

endeavors, the *Rock 'N' Roll* album proved a headache on almost every level for John, from creation to release. It's therefore not surprising that the experience left him ready for relief from contractual obligations for the next several years, savoring new fatherhood and a taste of freedom unknown since his art school days. He was, as he asserted in a song he would soon begin composing, "free as a bird."

A&M RECORDS VS. GEORGE HARRISON – 1976

Recognizing the imminent demise of Apple, and evidently still harboring dreams of mentoring new artists, George announced the formation of his own label, Dark Horse, in 1974. The new label's product would be distributed worldwide by A&M. Founded in 1962 by industry exec Jerry Moss and trumpeter Herb Alpert, A&M's chart success with the Tijuana Brass set the label on its way to becoming the world's largest independent record company within ten years. George may have been drawn to the label by Billy Preston who, after leaving Apple, began racking up a string of hit singles over at A&M. Though his own fortunes were tied to Apple and Capitol until 1976, George was carefully laying the groundwork for revisiting the ideals that Apple was set up to enact in 1968 (at least in talent-spotting).

With the ex-Beatle fronting the newly-minted subsidiary (though not contractually free to record on it for the first two years) and producing some of its acts, A&M was prepared to sink a bundle into making Dark Horse viable. Initial signings like Splinter, a Harrison-esque, Badfinger-like pop-rock act, and The Stairsteps, who (as The Five Stairsteps) had scored a hit with "O-o-h Child" back in 1970, seemed like solid enough investment. Where the deal went south was with George's own commitment. Freed from his ties to EMI, his first Dark Horse album was due to be delivered to A&M on July 26, 1976. It wasn't. The explanation given was that due to a serious bout of hepatitis, he had fallen behind schedule. Fair enough; also, the "My Sweet Lord" litigation was in full swing, with the "subconscious plagiarism" ruling coming in late summer.

But A&M's execs were getting nervous. Two years into the deal, none of the Dark Horse acts had really caught fire, and by August, rumors spread around the A&M offices was that Dark Horse was sending album artwork across town over to industry giant Warner Brothers. A month later, their personnel began packing up. With *Thirty-Three & 1/3* still unfinished, A&M decided to cut their losses before the meter ran too high. On September 26, they filed a $10 million suit against George and

Most of the non-Harrison Dark Horse roster found release during the A&M tenure between 1974 and 1976. White funksters Jiva, Ravi Shankar, Henry McCullough and Stairsteps were all acts whose Dark Horse association more or less ended when A&M pulled the plug. Only Attitudes, Splinter and Keni Burke (from the Stairsteps) transitioned into the Warner Brothers years.

Dark Horse for breech of contract, seeking to recover their investment and to nullify the distribution deal.

George expressed shock and dismay at the turn of events, telling interviewers that he had in fact passed up higher dollar offers from other labels to sign with A&M in the first place. Despite his hand-delivering the master tapes himself to A&M's office to personally smooth things over, the relationship had irrevocably broken down. Luckily for him, being an ex-Beatle who happened to be bearing his most wonderfully commercial album in years meant that he didn't have to lose a step in getting the goods to market. He took Dark Horse over to the welcoming arms of Mo Ostin at Warner's, where he was reunited with ex-Apple stalwart Derek Taylor, already on the payroll, as well as former Apple artist James Taylor—no relation. (Previous Apple signings Badfinger and Jackie Lomax had already released product on Warner's, but by 1976 had parted ways.)

It is likely that A&M had simply wanted out of a deal that upon closer examination offered them little more to show for their outlay of money than the prestige of having George Harrison within their stable. The label had been remarkably prescient in signing acts that, for a time at least, proved phenomenally successful, among them The Carpenters, Peter Frampton, Supertramp, and The Police. (A deal with the Sex Pistols in 1977—not so much.) But despite the quality of the Dark Horse acts, none had performed as expected, while George himself hadn't enjoyed a Top Ten hit since 1973's "Give Me Love." The label may simply have gotten buyer's remorse; *Thirty-Three & 1/3*'s delay provided the excuse to get out before money began to hemorrhage.

Their lawsuit was settled out of court for $4 million. George apparently bore no ill will toward his former partners; in fact, he dedicated *Thirty-Three & 1/3*'s lovely "Learning How To Love You" to Herb Alpert. Warner Brother poured a lot of muscle into the promotion of George's new album, which sparked his best reviews since *All Things Must Pass*. (The honeymoon would come to an end four years later, when George turned in what became the first draft of 1980's *Somewhere In England*.)

GEORGE VS. RINGO – 1976

This is the one rather inexplicable legal action that the least is known about, other than that *something* happened. Both George and Ringo publicly confirmed this: during a joint 1988 appearance on the British chat show, *Aspel & Company*, Ringo brought it up, leaving George to uncomfortably concur that yes, he was "cross" with his ex-bandmate over the recording of his song, "I'll Still Love You" on the *Ringo's Rotogravure* album.

Here's the exchange:

Ringo: *The last time we were cross was when Georgie sued me.*

George: *That was the last time. We are always cross.*

Ringo: *Yeah yeah, we are still cross. The last time he called he said "I'm going to sue you" - "You are not, George, don't say that" - "No no, I'm going to sue you," - 'cause he wrote this song and I had it mixed by somebody else, and he didn't like the mix (George laughs). So I said "Sue me if you want but I'll always love you."*

As is noted in chapter 14, "I'll Still Love You" was a song that George had had in his pocket as far back as *All Things Must Pass*, intended initially for either Ronnie Spector or Cilla Black, depending on what account you read. Ringo played on the backing eventually used by the latter; another version exists, recorded by Leon and Mary Russell. During his *Rotogravure* blitz, Ringo told interviewers in 1976 that he remembered playing on the track and since no one else had taken it up, asked George if he could. The latter responded, "Fine – it'll save me a job!" (Elsewhere, Ringo went on to say "I said to him to get me a demo of it because he was too drunk at the time to do it himself. Hohoho...")

In George's place on the recording was ex-Apple signee Lon Van Eaton, who delivered a completely suitable (and Clapton-esque) guitar solo. Atlantic duly produced a promo film for the track, as though it were under serious consideration as a single release, but ultimately this did not happen. In summation: Ringo's take was hardly an embarrassment. It is therefore baffling why George found the whole thing so upsetting that he threatened his friend with legal action. Had it been an unmitigated train wreck, surely all public blame would have found its way to Ringo's doorstep and not the song's author.

In the end, their differences were settled in private. Though no court battle took place, Ringo could still reference the event over a decade later as though it hadn't been completely forgotten, either.

APPLE CORPS VS. LINGASONG RECORDS – 1977

Well aware that a brisk under-the-table trade was going on among Beatle fans seeking live recordings—*any* live recordings—EMI was prompted to give a second look to the previously deemed "unreleasable" Hollywood Bowl recordings from the 1964 and 1965 tours. After consulting with George Martin, who conceded that maybe they could be tweaked sufficiently to bring them up to snuff, EMI prepared a massive promotional campaign to launch the album—a real gift to fans who had reason to feel burned by 1976's *Rock 'n' Roll Music*; a seemingly arbitrary repackaging of material every hardcore fan already owned.

At around the same time, rumblings asserting the existence of live recordings predating the Hollywood Bowl shows began to be felt. Word of an amateur recording documenting the Beatles' Hamburg club days began to spread, though in retrospect it's clear that no one within the Beatles' camp took the public issue of them very seriously. After all, they had already twice been passed over for purchase; once by Brian Epstein in 1963, and again by Apple around ten years later. Conventional wisdom was that they simply were too raw for public consumption and that no label would seriously invest the time and money necessary to make them even halfway listenable.

What Apple didn't count on was the tenacity of one Paul Murphy of BUK Records, a Polydor subsidiary. Recognizing the historic importance of the undeniably rough tapes, he invested over £50,000 to bring them up to the 1976 state of the art, as best as could be done. While still rough, the recordings absolutely reeked of atmosphere and

When your Granny wouldn't have liked them.

Talstraße

1962.
Rock was raw, girls wore beehives, and it seemed like everyone was just seventeen (well you know what I mean).
Four boys from Liverpool were playing the Star Club, Hamburg – a long way from home.
They were called the Beatles. They played till night for as much food and drink as they could consume. They played well. And the Star Club became the place for kids to dance, listen, and enjoy themselves.
The Beatles Live! – a two-record set – shows the way it was then. And the way it should be now.
Brash, rough, loud. Exciting.
Get it now, it may never happen again.

2 LPs
A piece of History...
THE BEATLES LIVE!
at the Star-Club
in Hamburg,
Germany;
1962.
includes 13 never before released Beatles tracks

2 LPs, 26 tracks –
including 13
never-before
released.
LNL 1.
Also available
on cassette
and cartridge.

The Star Club release was cannily marketed for what it was: a rough-and-ready act that did not resemble the über-accessible band the world was familiar with. Arriving during punk's heyday, it was a smart move, as was the inaccurate leather visual; these shows were from the post-Epstein smart suit days.

personality, showcasing the cover-heavy set of a band poised to take over the world. Though quite public with his intentions, Apple paid Murphy little mind. Occasional communications were exchanged, but beyond this, nothing in the months leading to the Star-Club album's release, on a label expressly set up for the purpose: Lingasong. Only when EMI recognized that their Hollywood Bowl set and the Star-Club tapes were on a collision course was Apple at last roused from their slumber.

Legal action to block the release of the Hamburg tapes represented a rare courtroom defeat for the Beatles and Apple. The reason for the ruling against them was fairly straightforward—Apple, well aware for some time of the pending release, simply chose to wait until the eleventh hour to file a grievance. It would appear in retrospect that Apple erred strategically on a couple of issues that could have tipped things their way.

First, they seemed to concede the point that the recordings were made with permission from the Beatles themselves. Ted Taylor swore in an affidavit that one of the Beatles gave him approval to record their act, in exchange for beer. Legally, of course, this verbal acquiescence meant nothing, but had Apple contested it, they might have stood a good chance of prevailing.

More devastating was the decision not to bring EMI into the case. Paul Murphy was decidedly vague about precisely dating the recordings, implying that they were made in 1961 (or early 1962). This was a smooth calculation on his part; if it could be proven that the tapes originated from late 1962 (which they did)—after the Beatles were under exclusive contract with EMI—then Murphy and Lingasong had no legal ownership. As it was, Polydor, who *did* have a contract with the Beatles in 1961 (for the Tony Sheridan recordings), contacted Murphy to clarify the matter. It would appear that some sort of understanding was worked out, which had the effect of bolstering the 1961 claim.

Clearly, Apple's inattentiveness to the Star-Club tapes resulted in fans being rewarded with a priceless window into the Fabs' nightclub days. Never again would the spirited foursome be so loose, so freewheeling, and so unvarnished before a paying audience. The spring 1977 release of both the Star-Club recordings and the more polished Hollywood Bowl set gave fans a true bonus—something that wouldn't have been possible had Apple gotten its way.

Conspicuously, no Star-Club tracks ended up years later on the *Anthology 1* release. In the intervening years, an older but wiser Apple had won a court case against the reissue of the Star-Club recordings on compact disc. In 2008, yet another cease and desist suit was filed, this time against a Florida entrepreneur who had acquired previously unknown Star-Club performances.

THE UNITED STATES VS. ALLEN KLEIN - 1977

Years of engaging in less-than-ethical business practices at last caught up with Allen Klein in 1977, when he was charged with failing to pay income tax on the proceeds generated by selling promotional copies of Apple product. The most egregious source of his secret income came from sales of the *Concert for Bangla Desh* album—a product specifically created to raise money to benefit sick and dying children. No stranger to tax complaints, Klein had been charged with failure to file payroll tax returns back in the 1960s—a fact that the Beatles could easily have found out, had simple due diligence been performed before signing any contracts. But the current charges were a felony—something far more serious. Klein was charged with three counts of tax evasion and another three counts of falsifying his federal tax returns.

Chief witness against him was Apple promotions man Pete Bennett, who told authorities that he had been in the practice of selling off copies of releases set aside for promotional purposes on Klein's orders. Normally, these "promos" were clearly marked, via a sticker, stamp, or hole punched in the jacket, to prevent retailers from selling them—these were not. According to the Bennett, some 5,000 copies of *each* album and single release earmarked for promotion were sold to retailers and distributors instead of being given away, with the proceeds being split between Bennett and Klein. The Feds charged that Klein had profited by nearly a quarter million dollars between 1970 and 1972.

In court, Klein and his lawyers did their best to discredit Bennett, an admittedly guilty man. As to witnesses who had seen large amounts of cash changing hands between the two, Klein asserted that Bennett was merely repaying cash advances Klein had given him. Ultimately, the old saw about no honor among thieves sufficiently muddied the waters; after six days of deliberations, the jury remained hopelessly deadlocked, with nine jurors convinced that they would be unable to reach a verdict on even one count.

Given the clear animosity between Klein and Bennett by this time, jurors had been hard pressed to determine who was being more truthful. Given the deadlock, U.S. District Judge Charles Metzner declared a mistrial. Klein appealed, his lawyers asserting that he'd been denied due process by this "premature" ruling. But their efforts failed and the case was retried. On April 27, 1979, Klein was at last found guilty and sentenced to two years in prison. Ultimately, he served two months and paid a $5,000 fine.

APPLE CORPS VS. EMI – 1979

Traditionally, successful recording artists have held a certain amount of mistrust toward their record labels, especially when hits are scored. Through accounting practices that are baffling to most—especially musicians—there are any number of ways to conceal the real sales tallies and routinely underpay the artists. Very few musicians possess the acumen to discern when they've been hoodwinked, even with a business background. (Mick Jagger actually studied economics in school; coupled with his own native instincts, this would immeasurably help the Rolling Stones pile up a fortune through the years, but even he had been bamboozled by Allen Klein, much to his financial detriment.)

One of Klein's first acts upon coming into the Beatles' orbit in 1969 was to conduct an audit of EMI's books. He uncovered thousands of dollars in unpaid royalties, impressing even Paul McCartney. Audits are standard operating procedure in any royalty-driven business, enabling the artist to uncover cut corners in payments that are otherwise well concealed. (It should be noted that not all underpayments are sinister—Klein himself would later be accused of sloppy bookkeeping.)

In 1976, the ex-Beatles' original deal with EMI had lapsed. Paul had re-signed for a couple of more years, only to switch to Columbia in 1979. Ringo had landed at Atlantic, though by 1978 he had moved over to CBS subsidiary Portrait. George's Dark Horse was attached to Warner Brothers, and John was a free agent. Thus, with no EMI ties to bind them, the time was right for a thorough revisiting of the books. What the ex-Fabs uncovered did not please them.

According to the lawsuit they filed, Apple believed that Capitol-EMI had been systematically classifying perfectly good product as "damaged" or "destroyed," writing off the loss while secretly selling these same records and pocketing over $19 million during a ten-year period beginning in 1969. In a suit filed in a Manhattan court, Apple claimed lost earnings and punitive damages amounting to $80 million.

The suit represented what would be the first of several clashes between Apple Corps and their long associated record label, typifying what would remain an uneasy relationship. For this first go round, the charge of fraud was eventually negotiated out, with the breach of fiduciary claim left intact. Damages were likewise whittled down to $30 million.

Ultimately, it took some ten years to traverse the accounting thicket, with matters at last settled out of court for an undisclosed monetary amount. As part of the agreement, the ex-Beatles received a raise in their royalty rate, while EMI committed themselves henceforth to adhering to "more stringent auditing requirements"—apparently meaning, "All right, you got us this time. Next time, we'll try better (not to be caught.")

Next time came soon enough, resulting in a second settlement in 1995, this time with a reported $35 million payout to the surviving Beatles and the Lennon estate. Yet *another* suit against EMI came in 2005, again for underpayment of royalties; this would be settled two years later. One would expect this to settle matters for good between the two parties but, judging by history, it isn't likely.

APPLE CORPS VS. BEATLEMANIA – 1979

By the year of Elvis Presley's death, impersonators had begun taking root, recognizing the public appetite for a concert experience they would otherwise never enjoy. As the decade unfolded, all four former Beatles established solo careers, giving little outward indication that they would be reforming anytime soon. Into this void, some enterprising souls stepped in to give the public what they wanted. While a straightforward impression by four bewigged musicians might have sufficed for some, rock impresarios Steven Leber and David Krebs had greater ambitions. Casting four look-alikes (more or less), gathering an array of iconic sixties images, and marrying the whole thing to a state of the art light show, they called the result *Beatlemania*. By word of mouth, the audio-visual-concert extravaganza was road tested before debuting at Broadway's Winter Garden Theater in May, 1977.

Though critics and purists may have quibbled with the end result, the show packed in the crowds, becoming a bona fide smash. At least seven sanctioned iterations set up shop around the country to fulfill the public's appetite for their "incredible simulation." But distracted though they might have been by their own careers, the four ex-Fabs individually became well enough aware of their appropriated music and image to take legal action against its misuse.

Two years after *Beatlemania* was launched, Apple Corps filed suit in Los Angeles against the shows producers. Contrary to common belief, it was not copyright infringement that they charged, but "right of publicity"—that is, that the show's producers were in effect "stealing" the Beatles' name, likeness, and sound for commercial purposes, robbing them of control of their own carefully crafted public personas. As the show was in no way sanctioned by Apple or the individual ex-Beatles, their own right to promote themselves was in effect being hijacked by outsiders.

THE BEATLES: AWAY WITH WORDS

A GIFT FROM
WRIF Rock'n Stereo 101
Good for any performance
Sept. 8th, 9th and 10th
Masonic Auditorium — 500 Temple

№ 4556

Prior to the arrival of the slick Broadway-style presentation of the Beatles' music as enacted in Beatlemania, this multi-media extravaganza toured the country, presenting Beatle music with visuals depicting the era. (Later editions were called The Beatles Rise Again.)

40

By injunction, the show was closed for good on Broadway in October, 1979 after over 1,000 performances.

For such an open and-shut-case, the litigation took some seven years to move through the judicial system (with appeals factored in), mostly to determine damages. In the end, Apple was awarded $10 million for the misappropriation of the Beatles' image. Considering that the show had grossed some $45 million, this wasn't too stiff a penalty.

What was truly revelatory about the case only came to light in 1986 with the conclusion of the litigation. Only then were the ex-Beatles' sworn depositions made public. John's was given on November 28, 1980 – ten days *before* his death. In it, he stated, "I and the other three former Beatles have plans to stage a reunion concert." The plan called for a one-off live appearance to be filmed as a finale to their years-in-the-making documentary, *The Long And Winding Road*. This astonishing admission must be examined within the context from which it came. Certainly, given the court case before him, it would have been in his interests to assert that the Beatles were not yet played out and that with a future live project before them, any usurping of the Beatles' name would be potentially damaging.

But in examining his latest pronouncements outside of court, one can detect a pattern of building up Yoko at the expense of his past. In 1980, in glaring opposition to statements he'd made during his last public utterances on the subject, John argued long and loud against the possibility of the four of them ever getting together again. Much of what he had to say in the *Double Fantasy* promotional interviews had the effect of down playing any future Fabness, while playing *up* the domestic and artistic union he and Yoko were enjoying. His oft-repeated debt of gratitude for Yoko's wisdom and clearheaded guidance smacks of overkill, suggesting a man-child with horrific dependency issues—a characterization still hotly debated.

We now know that much of what he told interviewers was nonsense: for example, the narrative that he stayed musically inactive during the house husband years until being struck with inspiration during his 1980 spring sojourn to Bermuda. This mythmaking was easily dispelled with the commencement of the *Lost Lennon Tapes* radio show during the 1980s, which revealed a trove of recordings made during this allegedly inactive period, among them "Free As A Bird" and the various iterations of what became "Real Love."

John's final publicity blitz came in support of a joint project with Yoko, who—between the two—seemed to have a greater grasp of the contemporary music scene. (Despite the buzz surrounding Lennon's return to recording, *Double Fantasy* was *not*—initially at least—the chart-tearing rocket he might have expected, especially in England, where initial reviews were lukewarm.) On the night of his death, he worked on what was expected to be Yoko's commercial breakthrough track: "Walking On Thin Ice." New York City newsstands were carrying an issue of *Soho Weekly News* proclaiming (ironically, as it happened) "Yoko Only." With most of the critical acclaim being directed toward his wife's *au courant* sound, John had good reason to believe that his own work might soon be eclipsed—perhaps by design.

His private opinions regarding a future with his ex-bandmates were another matter. In his relationship with May Pang, which continued beneath the radar long after it had publicly ended, he often expressed a desire to resume a songwriting relationship with Paul. (Producer Jack Douglas concurred.) Stories from multiple sources have circulated suggesting that in Lennon's last weeks, Paul was stymied in his efforts to reach John, very likely for pursuing this very purpose.

John, Paul, and George were making contributions to Ringo's upcoming album—perhaps this could have provided the catalyst for a discussion of working together; if not as "Beatles," at least as musicians and long-time acquaintances that intuited each other's musical moves very well. It must also be remembered that for the first time in his solo career, George had just had a completed album handed back to him, with complaints that it wasn't commercial enough. With Wings on the skids, Lennon back in business, and Ringo being Ringo, might not the planned get-together for the drummer's nuptials in early 1981 be a most opportune time to re-think a mutually beneficial collective future?

Whatever John was thinking when giving his sworn statement, it isn't too much of a stretch to conclude that he was keeping his options open. That he was putting tremendous energy into pushing Yoko as an artist in her own right whose time had come strongly suggests that he was willing to suspend their joint efforts, using the one-two punch of *Double Fantasy* / "Walking On Thin Ice" to launch *her* solo career, therein liberating himself. The answer to what his intents were will forever be debated, but his deposition gives a tantalizing glimpse into what might have been, had the events of December 8 played out differently.

Pete Bennett, at left, seen with Phil Spector, John and Yoko and Geraldo Rivera; backstage at 1972's One-to-One concert. Photo by Paul Schumach.

CHAPTER 3

MET THEM ALL THERE IN THE MATERIAL WORLD: BUSINESS ASSOCIATES, FRIENDS, LOVERS, AND GOFERS

F irmly within the orbit of the Fabs throughout the decade following their disintegration were a number of personas that, for a time, were vitally intertwined with one or more ex-members. Some (like Vini Poncia or Elliot Mintz) were already successful in their own right; others (like Pete Bennett) were Apple employees; still others (Seaman) toiled behind the scenes while remaining unknown to the public. All had a role to play within the scope of this book and are discussed here.

(Note: The McCartneys were fairly self-contained; no one fitting the description of some of those described here really occupied the same space in their lives.)

PETE BENNETT

Born Pietro Benedetto (like the famous singer Pete claimed as a "cousin," he'd Anglicized his name) in the Bronx, Apple's record promotion manager Pete Bennett was a legend in the industry. An Allen Klein associate (who looked the part), his roots in the business ran deep, having gotten his start as a record plugger in partnership with Berry Gordy back in Motown's early days. Bennett scored enormous successes very early on, helping make records by artists as diverse as Nat King Cole, The Shirelles, Bobby Vinton, and Sam Cooke, solid hits. His love of music coupled with a gregarious and pugnacious personality made him ideally suited to the rough-and-tumble business at a time when paradigms were being shaped.

Bennett was something of a rock and roll Zelig, well-placed (his collection of photos taken with celebs is legendary) and—at least to hear him tell it—around at the right time to influence key moments in history. He has described over Nat Cole's objections recommending that the singer record "Rambling Rose," a "corny" number that became his comeback hit. A few years later, some quick thinking on Bennett's part kept the FCC from banning the Rolling Stones' "Honky Tonk Women"

WOMAN IS THE NIGGER OF THE WORLD

NOVA

SHE: "WOMAN IS THE NIGGER OF THE WORLD..."

JOHN LENNON

PLASTIC ONO BAND

with Elephant's Memory
and Invisible Strings

SISTERS O SISTERS

YOKO ONO

PLASTIC ONO BAND

with Elephant's Memory
and Invisible Strings

Apple 1848

Had John found a way to rephrase the tag line/title of this single, without losing an ounce of the sting – a tall order, to be sure – neither Pete Bennett nor any other detractors would've been able to ignore the power within the performance.

from the airwaves; they objected to the line "I *laid* a divorcee in New York City," but he managed to convince them that Jagger was actually singing *"played,"* saving the day and helping the band score one of their biggest hits.

The prototypical fast-talking New Yorker, Bennett's manner fascinated the Beatles, both before and after the break-up. (Al Aronowitz once described him as "somebody you might think had been banned from the cast of *The Godfather* because the Italian Anti-Defamation League thought he looked too real.") Despite the alienation Klein's control of the Fabs' affairs wrought, Paul maintained as close and amicable a relationship with Bennett as did the other three. By no means was a new record by any of the ex-Fabs a surefire hit, and it was Bennett's job to glad-hand, cajole, and otherwise massage DJs and radio programmers into getting his clients' wares some airplay.

Often, this was relatively easy. *All Things Must Pass* was the gift that kept on giving, spawning two hit singles, one a worldwide smash. John's *Plastic Ono Band* was less of an easy sell, given the intensity of emotion and lack of an obvious feel-good ditty. John must've been disappointed in its chart performance, for Bennett had to pull him aside and let him know that next time out, he would have to "go more commercial" to match George's achievement. Sure enough, *Imagine* became his first number one album (though the title single itself fell short).

For Ringo, "It Don't Come Easy" would be his first *real* test as a solo artist. Bennett acted to reassure him that the song was top-flight: "I told him I loved it...'we will make it a hit.'" After the song was added to fifty stations and earned a "bullet" in *Billboard*, the drummer began checking in with Bennett every other day to learn the single's progress. As the song's continued ascent began shattering everyone's expectations, a disbelieving John began calling in to check on it himself.

As a world-class raconteur, much of Bennett's repeated stories needed to be taken with a massive grain of salt. One of them that made the rounds concerned the run-up to the Bangladesh benefit, which Bennett was apparently helpful in arranging. As he told it, George was determined *not* to film the show, purportedly because cameras made Bob Dylan nervous. Bennett says that *he* arranged to have a crew equipped with 16mm gear show up anyway and document the show from hidden locations (!). When George spotted a couple of cameras before the show, he demanded to know why they were there. Bennett: "I told him they were CBS, NBC, ABC – do you want me to throw them out?" The next day, George (according to Bennett) is said to have opined, "We should have filmed it," to which Pete told him – wait for it – "We did, George, we did."

There are many problems with the underlying premise, among them being the fact that George *knew* full well he was being filmed, as a chunk of backstage and rehearsal coverage showed. The notion that a crew was arranged on the sly was ludicrous: Apple *paid* for it and arranged for the director. George *did* have reservations about the way it was filmed, not wishing for large 35mm film cameras to be obstructing the audience's view; that was how it came to be shot on smaller cameras normally used for news events. Furthermore, it was always intended that the film's revenue would add to the potency of the event's cash-raising abilities.

A more plausible vignette is Bennett's assertion that he told John Lennon to his face that he would not promote "Woman Is The Nigger Of The World" on the basis of it being "racist" and not commercial—despite Lennon, as a president of Apple, being his boss. Instead of getting angry, John is said to have challenged Bennett, saying he would promote it himself and—if it reached number one, as he believed it would—Bennett would have to "kiss (John's) behind." While Lennon may have been a gifted artist, he was out of his depth as record plugger: radio stations he called happily taped interviews with him (to air later), but then played the song off the air. The single stalled at fifty-seven and Bennett won the bet. (Whether he collected is not known.)

Though demonstrably at the top of his trade, Bennett was evidently not satisfied with his position within rock's highest strata. Recognizing an opportunity to further enrich himself—like so many others exploiting their proximity to the ex-Fabs—he grabbed at the bounty before him. As standard industry practice, Apple/Capitol set aside some 5,000 copies of each new release for promotional purposes. Normally these copies would be distributed among radio stations, distributors, rack jobbers, retailers—anywhere that they could grease the wheels of commerce and spur goodwill. In cahoots with Allen Klein, however, Bennett—under Klein's direction—*sold* unmarked freebies under the table and together they split the proceeds. By 1977, a Federal investigation into Bennett's activities came to a head: in a deal brokered to spare his own hide, he turned star witness against his former benefactor and helped send Klein to prison on tax evasion charges.

It's a chapter he didn't care to share on his latter-day road show. Bennett passed away in 2012; not one obituary mentioned these sordid dealings, as the court records had long since been sealed.

NANCY LEE ANDREWS

A chance encounter in 1964 with legendary TV and radio personality Arthur Godfrey in New York City set seventeen-year old Nancy Andrews on her way to a successful modeling career. The lively New Jersey native was blessed with height, cheekbones, and vaguely exotic looks, being a mixture of Sicilian and Cherokee blood. Given this deadly combination, Godfrey managed to arrange a meeting for her with representatives of the Eileen Ford Modeling Agency, and from there, a career was born.

Her work soon found her being documented before the cameras of many of the field's heavyweights, including Bert Stern and Richard Avedon. It also put her in the orbit of rock and roll royalty, and she soon fell into a serious relationship with bassist Carl Radle (born in Oklahoma on the same day as Paul McCartney). Radle, of course, became famous through both his session work and his charter membership in Derek and the Dominoes. Thus, through Clapton and crew, Nancy met her first ex-Beatle, George, during the *All Things Must Pass* sessions and subsequently at the Bangladesh benefit.

The next ex-Fab to cross her path was John, most likely during the recording of Nilsson's *Pussy Cats*. As a visitor to the studio, she met May Pang and the two instantly bonded, bringing Andrews into the Beatle orbit for the remainder of the decade. Since Nancy was

In addition to the album covers for Ringo the 4th and Bad Boy, Nancy Andrews also served as the publicity photographer for 1978's Ringo TV special.

now living in Los Angeles, she offered May the use of her garage (to store the reddish 1968 Barracuda John had bought her) whenever she and John were in New York City.

On a return visit to the West Coast in May, the two women were reunited, this time at the rented beach house in Santa Monica that became the Hollywood Vampire's party central. There, on May 27, 1974, Nancy and Ringo met over a game of poker. A good impression was made on both sides, for two months later, when work on *Goodnight Vienna* was underway, the two renewed their acquaintance. Soon, with John's encouragement, Ringo and Nancy became an item.

Though not quite on the level of a John & Yoko or a Paul & Linda, a certain amount of collaboration marked the pair's relationship. Since her modeling days, a camera was always close at hand and with Ringo's encouragement, Nancy documented their lives and those within their circle with a vengeance. She would be responsible for two of his album covers, *Ringo the 4th* and *Bad Boy*, as well as the promotional photography for his 1978 *Ringo* television special. The two also wrote a song together, "Las Brisas," the mariachi pastiche issued on 1976's *Rotogravure* set. (The tune was inspired by a romantic evening at a hotel in Acapulco.) Nancy also appeared in *Bad*

Boy's "Tonight" video.

In 1977, Ringo declared to *People* magazine his desire to have children with Nancy. Their time together, unfortunately, coincided with the downturn in Ringo's personal and professional fortunes. Though they lived an exotic, adventurous life, globetrotting around the world as "elegant gypsies" (Nancy's words), the Ringed One's sensibilities were unquestionably dulled by the effects of massive alcohol consumption. Further, despite the great love between them, Ringo hadn't completely gotten over Maureen.

After copping to adultery, it had taken some years after the trauma of their divorce for Ringo and his former wife to reach a point of rapprochement. His settlement terms had been generous, and in interviews, he never ceased to speak glowingly of how wonderful a mother he thought Maureen was. Despite reports of Ringo's engagement to Nancy, some held that a reconciliation was not beyond possibility, particularly after the drummer's near-death emergency surgery that year.

While the ex-spouses never did remarry, things were undeniably wobbly throughout the Andrews-Starkey saga. During a seven-month break-up, Ringo enjoyed romantic interludes with a number of women, ranging from actress Shelley Duvall to singer Lynsey DePaul to Stephanie LaMotta, the teen-aged daughter of ex-boxer Jake "Raging Bull" LaMotta. Nancy remained loyal to the man she described as occasionally being a "jerk," but even she underestimated the effect that meeting actress Barbara Bach would have on him in 1980. "I thought he would come home to me," she told *Daytrippin'* magazine, but as he explained to her, "You can't fight lightning."

Nancy's photography career resumed full tilt after their split; she also accepted an acting role in the 1981 horror spoof, *Saturday The 14th*, starring real life husband-and-wife, Richard Benjamin and Paula Prentiss. Today, happily settled in Nashville with husband Eddie Byrnes, Nancy operates her own studio, shooting an array of country stars, as well as acting as director of photography for *Twang* magazine. She recently re-surfaced in Beatledom, publishing a stunning collection of her photographs taken during the seventies (after being prodded by her friend, former U.S. Apple head Ken Mansfield). The book is called *A Dose of Rock and Roll*—it's well worth checking out.

VINI PONCIA

Phil Spector was a record-producing dynamo in the early sixties.

In early 1964, he started up an offshoot label, Annette (named for his then-wife). One of his female back-up singers was to be launched from the new marquee as a soloist: the 17 year-old Cherilyn LaPierre. Her boyfriend Sonny Bono was a Spector protégé, as was the man credited with co-writing her debut single, Vini Poncia. The song (released under the "American sounding" name Bonnie Jo Mason) was a novelty cash-in on Beatlemania titled "Ringo I Love You." It was not a success; released one month after the Beatles played *The Ed Sullivan Show*, radio programmers were baffled by the singer's contralto voice and, fearing it was a pledge of homosexual devotion, shunned it.

For Poncia, the song was just one of many crafted for Spector's stable of artists. Born in 1942, the musician/songwriter became something of a jack-of-all-trades, learning the business through proximity to the industry's giants while recording and performing with several acts, most notably The Tradewinds ("New York's A Lonely Town" was a Top Forty hit in 1965). In 1968, he issued an album with his songwriting partner, Peter Anders (entitled, naturally *The Anders and Poncia Album*), produced by Richard Perry. After splitting with Anders, Poncia and Perry began a partnership of their own and such is how the writer of "Ringo I Love You" came into the ex-Beatle orbit.

By sheer coincidence, Ringo's future songwriting partner, Vini Poncia, co-wrote this one-off novelty song about him in 1964. It served as Cher's recording debut as a soloist, albeit under an alias.

At L.A.'s Sunset Studios, Poncia was on hand for the *Ringo* sessions, contributing guitar throughout but also co-authoring a pair of tunes, "Devil Woman" and the bouncy "Oh My My." He and Ringo hit it off; over the course of his next four albums, Poncia stayed a constant, becoming the ex-Fab's most prolific co-author. Two more tunes sprang from their partnership

51

for *Goodnight Vienna*: "Oo-Wee" and "All By Myself," followed *another* pair on *Ringo's Rotogravure* ("Cryin'" and "Lady Gaye.") With Ringo at last hitting his stride as a writer, it's little surprise that the two went all out for the next release: six of the ten songs on *Ringo The 4th* were joint credited, plus the non-album B-side, "Just A Dream." Unfortunately, the scathing reviews the album received spooked them into going back to the professionals for their next— and final—outing.

For *Bad Boy*, Poncia at last took over the production reins himself. It should be noted that he and Ringo weren't completely joined at the hip: Poncia had also been producing singer Melissa Manchester, whom he had brought into the sessions for Ringo's two Atlantic releases as a back-up singer. She of course had scored big with "Midnight Blue" in 1975; that and 1978's "Don't Cry Out Loud" were produced by Poncia, as were nearly all of her studio releases. He also helped out his buddy Richard Perry by assisting Leo Sayer with the writing of what became his first number one single. In polishing off "You Make Me Feel Like Dancing," based on a lick boosted from Jean Knight's "Mr. Big Stuff" after Sayer hit a writer's block, he earned himself and the singer a Grammy for *R&B* Song of the Year for reportedly *five minutes work*. (No one said life is fair, folks.)

Unfortunately, his hit-making capabilities were no longer transferable to Richie Snare. *Bad Boy* marked their last collaborative effort, despite the presence of "Who Needs A Heart," perhaps their strongest co-composition song since "Oh My My." That same year, Poncia undertook production chores for another drummer turned singer, Kiss' Peter Criss. Though regarded as possessing the best pop instincts of the group (Criss had sung "Beth," which he co-wrote, as well as "Hard Luck Woman"), the album sold poorly. Poncia did better when he produced the next Kiss album, 1979's *Dynasty*, which spawned the disco smash, "I Was Made For Lovin' You," therein earning the enmity of diehard Kiss fans.

ELLIOT MINTZ

Though a Disney-owned, conservative talk radio show today, Los Angeles' KABC-AM was quite different back in the early seventies. One of its more highly touted stars was Sunday night host Elliot Mintz. Mintz had made a name for himself in the late sixties for the show he'd hosted on progressive FM radio station

KPFK, where he was known for his array of counterculture topics, including interviews with guru Baba Ram Dass and shows on the Bermuda Triangle. (He also briefly MC'd a syndicated television rock showcase, *Headshop*.) Lured over to the AM powerhouse increased his listenership (while denting his "hip" credentials only slightly). Well on his way up, career-wise, he came off as a sort of West Coast Dick Cavett, substituting earnestness for wit.

By 1971, Mintz had switched again, back to FM and album rock station KLOS, where he anchored a weekend show. (This kept him in the employ of ABC, who occasionally tabbed him to act as television interviewer for their sister TV station.) That same year, he placed a call to the East Coast, seeking an interview with Yoko, who was in the midst of a busy year, what with the release of *Fly*, a re-print of *Grapefruit*, and a one-woman art show in Syracuse. The two hit it off on the air, as Mintz asked questions that seemed to be on a slightly higher level than what she was accustomed to. (For example: "Do you dream in Japanese or English?")

If Mintz was plotting some sort of Machiavellian plan to use Yoko as a stepping stone to insinuate himself into John's good graces, he could not have scored any better. For weeks after their interview, Yoko and Mintz continued the conversation with late night phone

When John and Yoko separated in 1973, one frequent visitor was Elliot Mintz. According to Jack Douglas and others, he was regarded as Yoko's friend and a "spy," reporting on John's doings directly to her.

calls, until finally John demanded to know who her friend was and what did he want? He got his answer when Mintz conducted an interview with John, one day after his thirty-first birthday in October. From then on, John saw Mintz as an effective instrument to communicate to the West Coast and cultivated him accordingly, via telephone.

Not until the spring of 1972 would the Lennons and Mintz meet face to face. The couple undertook a cross-country jaunt in early June, meeting up with Mintz in Century City. It was the eve of the release of *Some Time In New York City*—as an "exclusive," they gave him an advance copy to play on the air. Mintz milked the occasion for all it was worth, presenting the double album uninterrupted (while holding all commercials until after it had finished playing). He then opened up the phone lines for listener reactions. While that aspect of the evening could be judged a success, the show's sponsors were evidently less than flattered to be associated with a record that so brazenly courted controversy. As Mintz tells it, he was given his walking papers as a result of the broadcast.

Taking a hit for the cause put Mintz in solid with the Lennons, especially Yoko. With personal and unquestioned loyalty being the most desirable of traits, Mintz earned proximity, if not complete trust. When they separated in 1973 however, it became clear where allegiances lie. Mintz has maintained that he accompanied John to Los Angeles and hung out with him as an intimate. May Pang tells a different story: that Mintz has distorted or exaggerated events in his telling, expressly cutting her out of incidents where she was present—and had the photos to prove it. She further asserts that when he was around at all, it was on marching orders from Yoko to act as her eyes and ears. (Her dismissal of Mintz as not quite the close personal friend of John's that he claimed is not unique. Still, it's important to keep in mind is that both sides had a vested interest in spinning their stories as they did.)

In October 1982—nearly two years after Lennon's death — Mintz contributed heavily to an essay in *Rolling Stone* entitled "The Private Years." The basis of so much mythology concerning John and Yoko's marriage and what exactly he was up to during his five years out of the public eye sprang from here. It is known that Mintz flew out to Japan to meet the Lennons in 1977, around the time Elvis died. In the article, he described being summoned by a mysterious hand delivered message that included an air ticket and an elaborate set of instructions, detailing exactly how to proceed.

("...a man would meet Mintz and take him to a train station and give him a card with Japanese markings to indicate which train to take.") The picture painted by Mintz's descriptions of John's life seemed to amplify themes John himself propagated in his final interviews, as someone who'd finally found a kind of peace within a tight-knit cocoon containing himself, Yoko, Sean—and Elliot Mintz.

It's unfortunate for history's sake that there is no independent corroboration for much of what Mintz has described. The John Lennon described in his accounts borders on superhuman: the perfect nurturing father; the bread-making homebody; the living legend who turned his back on his livelihood, forsaking any musical creativity until his muse was reawakened during his sojourn to Bermuda in 1980. Going unmentioned are the many compositions written or started during the time-off; any talk of drug or health issues (between 1975 and the day he died, there were times when John's startling weight loss made him appear to be anorexic); or his less-than-idyllic married life that he and Yoko went into overdrive hyping during promotional chats for *Double Fantasy*.

It is known that May Pang sustained an intimacy with John for some years after the "Lost Weekend" ended; there are also accounts by people close to the couple detailing Yoko's plans to divorce John in 1980, perhaps to marry the New York City art dealer she's reputed to have been more than friends with. Yoko herself has since admitted her relapse into heroin addiction that same year, a subject that Mintz avoids completely, as well as her twenty-plus year "marriage" to Hungarian artist Sam Havadtoy, going full-time when he moved into the Dakota only months after John's murder. Remarkably casual romantic liaisons for a couple that publicly fancied themselves Robert and Elizabeth Barrett Browning incarnate.

Since Lennon's death, Mintz's bond to Yoko has come into sharper relief. Initially described as a close friend, he segued seamlessly into the role of spokesman, appearing as the public face of the grieving widow whenever trouble was afoot, which was often. When the members of Elephants Memory surfaced in the 1980s, demanding payment for their contribution to a charitable event, now being issued for profit, Mintz appeared before the press to declaim them as a "tenth-rate" band. When Macca publicly repeated his desire to reverse the name order on the credits of Lennon-McCartney songs that *he* had authored, Mintz dismissed Paul's wishes with a stretch of hyperbole that declared "Eleanor Rigby" had been "kidnapped."

Such implementation of language, falling somewhere between

Derek Taylor's sublime wordcraft and Tony Barrow's hackery, has of late been put to use for a list of clients falling somewhat short of the ex-Beatle's stature, among them Christie Brinkley, Don Johnson, and—most infamously—Paris Hilton. Many have wondered how Mintz came to find himself flacking for the talent-deprived dilettante; reasoned Mintz: "Young people today don't believe in politicians. They don't believe in leaders. They look to celebrities to represent them."

FRED SEAMAN

Battling the mythic spin generated by Mintz, Yoko, and Ono stalwarts Bob Gruen and Alan Tannenbaum (photographers both) was the counter-myth that emerged in the 1980s, infamously disseminated by necro-biographer Albert Goldman (*The Lives of John Lennon*), Yoko's tarot card reader, John Green (*Dakota Days*); writer Robert Rosen (*Nowhere Man: The Final Days of John Lennon*); and most notoriously of all, John's last personal assistant, Frederic Seaman (*The Last Days of John Lennon*). The portrait that emerged from their tellings depicted a drugged up, strung out, physically abusive depressive, fiercely jealous of Paul McCartney's achievements while seemingly incapable of defying the will of his occultist wife, who—naturally—stayed married to him to control his millions and attach herself, leech-like, to her famous husband in order to fulfill her rock star ambitions, like an updated (and thoroughly warped) Lucy Ricardo.

Unlike Goldman or Rosen, Seaman was a bona fide insider, employed by the Lennons as an all-purpose gofer. He came with the most sterling of credentials, being the nephew of Sean's nanny, Helen Seaman. Helen had achieved her position as wife of an old Yoko crony, Norman Seaman who, together with his brother, conductor/pianist Eugene, booked concerts in New York, including some pre-Lennon Ono performances in the early sixties. In any event, Fred began work in February 1979. His duties, often spelled out in long, hand-written notes from John, ranged anywhere from looking after Sean to running out to get groceries to acting as photographer on special occasions. Given such intimate contact with the family inside their domicile, Seaman would have been privy to their private goings-on; as such, he was required to sign a confidentiality agreement as a condition of employment. His detractors asserted that he never intended to honor the document.

Seaman was on hand when John began to demo material in earnest in the summer of 1980, flying down to meet him in Bermuda and acting as sounding board, roadie, and accompanist (banging out percussion) as John laid down the sketches of what became *Double Fantasy* and *Milk and Honey*. By his account, it was an idyllic trip, one that reignited John's passion to make music. (John declared he had been wary of listening to current pop music, fearing if it was bad, he would hate it, feeling he could do better; if it was good, he would become angry, because it *wasn't* him making it.) Hearing Paul's "Coming Up" finally spurred him to action, though it took him some time to shake off the insecurity that perhaps his time had come and gone.

Things were only bound to get more interesting with the Lennons resuming a musical career, but John's murder just weeks after the release of his comeback triumph brought things crashing down. Unbeknownst to Yoko or anyone else working for the couple, Fred—after asking for and getting time off for bereavement—formulated a plan. He began by removing certain items surreptitiously from the Dakota's Studio One offices. In addition to minor things like articles of clothing and electronic gear (John was constantly being gifted the latest gadgets by manufacturers, more than he could ever take the time to learn to operate; reportedly he'd frequently told Seaman to take home whatever he wanted, an invitation he did not act upon until after John's death), he also removed the entire lot of Lennon's personal diaries, covering the years 1975 until his death.

In his defense later, Seaman said that John had instructed him to make sure that Julian got them in the case of his demise. Apparently this brief extended to cassettes of unpublished songs (as well as the manuscript to John's third book, *Skywriting By Word of Mouth*, eventually made public in the 1980s). The spiriting away of Lennon materials from the Dakota might have continued indefinitely had not Yoko, upon catching Fred taking a bath during working hours (as well as wearing John's clothes—not simultaneously) fired him in 1982. Not long after, she was tipped off about the thefts: when efforts to recover the items failed, Yoko notified police and Seaman was arrested.

What emerged from his trial was a tale so bizarre that it could scarcely be imagined. First, Seaman had (per the prosecution) been plotting to secure a deal for a tell-all book (expected to sell millions) practically before John's body was cold. Two weeks after

John's death, a notarized contract was signed between Seaman and the aforementioned Robert Rosen, a college friend who held the materials Fred began gathering and agreed to collaborate on the book. "Project Walrus," as the enterprise was dubbed, grew to include a retired New York City diamond dealer (introduced to Seaman by his psychiatrist) as well as Rick DuFay, a journeyman guitarist (who played with Aerosmith in the early '80s until the return of Joe Perry). There was no love lost among the members of the cabal: Rosen recorded that each one wondered "who is the most contemptible among us."

Bankrolled by the diamond merchant, Project Walrus entailed establishing Fred Seaman as *the* heir to John Lennon's legacy while simultaneously tearing down Yoko as a fraud and seeding "the gossip market" with the most damaging and salacious tidbits they could contrive. Seaman embezzled from Lenono's petty cash to pay Rosen a retainer, delivering grocery bags of purloined documents and materials weekly, while the Lennon journals—ostensibly removed to fulfill John's wish that Julian get them—somehow never seemed to find their way to England. Rosen worked at transcribing them and generating a manuscript for over a year, until—after Seaman's dismissal—he was declared dispensable by the plotters and, while on an expenses paid trip Jamaica, unceremoniously cut from the conspiracy. His apartment was looted of all Lennon materials, a development that did not sit well with him.

Rosen contacted *Rolling Stone* publisher Jann Wenner and spilled all he knew; Wenner in turn put him in touch with Yoko and from there, Project Walrus quickly unraveled. Rosen exchanged information for immunity while Seaman attempted to extort cash for the return of the materials—failure of the negotiations landed him in court. Whatever self-righteous bravado he'd possessed until then evaporated in the face of massive legal bills and protracted litigation. On May 7, 1983, Seaman pleaded guilty to grand larceny in the second degree and received five years probation. Simon and Schuster canceled a book deal (that included a $90,000 advance), whereupon Seaman took his gathered materials, insider info, and axes to grind over to Albert Goldman. The result of their joining forces resulted in the second assassination of John Lennon in less than a decade.

One would think that having been through the legal wringer once would forever remove any temptations to further bait the limitless might of someone that will out-lawyer you every time. But no:

in 1988, in violation of the terms of his guilty pleading, Seaman went ahead anyway and published a book, 1991's *The Last Days of John Lennon*—his tale of the Lennon years. While Goldman let no opportunity to slander John pass in *his* book, Seaman did likewise with Yoko in his. To her credit, Yoko let it slide: ignoring his working with Goldman, the subsequent book, and a continuous stream of public badmouthing before again being forced to come down on him. And when she did, it was only in response to his first going after *her.*

The 1999 *Lennon Anthology* box set included in its packaging a number of photos Fred Seaman had taken while in their employ. In an act of hubris beyond comprehension, he elected to tug hard on the tiger's tail by laying claim to them. It was a bridge too far, as they say, and this time, he got the attention he'd apparently been missing. It took three years work its way through the courts, which concluded that he had no ownership of images taken at the Lennons' direction, with their camera. The thoroughly-shamed defendant stood in a Manhattan courtroom, admitting to his misdeeds. The settlement called for the return of Lennon letters he'd stolen and sold (to the tune of some $75,000); the return of 374 photos, and this public statement:

"I wish to offer this public apology to Yoko Ono. I did wrong by you and indeed am guilty of violating your trust. After more than 20 years, it is time for me to ask for your forgiveness for my actions.

I did in fact steal items from you that once belonged to you and John. These items include diaries, documents and more. I wrote things about you and your family in my book and various tabloids that were factually inaccurate, and I now realize how much pain and embarrassment I have caused. It is impossible to undo what has taken place. But it stops here and now.

I will return any remaining things that I have that are yours. I will refrain from ever writing anything about your family or about the time in your employ. I offer no excuse for my conduct and only ask that you can find it in your heart to forgive so I can move on with my life."

Since over a decade has passed since Seaman was last called into court by his former employer, who knows? He may have even meant it.

Billy Preston's gospel-flavored cover of George's biggest-selling single much more closely resembled the recording that inspired it: 1969's "Oh Happy Day" - not surprisingly, since his take featured the Edwin Hawkins Singers on backing vocals.

CHAPTER 4

ALL I HAVE IS YOURS: EX-FAB SONGS RECORDED BY OTHERS

T he Beatles' golden touch with crafting hits carried over well into their solo years. Each ex-Fab composed songs that were successfully covered by other artists, even Ringo. (Engelbert Humperdinck covered "Photograph" on his 1973 release, *My Love*, named for his cover of *Paul's* song.)

After their initial chart successes in 1963, the Lennon-McCartney songwriting team found itself in demand by other singers anxious for a touch of their compositional star power. Typically, John and Paul would dump sub-par material on other acts, but occasionally they would custom-craft a tune for an artist they liked. This practice carried over into their solo years, with George replacing John in that role.

Judging by his Fab-era output, it's not surprising that of the four, it was Paul who coveted the role of "writer of standards" the most. What is surprising is that, during the years immediately following the break-up, at least, it was *John and George's* solo material that tended to be covered the most, not Paul's. The following represents a good cross section of the diverse artists that found the songwriting of the ex-Beatles irresistible.

"MY SWEET LORD" RECORDED BY BILLY PRESTON – RELEASED 1970

Beginning in the last year of the Beatles' existence, George and Billy Preston became frequent collaborators on recording projects. When not assisting others on the Apple roster, they helped out each other, with George co-producing and playing on Billy's two Apple albums, *That's The Way God Planned It* and *Encouraging Words*. Billy would return the favor as a key player on George's *All Things Must Pass*.

Before that landmark album got underway, George offered Billy a song he'd composed in a fit of inspiration while touring with Delaney and Bonnie in the fall of 1969, sparked by the fluke success of the Edwin Hawkins Singers with "Oh Happy Day" earlier that year. Though the gospel-rock of Billy's "That's The Way God Planned It" didn't chart as well as expected, George felt that an exploration of the genre wasn't yet a lost cause. After co-writing "Sing One For The Lord" together, George offered up another composition that Billy was more than glad to have a go at. It was called "My Sweet Lord."

Performing on the funked-up arrangement were Keith Richards on bass, Eric Clapton joining George on guitar, and Ginger Baker on drums. The Edwin Hawkins Singers, augmented by Doris Troy, contributed backing vocals. It was released as a single in the States in late 1970, rising to ninety in the charts. It might have done better, had it not gone head to head with the version by the song's writer.

For his own recording, George decided to take the song in another direction. The majestic Spector "wall of sound" may have made the difference, but more likely it was his innate Beatleness that turned George's recording into a worldwide smash. It was released as a single against his initial wishes, once Apple divined that the track was getting massive requests for airplay. Perhaps if he'd gotten his way, the subsequent troubles the song later caused George might have been avoided.

In 2002, Billy and Eric were among the friends and colleagues gathered together at London's Royal Albert Hall to honor George on the one-year anniversary of his death. "My Sweet Lord" was performed, sung by Billy publicly for probably the last time. He died of complications from kidney disease in 2006.

"LOVE" RECORDED BY THE LETTERMEN – RELEASED 1971

Back in the day, a radio format geared toward listeners who could not stomach rock existed alongside Top Forty radio. "Easy Listening," "Middle of the Road" (MOR), "Adult Contemporary"— by whatever euphemism it was known, an entire stratum of singers that would never fit on a rock and roll station existed, typically featuring crooners from another era (i.e. Perry Como, Johnny Mathis) alongside younger artists (i.e. the Carpenters, Engelbert Humperdinck—the latter whom John once unfavorably compared Paul to).

Standard operating procedure for such acts was to take a breakout hit of the day and produce a smoother, mellower version, designed to please the ears of adults who, by now married with kids or preoccupied with their careers, could use the wallpaper to accessorize their daily lives. The Adult Contemporary format in radio exists today, but is downright raucous compared to what existed back in the sixties and seventies.

One of the more successful purveyors of this style was a trio (with a rotating line up) called The Lettermen. After signing with Capitol in 1961, this boy band's hit-making career began in earnest with a pair of standards, "The Way You Look Tonight" (still played at weddings) and Nat King Cole's "When I Fall In Love." As the sixties unfolded, their brand of lush vocalizing became a harder sell, competing against the likes of Motown, the Beach Boys, and the Beatles. But the act segued easily into the Adult Contemporary charts, enjoying a string of hits there for another decade.

In 1971, the group released their thirtieth (!) long player, the thematically programmed *Love Book*. Linchpin to the entire set was a cover of John's *Plastic Ono Band* ballad, "Love." (John himself was well aware of the tune's commercial possibilities; not wishing the song to represent the album in the singles market, he deliberately mixed it so as to fade up slowly, guaranteeing its unsuitability for airplay. After his death, the song was re-mixed with Phil Spector's piano intro at full volume and released as a single in England to promote the *John Lennon Collection* best-of.)

The Lettermen's version, arranged as a solo piece featuring singer Gary Pike, stuck close to Lennon's blueprint, with some McCartney-esque "aahs" and a bit of orchestration thrown in. The results being somewhat anachronistic in its day, the song made it only to forty-two on *Billboard*'s Hot 100—their last such appearance—but reached the Top Ten on the adult contemporary chart. Its success led the group to tackle John's "Oh My Love" on their follow-up LP, 1972's *1*.

"BEWARE OF DARKNESS" RECORDED BY
LEON RUSSELL – RELEASED 1971

It was through Delaney Bramlett that George first came into personal contact with this Oklahoma-born jack-of-all-musical-trades. A loose fellowship came into being, with George, Leon, Ringo, Billy Preston, Klaus Voormann, and Eric Clapton participating on projects together. In the fall of 1969, this aggregate assembled to assist in the recording of Russell's debut album, a collection that included his pop standard, "A Song For You."

A year later, sessions commenced for his follow-up, *Leon Russell and the Shelter People.* Included in the set was one of the newer songs composed for *All Things Must Pass*, "Beware of Darkness." Recorded more or less concurrently with the version by the song's author, it had a rather more elaborate arrangement, featuring tabla and sitar interludes (in nearly a parody of George's Indian obsessions).

Like "My Sweet Lord," it was significant as a validation of George's capacity for writing solid tunes that could be covered by other artists, even one as idiosyncratic as Russell. (It also must have pleased George to be included among the other covers included on the Leon's album—largely Bob Dylan's.)

At the Concert for Bangladesh in summer 1971, George graciously allowed Leon a turn on a verse of "Beware of Darkness," thereby heightening the latter's profile for the masses not yet turned on to his eclectic brand of music. The two would maintain contact, with Russell turning up onstage with George in Tulsa during the 1974 *Dark Horse* tour.

"MOTHER"
RECORDED BY BARBRA STREISAND
– RELEASED 1971

Very much a throwback to old-school entertainment when she burst upon New York's Broadway scene in 1962, Streisand nonetheless weathered the tide of Beatlemania quite well as the sixties unfolded. Successes on television and film followed, while her recorded output placed her in the upper ranks of best-selling artists.

By 1970, she'd re-invented herself as a more contemporary stylist of the era's best-known songwriters, notably Laura Nyro, whose "Stoney End" Barbra took to number six that year. For her follow up release, *Barbra Joan Streisand*, released in August 1971, Barbra extended the formula to include songs by Carol King, Bacharach and David, future Steely Dan mainstays Walter Becker and Donald Fagan, and John Lennon.

Imagine had not yet been released by the time Barbra began collating songs to record for BJS, but she did latch onto John's *Plastic Ono Band* album. For such a starkly personal and decidedly uncommercial record, Barbra showed astonishing good taste by tackling *two* tunes from the album: "Love" and "Mother." The first song was one that virtually anyone with ears could see was brimming with potential—

Produced by future Ringo collaborator Richard Perry, the Barbra Joan Streisand album was unloved at Rolling Stone magazine, whose reviewer called her take of "Mother" an "unqualified bummer."

the simplicity of the lyric, the plaintive, yet delicate melody, the universal sentiments.

But "Mother" was something else all together, being one of John's most personal and anguished compositions ever. To her credit, Streisand turned in a fine performance, showing what a singer with emotional empathy and chops aplenty could do. In a move that speaks volumes for the times, the song, produced by Richard Perry, was issued as a single—something not even imaginable in rock's far more formulated later years. While not a hit (reaching seventy-four on the Hot 100 and twenty-four on the AC chart), the fact of its existence speaks well of its creator.

In 2006, perhaps taking a cue from Barbra's rather obscure version, singer Christina Aguilera, no stranger to childhood trauma herself, took a crack at "Mother" on the star-studded charity compilation, *Instant Karma: The Amnesty International Campaign To Save Darfur*. She acquitted herself well.

"TRY SOME, BUY SOME" RECORDED BY RONNIE SPECTOR – RELEASED 1971

As George and Phil Spector's ongoing musical partnership unfolded in the wake of *All Things Must Pass*, it was inevitable that their attentions would be drawn to Phil's wife, Ronnie. Having retired from recording in 1966, it was a concern to Phil that the former lead singer of the Ronettes was in danger of being forgotten by the public. He desperately wished to re-introduce Ronnie to the marketplace: in a big way; who better to make this happen than the hottest former member of the biggest band on Earth?

For his own part, George too was anxious to expand his compositional horizons. Being a Ronnie fan from the beginning, he jumped at the chance to custom-tailor a song to her singular voice. His first effort was a real throw-back to the girl group days entitled "You." For whatever reason, while the backing was recorded, the track sat unfinished. A few years later, George, loath to squander his labors, dusted the tune off, overdubbed a new drum track, forced his vocals onto a song recorded just beyond his natural range, and released it as the lead-off single to his *Extra Texture* album in 1975.

The poppy "Lovely La-De-Day," "I Love Him Like I Love My Very Life" and—allegedly—a take of George's "Whatever" (later known as "I'll Still Love You" when recorded by Ringo) were also laid down by Ronnie. But it was another song he wrote that was judged the ideal vehicle for simultaneously expressing philosophic concerns while providing Phil the perfect platform for orchestrating his trademark Wall of Sound. While "Try Some, Buy Some" apparently fulfilled both men's needs, it fell far short of providing the singer with something to sink her teeth into. George's allegorical lyrics baffled her as much as her husband's insistence that this was the song to jumpstart her comeback. Her take on the end result? "It stunk!"

Ronnie Spector's assessment of the track may be too harsh and was perhaps colored by the single's failure on the charts. While peaking at seventy-seven in the spring of 1971, the song certainly had its fans, among them John Lennon. He was especially impressed with the string arrangement (by John Barham); later that year, he commissioned him to recreate the multiple-mandolin effect for his own "Happy Xmas (War is Over)" single. (Contrary to rumor, John did not participate in the Ronnie Spector recording, nor did Ringo. But a tape exists of John's 31st birthday celebration later that year, wherein John, Ringo, and a platoon of guests run through a number of songs, among them the flipside to Ronnie's single, the Harrison-Spector penned "Tandoori Chicken.")

Public indifference notwithstanding, George—as he would with "You"—decided that the studio effort was not worth squandering. In 1973, he replaced Ronnie's vocals with his own and issued his take as a cut on the *Living In The Material World* album. Ronnie's original saw official digital release at last in 2010, as part of the *Come and Get It: The Best of Apple Records* compilation, while in 2003, David Bowie recorded a version for his *Reality* album, offering evidence of what Spinal Tap might have termed the song's "select appeal."

"WHAT IS LIFE" RECORDED BY OLIVIA NEWTON-JOHN – RELEASED 1972

Today, the England-born, Australia-raised singer is largely remembered for her deathless role as Sandy in *Grease* (1978) or in her 1980s incarnation, as embodied by the song (and video) "Physical." But when the "Lovely Livvy" (as she was known earlier in her career) first entered America's consciousness, she was marketed as a country-rock chanteuse, with string of twangy hits like "Let Me Be There" and "If You Love Me (Let Me Know)" to her credit.

It all began for her on a major scale in 1971 with a cover of Bob Dylan's "If Not For You," modeled after George's *All Things Must Pass* version (complete with slide guitar). As an introduction, it did well, reaching number twenty-five in the U.S. Top Forty while topping the Adult Contemporary chart. Someone—either her handlers or Olivia herself—displayed an ATMP fixation when, for a follow-up, she recorded "What Is Life." Perhaps believing that George's *meisterwerk* possessed magical powers, Olivia threw a *third* cover of an *All Things Must Pass* song, George's paean to Bob Dylan,

"Behind That Locked Door" onto her follow-up album, which went unreleased in America.

Her perky take is recommended for her fans only—it's not truly awful, but not something most people need to hear more than once, either. A single release on the Uni label reached thirty-four on the Adult Contemporary chart in the States, perhaps predictably, since George's own version had already reached the Top Ten.

Prior to striking gold in the charts with this canny Dylan cover (by way of George), Olivia Newton-John was part of a bizarre sci-fi musical film project in 1970. Toomorow was masterminded by Don Kirshner, who later distanced himself from the end results and – reportedly – would not allow it to be shown.

Olivia's take did better in England, where the original hadn't been issued in 7" form.

"IMAGINE" RECORDED BY DIANA ROSS – RELEASED 1973

John's hymn-like appeal for universal brotherhood touched a chord with virtually everyone who heard it. Simple without being hackneyed and sweet without being saccharine, the song lent itself to a variety of treatments and settings, almost as much as "Yesterday" had for Paul. The charms of "Imagine" remain undiminished in the decades since its creation, with versions being recorded in recent years by artists as diverse as Dolly Parton and Madonna.

Like Lennon, former Supreme Diana Ross had segued nicely from being a member of a much-loved sixties act into uncharted solo territory. A re-make of the Marvin Gaye-Tammi Terrell hit "Ain't No Mountain High Enough" jump-started her career in 1970. More hits followed, along with a star turn in 1972's Motown-produced biopic, *Lady Sings The Blues*, with Ross cast in the lead role as singer Billie Holiday. The film's soundtrack scored Ross the only number one album of her career.

In its wake, she returned to the task of routine pop-making. What must have been evident to her was that the times had changed and that her peers on Motown, Stevie Wonder and Marvin Gaye, had raised the stakes by issuing albums that addressed topical concerns. While getting overtly political was probably beyond her interests (not to mention capabilities), "Imagine" offered the perfect opportunity to stay relevant while stopping short of straying too far from her standard sound.

The track graced her wildly successful *Touch Me In The Morning* album. Though not issued as a single, Ross' take was no mere filler. Tastefully produced, the singer's understated performance must rank as one the finest versions of this oft-covered track.

"THAT IS ALL" RECORDED BY ANDY WILLIAMS – RELEASED 1973

George's *Living in the Material World* was defined by its inherent spiritual undercurrent as well as some of his most adventurous singing to date. Never before—neither during his Beatles career nor on the sprawling *All Things Must Pass*—had he implemented falsetto crooning as much as he did on his second post-Beatles long-player. While as a solo artist, he rarely ventured into anything that might be considered hard rocking, he also wasn't exactly typed as a balladeer either. Either way, middle-of-the-road appeal wasn't what he was known for. (Only 1975's *Extra Texture* and the 1979 self-titled release ever came close to embracing Adult Contemporary values within the Harrison oeuvre.)

And yet, the album's concluding cut, "That Is All," would be recorded by *two* artists well represented on MOR-formatted radio. One was by Harry Nilsson, who issued his take on 1976's *...That's the Way It Is* album (where it functioned as opening *and* closing track). The other was by Andy Williams: the embodiment of the genre. His version came on 1973's *Solitaire* album: a release that featured some of the same players heard on the Harrison original (Jim Keltner, Klaus Voormann and Nicky Hopkins).

Williams was a kingpin of Easy Listening music during his recording heyday. Beginning in 1956 with "Canadian Sunset," he managed to keep charting hits throughout the rock era, including his take on "Moon River" (popular without actually being issued a single); "Days of Wine and Roses" and "Where Do I Begin (the theme from Love Story)." During the time of John Lennon's immigration troubles, Williams was a vocal supporter in his fight to stay in America. (This may—or may not—have earned him his the spot in the 1973 *Ringo* cover artwork, painted by Tim Bruckner.)

Produced by Richard Perry, *Solitaire* was a refreshingly contemporary-sounding package. In addition to the aforementioned Harrisong, it included Paul's "My Love"—no surprise, as it *was* more or less designed to be a standard—as well as Stevie Wonder's "You Are the Sunshine of My Life"; Neil Sedaka's title tune; a Nicky Hopkins original called "The Dreamer" (not to be confused with Joey Molland's Pete Ham tribute of the same name——which Nicky played on—issued in 1979 on *Airwaves*) and "Make it Easy for Me" by Peter Skellern (who penned "Hard Times," recorded by Ringo for *Bad Boy*).

Either Perry, or Williams, or both heard in "That Is All" the potential "That is All" possessed as a power ballad. Lushly orchestrated (as was the original), Williams did a terrific job, sinking his teeth into what, truth be told, was another installment in George's ongoing sub-genre of songs that could as easily be devotionals to a love interest as a supreme deity. Williams' version is one of those rare covers of Beatle-related material that's every bit as good as the original.

"MOVE OVER MS. L" RECORDED BY KEITH MOON – RELEASED 1975

No rock and roll legend was less qualified to record an album of his own singing than the Who's beloved drummer. Indeed, fans purchasing *Two Sides of the Moon* in anticipation of a drumming showcase may have been gobsmacked to discover that the hyperkinetic percussionist commandeered the kit for barely three of the LP's tracks, instead choosing to produce a collection of genre exercises ranging from rock to country to pop to oldies.

The project was built around the same loose musical posse that contributed to Nilsson's *Pussy Cats* album and Ringo's *Goodnight Vienna*, with assorted guests coming and going at will. Sessions for the Moon album amounted to an extended party taking place in a recording studio, horrifying record company execs that watched the budget spike into overdrive. Midway through the drug and drink-drenched proceedings, Mal Evans was sacked as producer by MCA, in favor of Skip Taylor, who re-recorded the exact same songs the exact same way.

It isn't hard to see why the resulting mess was shunned by the masses, but once modern listeners get past the point of cringing at Keith's vocals, they can appreciate the project for what it is: a snapshot of a long-gone era in the music industry, where celeb friends could hang out and have a good time for its own sake rather than to produce serious art, taken to

This John Lennon composition graced the B-side of "Solid Gold," a recording that featured Ringo as the "announcer." The single issue of Keith's take on the Beach Boys' "Don't Worry Baby" arrived with John's "In My Life" on the flip.

the extreme. *Two Sides of the Moon* serves as the flipside to *Ringo*, making one appreciate the quality control wielded by Richard Perry.

Conspicuously absent from the proceedings was John Lennon. A key member of the gang running amok in L.A., John's contribution to his drinking buddy's project was limited to one original song, "Move Over Ms. L." Stylistically, this stream-of-consciousness rocker might have been a better fit for John's *Rock 'N' Roll* covers album rather than *Walls and Bridges* (where it was slated to go) had he not penned it himself. While some have described the song as a "kiss-off" to his estranged wife, there is nothing in the lyric suggesting this, beyond a chorus that proclaims, "I wish you well."

In giving the song to Keith, John may have believed that since the composition required more of a rapid-fire delivery than actual singing, it would work well for the drummer's melodically-challenged pipes. In actuality, though, Moon lacked the breath support to achieve even this, coming up sounding winded and flat on the song's verse-ending ascension. Still, Keith's version merited selection as a B-side to his "Solid Gold" single (the latter of which featured a voice-over from Ringo).

Interestingly, another Lennon cover on *Two Sides of the Moon* drew special attention from the composer himself. John would proclaim Keith's heartfelt take on "In My Life" to be his favorite version of the *Rubber Soul* track. Playing it straight for once, the drummer's vocal limitations undoubtedly enhanced the song's inherent pathos.

"EVERY NIGHT" RECORDED BY PHOEBE SNOW – RELEASED 1978

For a man who had spent his entire career mastering the art of the perfect single, it's curious that Paul McCartney's debut album contained none (nor, some would assert, many fully-realized tunes). "Maybe I'm Amazed" was universally recognized as *the* stand out track, but the song did not get issued as a single until *Wings Over America*'s live version in 1977. Overlooked as a possible chart contender was the song "Every Night." Catchy *and* tuneful, it slipped beneath the radar of nearly everyone; radio stations did not play it, nor did its creator offer it in concert—at least initially.

It did get noticed by a young singer/songwriter named Phoebe Snow, who sprang from New York's Greenwich Village club scene.

Taking her performing name from a fictitious turn-of-the-century railroad advertising personage, the eclectic Ms. Snow reached number five on the *Billboard* charts in 1975 with "Poetry Man," her debut single. Her sound was a blend of jazz, pop, folk, and gospel; her four-octave vocal range and insightful lyrics made her a formidable talent in any genre.

She appeared as a frequent musical guest during *Saturday Night Live*'s early years, beginning with their premier show. A duet

After her debut single "Poetry Man," Phoebe Snow's biggest chart success was this gospel-pop duet with Paul Simon, which peaked at #23 in 1975.

with Paul Simon, "Gone At Last," gave Snow another hit, while a Grammy nomination for her debut album boosted her profile tremendously. Sadly, the rush of acclaim was tempered by professional and personal difficulties. Litigation against her record company took its toll, as did the birth of a brain-injured daughter (who passed away in 2007).

Luckily for her following, Snow's recorded output did not diminish in quality. She recorded "Every Night" for her fifth album, 1978's *Against The Grain*, turning in a fine performance that challenged McCartney's own for the final word. It may be a coincidence—or maybe not—but in 1979, Wings' last year of touring, Paul added the 9 year-old to the band's set. Sadly, Ms. Snow followed her daughter onto the next level in 2011 at the age of 60, having been some time in a coma following a stroke.

"GIRLFRIEND" RECORDED BY MICHAEL JACKSON – RELEASED 1979

The seeds for the dubious musical partnership between Macca and Michael were planted when the two met at a party in Beverly Hills during the seventies. Apparently, Paul had made mention at the time that he'd composed a song with the adolescent in mind. (Some accounts say that Paul and Linda actually *sang* it to him.) But Jackson never asked about it further and Paul proceeded to resurrect the tune for the *London Town* album.

Sad to report, the finished product was a wisp of a tune, sang mostly in an annoying falsetto. The song served up every element critics found grating in Paul's post-Beatles work: banal lyrics, sung over candy-ass harmonies in a production that was all shine and no edge. CD-era listeners could always hit the skip button, but perhaps it was McCartney's intent all along to set up side one's closing track, "I've Had Enough," to sound as fierce as possible by juxtaposing it with the froth that preceded it.

In any event, 1979 saw producer Quincy Jones and the gloved one choosing material for what would be Jackson's breakthrough solo album. Jones himself brought "Girlfriend" to the sessions, not realizing what had transpired earlier. This time, the song took, with Jackson recording it faithfully (save for dropping the minor key bridge that was actually its most interesting feature).

Upon release, *Off The Wall* proved to be a monster, spawning a string of hits, including "Rock With You," "Don't Stop 'Til You Get Enough," and the tear-streaked "She's Out Of My Life." Including a McCartney composition among the tunes, slight though it was, certainly didn't hurt Jacko's credibility as he transitioned into his musical adulthood.

"Girlfriend" saw release as a single in England where, though it stiffed, it still helped solidify *Off The Wall*'s rep as a hit-laden album and Michael's as a musical force on the rise. The 1980s would see the ex-Fab and the ex-Five get closer, dueting on "Say Say Say" and "The Man" for Paul's *Pipes of Peace* album, a year after he contributed vocals to "The Girl Is Mine" for Jackson's ubiquitous *Thriller* album.

Probably the weakest (if not to say most embarrassing) of *that* LP's seven singles, "Girl"—in remixed form—would grace a 25th anniversary edition, *minus* Macca's vocals. Considering the bad blood generated by Jackson's purchase of the Beatles' music publishing back in the eighties, maybe he felt he owed Paul a favor. Whatever lingering strain there may have been in relations between the two, it ended forever with Michael's death at 50 in 2009.

So long as John was able to keep Phil Spector on a short leash, their collaboration worked well, particularly on the Imagine album (shown here). But once John relinquished control, all bets were off.

CHAPTER 5

BUT I'M NOT THE ONLY ONE: STUDIO ASSISTANCE

During the Beatle years, it was relatively easy to track who the Fabs relied upon to transform their musical ideas into hit records in the studio, given the relative consistency of their recording team. But once four separate careers were underway, the list of players expanded exponentially, encompassing some of the biggest names in the business. Given that they could by then work with anyone they wanted to, the choices that they made—if anyone at all (since all four ex-Beatles would eventually shoulder production duties themselves)—are worth examining.

PHIL SPECTOR

As discussed in *Fab Four FAQ*, the legendary "Wall of Sound" producer was called in to raise the abandoned "Let It Be" session tapes from the dead, simultaneously producing an eminently salable "farewell" from the Fabs while stirring outrage from any number of detractors, not least one quarter of the fractured foursome and their former producer. The fact that he was willing to take on the misbegotten project in the first place and make something listenable out of it ("I didn't puke," damned Lennon with faint praise) raised his stock with at least two of the ex-Fabs, who contracted Spector's services straight away for their premier long players.

Odds of Spector working with Macca were remote, to say the least (although Paul *did* hire Richard Hewson—the orchestral arranger of "The Long And Winding Road" —to work similar magic on the *Thrillington* release; apparently all was forgiven.) As for Pete Best's successor, Richie Snare was on hand during the Spector *Let It Be* sessions for some overdubs. It is recorded that Ringo had to intervene on behalf of the engineers and musicians whom the drama-addicted producer was browbeating, letting the diminutive legend know in no uncertain terms that this was simply not how things were done at EMI's number two studio.

A study of bigger contrasts between Spector's work on *All Things Must Pass* and *Plastic Ono Band*—recorded back-to-back—cannot be imagined. While the overall sound and feel of John's debut represented more or less a fine-tuned version of the effect Spector had achieved on "Instant Karma" back in January 1970, being at once instrumentally sparse yet sonically full, George's project pulled out all the stops, employing so many musicians that some went uncredited.

At the onset of the sessions in May (not long after *Let It Be* was released), George ran through his new compositions for Spector's benefit, familiarizing his producer with the material. Accompanied only by his own guitar and—apparently—Klaus Voormann on bass, he performed nearly all the tunes that would eventually make it to the release as well as several others. Hearing the songs in such stripped down form (the tapes have been widely bootlegged) makes for some fascinating listening, as George offered up an "unplugged" performance decades before the term had been conceived. (George himself would later note that he'd been mightily tempted to strip some of the album's excessive echo and layers of instrumentation off the 2001 reissue, recognizing that at the very least, it tended to date the material, but ultimately he let it be.)

For someone whose confidence was rather shaky at such a precipitous time, George was quickly put at ease by Spector's praise for his songs and total belief in him as an artist, in striking contrast to Harrison's *last* producer. Phil midwifed the project at the onset, helping to turn George's simple demos and Band-like compositions into impenetrable, grandiose listening experiences. Though he never publicly commented on the *content* of George's pious pronouncements, the platform that Spector was erecting gave no doubt that he saw no percentage in subtlety. By architecting what would become Harrison's *meisterwerk*, he put the world on notice that Hari Georgeson was something more than a lucky sideman toiling in the shadow of Lennon-McCartney.

While grateful for Spector's support throughout the project, the manifestations of the producer's personal idiosyncrasies soon began to wear on George. For starters, there was his chronic lateness; Beatle sessions had been run with the efficiency of a well-oiled machine; apparently Spector was allowing himself to become a little too well-oiled before showing up, forcing Harrison to bear the load himself. Also, while both men were perfectionists, George would typically try to coax the optimum performances out of his musicians, dropping the matter if it just wasn't happening. Spector, on the other hand, would usually demand take after take, taxing the patience of the notoriously short attention-spanned players.

It has been said that there was no love lost between Spector and

England. As the sessions wore on, delayed by the illness and death of George's mother, the producer took to relieving his boredom in a place that was not home by drinking to excess, eventually failing to turn up at all. Harrison would complain "I was ending up with more work than if I'd just been doing it on my own." Spector's prolonged absences forced George to shoulder more of a burden than he might have expected, but given his natural bent toward self-improvement, he likely viewed the opportunity to hone his producer/arranger skills as his graduate school.

"Many Rivers To Cross"
A new single by Harry Nilsson
Produced by John Lennon

From his forthcoming album, 'Pussycats'.

John was always modest about his own skills as a producer. But by 1974, he'd shown that he was at last mastering the skills: Pussy Cats, on behalf of Harry Nilsson, represented a dry run for his success with Walls and Bridges later that year.

Spector eventually returned in time to assist with the mixing. The results seemed to justify the labor that went into his working methods, as a Cinemascope presentation of Harrisongs emerged from the thicket of multi-tracking. Spector further offered a detailed song-by-song analysis to George with helpful input based on a listen to the rough mix acetates. He was quick to notice George's insecurity about his vocals when the latter tended to bury what should have been upfront in the mix. ("I really feel that your voice has got to be heard...so that the greatness of the songs can really come through.")

Harrison took Spector's velvet-gloved advice to heart, therein gaining the confidence to produce himself on the follow-up, *Living In The Material World*. In between lay the Bangladesh concert recording. It was here that the relationship began to fray, as again Spector demonstrated a work ethic that left the heavy lifting to others while he popped in and out, mainly to demand "more audience" from the mix engineers. Spector nonetheless managed to generate a couple of oft-told anecdotes at the show. One came in the mobile recording truck, during the evening performance of "That's The Way God Planned It." When Billy, carried away by the spirit of the moment, rose from his bench to take center stage with his gospel-style dance, Phil—lacking the visual in the truck—suddenly flipped out when the organist's microphone went dead at the same time the applause reached a crescendo. "Where's Billy?!?" he demanded.

Another episode occurred earlier backstage, when security personnel, failing to recognize the industry legend, confronted him, nightsticks at the ready. As reported in Mark Ribowski's *He's A Rebel*, Spector—burdened with a fragile ego at the best of times—went berserk, playing the "Don't you know who I am?" card while his own bodyguard stood down. Finally, George, seeing what was going down, prompted Apple promo manager Pete Bennett to rescue him. The guards were hardly abashed however, one responding, "I don't care who he is—he's a nasty son of a bitch!"

As for his work with John, Spector's role on *Plastic Ono Band* was even less hands-on than it had been with George's. John purposely sought not to stray too far from his own home-recorded demos, requiring only that Spector reproduce the feel and sound of his self-productions while translating them into a commercially viable product. Given the emotional intensity of the material, Spector likely realized that draping the tunes with the suffocating blankets of brass and strings would serve no good purpose, even had that been an option. Instead, every nuance would be amplified and depicted in sharp relief.

With most of the tunes laid down as a three-piece unit, Spector's input on *POB*, such as it was, served to foster the illusion of richness without resulting in a collection of unfinished sketches. His chief contribution seemed to be in possessing the ears to know what technical touches would add detail and sonic texture; for instance, the splash of organ just past the 2-minute mark on "Isolation."

Yoko, Ringo, and Klaus have since confirmed that Spector had far less involvement with *POB* than has been supposed and indeed, was given more leave to do his thing on *Imagine*; documentation of the latter sessions seems to bear this out. Deliberately setting out to craft a more easy-listening experience for the *POB* follow-up, Spector was allowed to be Spector, orchestrating some songs—lightly—while presenting others as near-*Plastic Ono Band* out-takes, bearing a fuller sound.

John, to his credit, was comfortable taking on a strong personality for a musical partner. Spector doesn't seem to have abused the relationship—at this juncture, anyway—the way he had with George on *All Things Must Pass*. Predictably though, the two strong-willed individuals were certain to clash at some point. Phil the perfectionist going head-to-head with John the "bang-'em-out-and-get-'em-done" artist would butt heads on *Imagine* but given the passive-aggressive tendencies that marked the *Let It Be* sessions, these disputes were resolved mostly with John barking at others in Spector's place. (It's engineer Phil McDonald who Lennon lashes out at during the recording of "Oh Yoko!"—as seen in the *Gimme Some Truth* documentary—mostly for the sin of being around when it was Mr. Spector that seemed to be having difficulties: "What's wrong with you?!?")

Their next two collaborations were decidedly more up Spector's alley: the holiday sing-along of "Happy Xmas (War Is Over)"—complete with layered mandolins cribbed from the failed "Try Some, Buy Some" recording—followed the following year with the infamous *Some Time In New York City* release. Whatever beefs listeners and critics had with the album's contents—and there were many—no one could dispute the power of the production. Given a full time saxophonist (in the person of Elephant's Memory's Stan Bronstein) and John's own inherent fifties rock and roll bent, Spector was in heaven, creating thunderous, wailing backings to John and Yoko's shrill screeds.

The two took a sabbatical from each other in 1973 with *Mind Games* as John went back to producing himself for the first time since "Cold Turkey." This was followed by John and Yoko's separation and the nightmarish *Rock 'N' Roll* sessions, detailed elsewhere in this book. Suffice to say, the relationship had run its course, and Spector closed out the seventies collaborating with a string of other notable artists, including Dion, Cher, and Leonard Cohen, all of which stiffed. Only his work on the Ramones' *End Of The Century* in 1980 garnered any attention at all, hyped as a sort of "when two giants meet" moment. It wasn't a good fit.

GEORGE MARTIN

Whatever the regard the four ex-Fabs held for the producer who had guided them to stardom, John and George chose never to work with him again after the Beatles' recording career was finished. Ringo employed him during their waning days for his *Sentimental Journey* project (as well as an early stab at "It Don't Come Easy") but predictably, only Paul ever again used him on a level resembling old days. It was Macca who probably enjoyed the closest relationship with Martin, especially during their turbulent final years when he was more or less running the show for his three increasingly disinterested partners.

George certainly had his reasons to avoid revisiting the quiet torment that marked his tenure with Martin, despite their more or less collaborating on "Within You Without You." "I was always rather beastly to George," Martin admitted years later, citing his dismissive attitude toward the guitarist's ideas and all around condescension. Had he been more nurturing, as he was with John and Paul, it may have helped George's talents blossom and flourish that much sooner, but of course we'll never know.

As for Lennon, he famously dissed his ex-producer in the 1970 "Lennon Remembers" *Rolling Stone* interview, asserting that it was the Beatles that made *Martin* and not vice-versa. (For good measure, Phil Spector was equally patronizing, saying of his peer "He's an arranger, that's all!") Both men certainly had ego reasons for their shabby disrespect of Martin, but the fact was, he was exactly the partner the Beatles needed to thrive: patient, knowledgeable, willing to experiment, and thoroughly aware of their talent and potential.

His respect for them as individuals and as a collective was rather exceptional for the rock industry, a fact the Fabs would have done well to remember. (To his credit, Martin wasn't one to let Lennon's stinging criticism stand: he confronted John on it in Los Angeles in 1974, demanding an explanation. By way of apology, Lennon shrugged, "I was out of my mind, wasn't I?")

Contrary to established belief, 1973's "Live And Let Die" was not the first time Paul and his former Fab producer were professionally reunited: in fact, according to Dixon Van Winkle, an engineer with New York's A&R Studios, Martin was responsible (without credit) for writing the charts to "Uncle Albert/Admiral Halsey" for *Ram* in 1971, unquestionably lending the track a Beatle-esque quality absent on other Macca releases.

The following year (in October), "My Love" and "Live and Let Die" were recorded back-to-back at the same session (according to Henry McCullough, at least), utilizing the George Martin orchestra with their leader wielding the baton. (Interestingly, Paul copped the producer's credit for the former song while Martin was credited on the latter.) As pointed out in *Fab Four FAQ*, Martin had some experience with James Bond themes, having produced the deathless "Goldfinger" with Shirley Bassey in 1964, as well as mentoring Matt Monro, who sang "From Russia With Love" the year before.

Composer John Barry had handled the 007 scores from that latter film onward. It was he who was credited with composing the famous Bond incidental theme, conspicuously spoofed by Ken Thorne throughout the *Help!* soundtrack. When Barry took on another project that precluded his involvement in the eighth Bond film (and first with Roger Moore), Martin accepted the assignment. Paul had apparently been offered a shot at composing the title song to the previous Bond flick, *Diamonds Are Forever*, but was too busy forming Wings to accept. Martin's role in composing the soundtrack to *Live and Let Die* virtually assured that Paul would get a second chance at penning a title tune.

The two were clearly delighted to be working together again, virtually where they'd left off on *Abbey Road*. "Live and Let Die," like "Uncle Albert/Admiral Halsey" and the renowned side two medley, was assembled by stringing several distinct components together. (The reggae-esque middle-8th—"What does it matter to you?"—was publicly credited as Linda's inspiration.) Martin's orchestration, veering between bombastic and soothing, proved to be a powerful bonding agent (pun not intended) when applied to Wings' supporting ensemble. What on paper shouldn't have worked, did—spectacularly.

Interestingly, the film's producers did not want a Paul McCartney performance for their film. While they were pleased enough with his song (upon first hearing the finished track, they thought Martin was playing them an elaborately produced *demo*), they fully expected to substitute a different singer in the opening credits. *Live and Let Die*, for those who haven't seen it, was essentially a blaxploitation picture featuring James Bond; the studio therefore lobbied hard for someone like Thelma Houston to do the honors. But Martin held firm, and while Macca received his opening credit sequence (and a hit single), within the film, his vocal was replaced with a performance by B.J. Arnau.

The McCartney-Martin partnership would pick up again in late 1980. During the years between, Wings scored some astounding successes, as did Martin (as we'll discuss below). As it happened, by the time they rejoined forces, a major shift in perspective had occurred for both of them: Martin saw no particular need to cut an album with Paul's then-current sidemen, while Macca had by this time stopped looking at Wings as sacrosanct. The prevailing consensus rendered Messrs Laine, Juber, and Holley redundant, and so in early 1981, Paul again became a solo artist.

Martin had stayed quite busy since last working with the Fabs, who'd been reduced to a three-piece by the time they cut "I Me Mine" (on Martin's forty-fourth birthday) as 1970 began. Having opened his

COLUMBIA

© "Columbia," Marcas Reg.

45 RPM
DEMONSTRATION
NOT FOR SALE
3-10802
ZSP 164420
℗ 1978 RSO
Records, Inc.
Publisher:
Maclen
Music Inc.
(BMI)

**MONO
3:45**

**AEROSMITH
COME TOGETHER**
-J. Lennon - P. McCartney-
Produced by Jack Douglas
and George Martin

Don't let the label fool you: Aerosmith's take on "Come Together," recorded for the 1978 soundtrack to the Robert Stigwood's abysmal Sgt. Pepper film, was not a joint production between the two legendary producers.

own AIR Studios on Oxford St. in 1969, he maintained an active production schedule with artists ranging from Stackridge and the Mahavishnu Orchestra to the Paul Winter Consort and Jimmy Webb. (In 1979, he opened another facility, this one on the Caribbean island of Montserrat. Much beloved by artists like Eric Clapton, Dire Straits, and The Police, Hurricane Hugo destroyed it ten years later.) But perhaps his three most notable productions were with three conspicuously varied artists.

Martin's *second* most successful pop production involved a trio of military brats, raised largely outside of their "home" country. America had scored a pair of hits with their first two albums, beginning with the Neil Young sound-alike "Horse With No Name" in 1972, followed by "Ventura Highway" on their sophomore release. When their third release (1973's ambitious *Hat Trick*) failed to stir much interest, Martin was recruited to right the foundering band's career. The resulting alchemy produced a number three album with *Holiday*, which spawned two Top Five singles: "Tin Man" and "Lonely People."

Proving the success was no fluke, *Hearts*, the follow-up, generated a number one with "Sister Golden Hair" in June 1975, a tune featuring some Harrison-esque guitar (better late than never, George), as well as the McCartney-esque confection, "Daisy Jane." The string of Martin-America collaborations continued on through 1979, though truth be told, *Hearts* really was the high-water mark, chart-wise. (Lest anyone be wondering, yes—the band *did* make a practice of titling their releases with words beginning with 'H,' including a greatest-hits package called *History* that featured album cover artwork by the late comic actor, Phil Hartman. Yes, really.)

British guitar hero Jeff Beck's career path had meandered a bit since leaving The Yardbirds in 1966, ranging from the gut-bucket *blooze* of his acclaimed Jeff Beck Group albums featuring Rod Stewart on vocals to his more experimental jazz-rock collaborations with drummer Carmine Appice and bassist Tim Bogert in the early seventies. Following that outfit's demise, Beck got together with some new musicians and George Martin at the latter's AIR facilities in London. The resulting recordings represented a major commercial and artistic leap forward for both men.

Blow By Blow, released in early 1975, became the first million-selling jazz fusion album. Martin's sublime production, encompassing extended (but not overblown) solos, disciplined arrangements, superb material (including a complete reworking of the Beatles' "She's A Woman"), and his own tasteful orchestration gave Beck the platform to execute some of his most brilliant six-string explorations. Famously, the all-instrumental album included seventies FM radio staple "Freeway Jam," as well as a pair of Stevie Wonder compositions, "Thelonious" and the empyrean "Cause We've Ended As Lovers." The Martin-Beck collaboration was extended for another album, 1976's *Wired*, which included former Martin clients (from the Mahavishnu Orchestra) as additional support.

Beck's career took a number of turns thereafter, most of which did not include George Martin. But the two eventually did reunite in 1999 when, at Martin's request, Beck turned in a masterful instrumental reading of "A Day In The Life" for Martin's farewell to producing release, *In My Life*. Beck's recording is surely worthy of some sort of recognition as one of the finest Beatles covers *ever*.

The final George Martin high-profile production of within the scope of this book came in the summer of 1980 with American pop-rockers Cheap Trick. Following a string of hit releases with producer Tom Werman, the band was determined to stake out a new direction for themselves. As Beatle über-fans, it must have seemed like the opportunity of a lifetime to be on the receiving end of Martin's—as well as engineer Geoff Emerick's—magical powers. (Said bassist Tom Petersson: "I was in heaven when we started working with George Martin." Seconded guitarist Rick Nielsen: "George was the most brilliant producer, musician, and artist I have ever worked with.") For his part, Martin was likely wishing to revisit the melodic pop of his Fab heyday, this time with a muscular, guitar heavy ensemble containing a witty songwriter, a vocal chameleon, and possibly the tightest rhythm section he'd worked with since 1969.

The resulting album, *All Shook Up*, fully delivered on all the band's well-honed strengths while pushing their sonic boundaries into new, layered territory. References to both the Fabs and other rock heroes abounded, beginning with the album's opening track, "Stop This Game," which literally picked up musically where "A Day In The Life" ended. The prototypical power ballad, "The World's Greatest Lover" came with Robin Zander's most Lennon-esque vocal; it is not for no reason that it was chosen to represent the project on Martin's boxed set career overview.

Alongside his work with English rockers UFO (who Martin had produced a year earlier for the *No Place To Run* LP*)*, the album may have been the hardest rocking record Martin ever produced. Cheap Trick was on a roll professionally; coupled with the added buzz of the Martin association, expectations were high. Unfathomably, the release didn't perform as well as hoped for commercially. *All Shook Up* signaled the start of a decline for Cheap Trick, as marked by bassist Tom Petersson's exit from the band for eight years while label and management squabbles sapped their creativity for the next decade or so.

George Martin has never escaped the shadow of the Beatles. He penned a rather lightweight memoir in 1979 entitled *All You Need Is Ears*. (Later, his reflections on the most acclaimed album of his career were published as *With A Little Help From My Friends: The Making of Sgt. Pepper*.) He duly produced Paul's *Tug of War*, issued in 1982, as well as Paul's 1984 vanity film project *Give My Regards To Broad Street*. His oversight of both the *Anthology* project and *Love* lay beyond the horizon, but they'll be discussed in another time (and book).

JOHN BARHAM

One of the unsung heroes in the George Harrison saga is this man, a friend as well as uniquely gifted arranger and musician. Barham had been a student of music in London, specializing in arranging Indian ragas for *piano* (while still a teen) when he first came to the attention of sitar maestro Ravi Shankar. Given his command of Western music as well as an affinity for Eastern, Barham proved to be exactly in the right place at the right time when it came time for Ravi's collaboration with violinist Yehudi Menuhin. Barham's ability to translate Indian notation into a coherent transcription for non-Indians helped make Shankar's *West Meets East* album a classic within the World Music genre.

Shankar brought the youthful Barham along when he went to

George's home for the first time in 1966. The two young men bonded easily and soon became close, using each other as a sounding board for their compositions as well as turning each other onto new sounds. George invited Barham down to the studio for visits during the *Sgt. Pepper's* sessions, introducing him to John along the way. Only months later, the two first formally collaborated on a project, with George using Barham as his East-West liaison on the *Wonderwall* soundtrack.

Barham's introduction to the Beatles' inner circle paid immediate dividends when he found himself tabbed as arranger for various Apple projects, including Jackie Lomax, the Radha Krishna Temple, and The Iveys. For Billy Preston's Apple debut, Barham did an arrangement of the W.C. Handy song, "Morning Star." The song had special significance for Billy, for in the 1958 biopic, *St. Louis Blues*, the then-11-year old had played the composer as a boy, starring opposite Nat King Cole. Barham also played harpsichord on Yoko's "Who Has Seen The Wind?," issued as the flipside to "Instant Karma" in early 1970.

Not long after, George called on Barham to provide all the orchestral arranging on *All Things Must Pass*. Though a capable technician, Phil Spector typically used professional arrangers on his projects. For George, Barham was the ideal choice: possessing perfect empathy with both his musical *and* philosophical world view while straddling the East-West sensibility that informed Hari Georgeson's compositions. It is difficult to imagine George Martin achieving similarly striking results with the same material. His work on the title track as well as "Isn't It A Pity" are particular stand-outs. (Though individual credits are lacking, Barham is known to have played vibraphone on the album as well.)

Whatever else he thought of George's magnum opus, John was quite impressed with Ravi Shankar's protégé and immediately thought to use him for a pet Apple project. Filmmaker Alejandro Jodorowsky's *El Topo* was released with a score composed by the director. When John wanted to issue the soundtrack on Apple, it was discovered that the master tapes had gone missing (along with the actual notated musical score, apparently). No problem: he simply hired Barham to transcribe the music from the film itself and recreate it, enabling the label to issue it on vinyl after all. Having thus established a strong rapport with *two* former Fabs, Barham was brought along when George was invited into the *Imagine* sessions at Tittenhurst Park. There, he ended up playing harmonium on "Jealous Guy," as well as vibes on "How?"

Following the *Imagine* sessions, George and Barham worked together on Gary Wright's solo album, *Footprint*. The ballad "Love To Survive" was a particular stand-out, featuring Barham's orchestration and a vocal

85

choir. Both lyrically and sonically, it would inspire George's "That Is All," the closer on his next release, *Living In The Material World*. Though unburdened by the tension that came with Phil Spector and his ever-present bodyguards, sessions for the *All Things Must Pass* follow-up were marked by a notable seriousness in George, as if—Barham felt— he was undergoing a spiritual crisis.

The songs comprising the collection in large part reflected this somber tone, as though an unseen burden was driving the artist to seek solace by merging his musical and spiritual life more inextricably than before. Though not exactly inspiring

Made independently in 1970, Alejandro Jodorowsky's El Topo ("The Mole") found favor with John Lennon, who talked Allen Klein into picking up the US distribution rights. While critics were divided over the film's merits, it did have its fans, including Peter Gabriel, who sought out Jodorowsky to take on a film version of The Lamb Lies Down on Broadway – a project that has yet to see fruition.

listeners to rock, *Living In The Material World*'s ethereal milieu, underscored by Barham's lush but tasteful contributions, represented a rewarding listening experience for those of a more contemplative bent.

Barham's career soon took a different path and though he and George would remain friends until the latter's death, never again would they work together so closely. The multi-talented arranger had already produced a pair of albums for the English prog/jazz/raga rockers Quintessence; he would later add Who vocalist Roger Daltrey (*Ride A Rock Horse*) to his credits, as well as a score for Otto Preminger's final film, 1979's *The Human Factor*.

GLYN JOHNS

One of the real heavyweights of rock production was producer/ engineer Glyn Johns. His legacy of shaping recordings by the very cream of British rock royalty (The Rolling Stones, The Who, Eric Clapton) may be only slightly tarnished when one considers that his work with the Beatles constituted their lowest ebb. He had been called in to supervise recordings undertaken as cameras rolled during the *Let It Be* sessions, seemingly in the face of George Martin's complete distance from the project.

Johns thereafter spent many months toiling away on the resulting tapes, attempting mightily to fashion the proverbial silk purse out of a sow's ear. While strictly maintaining the project's "warts and all" conceptual purity, the results yielded a product that no one wanted to sit through, paving the way for Phil Spector's complete overhaul in 1970. Like those in the McCartney-Martin camp, Glyn too was unimpressed with the results: "(I) think it's an absolute load of garbage."

Despite the Fabs' ultimate rejection of *his* work, Johns' career proceeded without disruption as he went on to produce albums by Humble Pie (their eponymous third release), the Steve Miller Band (their first four, beginning in 1968), the Who's re-think of the aborted *Lifehouse* project, *Who's Next*, and the first two long-players from American country-rockers, the Eagles. Given his obvious mastery of a variety of styles as well as demonstrable hit-making abilities, it was not for no reason that Paul, coming off *Wild Life*'s commercial failure, was anxious to work with him, *Get Back* notwithstanding.

Given his rock and roll pedigree, what makes him worth discussing in this book is not what he did with Paul McCartney and Wings but what they *didn't* do together. Plans called for *Red Rose Speedway*, the first Wings album as a five-piece, to be issued as a double album. Some Laine and McCullough material, as well as Linda's "Seaside Woman" were recorded with the intent that they be included on the release. Ultimately, this did not happen, as EMI was unwilling to risk another ex-Fab two-record stiff, coming off the heels of John's *New York City* fiasco (as well as Paul's *Wild Life*.)

Still, tracks were being laid down with abandon. By the time Johns was called in to co-produce in March 1972, Wings had tracked a number of tunes in Los Angeles, including several like "Big Barn Bed" that were destined for the finished product. Work began with Johns at the helm at London's Olympic Studios (traditionally, the

Rolling Stones' stomping grounds) but before a month had passed, he gave Macca notice that he was through, never to return.

What had happened to this seasoned professional to make him walk out of a Paul McCartney project? It would appear that it was the band's air of undisciplined experimentation, ceaseless toking up and squandering of studio time that at long last got to Johns. Ex-Beatle or not, Johns was unwilling to sit back and police what was fast becoming amateur hour. Though Paul ultimately produced the album by himself, it would be engineered by a crack platoon who included Alan Parsons, David Hentschel, and Richard Lush.

It is therefore interesting to speculate what might have been had Johns stuck around and applied some needed discipline. Though the resulting work wasn't as self-indulgent as it might've been had the original plan held, *Red Rose Speedway* became the second of all too many Wings releases that would have seriously benefited from a strong outsider explaining to Macca the difference between genius and garbage. Had the Johns touch held and Paul released a *Band on the Run*-type blockbuster one album sooner, might this iteration of Wings have held together? Would we never have heard of Jimmy McCulloch, Joe English, Steve Holley, or Laurence Juber? It's impossible to know but fun to ponder the "what ifs." While *Red Rose Speedway* did make it to the top of charts—briefly—it was on the strength of the "My Love" single and little else; Paul himself later expressed the viewpoint of many objective listeners when he opined that he "couldn't stand" the album. Meanwhile, Johns continued to demonstrate his command of the hit record, producing "Jackie Blue" for the Ozark Mountain Daredevils; "Squeeze Box" from *The Who By Numbers*; and Eric Clapton's *Slowhand*, featuring "Cocaine," "Lay Down Sally," and "Wonderful Tonight," as well as many other classic recordings.

RICHARD PERRY

One could easily make the case that what George Martin and Holland/ Dozier/Holland were to the sixties, Richard Perry single-handedly was to the seventies. At least it seemed that way, with Perry responsible for producing a stunning array of hit records for a wide range of artists during that decade. Before name-dropping his star-studded clientele, some background is in order: Perry started in his teens as a singer in the early rock and roll group, The Escorts. Not particularly successful, the group split in 1963 and, after completing college, Perry landed a gig as a staff producer with Warner Brothers. Captain Beefheart's *Safe As Milk* was a notable early achievement, as was Tiny Tim's "Tiptoe Through The Tulips."

Aging better was his work reviving the fortunes of the iconic Fats Domino. (1968's *Fats Is Back!* featured covers of "Lady Madonna" *and* "Lovely Rita"; the following year, he recorded "Everybody's Got Something To Hide Except For Me And My Monkey" with Perry at the helm.) Perry left Warner's in 1970 to work as an independent (echoing George Martin's move five years earlier). Among his first clients was Barbra Streisand; Perry masterminded her chart comeback with *Stoney End* (the song and LP), as well as the follow-up, 1971's *Barbra Joan Streisand*. Perry's skills were drawing notice, and he soon began numbering Carly Simon, Harry Nilsson, and Art Garfunkel among his success stories.

It was while working on *Nilsson Schmilsson* in 1972 that Ringo and Perry became reacquainted. Back in late 1969, Perry had been one of the arrangers who the drummer had tabbed to contribute to *Sentimental Journey*—the title cut in fact. (Given his success at the time with Tiny Tim and Fats Domino, it certainly seemed that getting *way* back would be right up his alley.) This was, of course, a one-off genre exercise and as Ringo had George pretty much at his disposal for his first actual rock recordings, ("It Don't Come Easy" and "Back Off Boogaloo"), not until the drummer was ready to seriously tackle an LP's worth of tunes was the idea of producer shopping even contemplated.

Perry had asked Ringo to serve as co-presenter (with Nilsson) in early 1973 at the Grammy Awards, being held that year in Nashville. Perry and Starkey had established a comfortable relationship by this time, with Ringo expressing his desire to work with Perry "some day." But this time Perry called his bluff: what about *now*? Ringo then offered the novel suggestion of creating a truly global recording project, with tracks cut literally around the world: in Nashville, New York, London, and so forth. The more practical of the two, Perry responded, "How's L.A. sound?"

Ringo agreed and without much fuss, the two—abetted by a cast of supporting players drawn from the Starr's Rolodex—quickly knocked out five tracks in five days. With goodwill running high, Perry instinctively recognized the best way to build a project around someone not exactly known for his compositional skills or ability to pull together a full-length concept with mass appeal on his own: instead of letting his musical gifts as a *singer*—dubious as they were—be the center attraction, Perry crafted a setting that allowed Ringo's *personality* (or at least the public's perception of it) to shine through.

Beyond the expectations of most everyone but the album's makers, *Ringo* became a left-field smash, peaking at number two and eventually going platinum. No other ex-Fab project produced *two* number one hit singles, not even *Band on the Run*, issued a month later. Critics were pleasantly surprised at how much they enjoyed the album; *Rolling Stone* called it a "document of the good time had in its making," while industry bible *Billboard* gushed, "the best Ringo Starr album ever."

Seeing no reason to tamper with the formula, Perry and company reconvened in Los Angeles in the summer of 1974. This time though, some slight changes were in order: both George and Paul were quite busy and sent regrets, but their absence was made up for with contributions from others, namely the addition of Elton John to the mix, as well as John's stepped up participation. *Ringo*'s success guaranteed that others too engaged with their own careers were now eager to lend a hand to what promised to a surefire hit. In comparison to its predecessor, *Goodnight Vienna* seemed distinctly more focused, as though more musical cohesion and less scattershot stylistic variance was the priority.

Like the album that preceded it, *Goodnight Vienna* also generated three hit singles, though not quite on the same blockbuster level. Likewise, the album's chart performance was very good in the states (where it went Top Ten), less so in England. This may be attributable to the lack of a faux Fab reunion to stir interest; also, that the novelty of Ringo out on his own had worn off. But musically, the album was no embarrassment. (The artist himself has declared that he preferred it to the more acclaimed work that put him on the map.)

By the time the second Ringo-Perry project had run its course, Apple was winding down as a label. His contract was closed out with *Blast From Your Past*, a singles collection that summed up his post-Beatles career to date nicely. Had EMI elected to make a serious offer to re-sign the Starr drummer, it is entirely likely that Perry would've manned the helm of the next project. Instead, Ringo signed with Atlantic, who paired him with staff producer Arif Mardin, thus ending a partnership that enjoyed a staggeringly successful commercial run.

Perry's trajectory continued onward through the decade, as he continued his string of chart successes with Leo Sayer ("You Make Me Feel Like Dancing," "When I Need You"); ex-Guess Who singer Burton Cummings("Stand Tall"); and most consistently, with the Pointer Sisters ("Fire," "He's So Shy"), whom he signed to his own Planet Records. It might have made for a productive reunion in the early 1980s had Ringo, without a record deal, been offered a lifeline from Perry: a home on Planet Records and a third collaboration with his most successful producer, just when he needed it most. It didn't happen (though eventually Ringo would find his footing again in the 2000's with Mark Hudson manning the desk).

THE RECORD PLANT CREW: ROY CICALA, SHELLY YAKUS, JIMMY IOVINE, THOM PANUNZIO

New York City's Record Plant was once the hottest recording facility this side of Abbey Road. Opened in 1968, Jimi Hendrix's *Electric Ladyland* put the facility on the map. In the wake of that success, the studio's early years saw an array of talent pass in and out of its doors, including Frank Zappa, Vanilla Fudge, Miles Davis, Todd Rundgren (who doubled as an engineer), and The Who. What set the 10th floor studio apart was the fact that it was set up with the artist's comfort in mind, with a "living room"-style environment so relaxing that jaded rockers wanted to move in.

Among the early staffers were Roy "I Only Like Singles" Cicala; Shelly "I Can't Take The Pressure" Yakus; and Jim "What It Is" Iovine (each as credited on *Walls and Bridges*). Cicala and Yakus had years of experience by the time John Lennon first began frequenting the place for work on *Imagine* but Iovine and Jack Douglas (more on him below) were barely out of their teens. The group became John's engineers of choice for whatever project he and /or Yoko were working on at the time. Despite the presence of a Phil Spector, John always relied heavily on the up-and-coming talent around him to get the sounds in his head onto tape. They, in return, revered him as someone they'd idolized in their youth, that nonetheless came off as just a regular guy, according them kindness and respect, despite his stardom.

The facility was also used by George and Spector to prepare the *Concert For Bangla Desh* release. As an interesting footnote, the facility's audio library kept applause from the show on hand to use as "sweetening" for future recordings by other artists. Rumor has it that among the acts benefiting from some canned Bangladesh love was Cheap Trick—on a Beatle song, no less. Their 1979 live recording of "Day Tripper" had to be scrapped for technical reasons and recreated in the studio, with audience sounds added. If true, the irony is delicious.

During the seventies heyday, the rivalry between The Record Plant on West 44th Street and The Hit Factory, over on West 54th was intense.

91

Loyalties were attached to one studio or the other, and the idea of a client working between the facilities indiscriminately was viewed by staffers as something akin to treason. (At the end of his life, Lennon began the *Double Fantasy* sessions at the Hit Factory, raising eyebrows among his past stalwarts, but Jack Douglas, who of all people should have known better, pointed out that the choice was made due to the studio's slightly more isolated—and therefore overlooked—locale and not out of preference per se. He did, though, make sure that the tapes were brought back to his old stomping grounds on 44th street for mixing.)

While generally upholding an all-business approach to his work, John was not above occasionally "punking" his studio help. During the *Mind Games* sessions, he announced to the staff that he was bringing the album's master reel into the studio's cutting room, ostensibly to oversee the final stage of creating the finished production tape. Cicala ducked out for a moment; when he returned, he found a forlorn looking Lennon sitting in a room strewn with snippets of recording tape everywhere. In shock, Cicala immediately fled the scene to "count to 100 or something" before John and the others that were in on the joke caught up with him: the tape had been blank.

John's magnanimity further ingratiated him with the crew. Just a few weeks into his job at the Record Plant, Thom Panunzio was tasked with some basic duty as an assistant's assistant on the *Rock 'n' Roll* project. (Though a rather prestigious gig for a novice, Cicala had vouched for him.) His inexperience immediately demonstrated itself when he accidentally stretched—thereby destroying—the master tape to the re-make of "Bony Moronie." Certain that his career was over, he broke the news to John the next day. "Didn't like that one, huh?" was Lennon's response. Laughing, he had Cicala (who must have been equally relieved at John's reaction) take out his camera and document Panunzio's bloodless face. "We'll show you this picture someday when you're a great producer, you dumb fuck."

Indeed, all of the crew who John worked with ended up with illustrious careers. Panunzio's future included engineering or producing a host of acts, ranging from New York folk-rocker Willie Nile to Bruce Springsteen and Motörhead. Jimmy Iovine became one of rock's most successful and renowned producers, beginning with artists like Patti Smith, Meatloaf (on the mega-selling *Bat Out Of Hell* album), Dire Straits, and most successfully, Tom Petty and The Heartbreakers. (Against Iovine's initial wishes, Petty recorded the duet "Stop Draggin' My Heart Around" with Fleetwood Mac's Stevie Nicks; the song became a hit while Iovine and Nicks became an item.)

Iovine was also responsible for helping to craft a bizarre hoax in the 2000s, centered on a fictitious act called Platinum Weird. The full details are better discussed elsewhere, but is worth mentioning due to the fact that both George and Ringo were involved. Iovine often worked in tandem with Shelly Yakus; together, the pair left their mark on the decade with records by The Raspberries, Grand Funk Railroad, Blue Öyster Cult, and Graham Parker—among many other acts—to their credit. (Less commendable was Iovine's involvement with TV's *American Idol* as a mentor. The show and its ilk have spawned a generation of singers bent on doing to popular music what the Visigoths once did to Rome.)

Roy Cicala went from head engineer to part owner of The Record Plant, eventually selling it to Chrysalis Records. (The label had bought George Martin's AIR Studios in 1974, with Martin retaining his position. Seven years to the day after John was murdered, George Martin became an investor in Lennon's favorite recording facility.) Cicala bears a distinction few others share – a co-writing credit with John Lennon. In July 1974, during the *Walls and Bridges* sessions, Cicala added music to some lyrics John had jotted down, resulting in a composition entitled "Incantation." (Lest anyone dismiss this as a pure throwaway, Lennon *did* take the step of copywriting the tune four months later, though he never actually recorded it.)

ARIF MARDIN

Within the world of popular music, producer Arif Mardin was a legend well before the 1960s had ended. The Turkish ex-pat had relocated to New York during the 1950s, and in many ways his life journey paralleled that of his boss, Atlantic Records founder Ahmet Ertegun. Both were sons of powerful men *not* in the music industry that had expected to groom them for other careers. But a compelling love of music—specifically, jazz and blues—held sway over them and both Turks found their way to America: Ertegun to launch Atlantic Records and Mardin to become one of its most acclaimed producers.

It took some years to reach that esteemed role. A chance encounter in his native country with Quincy Jones, then a trumpeter with Dizzy Gillespie's band, led Mardin to accept a scholarship to study music theory in Boston. Not long after, he met Nesuhi Ertegun, Ahmet's brother, at the Newport Jazz Festival. The ever-charmed Mardin thereupon landed a job as Nesuhi's assistant at Atlantic. There, he learned the ropes in the studio, studying alongside the likes of Jerry Wexler and Tom Dowd as he enjoyed a ringside seat to some of the greatest names in the business laying down tracks.

His duties included quality control, managing bookings at the studio, and eventually, arranging. Though not a pop music fan per se—at least at first—Mardin got his big break at the same time as The Young Rascals, by producing and arranging "Good Lovin'" for them in 1966. The single reached number one, propelling the careers of both the group and Mardin. From then on, Mardin was regarded as "the fifth Rascal," producing or arranging nearly every hit they had from then on. He also worked with King Curtis and Aretha Franklin, helping to architect the latter's breakthrough single—"Respect"—in 1967.

Mardin's reputation as an exquisitely gifted hit-maker grew with successes such as Brook Benton's "Rainy Night In Georgia," the Roberta Flack-Donny Hathaway duet "Where Is The Love," and the first Hall & Oates hit, "She's Gone." By 1974, as the first ripples of what would dominate the charts for the rest of the decade—disco—began to be felt, Mardin was at the forefront, producing hits like Average White Band's "Pick Up The Pieces" and the Bee Gee's breakthrough *Main Course* album. Lest anyone think that he only involved himself with mainstream acts, Mardin also produced folkie John Prine's first few releases as well as a gospel album by Willie Nelson (*The Troublemaker*).

Ringo's high-profile signing with Atlantic increased the probability that only the label's most successful all-around producer would do for an ex-Beatle. (The two already had a nodding acquaintance from Stephen Stills' solo debut.) And so it was that they set about working from the Richard Perry template for his post-EMI debut: an oldie; a song each from John, Paul, and George; some heavy guests (Clapton, Peter Frampton). *Ringo's Rotogravure* cut across a swath of musical stylings, ranging from country ("Cryin'") to dance-grooved rock ("A Dose of Rock and Roll") to faux-mariachi ("Las Brisas"). Whatever else can be said, the partnership put Mardin's eclectic background to good use.

Unfortunately, the album was not a hit. In retrospect, its commercial failure can be seen as more of a reflection of the record buying public's taste than any particular fault with the music. Track by track, Mardin did a good job of tailoring each tune to Ringo's unique skill set, generally with good results. But the label was a little rocked by the record's lack of traction and, with the apparent concurrence of artist and producer, ditched the Perry paradigm completely the next time out. The resulting *Ringo the 4th* marked the beginning of an artistic decline that took years to undo. Blame for the less than stellar results cannot be laid at Mardin's feet—entirely. The fact was, he was dealing with an increasingly disengaged Starr and shifting musical tastes. His attempt to drop Ringo into the hottest genre of the day and make it work shows at least a willingness to take chances, misbegotten though they were.

At least Mardin's own career didn't suffer. Though Atlantic quickly washed their hands of the ex-Fab, his former producer managed to move forward without missing a step, enjoying successes in the remainder of the decade with Carly Simon and Leo Sayer (seemingly making a habit of taking on Richard Perry's previous acts) as well as Chaka Khan, Bette Midler, and Melissa Manchester.

Arif Mardin can be credited—at least in part—as the mastermind behind the Bee Gees' astonishing comeback as a hardcore disco act. Though 1975's Main Course, which featured this #1 hit, would be the last he worked them on (due to their label change), it was Mardin that encouraged Barry Gibb to begin using what would be his trademark falsetto voice.

RUSS TITELMAN

The executive chores that befell George as the head of a record label were many. Added to this were other duties, including sometime producer and occasional guest musician for acts on the Dark Horse roster. Beyond these obligations, there were of course the aspects of his own career to look after. 1976 had been a particularly grueling year, and to no one's surprise, he took the following year off. He would say later that he wrote no songs during 1977, just took it easy, got a perm, and recharged his creative battery while indulging interests in travel and Formula One racing.

By the time he remembered that he owed some product to Warner Brothers, it was early spring 1978: Dhani was on the way, and having stepped out of the marketplace for what amounts to an eternity in industry terms, George's confidence in his own abilities was not what it had been. For that reason, he met with label staffers Lenny Waronker, Ted Templeman, and Russ Titelman before commencing work on the new project, soliciting from them their opinions and a sense of direction. Among the conclusions he reached was that he wanted a *real* co-producer this time— unlike a Spector who, when not phoning it in, showed up long enough only to provide some drama—and chose Russ Titelman.

Titelman was born in Pennsylvania but moved to Los Angeles early on. His parents, while not musicians themselves, filled their home with a variety of music ranging from The Weavers to Nat King Cole. Before his teens, Russ was studying jazz guitar, while his older sister was dating a member of a trio calling themselves The Teddy Bears. The ensemble scored a hit in 1958 with a song written by 17 year-old Phil Spector called "To Know Him Is To Love Him" (a phrase lifted from his father's tombstone). Spector, the male member of the group that Susan Titelman wasn't dating, encouraged young Russ's interest in the record industry, occasionally using him as a session player.

Titelman ended up singing back-up and playing guitar on recordings by The Paris Sisters, including "I Love How You Love Me." But at the same time, he was doing a great deal of songwriting. Titelman managed to parlay his Spector connections into a job at Screen Gems in New York, writing with Brill Building legends Barry Mann and Gerry Goffin. (One of his early tunes, "Yes I Will," was recorded by The Hollies. Re-titled "I'll Be True To You," it sold millions as a cut on The Monkees' debut album.) He also did some writing with head Beach Boy Brian Wilson, including a song called "Guess I'm Dumb."

In the long run though, his writing didn't generate the hits necessary to sustain a career. But Titelman was able to use his networking to segue into a career as a musician-for-hire, first as one of the "Shindogs"—the house band on the television show *Shindig!* (placing him in the company of future Harrison intimates Billy Preston and Leon Russell) and later, in the studio with producer Jack Nitzsche. He played alongside his future brother-in-law, guitarist Ry Cooder on Mick Jagger's "Memo From Turner" from the film *Performance*. The one-off gig opened the door to a full time one at Warner Brothers, which is where his reputation really begins.

Lowell George's Little Feat became Titelman's first production job. Although the album didn't exactly set the charts ablaze, Titelman's ascent came at a time when record companies still believed in nurturing talent over the long haul instead of demanding hits instantly, thereby giving him a certain amount of latitude to master his role. Certainly, the talents he was assigned to work with helped, as he co-produced (with Lenny Waronker) albums by Randy Newman, James Taylor, and Rickie Lee Jones.

Part of George's criteria was someone he could get along with personally. Titelman's laid-back hippie style (he'd actually studied sitar during the sixties) and deep roots in pop music assured this. As for Titelman, once he overcame his initial reverence ("There was a certain awe I had to

Recorded in 1964 and originally intended for the Beach Boys, "Guess I'm Dumb" - one of two co-writes between Russ Titelman and Brian Wilson – was eventually given to Glen Campbell as a "thanks" for helping out with live dates. Issued in June 1965, the Bacharach/David-like composition did not chart.

get past"), the two got on well, although George's habit of taking the producer on high-speed drives along England's back roads convinced the white-knuckled passenger that Hari Georgeson was hell-bent on introducing him to his Lord sooner rather than later.

Titelman believed in an uncluttered production style that allowed listeners a touch of intimacy with the artist. Not for him the Wall of Sound of his earliest mentor, or even the snappy-brass styling of Tom Scott from George's *Thirty-Three & 1/3*; instead, electric piano, and 12-string guitars provided a foundation for colorful splashes of marimba, mini-Moog, and even harp. The lush musical bedding offered sonic support to George's close-miked vocals and signature slide guitar, resulting in a modicum of breathing space that avoided swamping the compositions.

George's notorious *"White album"* leftover, "Not Guilty" was re-cast as a lightly-jazzy acoustic piece, while the racing theme of "Faster" was augmented—tastefully—with actual race track sounds recorded at the 1978 British Grand Prix. ("Soft-Hearted Hana" likewise contained a field recording taped at George's local, The Row Barge.) Sales of *George Harrison* were boosted by a song ("Blow Away") so catchy, it was "embarrassing" (George's word). Still, the self-named release was a hit; its American chart performance was bested only by Canada's, where it peaked at number three.

For what was indisputably a return to form, it is somewhat baffling that George and Russ didn't work together again. For his next outing, *Somewhere In England*, George co-produced with Ray Cooper, long noted for his percussion work with Elton John rather than for any particular hit-making ability. One may well wonder the cost of foregoing Titelman's services, since the resulting product was handed back to him by Warner's on the grounds that Mo Ostin just couldn't hear a hit on it. As for Titelman, he had nothing but deep praise for the ex-Fab: "George... brought both a very confident spiritual dimension and a knowledge of world music to pop music that it had never had previously. Things like that take guts and an inner will."

CHRIS THOMAS

Chris Thomas was a musical prodigy. As a child, he studied both violin and piano, though once rock and roll—and the Beatles—caught his ear, he was quick to abandon his classical studies. He gravitated toward bass and ended up in a South London band called The Cat, which featured on drums the late John Keen. (As "Speedy" Keen, he would front the Pete Townshend-produced band, Thunderclap Newman in 1969, which featured future Wings guitarist Jimmy McCulloch.) Ultimately though, Thomas became more interested in crafting sounds rather than merely gigging. To further that goal, he wrote a letter in 1965 to George Martin asking how to get started. The Fabs' producer duly responded, though it took another two years before Thomas followed his advice. This time, his efforts resulted in a six-month trial apprenticeship, not with EMI, but with Martin's AIR production company.

Readers of *Fab Four FAQ* may recall that, as a young engineer, Thomas was pressed into service to act as *de facto* producer for the Beatles in 1968 during the "White album" sessions while George Martin absented himself. Though initially horrified at the prospect of being thrown in the deep end, he acquitted himself well (and even contributed instrumentally to a couple of tracks). He quickly found his niche in a very competitive industry, working with artists ranging from John Cale to Pink Floyd. But his most sustained success came from his working relationship with Procol Harum. Between 1970 and 1975, he produced five releases, including their live album, which spawned the 1972 hit single "Conquistador."

That same year, Apple's Tony King, a fan of Thomas' work, brought him to the attention of Badfinger, who were then struggling with self-producing their final release on the label, *Ass*. Not surprisingly, Thomas and the band proved a good fit. After an initial run as sole producer for their self-titled Warner Brothers debut, Thomas collaborated with the band to produce their finest achievement, 1974's *Wish You Were Here*. At last poised on the brink of receiving their due ("I thought it was the best album I'd made to that point"), Badfinger's momentum was arrested permanently when the album was recalled by Warners in the face of shady managerial dealings. (Thomas is said to have wept when he heard the news.)

Still, in all other respect's his career was proceeding nicely, scoring hits with Roxy Music from one extreme to the Sex Pistols on the other. Always acutely attuned to the goings-on in his professional world, Paul McCartney recognized that his former engineer had blossomed into a world-class *artiste* with enviable range. Having decided that his newest project needed the benefit of an outside producer as well as someone plugged into *au courant* tastes, Macca decided that Thomas was his man.

The newest (and final) iteration of Wings gathered for sessions at Lympne Castle, located outside of Kent, England. (Ever on the lookout for an exotic locale to record in, this one at least didn't require leaving the country.) As always, McCartney and company ended up laying down more material than was needed to fill out an LP. Paul was interested in offering up something rawer and more in keeping with current tastes than *London Town* had, despite that last album's success. Through his daughter Heather, he'd cultivated an acquaintance with punk. (Paul would in fact pen a "punk" tune, a tongue-in-cheek take on adolescent anxiety entitled "Boil Crisis.") For that reason, Thomas was charged with drawing out an edginess not typically found on a Wings product.

In the end, *Back To The Egg* did not live up to the talents of those involved, being hamstrung by the overall weakness of the material and Paul's chronic inability to decide on a path and stick to it. Not unlike the eponymous Badfinger album he'd produced, *BTTE* worked on a song-by-song basis without jelling as a whole. Though Thomas duly channeled the group's capacity to rock on tunes like "Getting Closer" and "Spin It On," he evidently could not control McCartney's penchant for incongruously placing such tracks alongside, for instance, his Mills Brothers tribute, "Baby's Request," or the light-pop crooner, "Arrow Through Me." The resulting schizoid approach proved alienating to people of *all* tastes.

It represented a real waste of opportunity for things to play out with

Produced by Chris Thomas, Badfinger's Wish You Were Here – released in October 1974 – is rivaled only by 1971's Straight Up as their tour de force.

such disappointing results, for Chris Thomas was probably the closest Paul came to a George Martin with a modern sensibility. Given his skill at balancing raw energy and pop tunefulness (as evidenced with *The Pretenders* album, or Pete Townshend's *Empty Glass*), what should've given Wings a new lease on life ended with a critical and commercial letdown. Eventually Paul and Chris would get back together, with far stronger results, on 1999's *Run Devil Run*. The crisp production and tightly-focused performances harnessed the raw emotion generated by a grieving Macca in the wake of Linda's death.

JACK DOUGLAS

This New York-based studio legend, long associated with hard rock, began his musical life as a folkie, one with a political bent. In 1964, Douglas was officially designated staff songwriter to Robert Kennedy's New York senate campaign. After Kennedy's victory, Douglas' head was turned: after all, this was the year that the Beatles conquered America. Earnest strumming on unamplified instruments became passé overnight, so Douglas, like so many others, got caught up in a wave that placed him in his first rock band; unlike most, his fervor literally took him to the backyard of his idols: Liverpool.

He and his partner-in-crime, Ed Leonetti, arrived in England via tramp steamer (right around the time *Rubber Soul* was released) but without proper papers and thus weren't allowed off the ship at first. Their saga became a *cause celebré* in the local papers until at last, the two batty Yanks were given a 60-day visa. The story is worth mentioning because years later, when Douglas met John Lennon while engineering *Imagine*, it became their icebreaker, as Lennon recalled laughing over the story with his fellow Fabs.

In 1969, Douglas had his professional epiphany. It came during the mixing process of his band's debut long-player. Privilege, as the outfit was called, were signed to T-Neck Records, owned by the Isley Brothers (of "Twist and Shout" fame—see how it all ties together, folks?). Fronted by his old friend Leonetti, who'd scored two years before as a member of the Soul Survivors ("Expressway To Your Heart"), the band aspired to a sort of Hendrix-esque sound, augmented by keyboards. Bassist Douglas, however, was not happy with the album's production, which featured a slathering of horns and backing vocals. Much to his surprise, he was given leave to have a go at the faders himself and therein, a studio career was born.

After completing schooling at the Institute of Audio Research (the first graduating class), Douglas found work at the Record Plant—as a janitor. But proximity gave him invaluable insights into the process, as well as opportunity. It came in March 1971, when The Who were in town, attempting their first crack at what was expected to be the multi-media follow-up to 1969's *Tommy*, a futuristic concept piece entitled *Lifehouse*. With their longtime manager/producer Kit Lambert in sway to the heroin addiction that proved one more nail in his professional coffin, the band entered the studio intending to use house engineer Jack Adams as their producer.

But Adams, an R&B fanatic, hated rock music and was none too impressed with The Who. Growing weary of "Won't Get Fooled Again," "Pure and Easy," and "Behind Blue Eyes," he contrived an excuse (that the houseboat he lived on was ablaze) and vacated the producer's chair to the by-now assistant engineer, Douglas. It proved to be his big break, as Townshend and company hit it off with the stunned novice and—though they eventually scrapped the New York tapes for re-takes back in England (as *Who's Next*) with Glyn Johns—their association put Jack Douglas on his way.

He quickly made a reputation at the Record Plant, engineering for artists ranging from The James Gang to Miles Davis. When the Lennons arrived in New York to work on the soundtrack and subsequent album accompanying Yoko's *Fly*, Douglas proved to be a versatile and open minded member of the engineering team, making a positive impression. When John arrived in June to add some vocals, sax, and strings to the *Imagine* tracks started in England, Jack Douglas was on hand, bonding with the man who had made such a lasting impact on his life from afar.

Douglas engineered on the Apple-issued *El Topo* soundtrack, as well as Yoko's next two albums, *Approximately Infinite Universe* in 1972 and *Feeling The Space* in 1973. But his horizons were further expanded with projects by artists like the New York Dolls and Alice Cooper. In 1974, a Boston-based outfit preparing for work on their second album came his way, initiating his close working relationship with Aerosmith that would last over five albums, encompassing their most creative (and

Cheap Trick Live in Japan
The Biggest Thing Since Transistors!

Jack Douglas produced Cheap Trick's 1977 debut album; an acclaimed but largely ignored effort. Two studio albums followed, but only after radio stations began airing the concert recording of "I Want You To Want Me" from Japan did popular demand force the stateside issue of the release that at last broke them in America.

drug-addled) period. 1977 saw Douglas help secure a recording contract for his own discovery, a Midwestern powerhouse called Cheap Trick he'd spotted in a Wisconsin bowling alley. He went on to produce their magnificent (though largely ignored) self-titled debut.

Sometime in the summer of 1979, Jack and John bumped into each other at a health food store. "You're a big producer now," John observed. He invited the still somewhat awe-struck studio artiste to come hang out at the Dakota, even slipping him his phone number. Douglas, busier and more in demand than ever, never took him up on the offer while regretting it profusely. But opportunity afforded him a second chance when Yoko called him up a year later. In a vignette that might have come out of a spy movie, she directed him to show up an East River pier at a designated time, where a seaplane spirited the bewildered but intrigued technician out to the Lennons' home at Cold Spring Harbor.

Upon his arrival, Douglas was presented with an envelope bearing the inscription: "For Jack's ears only." It contained a letter from John and a cassette of home demos. Yoko told him that John was ready to record again and that he—Jack Douglas—was his choice for a producer. "But you must keep this a secret," she warned him. John, who phoned Douglas from Bermuda soon after, cautioned that he was uncertain of his place in a musical world that had changed since he'd absented himself; therefore, the entire project was to be considered classified until further notice. (Yoko then took the opportunity to hand him a stack of reel-to-reel tapes—*her* demos—and informed him that "John doesn't know it yet, but I'm going to have a couple of songs on this album.")

The resumption of John – and Yoko's – recording career in the summer if 1980 saw a renewal of Douglas' relationship with the Lennons. In addition to being a part of an almost-guaranteed blockbuster, he was pleased to have the challenge of producing a straight pop record, something he'd successfully steered clear of to this point. Yoko's tunes, at least, seemed remarkably current with their raw edginess, while John was apparently happy to churn out some rather safe-sounding compositions not too far removed from his pre-*Pepper* Beatle heyday. Still, with all the energy Lennon was prepared to put into it, Douglas saw the opportunity to hone their material in a way that could engage the masses without sounding stale.

In addition to secrecy, John requested that Jack book studio time (at the Hit Factory) and put together a band of professionals, ones that would understand his musical background and not offer a blank stare if he referenced an obscure fifties record. It was very much a part of John's design that the work be all business and that none of the usual party atmosphere disrupt the proceedings. For that reason, old friends like Jim Keltner, Klaus Voormann, and so forth were not asked. (Session superstar Steve Gadd *was* invited, but never returned Jack Douglas' call, paving the way for drummer Andy Newmark's participation.)

Douglas fulfilled his brief well, both in maintaining the secrecy among his musicians (who were not told who they were working for until the day before recording started, though a couple of them had guessed) and in getting them rehearsed before John showed up, ready to begin. (They'd learned the tunes via John's demos while Douglas led them through the tunes, providing the vocals himself.) John was acquainted with a few of the men, but some, like bassist Tony Levin, were new—and impressive—to him. So efficient was the ensemble that by the time the sessions wrapped up in early September, the five productive weeks had generated nearly enough completed material for two albums.

The final evening of John's life was spent with Douglas at The Record Plant, working on mixes of Yoko's anticipated breakthrough single, "Walking On Thin Ice." The atmosphere was, by all accounts, celebratory. (At one point, David Geffen popped in to announce that *Double Fantasy* had gone gold after only two weeks out.) But despite the apparent buzz, Douglas would later report rather cryptically that there were things said that night by John that were just "too painful" to air publicly and afterwards, he erased the covert recording he'd made.

He and John said their goodnight outside an elevator at the studio just past ten o'clock. Before an hour had passed, his girlfriend burst into the facility with the news she'd just heard on the radio that John had been shot. For Douglas, a light in his life had just gone out, ushering in a darkness that would take some years to emerge from. He spent the night walking—just walking—in an effort to make some kind of sense of the terrible news. Twenty-four hours later and still in shock, he appeared in Tom Snyder's *Tomorrow* show, offering his thoughts on John and the last four months.

In March 1981, Yoko re-entered The Hit Factory to begin work on a cathartic album entitled *Season of Glass*. She gathered the same musicians that Jack Douglas had assembled, but this time she reached out to a partner from the past to co-produce with her: Phil Spector. Over time, it became increasingly clear that Douglas was on the outs with her and he did not know why. In February 1982, Yoko and Sean appeared at the Grammy Awards to accept the Album of the Year award for *Double Fantasy*. Douglas was entitled to pick up a trophy, but the word from the Yoko camp was "stay away."

It proved the final straw in the strained relations that followed John's murder. Douglas had not been paid for his work on either *Double Fantasy* or the still unreleased *Milk And Honey*, being put off with one excuse after another. When personal appeals to Yoko went nowhere, he filed suit in March 1982 for his unpaid royalties. While—bizarrely—Yoko tried to characterize their contract as "fraudulent" and Douglas a mere "nobody," right was on Douglas' side and the court ruled that Yoko had to pony up over $2.5 million, plus interest. It was a shabby end to the partnership that gave the world John Lennon's final musical statement. The postscript would come decades later, when in 2010, the two made nice again, commemorating what would have been John's 70th year with the *Double Fantasy Stripped* project and Jack's involvement in the PBS documentary, *LennoNYC*.

Splinter's soft-rock tunefulness should have been an easy sell during the second half of the seventies. But though evoking George at his listener-friendly best, the head of Dark Horse once again learned that spotting talent is far easier than marketing it.

CHAPTER 6

LADIES AND GENTLEMEN A BRAND NEW STAR: PROTEGES

In *Fab Four FAQ*, some of the acts signed to Apple early on (Mary Hopkin, James Taylor) were discussed at length. But the Beatles' attempts at talent scouting didn't end with their dissolution as a group. Once in the mode of spotting and nurturing, it was hard for them to stop. The practice continued even after Apple was no more, as both George *and* Ringo set up their own boutique labels (as though they hadn't learned *anything*).

The following roll call presents acts that were associated with individual members of the Fabs during the seventies. Some, like Badfinger, were first mentored during the Beatle years. Others, like the Van Eaton brothers, were musicians who got their own shot at the brass ring while helping out on ex-Fab projects. Still others were intimates (Yoko, Linda) who burned up studio time because they could.

Each act enjoyed hands-on involvement from an ex-Fab, requiring a commitment that took time away from their own career. From this, we can conclude that each must've really felt strongly about making these artists successful.

YOKO ONO

Just as it's a mistake to fall into the "Yoko broke up the Beatles" mindset (the truth is far more complex than that; does anyone really believe that they would've stayed together if John *hadn't* met her?), so it is equally unwise to paint her work with a broad brush and dismiss it out of hand as talentless noise. Hers is an acquired taste (like, say, Frank Zappa is) with its own devoted fans among those whose preferences run to the experimental. Though Yoko released four Apple A-side singles, she really wasn't competing with Top Forty acts and one shouldn't judge her work within the pop paradigm.

That said, John's own insistence that they were artistic equals and that Yoko's music was on par with any other rock pioneer ("Listen to 'Don't Worry Kyoko.' It's one of the fuckin' best rock and roll records ever made.") undoubtedly further hurt her public standing. With an arrogance that bordered on zealotry ("It's as important as anything we ever did"), he unwittingly invited blowback and may have turned off that tiny segment of the audience who might otherwise have given her a chance.

Not counting the trio of experimental long players (*Two Virgins*; *Life With The Lions*; *Wedding Album*), the concert recording (*Live Peace in Toronto*) released during the Beatles' lifetime; the pair of joint credited albums (*Some Time In New York City*; *Double Fantasy*) issued subsequently, Yoko Ono was responsible for four solo releases: two single and two double albums. (Another collection, *A Story*, was recorded in 1974 but remained unissued for another twenty years—possibly because Apple was in its death throes as an active label at the time.)

For her solo debut, Yoko unleashed—in tandem with John's *Plastic Ono Band*—an avant garde tour de force. Recorded with instrumental support from Klaus, Ringo, and her husband, *Yoko Ono/Plastic Ono Band* was a wordless affair, containing the archetypical Yoko repertoire of wails, warbles, and other unsettling noises not ordinarily associated with a non-institutionalized human being. *YO/POB* delivered what John's album only hinted at: a cathartic unleashing of pent-up anguish that transcended mere speech, bolstered (if not unlocked) by the treatment of Dr. Arthur Janov. Indeed, at one point, John's release was to be titled *Primal* and Yoko's, *Scream* before the two thought better of it.

It should be noted that, just as John's screaming on record in the years before he met the good doctor was inspired directly from rockers like Little Richard, Yoko's vocal style had precedent that she herself acknowledged. Jazz vocalist Patty Waters released an album in 1966 that featured a thirteen-minute workout of the Appalachian chestnut, "Black Is The Color Of My True Love's Hair." The recording resembles nothing so much as a tortured exorcism, featuring the word "black" shrieked and moaned in a variety of ways, presaging Yoko's similar excursions found on *Live Peace In Toronto*'s second side.

For those not yet convinced of her musical bona fides, the album contains one cut recorded separately from the rest of the sessions: "AOS," a collaboration with free jazz legend Ornette Coleman, recorded in February 1968 (around the same time John was getting a handle on "Across The Universe.") Other tracks are augmented with found sounds, such as a train ("Paper Shoes") and a falling tree ("Touch Me"). But most notable are the musical performances: Ringo's playing is suitably intense, while John—never much noted for possessing a distinctive guitar voice—is incendiary. Well aware of his shortcomings as an

Though still very much an experimental avant garde artist, Yoko expanded her palette with 1971's Fly to encompass a straightforward pop approach, typified with this fittingly Lennon-esque single.

instrumentalist, on *YO/POB*, John displayed an inventiveness unheard of again until his work on Yoko's "Walking On Thin Ice" ten years later.

Fly was a double album, released alongside *Imagine* in September 1971. In addition to featuring the cast from her prior release, she added Joe Jones and the Tone Deaf Music Co. This ensemble, part of New York's conceptual art community, specialized in producing sounds from "self-playing" instruments. *Fly* represented a step toward traditional rock values, featuring some cuts that displayed conventional compositional motifs. "Midsummer New York", the album's boogie opener, would not have sounded out of place coming from any of the quirky female artists who populated the so-called New Wave scene of the late seventies. Another track, "Mrs. Lennon," is a piano-based ballad featuring atmospheric production and an increasingly idiosyncratic turn-of-the-phrase ("Husband John extended his hand…and suddenly he finds that he has no hands.")

Indeed, it would be attempts at wedding her unique lyricism to a steadily more traditional pop/rock setting that defined Yoko's next release. Backed by Elephant's Memory, 1973's *Approximately Infinite Universe* built upon her *Some Time In New York City* political screeds, but to more focused—and ultimately, more satisfying—results. "Move On Fast" rocks convincingly, while the ballad "I Want My Love To Rest Tonight" admonishes her feminist sisters not to judge their men too harshly. Though the release as a whole demonstrated a real breakthrough in terms of crafting meaningful yet mainstream material, aficionados of her earlier work were less impressed with her "selling out."

Credited to "Yoko Ono with the Plastic Ono Band + Something

Different," 1973's *Feeling The Space* represented the culmination of her pop studies to this point. Pared down to a single disc, the album—an exploration of feminist themes—demonstrated a grasp of contemporary sounds that occasionally outdid her husband's. *FTS* featured a superb supporting cast (though John's participation was minimal), comprised of the same musicians on the concurrent *Mind Games* album, augmented by the Something Different Chorus. (The album's playful packaging provided the "measurements" and phone numbers of all the male musicians—'cepting John's, which was given as "not for sale.")

The anthemic "Woman Power" saw canny but fruitless issue as a U.S. single, though *FTS* contained several candidates for chart success, including "Run Run Run" (which was released in the U.K.) and "Coffin Car." The penultimate non-Beatle Apple release hit the stores just as the couple was separating. Yoko stayed musically active in the interim, touring and recording *A Story*, which contained several songs that were revisited later. After John and Yoko reconciled, she put aside her musical career to concentrate first on her pregnancy, then business.

Upon the fabled re-awakening of John's muse in 1980, Yoko assembled a collection of her own demos to round out the release. Jack Douglas, who had worked with the both of them, recognized early on that he would need to keep the couple separated in order to get anything done. To that end, the producer established a procedure where Yoko's cuts were recorded early in the day and John's later, so he could minimize their actual overlapping time in the studio.

Double Fantasy generated the finest reviews of Yoko's career. Indeed, to many critics, John's sound was old hat, while *her* tracks possessed a freshness and energy that competed with the best of the current scene. It appeared that the world and Yoko had met each other halfway, as tunes like "Kiss Kiss Kiss" and "Give Me Something" began getting spun in clubs. (Quite a contrast to the art snob who harangued John over the Beatles' use of simple beats back in the day.)

Their collaborative culmination came with a song held off the release: a powerfully haunting (yet über-danceable) track entitled "Walking On Thin Ice." Powered by some elastic guitar work (inspired by, of all things, a minor 1956 hit by Sanford Clark called "The Fool") from John and Earl Slick, the song was the ultimate encapsulation of Yoko's singular vocalese, fused to a hypnotic piano line, an insistent disco rhythm and produced with a hard rock sensibility.

WOTI was fully expected to be *the* song to at last bring Yoko out of her husband's shadow as a recording artist. A 12" EP entitled *Yoko Only* would present the new track alongside the once-controversial

"Open Your Box," plus a pair of other club-friendly recordings. John himself predicted "I think we've just got your first number one, Yoko." It took another twenty-three years and a remix to make his forecast come true, but it did – on the U.S. Dance charts. (The then-seventy year-old set a record as the *oldest* artist to score a chart-topper.)

BADFINGER

In the wake of the Beatles' dissolution, Apple's greatest hopes for sustained success were pegged to the half-Welsh, half-Liverpudlian quartet who came to them as The Iveys. Badfinger— comprised of Pete Ham, Mike Gibbins, Tommy Evans, and Joey Molland—were a singular outfit containing *four* capable singer/songwriters, a superb work ethic, and a decided lack of ego that should have propelled them to rock's top tier. That their story played out with such tragic results speaks to the truly brutal nature of the rock industry, a side seldom seen with such chilling clarity.

With one Paul McCartney-penned hit under their belts, Badfinger

was now keen to achieve success under their own steam. After apprenticing on recordings for George (*All Things Must Pass*) and Ringo (Tommy and Pete sing on "It Don't Come Easy"), the band offered up one of their own compositions, Pete's "No Matter What," for selection as their next single. Trouble was, the powers-that-were at their label didn't see things the same way and refused to issue the Mal Evans-produced track. Not until Al

If Paul McCartney and George Harrison were still making music together in 1971, the results might have sounded like this. Badfinger's Pete Ham possessed the former's way with melodic pop, while the Harrisonian productionwork on "Day After Day" gave it an ambience that left the band with very mixed feelings: being more his sound than their sound.

Steckler, an Allen Klein crony, heard the song and approved, was it greenlighted as the "Come And Get It" follow-up. Issued in the fall of 1970, "No Matter What" gave Badfinger its second straight U.S. Top Ten single, a feat that no non-Beatle had achieved at Apple.

The accompanying album, *No Dice*, was similarly well-received, although the band *was* quickly discovering an albatross around their necks in the form of endless Beatle comparisons. In that *No Dice* offered a collection of sensitive ballads and gritty rockers featuring exquisite harmonies, adroitly produced and performed, the band *were* Beatle-esque; so too were half of their peers (the Bee Gees, Marmalade, the Raspberries, etc.). But having conspicuous Beatle sponsorship and sharing their label branded Badfinger in a way that the other acts weren't. What had been good fortune had now turned into a double-edged sword that would bedevil them for the whole of their career.

Having achieved success with their first true band outing (Joey wasn't on the earlier *Magic Christian Music* release, which had been cobbled together with Iveys tracks), the band was ready to repeat the formula. Again, Geoff Emerick was recruited to produce, and an equally eclectic blend of material was laid down in early 1971. Despite the obvious ambition shown in both writing and arrangement, Apple again balked at releasing the album, feeling it was a little too "beat group" sounding for contemporary audiences.

George Harrison agreed. As with Jackie Lomax earlier, George was loath to let an Apple protégé he had a personal interest in struggle to find a place in the marketplace. While much of the material was fine, George felt that it simply didn't hold together as an album—not to *his* standards, anyway. Believing Badfinger capable of greater things, he offered them another shot with himself in the producer's chair – a deal they scarcely believed possible.

But George was serious and to that end, he convened the band at EMI's Abbey Road facilities in late May. Among the first tunes he chose to take on was Pete's "Name Of The Game." Perhaps something about the "existentialist ballad" struck a chord with the philosophical ex-Beatle, but in any case, he transformed the rough gem into something approaching an *All Things Must Pass* out-take. Next up was a Joey Molland composition called "I'd Die, Babe." The composer himself regarded it as little more than "a bunch of nonsense" before George worked his magic, adding his own lower register guitar riff and a touch of keyboard, resulting in a "great little number" (per Joey) that *swings*.

Less appreciated was George's edict on Molland's "Suitcase." The song was an encapsulation of the band's touring experience, including an explicit reference to the purveyors of illegal substances found backstage at every gig. George took what had been an impressionistic, guitar-driven life-on-the-road tale and produced (with an assist from Klaus Voormann and Leon Russell) a catchy piece of ear candy, replete with slide guitar and electric piano—not exactly Badfinger's signature sound. Further adding insult was Hari Georgeson's insistence that the "pusher pusher" language had to go, otherwise the song would never be played on the radio. For the twenty-three year-old guitarist, hearing this from a hero—someone he regarded as the paramount of the anti-establishment—was stinging. Joey duly changed the words to "butcher butcher" (though not in concert), hoping his veiled meaning would get across, but the perceived rebuke stayed with him ever after.

Happier results were achieved on Pete's "Day After Day" (as discussed in detail in *Fab Four FAQ 2.0*), though the sense that the band had been remade in George's image remained. Still, Badfinger was gratified to be given a second shot at *Straight Up*, as the album was now titled. But before more than the first four tunes were finished up, duty beckoned George away to organize the Bangladesh relief effort. For him, the Badfinger chapter had ended, but not before offering the consolation of a slot at the Madison Square Garden benefit.

It's somewhat disappointing in retrospect that Badfinger was not given a turn in the spotlight at the show, perhaps performing "No Matter What," or previewing the freshly recorded "Day After Day" (with Leon present and a cast of dozens, it would have been their one opportunity to replicate the record). Alas, it not to be, though Pete and George's duet on "Here Comes The Sun" must rank as a something special. Without the benefit of a rehearsal, Ham had to practically wing it, learning the tune from a tape of *Abbey Road* he bought in New York.

Straight Up was completed with the help of Todd Rundgren, per George's direct intercession. Essentially tied up with Bangladesh matters for the next year and a half, his dropping out represented the dissolution of the last direct tie between the ex-Fabs and Badfinger. Temperamentally, Rundgren was a complete departure from George, leaving the band feeling alienated from the record making process by what they perceived as a dictatorial method of operation. (For his part, Rundgren griped about the omission of credit on the finished album for his work on completing the tracks that George had started.)

Badfinger's success streak as a chart act ended with *Straight Up*. The album peaked at thirty-one in the states (to *No Dice*'s twenty eight), though it did spawn two hit singles, "Day After Day" (four on the charts) and "Baby Blue" (fourteen). It would be nearly two years before a follow-up hit the stores, 1973's *Ass*. Delays owing to the unsuccessful renegotiation of their Apple contract as well as considerable management woes arrested their momentum, despite the quality of the material. A morose farewell to their label was issued as a single: Pete's "Apple Of My Eye." (A distracted George was reportedly livid that no one told *him* that there were troubled relations between Apple and the band.)

At Warner Brothers, the original band cranked out two more albums in rapid succession, 1974's self-titled release, followed nine months later by their masterpiece, *Wish You Were Here*. Under the able production hand of former Beatles engineer Chris Thomas, Badfinger had unleashed their magnum opus, informed by the internal turmoil that would splinter the band and result in Pete Ham's suicide within six months.

The what-ifs in Badfinger's story are many: what if they had been signed to another label without the crippling Beatle association, where they might have flourished? What if one of their numerous mentors had stepped in when needed to help sort out their financial entanglements? What if the band unity hadn't fractured over their management issues and they'd fought back as one? What *is* clear is that the sordid going's on that led to their sad fate remained a sensitive subject with the ex-Fabs, every one of whom balked at publicly telling their side of things for the record. The silence, as they say, is deafening.

PERCY "THRILLS" THRILLINGTON

In 1966, Paul composed a song for Peter and Gordon entitled "Woman." Though the duo had already recorded and scored hits with other material from his pen, on this outing, Paul thought it clever to see if the composition would make it on its own merits rather than because fans would blindly lap up anything with his name on it. A cover story was concocted claiming that the song was actually written by a student named Bernard Webb (in some markets, the credit ran "A. Smith"); upon release, the single duly made the top twenty before the ruse was revealed. In short, the exercise displayed a Macca penchant for working under a pseudonym, one that would culminate with his electronica releases in the 1990s under the "Fireman" moniker.

Between these two excursions came the *Thrillington* release. Issued in 1977—six years after it had been recorded—it was the most elaborate vanity project ever tossed off by an ex-Beatle, released to little fanfare and basically left for the public to discover on their own. (Rock's closest precedent may be the bizarre record issued by Michael Nesmith at the height of Monkeemania entitled *The Wichita Train Whistle Sings*, an all-instrumental collection of his own compositions.) The record was simply a track-for-track recreation of the *Ram* album, scored for and performed by an orchestra. *Who* exactly Paul thought the audience for such a release was remains a mystery, but he cut no corners in its production, offering a pleasing but baffling alternate version of tunes that he was obviously quite proud of.

After *Ram* was completed but before it was issued, Paul summoned arranger Richard Hewson, a Peter Asher protégé, to offer him the assignment of putting together orchestral arrangements of the entire album. Though Hewson was well known to Apple, having arranged the old-timey instrumentation on Mary Hopkin's "Those Were The Days" and subsequent singles, as well as James Taylor's debut album, he was a curious choice for Paul to have made. In 1970, Hewson was tapped by Phil Spector on very short notice to put together a slathering of orchestration for *Let It Be*'s "The Long And Winding Road"—an arrangement famously *despised* by Paul. Whether he was aware of who was responsible is unknown, but he nonetheless hired Hewson (who wasn't about to bring it up) for the *Ram* project.

The sessions began at EMI's Abbey Road studios in June and ran for three days only. Assisting were EMI engineer Tony Clark, who had worked with the Fabs as a mastering engineer beginning with "Paperback Writer" in 1966; also, Alan Parsons, who got his start as a tape operator on *Abbey Road*, would work on Paul's *Red Rose Speedway*, and ended the decade fronting the *Alan Parsons Project*. Among the musicians hired were bassist Herbie Flowers (whose signature riff propelled Lou Reed's "A Walk On The Wild Side" and would later record with both George and Ringo) as well as the Mike Sammes Singers (contrary to reports that credit the Swingle Singers), who appeared on both "I Am The Walrus" and "Goodnight.")

It is astonishing in retrospect to see the amount of trouble Paul put into creating a hand puppet to front the project, contriving an elaborate back story for "Irish bandleader" Percy "Thrills" Thrillington. Introduced as an eccentric yet gifted socialite, Thrillington's name began popping up in the gossip pages of the British press (and *Rolling Stone*), with tidbits spoon-fed to columnists by Paul as part of a campaign to lay the groundwork for the upcoming release. The fictitious details went duly reported without question, but then as suddenly as his emergence was announced, all Thrillington reports ceased.

What had happened in the summer of 1971 was that Paul decided instead to act on his desire to get a viable performing group together, putting his energics to better use with the creation of Wings. The completed album was quietly shelved and there it sat until, during the lull between the release of *Wings Over America* and *London Town*, Paul revisited the project and quietly issued it. Lacking any promotional push, it was—if noticed at all—regarded as a Beatle-related novelty, like so many other instrumental treatments of their material, and ignored.

No one initially connected Paul directly with the project, though he had in fact produced it (credits read "Thrillington"). He also, under the "Clint Harrigan" pseudonym, penned the liner notes. (This fictitious journalist also received the by-line for the cringe-worthy essay featured on Wings' *Wild Life* LP—a point that largely escaped *everyone* with the exception of the ever-alert John Lennon, who publicly called Paul out on it.)

The album itself, simply titled *Thrillington*, is something far more than the "Muzak" Paul has been accused of making throughout his career. Hewson re-imagined *Ram*'s varied styles with taste and intelligence that enhanced their inherent melodicism. As a whole, the album is rife with musical invention and freshness that almost makes one wish for similar treatments of other ex-Fab work. (Indeed, Ringo's eponymous smash was accorded a similar re-thinking; see David Hentschel below.)

"Eat At Home," for example, was offered up as a reggae piece—something that must have greatly pleased the McCartneys. "Uncle Albert/Admiral Halsey" marked the first appearance of a smoky piano lick that would recur later in the concluding "Back Seat Of My Car"—a deliberate homage to Nelson Riddle's recurring motifs on his "Quarter To Three" Sinatra productions.

Had *Thrillington* been released upon its completion in 1971, it would have been on the Apple label. Its delayed vinyl appearance came on Capitol; it has since been reissued twice on compact disc (including as a bonus with 2012's *Ram* remaster), making it accessible to anyone interested in a re-approach to *Ram*, or simply wanting to hear some really well-presented Macca tunes.

BILL ELLIOT/SPLINTER

In 1970, a Newcastle group called Half Breed crossed paths with the soon-to-be-former Beatles' road manager, Mal Evans. Believing he had another Badfinger on his hands, Mal took them into the studio to produce a demo for Apple. Turns out he was half right; the label *was* interested in exactly half of Half Breed (Quarter Breed?)—singer Bill Elliot and songwriter Bob Purvis.

The duo's proximity to the ex-Fabs paid off almost immediately. As luck would have it, an underground satirical rag, *Oz*, was on trial for its very existence in England, charged with obscenity. Unwilling to turn down any counterculture cause that caught his fancy, John pledged his support for their legal defense fund by producing a single to raise money and draw attention to their plight. Just as George would soon do his bit for the starving refugees in Bangladesh, John chose some sophomoric wise guys for *his* largesse.

Though willing to lend his compositional pen to the cause, John wasn't about to put his voice out in front. To that end—through Mal's intervention—Bill Elliot was tabbed to cut the lead vocal, after one "Magic Michael" flubbed his shot due to a basic lack of recording studio experience. Backed by John, Ringo, Klaus, and augmented by the brass of Bobby Keys, "God Save Us" was a catchy if repetitive slice of fifties-ish rock, released under the nomenclature "Elastic Oz Band." (The flipside featured Lennon himself on lead vocals for a noisy piss-take of "The Hokey Pokey" called "Do The Oz." It has since been issued as a bonus track to the *Plastic Ono Band* CD release, while John's guide vocal on the A-side was released on the Lennon *Anthology* box set in 1998.)

The single would have made a fine high-profile recording debut, had anyone heard it, but "God Save Us" failed to chart. Just the same, Elliot and Purvis maintained their esteem among the ex-Fabs. After some time apart, the pair reunited to cut some demos. One song, "Another Chance I Let Go," was deemed a superb addition to the soundtrack of a film that Apple was producing, a cinematic treatment of the play *Little Malcolm*. With lyrics written almost entirely by Mal and featuring Badfinger's Pete Ham on guitar (at George's behest), the song—re-titled "Lonely Man"—was included in the film (as were Purvis and Elliot), bringing the duo further into the ex-Beatle orbit.

Since it was clear that Apple had reached its end of days, George made Purvis and Elliot—now dubbed "Splinter"—his first signing to the newly-formed Dark Horse Records in 1974. Additionally, he put his money where his mouth was by producing their debut long player, *The Place I Love*, providing guitar throughout, as well as synthesizer and percussion (under a variety of pseudonyms, of course). Also present were the usual crew: Keltner, Preston, Voormann, Wright, plus guitarist Alvin "I'm Going Home" Lee.

"Costafine Town" was a lilting but catchy slice of piano-based pop, sounding a bit like a Harrisong performed by Marmalade. Released in the U.S. in November 1974, the song peaked at a disappointing seventy-seven; in other markets, however, it was a genuine smash, hitting the Top Twenty in England and the Top Ten in Australia and South Africa. The parent album itself was a Harrisonian delight, reminiscent of Badfinger in places but possessing slightly less edginess, lacking the firepower of the Ham-Molland guitar axis.

Every major country has a screw in its side, in England it's Oz. Oz is on trial for its life. John and Yoko have written and helped produce this record - the proceeds of which are going to Oz to help to pay their legal fees. The entire British underground is in trouble, it needs our help. Please listen - 'God Save Oz'.

Co-produced by Phil Spector

Apple 36

As George also discovered later with his "Faster" single, John learned good intentions were not enough to entice the public into buying your charitable efforts: "God Save Us," earmarked for the Oz defense fund, did not chart.

For A&M, who had agreed to take on the Dark Horse roster mostly for the sake of having an ex-Beatle in their midst, Splinter's success was gravy—an unexpected bonus. It is therefore not surprising that they really weren't prepared to build upon Splinter's debut, making what followed become steadily more marginalized. *Harder To Live*, their sophomore effort, featured George on only one cut, the aforementioned "Lonely Man." Produced by horn player Tom Scott, it marked an increased slide toward Los Angeles-style light rock, perhaps in keeping with the prevailing non-disco trend of the day. Unlike its predecessor, it spawned no hits.

The Dark Horse shake-up, which saw distribution switch from A&M to Warner Brothers, disrupted their career briefly; *Two Man Band* came in 1977, over a year after *Harder To Live*. Sadly, the effect of George's increasingly hands-off involvement manifested itself in increasingly bland production that downplayed the duo's unique charms, seemingly in an effort to tailor their sound toward the marketplace. While acts like Firefall, England Dan and John Ford Coley, and the newly revamped Fleetwood Mac were producing soft rock hits effortlessly, Splinter struggled, maintaining a foothold only in Japan.

George contributed some guitar to *Two Man Band* but the album marked their U.S. swan song. Though they would go on recording together till 1984, Splinter never lived up to their early success, making Dark Horse's only non-Harrison hit-makers a Fab footnote.

ELEPHANTS MEMORY

In retrospect, it is unfortunate for their reputation that this New York-based band is renowned today mostly for backing up John on his worst regarded solo album as well as at the wobbly *One To One* concert. Given the sub-par material on the first and the under-rehearsed performance on the latter, the band's musical invention and undeniable chops were somewhat lost, fueling comparisons akin to Janis Joplin's Big Brother and the Holding Company in that they were little more than a glorified bar band that got lucky.

In fact, Elephants Memory were viable artists in their own right who—saddled with record label woes and a revolving door line-up—never really lived up to their potential. Formed by saxophonist Stan Bronstein and drummer Rick Frank in 1967, the group initially seemed like just one more horn based rock band, much like Blood, Sweat and Tears and Chicago. Where they differed was their avant garde musicality (a good comparison would be the Mothers of Invention, minus the satirical bent) and overt politicism. (Though Chicago's earliest albums were also somewhat didactic, this direction was abandoned by 1973.)

Before their debut long-player in 1969, the band's members included vocalist Carly Simon, who contributed material and arrangements. (Their parting was apparently not amicable and songs she'd written were *re-written*.) The band scored a minor hit with the single "Mongoose," a political allegory; they also contributed to the soundtrack of *Midnight Cowboy*.

But their self-titled debut LP (whose cover art depicted an actual elephant, as well as the band members nude but for some body paint) was not a success and in 1971, they were still hardwired into New York's club circuit when Jerry Rubin put them into John Lennon's orbit. After some spirited getting to know each other at Max's Kansas City, the band was ready to back up John and Yoko on the *Mike Douglas Show* in February 1972. By now thoroughly steeped in the radical-chic politics of that time and place, John and EM began recording *Some Time In New York City* soon after their television appearance.

While John's long-range plans included the possibility of undertaking a tour, the distraction of his ongoing immigration problems kiboshed that. But the band *was* given sponsorship for release through Apple and *Elephants Memory* (the *second* time this title had been used) appeared in 1972, produced by John and Yoko. Though "Liberation Special" was duly issued as a single, the album was not a success. (Release of a second single, "Everglade Woman," was scrapped.) (Because the Elephants, like David Peel, were never *signed* to an Apple deal, their recordings have not been reissued along with the other back catalog material: the masters are believed to be owned by the Lennons and unless Yoko licenses them out, in the vaults is where they will stay.)

ELEPHANTS MEMORY

POWER BOOGIE ＊ LIBERATION SPECIAL

Apple　45

Though more than capable instrumentalists, the lack of a distinctive vocalist or songwriter doomed any chances Elephants Memory might have had for mainstream success, despite the heavy duty sponsorship.

However, the band *was* tapped for support on Yoko's sprawling *Approximately Infinite Universe*, collectively their finest hour musically and artistically. In contrast to the poppier but ultimately less cohesive production of Jack Douglas and hired studio guns on the subsequent *Feeling The Space*, *AIU* works, due in large measure to the sensitive and utterly simpatico arrangements provided by the Elephants. With little exaggeration, one might make the case that Yoko's brutally direct "Death Of Samantha," detailing a lover's betrayal (and believed to be inspired by John's election night cruelty) is as strong as anything her husband ever recorded.

By that time, John had given Elephants Memory their walking papers, concerned that his troubles on a variety of fronts would be detrimental to their own livelihoods. The band provided support to Chuck Berry on his 1973 album *Bio* before disbanding soon after. Bronstein continued as session player through the years (including work for the Clash).

But in the 1980s, the band would resurface in the press when the members filed a $104 million lawsuit against Yoko, citing the album and video release of their 1972 charity concert as *Live In New York City*.

Since the event had been a benefit, no one was paid at the time, making it galling to issue their work later for profit. Yoko's spokesman, Elliot Mintz, dismissed both the charges and the band, calling them "tenth-rate" musicians. They say an Elephant never forgets; not so Yoko.

DAVID PEEL AND THE LOWER EAST SIDE

Being a Beatle aficionado and/or a collector of Apple releases can be at times an extremely taxing job, given the—shall we say—broad tastes that the ex-Fabs exhibited. Whether a Ravi Shankar raga; some Yoko Ono "unfinished music," or the western swing of the Sundown Playboys, the patience of even the most open-minded listener can be put to the test. Though many of the acts sponsored by the label's owners certainly possessed the talent and potential to sustain long-term careers, others were unquestionably signed on the basis of striking their individual fancies at just the right moment.

Falling into this latter category was the self-proclaimed street musician David Peel. This fixture of Washington Square had already enjoyed a bit of underground success on the Elektra label with a pair of releases, *Have A Marijuana* (1968) and *The American Revolution* (1970) before Lennon first laid eyes on him. (Indeed, labelmate Jim Morrison was quoted describing the singer as "the only man I've ever known whose subconscious craziness is on par with mine!")

Backed by a loose aggregate of fellow travelers called The Lower East Side, Peel's music—such as it was—took the form of unsubtle rants, typically spewing anti-authoritarian screeds extolling the virtues of cannabis while voicing complaints against the police over an acoustic, percussive backing. His work was not without a sense of humor, however, and unlike most comedy records, it is his sly wit that rewards repeated listenings.

In addition to his lefty politics and his very embodiment of the man-of-the-people ideal that Lennon aspired to, Peel's philosophic bent proved equally appealing. John was present at a Peel event where the street musician rhetorically asked the assembled, "Why do you have to pay to see stars?" No star, he asserted, ever paid to see *you*. Given John's goal of shedding stardom that he sought upon his New York landing, it seems pretty clear that he looked to Peel as someone ideally suited to show him the way—in effect, his latest Maharishi.

Peel's ragtag ensemble backed the Lennons along with Yipsters Jerry Rubin and Abbie Hoffman at the Ann Arbor concert in December 1971; not long after, they taped a performance for the David Frost show

121

(airing in America on January 13, 1972). In it, John—playing stand-up string bass—supported *Peel*, as he made his network television debut. (Their reception was mixed, to say the least.)

In any event, Peel was rewarded with the standard ex-Fab honor: an Apple record deal (but not a recording contract; that would've taken overcoming the objections of two of the label's co-owners: Paul and George.) With John and Yoko credited as producers, the results of their collaboration was issued in 1972 as *The Pope Smokes Dope*, a title calculated to provoke and earning the ban throughout the world that its creators undoubtedly expected.

Like *Some Time In New York City*, TPSD was replete with journalistic-style observations on an array of topical concerns. "The Ballad of New York City" celebrated Peel's life-changing meeting with John and Yoko, while "Hippie From New York City" was a self-descriptive reply to Merle Haggard's "Okie From Muskogee." A reworking of a time-honored comedic bit, "F Is Not A Dirty Word," was actually considered for release (in censored form, of course) as a single, making it as far as the promo pressing stage before wiser heads prevailed.

Peel's undeniable counter-culture appeal, fearless provocation, and do-it-yourself ethos made him, in effect, a punk rock pioneer: all that was missing was the amplification. The extent of his influence can be measured with the success of the leather-clad rockers that sprang up in his wake in mid-seventies

David Peel
& the lower east side

PRODUCED BY JOHN LENNON / YOKO ONO

APPLE SW3391

David Peel – represented here with the image the FBI kept on file as "John Lennon" - had issued two albums on Elektra prior to coming into John's orbit. The first, 1968's Have A Marijuana, was much more of a straightforward street performance than its successor, 1970's The American Revolution, which featured amplification and a semblance of studio craft.

New York, notably The Ramones. Among Beatle folk, Peel's unabashed fandom of the Fabs resonates with subsequent post-Apple releases such as "Bring Back The Beatles" and "John Lennon For President." (Indeed, at least one Beatlefest in the 1990s featured an onstage performance by an ensemble of fans paying tribute, featuring an impersonator as David's brother, "Orange.")

Following his Apple album's descent into obscurity and the Lennons withdrawal from the causes that brought government prosecution down upon themselves, Peel started up a label of his own, called—wait for it—Orange Records. The label became an outlet for his own prolific releases, as well as for other provocateurs, such as shock-rocker G.G. Allin.

LON AND DERREK VAN EATON

New Jersey siblings Lon (guitar) and Derrek (vocals) Van Eaton possibly came the closest to fulfilling Apple's ideal in plucking unknowns from obscurity and attempting to launch them. (Virtually everyone else signed to the label had some connection or direct sponsor.) Formally of The Trees and Jacob's Creek, they put together a four track demo following the latter's dissolution after one album in 1971, recording layers of guitars and vocals (while simulating drums by banging on walls, tables and books). Amazingly, the resulting tape was actually heard at Apple and brought to the ex-Fabs' attention (whether by Tony King or Allen Steckler is in dispute).

Given the inherent spiritual bent of their music, it was natural that the brothers found a kinship with George. When in New York for the Bangladesh benefit, he met with them and deputized Klaus Voormann as his proxy. Klaus sounded them out at their New Jersey home and, liking what he heard, brought them over to London in September 1971. Despite bigger money being offered by other companies, the boys decided to sign with the Beatles' label based on their desire to work with "evolved" people.

The first fruit of their musical collaboration was the song "Sweet Music," produced at Abbey Road by George and featuring Ringo on drums and an unbilled Peter Frampton on lead guitar—not a bad beginning. "Song of Songs," tabbed for the flip, was produced by Klaus at the newly-opened Apple Studios on Savile Row. Released in March 1972, the single, not dissimilar in sound from George's, got rave reviews from *Rolling Stone*, which compared it favorably to "My Sweet Lord" (though musically, "Isn't It A Pity" would've been a better comparison).

123

Despite the praise and talent involved, the song struggled for survival in the marketplace, prompting a peeved George to fire off a telegram to New York: "For fuck sake do something with 'Sweet Music'…It's a potential no. 1 hit." Despite its quality and talent involved, the song did not chart. (A year later in England, Apple issued "Warm Woman," which performed similarly.)

Not until September of 1972 was an actual album's worth of material ready for issue. *Brother* was a relentlessly tuneful affair, containing further contributions from Ringo and any number of finely crafted originals. Adroitly produced by Klaus, the package included a zoetrope: a cardboard strip depicting a series of images of each Van Eaton. When placed on a turntable and viewed through the die-cut slots, a "video" loop resulted.

Despite the thoughtful production, strong material, and evident care put into the whole shebang, *Brother* garnered little more than positive notice in the rock press. More than ever, the assumption that Fab sponsorship automatically anointed one to the A-list was proven false and the brothers waited around for further word of what Apple planned next.

In the interim, they were dispatched to Los Angeles to meet with Richard Perry, then at work on *Ringo*. There they sat in, contributing percussion to "Photograph." It soon became evident that, despite their hopes at the onset, Apple was a sinking ship. The brothers were released from the label; thereafter (with George's help), they signed with A&M, recording one Perry-produced album, entitled *Who Do You Out Do*. Abetted by Klaus and Jim Keltner, the group toured Japan but large-scale success remained elusive.

Given the circumstance, it would be natural for that to be the end of things between the boys and the ex-Fabs, except it wasn't. Though Derrek

Though their stint on Apple didn't click with the masses the way George had hoped, Lon and Derrek Van Eaton got another shot in 1975, this time on A&M. Richard Perry handled production, but despite its inherent quality, support from the likes of Jim Gordon, Jim Keltner, Klaus Voormann and Gary Wright and a tour of Japan, Who Do You Out Do misfired

eventually retired from active pursuit of a recording career, Lon found his talents tapped for several Ringo releases, including *Goodnight Vienna*, *Rotogravure*, *Ringo The 4th*, and (pseudonymously), *Bad Boy*. Both brothers appeared on George's *Dark Horse* as well, while as much as an entire album's worth of material recorded with George and/or Ringo sat in the vaults for years. (It finally surfaced in 2013 as part of their self-issued CD, *Anthology 1968-2012*.)

Today, the Van Eatons remain as idealistic as ever. Lon runs an organization devoted to effecting change through performance media called *Imagine A Better World*. In 1996, the two reunited, contributing a heartfelt remake of Pete Ham's "Apple Of My Eye" to *Come And Get It: A Tribute To Badfinger*. This very public reminder of their talents prompted calls from the faithful for a follow-up, resulting in the 1998 release, *Black and White* (available through their website). *Brother* saw CD reissue in 2012 (as an import on RPM, supplemented with bonus demo tracks).

MIKE MCGEAR

At the height of Beatlemania, Paul's brother Michael, under the name of "McGear" (for fear of being seen as exploiting family ties) enjoyed some notoriety in England as part of a singular trio known as The Scaffold. Not quite a rock band, McGear, along with Roger McGough and John Gorman, blended music, poetry, and comedy in a rather unique exercise that completely escaped American audiences while scoring several U.K. hit singles, including the 1968 number one, "Lily The Pink" (doubtless familiar to *Dr. Demento Show* listeners).

As the seventies unfolded, Scaffold achieved further recording success by augmenting their membership with a pair of ex-Bonzos (Vivian Stanshall and future-Rutle Neil Innes) as well as ex-Undertaker Brian Jones (no, not *the* Brian Jones, but both men *did* play saxophone) and calling the ensemble Grimms. McGear's departure from Grimms in 1974 coincided with a period of Wings rebuilding after the departure of Henry McCullough and Denny Seiwell just as things were about to take off with *Band on the Run*.

Recognizing the opportunity to: 1) stay busy while running out the clock on his Apple contract; 2) help out his brother; and 3) audition new musicians, Paul seized the opening to produce what's been regarded for years as a "lost" Wings album, *McGear*. Macca wrote or co-wrote all but one of the album's ten tracks (and that last one was a cover of Brian Ferry's "Sea Breezes"), provided multi-instrumental support, and pro-

Mary had a little lamb / His brother's name was Mike: though an accomplished artist in his own right by the time of 1974's McGear, comparison's to the ex-Beatle would dog Mike McGear always, detracting from efforts to step outside his shadow.

duced the entire release. The album featured—besides Paul and Linda—three former, present, or future Wingsmen: Denny's Laine and Seiwell, plus Jimmy McCulloch.

The original plan had been to merely record a single ("Leave It," possibly the album's finest track) but circumstance allowed for Paul to go all out, using the opportunity to put together what could have been a Wings album, had his writing been a little more tongue-in-cheek. For this, his second solo release, Mike acquits himself well, providing (naturally) vocals that are McCartney-esque, as well as a certain detached humor not typically found in Paul's work.

Given the pedigree of the players, *McGear* is an expectedly well-produced state-of-the-art pop album. There are no real surprises (save, perhaps, the T. Rex impersonation on "Giving Grease A Ride") and as a whole, the release lies somewhere between *Red Rose Speedway* and *Venus and Mars* in terms of overall memorability. But upon its October 1974 issue (around the same time as *Walls and Bridges*, nearly), his label, Warner Brothers, did nothing to exploit the relations, thereby sentencing *McGear* to obscurity and the cut-out bin. (The album cover's artwork, featuring an inverted McGear as a Gulliver-like giant, bound to the ground and surrounded by Lilliputians, *did* feature Paul's image among the onlookers, but unrecognizably: as a child.)

For Wings aficionados, the 1990 CD reissue from Rykodisc (now out of print) is well-worth seeking out (augmented by a bonus single, the disco parody "Dance The Do"). Replete with the unmistakable vocalizing of Paul, Linda, and Denny, and Jimmy McCulloch's signature sound, *McGear* remains a worthy novelty.

126

DAVID HENTSCHEL

Despite, or perhaps *because* Ringo was not offered a new recording contract from EMI when it lapsed in 1975 (his string of successes notwithstanding), Ringo decided to start up his own label: "Ring O'Records." Ultimately, the company would issue but one album in the states, plus thirteen (a reissue of the Apple release, John Tavener's *The Whale*, was among them) in Europe before folding in 1978. David Hentschel's *Startling Music*, the sole American release, ranks alongside Paul's *Thrillington* as a rather odd excursion into revisiting one's own work as an instrumental release.

Hentschel began his professional career as an assistant engineer at London's Trident Studios. (Early on, he worked on George's *All Things Must Pass* in the course of his duties; later, he engineered on Paul's *Red Rose Speedway*.) But the act he is most associated with is Genesis, having engineered or produced all of their albums from 1971's *Nursery Cryme* through 1980's *Duke*. He was also an accomplished synthesizer pioneer: his work with the then-new ARP 2500 can be heard on Elton John's "Rocket Man" as well as "Funeral For A Friend."

It was this singular skill that served him in good stead when Ringo began recruiting talent for his label. While it is unknown whether or not he was aware of Paul's then-unreleased *Thrillington* project, the Ringed One was clearly thinking along similar lines when he decided

to commission a synthesizer-based track-by-track cover of his magnum opus: *Startling Music*, released in February 1975.

Assisting on the album was drummer Phil Collins, who would soon take over as Genesis' lead singer in the wake of Peter Gabriel's pending departure. Ronnie Caryl, Collins' bandmate from his pre-Genesis group Flaming

Of all the offerings on the Ringo O'Records roster, David Hentschel's Startling Music made sense for US issue as the most likely to click with American record buyers. Much of the rest of the artists possessed even less appeal than this synth-driven prop project.

Youth contributed guitar. The album was recorded in late 1974 at the newly-renamed Startling Studios (formerly Ascot Sound Studio) at Tittenhurst Park, John's former residence currently occupied by Ringo.

Given the richness of melodies found on *Ringo*, it's not too surprising that they would be so readily adaptable to a variety of styles. What's clear is that Hentschel's imagination was given leave to reinvent the tunes with much latitude, given the synthesizer's limitless possibilities. The opener, "Devil Woman" (yes, the running order was reconfigured) became a showcase for Collins' virtuosic drumming, while the country hoedown of the original "Sunshine Life For Me" was swapped out for a bagpipe-drenched march. "Oh My My" was issued as a single but predictably bombed (despite the original having peaked at six one year before).

Only a total prog-snob would dismiss the truly exciting arrangements found throughout *Startling Music*. Indeed, much of the material would have fit just fine on a Gabriel-era Genesis album, or even ELP. True, some of the synthesizer flourishes sound dated nowadays, but then isn't that part of the genre's attraction? Out of print as a CD, vinyl copies still pop up on Ebay. To anyone wishing to relive the prog side of seventies pop, this *Ringo*'s for you.

ATTITUDES

When George started up Dark Horse, it was in part to rectify the mess that Apple had become. Freed of Allen Klein's tyranny and perhaps having learned a lesson or two, both Ringo and George still had some residual idealism when it came to nurturing talent. But the record business can be deceptively tricky to navigate, and with so much success achieved, George, like his fellow ex-Fabs, may have naively felt their own collective goodwill could be passed along to any worthy act they desired, reality notwithstanding. Still, he may have convinced himself that as long as he was calling the shots, artists that he cared about would be treated properly and given the attention their talent warranted.

Among the acts signed to his label were Ravi Shankar—an obvious choice as someone he revered; The Stairsteps—a soul group who, as the Five Stairsteps, scored a smash hit in 1970 with "O-o-h Child"; Keni Burke, the aforementioned group's singer and bassist, following their disbanding; Jiva—a white funk outfit that deserved more attention than they ever got; and Attitudes, a band of sessioneers anchored by Jim Keltner.

Three of the group's four members—Keltner, keyboardist David Foster and bassist Paul Stallworth—had played on George's *Extra Texture* album (Stallworth is credited with coming up with the title). That is likely where the notion for their "supergroup" began. The fourth member was legendary session guitarist Danny "Kootch" Kortchmar, who'd gotten his start in James Taylor's Flying Machine in the sixties before going on to cut a swath through L.A. that included best-selling discs by Taylor, Carole King, and Linda Ronstadt.

The group released a pair of albums, 1976's self-titled debut, and 1977's *Good News*. Neither faired particularly well, although the first album included a Kootch tune, "Honey Don't Leave L.A.," that became a minor hit for James Taylor a year later. (*Good News'* "Sweet Summer Music" barely made the Hot One Hundred, peaking at ninety-four.)

The overall problem with Attitudes was that, despite predictably excellent performances (which included guests like Ringo, guitarist Waddy Wachtel, Booker T. Jones, Jesse Ed Davis, and the Tower of Power Horns), their self-penned material itself was a bit on the bland side. Session bands like the Atlanta Rhythm Section and Toto, faceless though they were, at least had some halfway decent songs to engage radio programmers. Dark Horse's lack of effective promotion couldn't have helped either.

Foster had played on George's *Thirty-Three & 1/3*, as well as Ringo's *Goodnight Vienna* and *Ringo the 4th*. (Despite his resumé claiming he'd recorded alongside John Lennon, perhaps what he meant was that John was in the room when he worked with Ringo.) He'd gotten his start in the Canadian band Skylark, who scored their one big hit in 1972 with "Wildflower." (Ironically, though Foster was the band's leader, he doesn't appear on their signature tune, as it was felt that it didn't need keyboards.) He would later become one of the most successful producers in the business, with names like Whitney Houston, Barbra Streisand, and Josh Groban among his clients.

Stallworth's playing turned up on recordings by artists as varied as Tommy Bolin and Al Jarreau. As for Keltner, his membership in supergroups was just getting started. In 1988, he provided percussive support to the five rhythm guitarists who comprised the Traveling Wilburys; in 1992, he joined forces with singer/songwriters John Hiatt and Nick Lowe and guitarist Ry Cooder to form Little Village, a group that lasted exactly one album.

LINDA MCCARTNEY

Unlike John's missus, the former Linda Eastman possessed no musical ambitions of her own. Prior to hooking up with Paul, her melodic interactions came either as a listener or on a more *intimate* level (sometimes involving photography). Her first vocal with her husband on record came unexpectedly, for "Let It Be." After Mary Hopkin—the intended singer—left the studio early, Linda was pressed into service to provide the high harmony. (Of course, this came *before* Paul's declaration, in the wake of the band's disharmonious break-up, that he would *never* put a woman's voice on a Beatle record.)

By the time Paul got around to laying down tracks for what would become his first proper studio album, John and Yoko had issued two singles and one live album, establishing musical identities that—to that point—didn't really rise to the level of collaboration. (There were joint releases, and co-credits even, but the couple didn't engage in any real duets until 1971's "Happy Xmas (War Is Over)" single.) Paul, on the other hand, recruited Linda in late 1969 to flesh out his own vocals and provide a sort of unschooled element that gave texture against his pop slickness.

Linda's harmonies appear throughout the *McCartney* and *Ram* albums. (For the latter release, she is recalled by others present as having actually composed her own vocal lines.) But not until the formation of Wings in mid-1971 was the complete novice compelled to formally learn an instrument, courtesy of Macca. While it is doubtful that John ever had to coax Yoko onto a stage, Linda had to be badgered, begged, and browbeaten into becoming a full-time member of Paul's post-Beatles act.

His insistence that she accompany him onstage in Wings compelled the neophyte to take a crash course in keyboards, making her—in spirit anyway—a musical partner. But not until Sir Lew Grade questioned her qualifications to appear on a composition's byline was Linda actually compelled to sit down and write a song herself. "Seaside Woman," a reggaefied trifle, was the result. (It was recorded by Wings on November 27, 1972.)

Though Macca was frequently at a loss to explain why he demanded Linda's presence, the answer is really simple: she was his emotional support (just as Yoko was for John) and he felt that by putting her on an instrument he'd justified her position to the critics—including the ones in the band. It was an entirely thankless role that Paul forced

 LINDA aud PAUL McCARTNEY

It's hard not to conclude that Linda McCartney would rather have stuck to photography than take on a career in music. Eventually, she learned to have fun with it, but compared to say Yoko Ono (as people do) she certainly showed no signs of possessing the drive to push herself as a recording artist.

her into, literally subjecting her to a world of abuse, while testing their marital ties as much as it demonstrated her love for her man.

It took a long time for Paul's compositional stranglehold on Wings' recorded output to loosen up enough to allow a song authored by Denny Laine to be issued; for Linda, who'd been with the ex-Beatle from the group's inception, that day never came. Within Wings' seven studio albums, she received exactly one solo lead vocal, on a song—"Cook of the House"—penned by her husband. Meanwhile, during the Wings years, she recorded some seven original tunes (plus two oldies covers: "Mr. Sandman" and "Sugartime"): all but one single's worth went unreleased in her lifetime—and *that* pair of songs was issued under a pseudonym.

That the band spent studio time laying down songs that Linda had taken the trouble to write (or co-write), only to then languish in the vaults begs the question: why? If Linda was in fact an essential component of Wings, as Paul so defensively proclaimed, why was her work not accorded the dignity of a public issue that even Jimmy McCulloch earned his first time out? The question cannot be answered without a certain disingenuousness creeping in, regarding either Linda's musical viability or Paul's protestations that "Wings is a band—*I'm* not Wings." It was *Paul* who ultimately decided what was and wasn't issued; with the lion's share of Linda and Denny compositions recorded but unreleased, the hypocrisy is demonstrably clear.

In any event, "Seaside Woman" came out in 1977, during the "dumping" period between *Wings Over America* and *London Town* that saw the issue of the similarly shopworn *Thrillington* album. The song itself is a pleasant enough novelty, with enough Macca backing vocals slathered on to effectively mask any shortcomings from the song's author. Given that the McCartneys had been discussing the song's existence for years (and even the pseudonym it was produced under), it didn't really generate much buzz among radio station programmers, peaking at fifty-nine on the U.S. charts; lower than any Wings single but higher than several of Ringo's.

Her next recorded composition was far more intriguing. "Oriental Nightfish," recorded by the same Wings trio in October 1973 that produced *Band on the Run*, was an atmospheric electric piano piece, augmented by flute and electric guitar. Not a song exactly, in that it's really more of an instrumental in support of a spoken word narrative, it ended up accompanying a rather trippy post-*Fantasia* piece of animation by Ian Emes, (directed by Linda) in 1978. The clip, featuring a nude blonde, was nominated for a Golden Palm Award at Cannes as best short film.

Other Linda compositions include "I Got Up," cut in Paris during the late 1973 sessions that served as Jimmy McCulloch's audition, along with the equally annoying "Wide Prairie"; 1975's "New Orleans"—a not-bad girl-group type of throwback (like "Seaside Woman" and "Cook Of The House," it too features a preoccupation with food); and 1980's "Love's Full Glory." This last tune was perhaps the most ambitious song Linda ever recorded, being—as its title suggests—a glorious romantic ballad. It featured orchestration scored by Tony Visconti, as well as his then-wife, Mary Hopkin, on backing vocals (alongside Stiff's Lene Lovich).

All of the songs were collected and issued with later recordings on the *Wide Prairie* album, released six months after Linda's death in 1998. (She had literally been working on some of the tunes in her final weeks to prepare them for release.) While like Yoko, Linda's work isn't to everyone's taste, some of it does possess a certain charm. Why nearly none of it was released during her lifetime (when she could have received the feedback that every artist craves) is a question only Paul can answer.

The first of two iconic images tying John to the Statue of Liberty came in the form of a post card packaged with 1972's Some Time in New Your City album.

CHAPTER 7

THE STATUE OF LIBERTY SAID "COME": THE U.S. VS. JOHN LENNON

The inimitable Norman Pilcher busted John and Yoko for drug possession on October 18, 1968. To put what he saw as an especially heavy-handed frame-up behind him, John pleaded guilty to misdemeanor possession of *cannabis resin* (that's hash to all you non-heads) and paid a fine. Little did he realize the repercussions of his actions, for in doing so he unwittingly handed the incoming Nixon administration a weapon to use against him in his efforts to settle in New York just a few years later.

The first hint of the implications came the following May, when—after having used the occasion of his nuptials to stage an Amsterdam Hilton "bed-in" for peace—Lennon was denied an entry visa to the states for an encore in New York. (He instead held his second such "happening" in Montreal, recording "Give Peace A Chance" in the process.) Not until the summer of 1970 was John again allowed to travel freely to and from America, possibly on medical grounds, as it was for the purpose of receiving Primal Scream therapy from California doctor Arthur Janov.

But his increasingly high-profile political activities proved impossible to ignore, once again drawing the ire of Nixon's government the following year. An all-out war between the ex-Beatle and forces within the INS and FBI under the direction of the president's political allies erupted, reinforcing the characterization of the administration as inherently corrupt and punitive once the details became public knowledge. The whole affair has been the subject of a fine book (*Come Together: John Lennon In His Time* by Jon Wiener) as well as a documentary (2006's *The U.S. vs. John Lennon*), both detailing the extraordinary effort to "neutralize" him, therein affecting his life, career, and art. Here are the key events in a struggle that bedeviled the Lennons for the first half of the decade.

SUMMER 1971 – JOHN AND YOKO AWARDED CUSTODY OF KYOKO COX

Like her third husband, Yoko too became a parent in 1963: to daughter

Kyoko, who was later celebrated in song, after a fashion ("Don't Worry Kyoko.") Also like John, Yoko's efforts at parenting were mixed at best, most often bordering on neglect (she would later justify her disinterest by asserting that "in general, mothers have a very strong resentment toward their children"). Once John and Yoko were together, Kyoko and Julian were brought along on various outings, but after the child's father, artist/filmmaker Tony Cox and Yoko were officially split, it was he that retained custody.

Yoko's maternal instincts were eventually awakened and in April 1971, the couple tracked down Cox—with Kyoko—at a retreat in Majorca, Spain (run by, of all people, the Maharishi). They spirited the child away to their hotel in Madrid, intent on bringing her back home to raise, but legal authorities intervened, resulting in a custody hearing, which declared Cox the legal custodian. Two months later, Yoko filed for custody in the Virgin Islands (where the divorce had been granted) and prevailed. The trouble was, Cox and Kyoko had vanished, reportedly to Texas.

So began an odyssey that would occupy the Lennons for years to come, as hired investigators attempted to track down the wily Cox, who had re-married, and Kyoko, soon to be known as Rosemary. The Coxes belonged to a fundamentalist group known as The Walk; it was their belief that John and Yoko were, as admitted drug users, unfit to raise the girl, and that they were therefore justified in defying the court order to turn over the child to Yoko. On the advice of their attorneys, the ongoing fight necessitated that the Lennons stay in America, giving their subsequent legal arguments more urgency.

AUGUST 31, 1971 – JOHN QUITS ENGLAND

The summer of 1971 was particularly busy for the ex-Fabs. With some help from George, John recorded a follow-up to *Plastic Ono Band, Imagine*, fairly quickly. Paul, enjoying the rise of his first solo number one single ("Uncle Albert/Admiral Halsey") formed Wings, while Ringo labored in Spain on a rather downbeat shoot-em-up, *Blindman*. The biggest share of the limelight, however, went to the former group's dark horse, George, for organizing the all-star relief effort for the refugees of the Bangladesh war. John had ample opportunity to contribute to the event, but ultimately opted out. Given all that was on his plate, his non-appearance wasn't completely unexpected.

Travel between London and New York was necessitated by work

completing *Imagine*; promotion of the reprint of Yoko's *Grapefruit*; supporting *Oz* magazine during their obscenity trial; and attending Allen Klein's birthday party, among other things. With all the attendant jet lag becoming tiresome, John at last decided that the time had come to cut the cord with his home country (a place he compared rather disdainfully to Denmark). Though it was certainly not his intent, John Lennon would never see England again.

Given their determination to use their celebrity to advance any number of political causes as well as the cultural diversity of what Yoko considered to be her hometown, the couple pulled up stakes at their Tittenhurst Park home and set up a base in the Big Apple. From there, they could still be at the center of all things hip while keeping tabs on the Kyoko situation. Whatever his long term plans were for settling in the New World, John and Yoko were granted entry on a six-month visa.

DECEMBER 11, 1971 – THE JOHN SINCLAIR FREEDOM RALLY

No sooner had the couple moved into the St. Regis Hotel than they made the acquaintance of Youth International Party (or "Yippie") co-founders Jerry Rubin and Abbie Hoffman. Though the pair was notorious throughout Middle America for the provocative antics that landed them in court as part of the Chicago Seven, they found that they had much in common with the Lennons and became instant BFFs. No novice to media manipulation, Lennon saw a pair of kindred spirits who, like himself, presented their messages with a theatrical flair.

It was through Rubin and Hoffman that John met street singer David Peel, as well as Elephant's Memory. With these and other connections, Lennon found a practical conduit for harnessing his innate anti-Establishment tendencies. The combination of Lennon's desire to put his money where his mouth was and the New Yorker's sense of where best to place it resulted in numerous live appearances in support of whatever the cause of the day was. John Sinclair's "ten for two" case offered the perfect opportunity to display his commitment to justice.

As described in *Fab Four FAQ 2.0*, the Ann Arbor concert marked John's first meaningful commitment of solidarity with the American counterculture. In so doing, he played right into the hands of the Nixon administration's chronic paranoia. Already alerted to the "un-American" tendencies of the Beatles by none other than Elvis Presley himself— personally, just one year earlier—John successfully placed himself on Nixon's enemies list that night with his participation. The first practical step toward eradicating this imported problem would be taken less than two months later; in the meantime, the Lennons' activities would be closely watched.

FEBRUARY 4, 1972 – STROM THURMOND'S MEMO

This "smoking gun" document marked the official start of the Nixon Administration's war on John Lennon. South Carolina Senator James Strom Thurmond, a member of the Senate Judiciary Committee, was one of President Nixon's strongest allies. In a political career which began just after World War II, he distinguished himself mostly for his staunch segregationist views: first, challenging his party's presidential nominee, Harry Truman, in 1948 as an anti-integration "Dixiecrat"; later as the record-holder of the longest filibuster in Senate history in opposition to the 1957 Civil Rights Bill. This despite having fathered a baby with the teen-aged daughter of his family's black housekeeper back in the 1920s, a child whose existence he never publicly acknowledged.

Rank hypocrisy aside, Thurmond, now officially a Republican, was a powerful man in Washington, having the White House's ear as needed. An internal memo written by staffers of the Senate Internal Security Subcommittee brought to Thurmond's attention Lennon's association with the already "risky" former Chicago Seven defendants, as well as his participation in the John Sinclair rally. A "mole," infiltrating the operation, had reported to the FBI their talk of staging a series of events throughout the presidential campaign year, encompassing concerts, get-out-the-vote drives, and anti-Nixon protests—this in the first year that 18 year-olds could legally vote. The potential for the former Beatle to influence the country's newly enfranchised youth against the administration was boundless and Thurmond knew it.

On February 4, he summarized the findings of the internal memorandum in a letter to Attorney General John Mitchell. According to Thurmond, any threat to the President's reelection could be dealt with easily: simply remove the head of the monster, in this case Lennon, by way of the Immigration and Naturalization Service (INS). By deporting the superstar, the "Dump Nixon" faction could be rendered fangless— or so Thurmond believed.

The notion of implementing an arm of the United States government against a perceived foe originated with White House counsel John Dean, who first introduced the concept in a memo he wrote only months before, suggesting that the White House "use the available political machinery to screw our enemies." The INS was the perfect weapon to deal with someone possessing the vulnerability that John had with his previous drug conviction. Thurmond's head's up found a receptive audience.

MARCH 6, 1972 – INS TURNS DOWN JOHN'S VISA RENEWAL

Mitchell's deputy, Richard Kleindienst, sought assurance that Thurmond's suggestion was even actionable. "Do we have any basis to deny his admittance?" he asked INS commissioner Ray Farrell. (Kleindienst was a little behind the curve; had he been a fan of *The Mike Douglas Show*, he would have learned that not only was the former Beatle already in the country, but that he was hosting the show that very week.) At this point, the administration's biggest fear was the prospect of an encore of the demonstrations held at the 1968 Democratic convention in Chicago, this time against the Republicans. The "law and order" president was genuinely frightened at the prospect of hippie hordes running amuck at their San Diego celebration with John Lennon as their ringleader.

It apparently didn't take much pressure from the White House to unleash the INS dogs. Just one month after Senator Thurmond's memo reached the West Wing, the INS fired the opening salvo, declining to renew John's visa, citing his 1968 drug conviction as making Lennon an "undesirable." This action set the stage for a series of deportation hearings beginning that very month. The Lennons secured the services of immigration attorney Leon Wildes to fight the proceedings, initially accentuating the Kyoko custody battle while downplaying the politics they believed to be behind the action.

It's interesting to note that, in light of all the adoration directed toward John during the Beatle years and after his 1980 martyrdom, virtually *no one* from the rock community offered public support in the fight. While luminaries ranging from conductor Leonard Bernstein to New York City Mayor John Lindsay provided glowing tributes to John as an influential artist and provider of good works to the community, *none* of his fellow musicians could be bothered to take a public stand. The situation was articulated in a blistering op-ed published in *Rolling Stone*, written by co-founder Ralph J. Gleason.

Noting that virtually everyone with a song on the radio owed the opportunity for their success to the Beatles and John Lennon, he asked,

"Where the hell is everybody?" He also put his finger on what would become an obvious issue to Lennon and his lawyer about the "selective enforcement" by the INS (while further asserting that John posed far less of a threat to the future of the republic than did Richard Nixon). The effect of Gleason's rant was swift, with Phil Spector seconding the "sickening" apathy from his fellow artists in a follow-up letter. The public soon followed, with letters of their own flooding the offices of the INS. Still, the silence from his peers was deafening.

MARCH 23, 1973 – INS ORDERS JOHN TO LEAVE U.S. WITHIN 60 DAYS OR FACE DEPORTATION

In fact, John had never agreed to take part in what Nixon's people feared, at best being willing only to partake in one-off shows. By the time the administration began fixating on him as key to all the shenanigans dreamed up by Rubin and company, he had begun to back off on any commitments, particularly where the prospect of violence loomed. While initially happy to play the part of the topical troubadour, he was no less resistant to being ill-used for his celebrity than he'd been in the Beatle days. Furthermore, the deliberately open surveillance of his every move put him under enormous strain.

In the year since the INS initiated proceedings, John had made numerous television talk show appearances that showcased his newfound support of so-called radical causes, be they equality for women, the Irish against the occupying Brits, or the inmates at New York's Attica State prison. The cover artwork to *Some Time In New York City*, released in June 1972 (around the time of the Watergate break-ins), featured a doctored photo of Richard Nixon and Chairman Mao dancing naked together; this could not have endeared him to the White

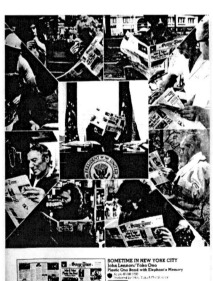

If there were any doubts as to the power that John Lennon could wield upon newly-enfranchised 18 year old-voters, the fine print in this Some Time in New York City ad underscored the point.

140

House. Recognizing that his overt political actions—first amendment rights notwithstanding—were turning off his fan base while drawing governmental heat, he began a retreat. The only live appearance he made that year was at the *One To One* benefit; the dreaded disruption of the Republican convention never occurred.

The president's successful reelection aside, the INS would entertain no more delaying tactics. On March 23, they granted Yoko permanent residency while ordering John to leave the country within sixty days or face deportation. (In the year since they first initiated their action, the government had apparently learned that Yoko did *not* have a drug conviction and was therefore not subject to the deportation order.) But the action would force Yoko to choose between her daughter and her husband, a less than humane solution. Unwittingly, the INS had handed the Lennons an effective public relations tool.

Seizing the moment, John and Yoko issued a proclamation of their own: "Having just celebrated our fourth anniversary, we are not prepared to sleep in separate beds" (though by the end of the year, they would be). Underscoring the human aspect of the story rallied supporters to their side, including one of the least likely. Never known to either traffic in the counterculture or criticize Republican administrations, the *Wall Street Journal* commented that the situation was "intolerable" and that "if the law does not reflect the human equities, it is the law that needs to be changed."

In a follow-up editorial, *Rolling Stone*'s Gleason full out blasted the selective prosecution of Lennon, noting that plenty of show biz celebrities had drug convictions (like, for instance, George Harrison and Paul McCartney) and were allowed to travel freely to and from the states. In fact, this was one of the very strategies that Leon Wildes was focusing on, another being that the very crime he'd been convicted of in the U.K. was not an offense in America. (Cannabis resin was not classified as a narcotic; therefore, possession would at best be a misdemeanor.)

Furthermore, Wildes noted in his appeal that the government had already pre-judged the case, based upon documents he'd found after filing a Freedom of Information Act suit. A memo surfaced explicitly instructing INS district manager Sol Marks to deny all of the Lennons 'applications. (Marks had as much as told Wildes this already, off the record.) John and his attorney filed a countersuit in October, demanding that the government either confirm or deny their surveillance. Admitting their actions would have made it impossible to claim that the INS case was "routine." Well-armed with this array of defenses, Wildes felt confident that right was on his side.

JULY 17, 1974 – INS DENIES JOHN'S APPEAL AND AGAIN ORDERS HIM TO LEAVE WITHIN 60 DAYS

Unfortunately, the attorney hadn't counted on governmental inertia. Though by the following summer, the embattled Nixon administration, thoroughly under siege, was on its way out the door, the INS seemed impervious to changing events, doggedly sticking to its path, denying the appeal. (As John would later lightheartedly describe it, he was in a cab when the word came over the radio that once again, he was being ordered out of the country by the INS: "So being jocular, I said 'Take me to the airport, Sam!'")

Ten days after the ruling against John, the Senate Judiciary Committee voted to recommend that the House impeach the president. Less than two weeks later, the Nixon administration was history, as were most of Lennon's antagonists. But as the case dragged on, evidence was mounting of the extremely political nature of his being singled out. Wildes found over a hundred applicants whose convictions ranged from heroin possession to violent crimes that *still* managed to stay in the country, therein debunking the claim that John's prosecution was "by the book."

It was perhaps with this obvious injustice in mind that George Harrison, upon his December 1974 Oval Office photo op with the newly-installed Gerald Ford, asked the president personally if anything could be done on John's behalf. Perhaps mindful of the shit storm he'd stirred by pardoning his predecessor, Ford demurred. (In private conversation, novelist Terry Southern—author of two Ringo film properties, *Candy* and *The Magic Christian*—tried to cheer John by putting the best face on the case: "The conservatives are happy 'cause they're doing somethin' about ya and the liberals are happy 'cause they haven't thrown you out. So everybody's happy! Except you!")

If the government thought that they could wear John down in their zeal to make him their latest Charlie Chaplin, they were mistaken. (Chaplin, another English leftie, left his home in America in 1952—at the height of the Red Scare—to promote his latest film, *Limelight* in Europe, only to find that the INS had revoked his visa. For a full twenty years, the U.S. kept the door locked until an aging Chaplin was allowed back in 1972 to accept a special Oscar; all was forgiven.) Wishing to avoid Chaplin's fate, Lennon made his plea directly to the public in numerous interviews, expressing his love of America while noting that "I might get into the occasional spot of trouble but nothing that's going to bring the country to pieces…I think there's room for an old Lennon or two…"

OCTOBER 7, 1975 – U.S. COURT OF APPEALS OVERTURNS THE INS DEPORTATION ORDER

In the battle to keep America on his side, John scored possibly one of his biggest public relations coups courtesy of his friend, photographer Bob Gruen. On October 30, 1974, Gruen did a series of shots of John

Though public support from high-powered fellow artists tended toward the non-existent during the immigration battle, this 1972 single – largely unheard – represented an effort. The "Justice Department" was a studio creation, coming from Tommy James collaborator Paul Naumann and former Third Rail member Artie Resnick, the co-writer of "Good Lovin'" and "Under the Boardwalk."

around the city—several of which have become iconic. Perhaps the best known frame is the one depicting John in front of the Statue of Liberty, arm raised in a peace sign. This image, published around the world, did much in the post-Nixon world to soften any lingering associations the public might still have held of the former Fab palling around with "terrorists."

The steady drip of stories detailing the obviously political prosecution of John Lennon made the government's case more and more untenable. In December 1974, the *Chicago Tribune* ran an article summing up all that had already ran in *Rolling Stone*, adding further details and providing the public with a rather clear pattern of abuse of power. With the Thurmond memo now public, the article noted what had already been pointed out by Lennon and his attorney: the INS went after him only after reports surfaced that he was making plans to disrupt the Republican convention. Coming from a right-leaning newspaper, the charges were particularly damning.

Not to be overlooked on the subject of why John and Yoko reconciled in early 1975 is the impact the couple's being together had on his immigration case. Early on, Wildes had urged them to appear in court dressed similarly and to keep holding each other's hand, no matter what. It was easy to reinforce the image of their devotion to each other and united front in pursuit of Yoko's missing child. But over time, strains in the relationship led to their separation. John's well-publicized antics in Los Angeles, overplayed though they were, did not help elicit sympathy from either the public or the courts one bit. Whatever else Wildes was feeling about their case, word that John and Yoko were back together and that furthermore, Yoko was expecting was the best news he could have gotten.

Her pregnancy marked the beginning of what was inexorably moving toward a complete vanishing act by John, as far as the public was concerned. He began 1975 with the release of the ill-starred oldies project, plus the Bowie collaboration "Fame," but beyond this he made fewer and fewer public appearances (just as Paul's star was in ascent as he geared up for his first world tour). Time out of the limelight was well-spent as he and Wildes concentrated on winning the case once and for all. Their January 2 court victory gave them the right to examine, for the first time, the government's "evidence" against him.

What they found was astonishing, not least because so much of what was gathered was so completely off the mark. For instance, a report in the files suggested that Jerry Rubin and fellow Chicago Seven defendant Rennie Davis were avoiding Lennon, put off by the ex-Fab's "heavy use of narcotics." Even more amusing was a "wanted" style flier, distributed by the FBI for the benefit of local law enforcement officers in case they found John Lennon in their sights. Despite possessing one of the most instantly recognizable mugs on the planet, the photo they used was of David Peel.

In the end, the court was less than concerned about the administration's fear of a disrupted convention; such paranoia merely reinforced what the country had become accustomed to learning throughout a year of Watergate hearings and investigative reporting. Instead, Judge Irving Kaufman vacated the deportation order on the slimmest of technicalities. The law in England that John was convicted on in 1968 differed from American statute on the point of whether the accused needed to know of their possession: in the U.K., one could be guilty whether one knew there were drugs on premises or not, whereas one could only be found guilty in the states if awareness of the presence of illicit substances was *proven*.

For the INS—and by extension, the former Nixon administration—to hang their case for deportation on such hairsplitting smelled like a deliberate misreading of the law that only underscored how weak the government's position was: if *this* was all they had for grounds, then the rather severe remedy they called for surpassed "all but the most

Draconian criminal penalties." No stranger to high profile political cases (he was, after all, the judge who had sent the Rosenbergs to the electric chair twenty-four years earlier), Kaufman recognized what was behind the action and said so: "The courts will not condone selective deportation based upon secret political grounds..."

Against the concentrated efforts of the federal government, Wildes had scored an unprecedented victory. John thanked all their supporters with a note to *Rolling Stone* shortly thereafter: "We couldn't have done it without you." (It was signed with an addition to his usual John & Yoko self-portrait: an image of baby Sean—"three virgins.")

JULY 27, 1976 – JOHN IS AWARDED PERMANENT RESIDENCE IN THE U.S.

The ruling effectively ended the case. Duly chastened (the court had further asserted that "Lennon's four year battle to remain in our country is testimony to his faith in this American dream"), the INS was forced to place him in line with all other, non-harassed applicants. His hearing came the following summer. Taking no chances, Wildes presented a full slate of celebrity "character witnesses," generally but not exclusively people from the arts that were prepared to vouch for the former Beatle. Novelist Norman Mailer; then-journalist Geraldo Rivera, and silent screen siren Gloria Swanson were among those who sang his praises. (As a pragmatic measure, the ironically named Sam Trust, president of ATV—John's music publisher—noted on the stand the revenue John's songs generated that might go elsewhere should he not be allowed to stay.)

The performance was merely an entertaining encore, for John's fate had been determined in October. Nonetheless, shortly after Ira Fieldsteel of the court's immigration division (the same judge who'd delivered the deportation order in 1973) asked if John was likely to become a state charge (i.e. a welfare case), drawing laughter from the assembled, he ruled "I find him statutorily eligible for permanent residence." The celebration that erupted was moved to an adjoining room, where John was presented with tangible proof of his long-coveted legal status. After years of ordeal, there was one final surprise: the card wasn't green. It was blue.

It took over four years, but in the end, the fight to obtain this legitimizing little document was a hard won but sweet victory; though fans can be forgiven for believing, in the end, John would have been better off had he been deported.

TRUE LOVE

Music and Lyrics by COLE PORTER

M-G-M PRESENTS
IN VISTAVISION

Bing *Grace* *Frank*
CROSBY · KELLY · SINATRA

IN "HIGH SOCIETY"

CO-STARRING
CELESTE HOLM · JOHN LUND · LOUIS CALHERN · SIDNEY BLACKMER
and LOUIS ARMSTRONG AND HIS BAND · JOHN PATRICK · MUSIC AND LYRICS BY COLE PORTER

MUSIC SUPERVISED & ADAPTED BY JOHNNY GREEN AND SAUL CHAPLIN · COLOR BY TECHNICOLOR · DIRECTED BY CHARLES WALTERS · A SOL C. SIEGEL PRODUCTION · Price 60c

CONTENTS: MIND IF I MAKE LOVE TO YOU   LOVE YOU, SAMANTHA   YOU'RE SENSATIONAL
NOW YOU HAS JAZZ   LITTLE ONE   TRUE LOVE
WELL, DID YOU EVAH?   WHO WANTS TO BE A MILLIONAIRE?

BUXTON HILL MUSIC CORPORATION
RKO BUILDING · Rockefeller Center · NEW YORK
Sole Selling Agent
CHAPPELL & CO., INC.

Cole Porter's "True Love" was in the early Beatles' repertoire; not surprisingly, given it had also been covered by Elvis, Ricky Nelson and the Everly Brothers, among others.

CHAPTER 8

MUSIC TOUCHING MY SOUL: COVERS OF OTHERS

T hough the ex-Fabs were prolific songwriters (with the exception of their drummer), they were not above occasionally recycling work *not* of their own creation; sometimes as an exercise in re-working another artist's material, other times as a straightforward homage.

It isn't uncommon for those thoroughly steeped in music to enjoy revisiting the tunes from their youth. As warm-ups in the studio or just for fun, this is exactly what most musicians do. (In fact, the documented-to-a-fault "Get Back"/*Let It Be* sessions are rife with the band's attempts to do anything *but* get down to the business at hand by taking stabs at virtually every song that they ever liked.)

During the solo years, each former Beatle tackled hit material from others. Mostly these little excursions down memory lane added a bit of familiar color to their collections of otherwise self-penned songs. Ringo, still finding his legs as a composer, actually scored a pair of hits by re-working the oldies. John and Paul, of course, would go on to record entire LPs worth of classic rock and roll, but those were concept albums, rather than the occasional detour that we explore here.

"LOVE IS STRANGE" – FROM *WILD LIFE* RELEASED DECEMBER 7, 1971

It is interesting to note that—Ringo excepted—nearly any cover that ended up recorded and issued by an ex-Fab was seemingly selected arbitrarily. (See John's "Ya Ya" and George's "Bye Bye Love.") Nowhere was this truer than on Wings' debut album, when an attempt at laying down a reggae backing morphed into a cover of a familiar oldie.

After spending some time on a Jamaican holiday in 1971, Paul and Linda returned to England thoroughly smitten with the native music they were exposed to. The couple brought back with them a supply of reggae tapes, seeing as they provided the perfect ambience for evenings spent reliving the trip while sharing a spliff. During the sessions for the first Wings album, the group began laying down a reggae-ish jam.

With no further intent other than to simply emulate the sounds they had been steeping themselves in, a serviceable backdrop was created, but for what?

The answer came when they realized that the three chord pattern they been jamming on fit perfectly the melody line to Mickey and Sylvia's 1957 hit, "Love Is Strange." *That* song, boasting a Latin-esque arrangement and sexually charged vocal interplay between the male and female vocalists, just missed *Billboard* Top Ten. (Interestingly, the recording featured session legend Bernard Purdie, who would later soil himself by inexplicably claiming to have replaced Ringo's drumming on Beatles recordings.) The song also proved something of an evergreen, being successfully covered by the Everly Brothers, Buddy Holly (in an eerie posthumous release), and R&B duo, Peaches and Herb.

Alas, the Wings version proved to be something less than a groove thing. Torpedoing the otherwise tolerable track were the shrieky, mixed-way-too-loud vocals of the Lovely Linda. Had Paul not been so hell-bent on attempting to replicate Bob Dylan's working methods by finishing an album in one week and instead worked on the mix with the craftsmanship that was his hallmark, better results might have been achieved.

"Love Is Strange" was originally penciled in for English release (Apple 5932) as Wings' premier single, but ultimately the honor went to the politically charged "Give Ireland Back To The Irish." Probably for the better.

"YOU'RE SIXTEEN" – FROM *RINGO* RELEASED NOVEMBER 2, 1973

With a pair of successful rock (as opposed to pop vocal or country and western) singles to his credit by early 1973, Ringo, bolstered by producer Richard Perry, was at last ready to extend his exploration of the idiom into an LP's worth of tunes. At Perry's suggestion, an oldie was thrown into the mix of Ringo co-compositions and tunes contributed by his ex-bandmates: Johnny Burnette's 1960 Top Ten hit, "You're Sixteen."

The song was composed by Richard and Robert Sherman, who first struck rock and roll gold with Mouseketeer Annette Funicello's 1958 hit, "Tall Paul." The brothers later gained considerable renown from their film scores, often—but not always—for Walt Disney's studio. *Mary Poppins*, *The Jungle Book*, and *Chitty Chitty Bang Bang* were among their credits—they also penned the migraine-inducing jingle,

"It's A Small World." (Their "Let's Get Together" from *The Parent Trap* featured a "yeah, yeah, yeah" refrain in December 1961—nearly two years before "She Loves You.")

Apparently, the notion of a thirty-two year old ex-Beatle luring a girl half his age into his car caused hardly a stir among the record buying public, who gamely accepted the premise and gave Ringo his second straight number one. As of 1973, no other ex-Beatle had scored back-to-back chart-toppers.

The recording featured Ringo and John's drinking buddy, Harry Nilsson, on backing vocals, along with Paul and Linda. Having already completed most of the album in Los Angeles with input

"You come on like a dream, peaches and cream,
Lips like strawberry wine,
You're sixteen, you're beautiful and you're mine." *

RINGO'S NEW SINGLE, "YOU'RE SIXTEEN"

1870
Produced by Richard Perry

Ringo's recording of "You're Sixteen" (as rendered by Klaus Voormann for inclusion in the Ringo album package) bested Johnny Burnette's 1960 original, chart-wise; #8 vs. Ringo's #1.

from John and George, Ringo was careful not to exclude Paul from the proceedings. "You're Sixteen" was completed in England with Paul contributing what to this day much of the world believes to be a kazoo on instrumental break. It isn't—it's simply Paul's verbal approximation of a sax solo, but seemingly no one believes this.

In 1978, as part of his *Ringo* (aka *Ognir Rratts*) television special, Ringo would showcase the song as a duet with the then-hot actress, Carrie Fisher, fresh off the success of *Star Wars*. The performance qualifies as one of those "must be seen to be believed" moments.

"YA YA" – FROM *WALLS AND BRIDGES*
RELEASED SEPTEMBER 26, 1974

A litigious hairball was stirred by John's ill-advised appropriation of a single line from Chuck Berry's "You Can't Catch Me" for "Come Together." The ensuing legal battle proved a prolonged headache, one that John apparently thought he could brush aside by the inclusion of this half-baked nugget on his penultimate album of otherwise original compositions.

Lee Dorsey was a frequent collaborator with Allen Toussaint. In 1970, he recorded "Occapella," which was in turn covered by Ringo four years later for Goodnight Vienna.

Big Seven Music, headed by industry honcho Morris Levy, owned Chuck Berry's publishing. An agreement struck to settle their lawsuit over the passing reference to Berry's song called for John to record *three* Big Seven tunes for his *Mouldies... but Goldies* project, an album begun under Phil Spector's supervision but which languished by mid-1974 due to certain less than lucid episodes involving Spector and the master tapes. Nonetheless, apparently as a gesture of good faith while the oldies project festered, John decided to tack a Big Seven tune onto *Walls and Bridges* as a coda. If he had hoped the addition of Lee Dorsey's "Ya Ya" would appease Levy, he was sorely mistaken.

As heard on the release, the performance consisted of John on piano and 11 year-old Julian on snare drum. It lasted barely a minute before fading and came off exactly like what it was: a moment of father and son bonding in the recording studio. Suffice to say, Levy was not the least bit amused, while what John had intended as a pleasant surprise for Julian left the latter mortified that his half-hearted run through had been enshrined in vinyl.

The song itself was ex-boxer Lee Dorsey's first hit. The New Orleans native and protégé of producer Allen Toussaint would later score with 1965's "Working In A Coal Mine." (In 1974, Toussaint contributed "Occapella" to Ringo's *Goodnight Vienna* album.) "Ya Ya" was actually based on a bit of kid's doggerel heard in Toussaint's neighborhood, though one may wonder whether he realized that the title was meant as a euphemism for a bowel movement. The song's scatological origins mattered not, for it landed safely in *Billboard*'s Top Ten in 1961.

A more fully realized recording of the song was indeed later issued on John's re-titled *Rock 'N' Roll* album in 1975, undoubtedly placating Levy. Conspicuously absent was Julian.

"ONLY YOU (AND YOU ALONE)" – FROM
GOODNIGHT VIENNA
RELEASED NOVEMBER 18, 1974

On the follow-up to his smash album *Ringo*, the drummer happily made use of John's considerably increased input. Relocated to L.A. during much of his estrangement from Yoko and spending most of that time in the studio for himself as well as others, John ended up penning the title tune; furthermore, he contributed an arrangement to an oldie custom-suited to the Starr's unique vocal abilities.

On paper, the notion of Ringo tackling the crooner's showcase best known by The Platter's 1955 version seems incongruous. But with the effortless charisma that his best recordings possessed, "Only You" was magic. Abetting the recording was a blueprint sketched out by John, who contributed acoustic guitar and a guide vocal that was arguably better than the one on the finished product. (The world would finally get to hear this performance on the *Lennon Anthology* set, released in 1998.)

Also in vocal support was the ubiquitous Harry Nilsson, who along with John added some smooth "oohs" beneath Ringo's lead. (A version of the track exists with Nilsson's scratch vocal—enterprising bootleggers have fused the performance with John's, creating a rough duet.) The backing was comprised of Billy Preston on electric piano; Klaus Voormann on bass; Jesse Ed Davis and Steve Cropper on guitars; and Jim Keltner on drums.

Released in advance of the *Goodnight Vienna* album, "Only You" reached number six on the American charts, solidifying Ringo's impressive track record as a singles artist. Having taken a reworked oldie to the Top Ten twice, the formula became established operating procedure for future Ringo projects, though never again to such great commercial success.

"BYE BYE LOVE" – FROM *DARK HORSE*
RELEASED DECEMBER 9, 1974

The ill-starred *Dark Horse* project—both album and tour—was plagued by a number of elements that taxed the patience of even the most loyal Harrisonphile. First, there were the strained vocals, of course. George's dogged determination to inject Lord Krishna into the proceedings—in song ("It Is He," for one example); in packaging (the "om" symbol was rapidly becoming George's corporate logo); and in ambience (the tour's stage dress came replete with burning incense)—increasingly rankled the loyal following he'd generated in the wake of the Beatles' dissolution.

Then there was this, a new element that couldn't help but make listeners squirm uncomfortably. A notoriously private man, George now chose the full glare of publicity surrounding a national tour to turn a spotlight on his marital situation. Conspicuously included in the product being promoted by the tour was a recording that existed apparently for no other purpose other than to allow the performer to publicly vent.

Had he been in top form, "Bye Bye Love," the 1957 Everly Brothers chestnut, might have made a fine showcase for George's rockabilly skills. But in the hands of 1974's seriously disturbed ex-Beatle, heretofore personal concerns were now put on full display, codified as part of his permanent Harrison record. Unsuspecting listeners found themselves suffering through the audio equivalent of an acquaintance crying in his beer.

While the rough parameters of the breakdown of his marriage to Pattie and her subsequent taking up with Eric Clapton were at least vaguely familiar to some, never were the salacious details so gratuitously shared with a mass audience. This shambling mess of a recording reworked the lyrics to explicitly offer George's take on the break-up: "There goes our lady with 'you know who.' I hope she's happy and old 'Clapper' too." He goes on to announce that after he "...threw them both out," he is now into romance but shies away from love. (This claim must be taken with a grain of salt, seeing as how George made of point of featuring future wife Olivia Arias' face on the record's label.)

Perhaps George saw his narrative as an effort to save face, declaring that his ex "did me a favor." But *Dark Horse*'s "Bye Bye Love" ultimately stands as an exercise in self-indulgence that no fan cared to be a party to. (Adding to the perversity is George's credit to Clapton for lead guitar on the track and Pattie herself on backing vocals: false on both counts.)

"CROSSROADS THEME" – FROM *VENUS AND MARS* RELEASED MAY 27, 1975

One might have expected "Bye Bye Love" to be the last ex-Beatle excursion into soap opera territory. But with the next Wings album,

Paul McCartney *literally* took on a daytime drama, laying onto wax his take on the theme to Britain's popular television weeper, *Crossroads*. The resulting recording was sequenced just after the last McCartney original on *Venus and Mars*, the "Treat Her Gently/Lonely Old People" medley. Its positioning was no accident—Macca apparently felt that invoking familiar (to Brits) lowbrow entertainment after "Lonely Old People" was a clever move.

While some appreciated his little joke, many English fans were outraged that a rock musician would immortalize such featherweight tripe. Sadly, it would not be the last time this former Fab would elicit that reaction from listeners. Americans, on the other hand, possessing no such frame of reference, were well-placed to judge the instrumental on its own merits. Context aside, it's a pleasant enough melody, written by U.K. music legend Tony Hatch, mostly known for his work on songbird Petula Clark's hits. Guitarist Jimmy McCulloch used the song as a vehicle for some superb fretwork, bringing the brief but memorable melody to a pleasing finish.

Among those who enjoyed Wings' take were the show's producers, who actually swapped out the original recording for McCartney's version. *Crossroads*, which had begun on English television in 1964, lasted until the 1980s, becoming an institution that was tolerated if not lauded.

"HEY! BABY" – FROM *RINGO'S ROTOGRAVURE* RELEASED SEPTEMBER 17, 1976

When touring England in June 1962, American singer Bruce Channel made the acquaintance of the Beatles as they shared a bill at the New Brighton Tower. Channel was riding a wave of popularity spawned by "Hey! Baby," a country-esque shuffle distinguished by its catchy harmonica hook. Texas blues harpist Delbert McClinton's work caught the ears of the ever-attentive Lennon, who cornered the musician and demanded a lesson in achieving the same effect. Famously, he applied McClinton's technique to "Love Me Do."

Fourteen years later, fond memories of both the song and the encounter must have stayed with Ringo, who chose to cover the song on his Atlantic debut. One could have hoped that John, who contributed a song ("Cookin'") to the sessions, might have seized the opportunity to recreate McClinton's riffing. Unfortunately, Ringo's version, as produced and arranged by Arif Mardin, dropped the part completely.

Still, the end result was as good either of the oldies produced by Richard Perry on the Ringed One's behalf. Unfortunately, the formula was wearing thin: Ringo's single reached only seventy-four in America and missed the charts completely in the U.K. In contrast, Channel's original had topped *Billboard*'s listings for three straight weeks in early 1962.

It was a shame that the song performed so poorly upon its release, but the inclusion of "Hey! Baby" on subsequent "best of" collections assured the track an audience years later. The same could not be said for Ringo's further oldies recyclings.

"TRUE LOVE" – FROM *THIRTY-THREE & 1/3* RELEASED NOVEMBER 19, 1976

In 1956, Bing Crosby and Grace Kelly starred in *High Society*, a musical remake of 1940's *The Philadelphia Story*. Boasting a superb score by Cole Porter, the film included performances by co-star Frank Sinatra and jazz legend Louis Armstrong. Given this array of talent, it's hardly surprising that the film's soundtrack spawned a hit single. What *is* surprising is an unlikely pairing of the film's topped-billed stars.

"True Love" provided one of the film's most memorable scenes, wherein the couple, in romantic reverie, sings the song on a boat: the future princess chirps somewhat sparingly (truth be told) while the aged crooner pumps away on a squeeze box. The dreamy tableau undoubtedly made an impression on the future Fabs, for by the time of their Hamburg stints beginning in 1960, they were performing the song in their night club sets. (Though undocumented as to who sang lead, it's hard not to conclude it was Macca.)

In 1976, George offered up his take on the song (correcting Porter's "wrong" chords, as he cheekily asserted) on his astonishingly upbeat "comeback" album, *Thirty-Three & 1/3*. Pared down to the song's essence, George cast aside a superfluous intro and produced a snappy arrangement, replete with his usual first-rate slide guitar fills. The results were loved largely by those unfamiliar with the earlier version and viewed as something akin to blasphemy by everyone else.

Sadly, his efforts on the album went under-appreciated at the time. "True Love" was released as a single in England, where it failed to chart, despite the comic video George produced to promote it. With punk rock in its ascendancy, could anything in 1976-1977 Britain be less hip than an ex-Beatle recording a song at least one generation too old?

"GO NOW" – FROM *WINGS OVER AMERICA*
RELEASED DECEMBER 10, 1976

By late autumn 1964, the Beatles had truly conquered the world. As they prepared their fourth long player for release, a Birmingham quintet by the name of the Moody Blues scored a number one single in England (number ten in the U.S.) with a cover of Bessie Banks' soul waltz, "Go Now." The tune, featuring a lead vocal by guitarist Denny Laine, established the band as one of many from England that, lacking a strong songwriter, got by with covers of American R&B chestnuts.

Denny Laine (at right), as seen with the Moody Blues on the cover of their self-titled 1965 EP.

Laine departed before the band shifted their focus toward a successful blend of ponderous psychedelia. But "Go Now" became something of a signature song for him. Once he joined Wings, the cover was frequently included in their early sets, but eventually dropped once their body of originals built up.

Though technically not a lead performance by an ex-Beatle per se, "Go Now" merits attention as a stand-out oldie included on the Wings live album. In 1976, as the band mounted their most ambitious tour ever, the song was pulled out of mothballs and staged as a Laine showcase, augmented by a typically stunning Jimmy McCulloch guitar solo. (Oddly, the Paul Simon song, "Richard Cory" was also included in Wings' set and sung by Laine—seemingly with no other justification than he *liked* it.)

Most sources assert that "Go Now" was performed only at the L.A. Forum in late June at the tour's conclusion; therefore, the performance included on the *Wings Over America* album must have originated from these shows. However, the song *is* in the concert film, *Rockshow*, which was shot at the Seattle Kingdome on June 10. (Paul and Linda, in the role of back-up singers, are seen clowning as they share a microphone.)

"Go Now" provided fans with the reminder that Laine was indeed someone with a hit-making past and not merely a moderately talented cipher who got lucky when Mr. McCartney came calling. Laine included a re-make on his *Japanese Tears* album released in the wake of Wings' break-up, and continues to perform the tune today at fan gatherings.

"WHERE DID OUR LOVE GO" – FROM *BAD BOY*
RELEASED JUNE 16, 1978

As the decade headed to a close, Ringo's meteoric recording success began its downward arc. After a spectacular chart run on Apple, nothing he did ever after in the 1970s came close to capturing the public's attentions. His stint on Atlantic terminated after two albums, a new deal with CBS's Portrait label signaled a shift in strategy, away from celeb guests and more recent efforts to re-cast the would-be crooner as a dance club divo.

Retained was the practice of adding a song from his youth to the mix; in this instance, a pair of songs. Benny Spellman's "Lipstick Traces (On A Cigarette)," written by Allen Toussaint, was a minor hit in 1962. Ringo's version was released as a single and promptly died a death, but the sheer bland inoffensiveness of his treatment does not interest us.

What does is the wretched decision by someone for Ringo to tackle a hit by the Supremes. Back in their day, the Beatles' domination of the pop charts was rivaled and sometimes bested only by the hit-making machinery of Motown's Holland-Dozier-Holland songwriting team. "Where Did Our Love Go" was the first smash by the trio (following a few false starts), but once they'd arrived, there was no stopping them.

The drummer's feelings toward the Supremes' music were/are unknown, but it's hard to believe that he was much of a fan. Certainly his reading of this standard betrays something far short of an innate feel for the material. Given a sympathetic backing, comprised of peers that understood his strengths, as well as his limitations, Ringo was capable of pulling off wonders, as his run of hits attested.

But dropped into a pop-making apparatus more concerned with fitting in with current trends than recognizing his idiosyncrasies, Ringo's charm dissipated. On "Where Did Our Love Go," he sounds wholly uncommitted to the sentiments, swamped by the power of the "baby, baby" backing singers over an instrumental bed that reeked of anonymity. The performance may well rank as among the most irretrievably embarrassing of any ex-Beatle's career during the 1970s— and that's saying something.

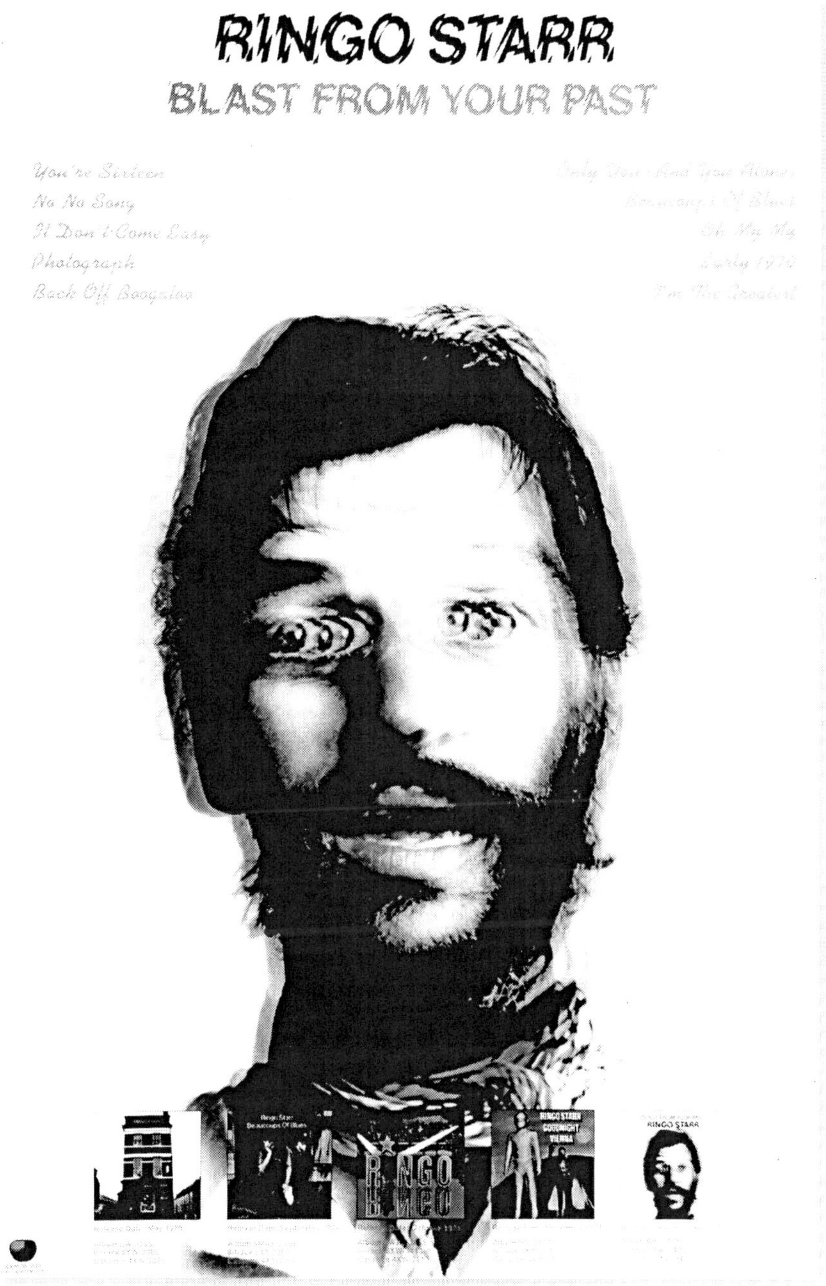

RINGO STARR
BLAST FROM YOUR PAST
You're Sixteen
No No Song
It Don't Come Easy
Photograph
Back Off Boogaloo
Only You (And You Alone)
Beaucoups Of Blues
Oh My My
Early 1970
I'm The Greatest
Ringo Starr
Beaucoups Of Blues
RINGO
RINGO STARR
GOODNIGHT
VIENNA
RINGO STARR

Covers of oldies would become a standard component of Ringo's recorded output from 1973 through 1983. But as 1975's Blast From Your Past showed, he didn't need to rely on the purely familiar to produce hits.

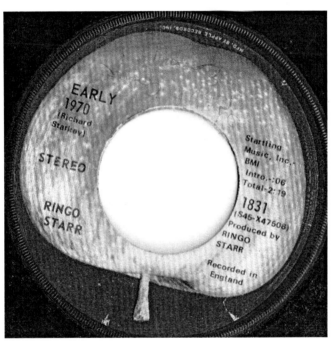

"I don't know how / You were inverted"

CHAPTER 9

I'VE BEEN ACROSS TO THE OTHER SIDE:NON-ALBUM B-SIDES

Back in the day, when hit singles were the currency of the recording industry, giving little thought to the back of the "plug" side was the rule, rather than the exception. Several artists came along to buck that practice: the Everly Brothers (and later, the Beach Boys), who favored backing an uptempo song with a ballad; Buddy Holly, whose second-tier material was typically as strong as the hit side; and the Beatles, who aggressively challenged radio station programmers with 45s of equal value on *either* side. (Until the mid-seventies, record industry bible *Billboard* magazine would place B-sides receiving airplay alongside A-sides within their Hot One Hundred.)

As the record business evolved, while a hit single was still something to strive for, the B-sides became (when not used as samplers for the parent album) a venue for artists to issue more experimental material, or songs that might not have fit onto the album release. For the ex-Fabs, who tended to be prolific in their recording habits, only rarely was the flip side of a hit used as a dumping ground for uninspired material.

The following list is notable for a couple of reasons. First, it demonstrates that the former Beatles adhered strictly to the aforementioned formulas when selecting flipside material, while adding another: the occasional flips that were *better* than the A-side, but were for some reason, undervalued by their creators. Though historically radio programmers exercised their option to decide which side of a release warranted airplay, this practice had essentially ended by the seventies, therefore leaving it to others in hindsight to point out the occasional flawed artistic judgment.

The glimpse into the artist's heads that this roll call affords us is noteworthy for another reason: though most of these songs live on today as bonus material tacked onto standard CD issues, the artists themselves originally chose to release these tracks via the transient media of the 45 record, with the apparent intent that they *would one day vanish*. Viewed through *that* prism, the choices they made are worth examining.

"COOCHY-COOCHY" B-SIDE TO "BEAUCOUPS OF BLUES" RELEASED OCTOBER 5, 1970

The *Beaucoups Of Blues* sessions were possibly the most efficiently run that Ringo had participated in since the recording of the *Please Please Me* album seven years earlier. Over the course of one week, he had selected songs, rehearsed them and laid down an LP's worth of vocals, completing an album in less time than the Fabs had since their debut. (Arguably, Paul would pull off the same trick a year later with *Wild Life*, but with far less convincing results.)

Unique among the material committed to tape was this, Ringo's third recorded sole-credited composition. (The "It Don't Come Easy" / "Early 1970" single had been cut but remained unissued.) While all the tracks that made it to the album were authored by seasoned Nashville pros, Ringo's sole original was relegated to the sole single's B-side.

It's unlikely that anyone questioned whether he had any help with the tune, bereft as it was of any Harrisonian passing chords or elaborate motifs. That said, "Coochy Coochy" was no embarrassment, being a rather standard country workout elevated by the peerless musicianship of the parties involved. Lyrically, the sentiments rang true, as an older but wiser Ringo observed in the aftermath of the Beatle years: "I've traveled all over…I've got everything that I ever wanted, done everything I ever wanted to do."

Of course, as the A-side proved a disappointment on the charts, it would only be the hard-core Beatlephiles that ever heard "Coochy Coochy." Only through the advent of the compact disc was the track rescued from certain obscurity, as a bonus alongside an edit of "Nashville Jam" on the *Beaucoups of Blues* reissue.

"OH WOMAN, OH WHY" B-SIDE TO "ANOTHER DAY" RELEASED FEBRUARY 28, 1971

Recorded with the basic *Ram* crew of Denny Seiwell on drums and David Spinozza on guitar, this rather bizarre, atypical (for McCartney) *blooze* track began life exactly as one might have expected: as a studio jam that grew legs and became fleshed out. Burdened with a rather unwieldy title, "Oh Woman Oh Why" comes off as a custom-recorded make-weight, designed to fill B-side space and nothing more.

Though the song has its fans, compositionally, little about it merits repeat listenings. Bearing a thematic resemblance to tunes like "Hey Joe" or Neil Young's "Down By The River," Macca waxes anguished about his "woman" and "that gun" in a manner most comparable to "Why Don't We Do It In The Road?," lacking only the wit and melodic sensibility of *that* recording. As if to underscore the gravity of the premise, the recording is punctuated by seven gunshots. (A photo of Paul pulling the trigger in the studio exists.)

Given his intensely prolific songwriting, his well-documented workaholic tendencies (no McCartney album session from 1971 on ended *without* surplus tunes in the can), and his well-honed sense of presentation, it seems rather odd that Paul would have deliberately squandered the flipside of his debut solo single on this. To look for the positive, the guitars do crank grittily and Seiwell's drums do provide some power. Paul never committed a half-hearted vocal to vinyl ever, so the raw ingredients for something special are there. The song simply lacks the basic appeal of what listeners expect from a record bearing his name: a well-defined melody and/or some halfway decent hooks.

Interestingly, in the 90s CD era, the song was finally given a second life: not attached to *Ram*, as might be expected, but to *Wild Life*, a collection predestined for obscurity. All in all, a sound decision.

"DEEP BLUE" B-SIDE TO "BANGLA DESH"
RELEASED JULY 28, 1971

Between the majesty of *All Things Must Pass* and the more subdued approach to his spirituality on *Living In The Material World* lies "Deep Blue," a song penned by George as he watched his mother battle her final illness. This musical "orphan" reflected upon the helplessness felt by those watching their loved ones suffer and their inability to mitigate the pain.

The song was rare excursion into folk-blues, informed by George's friendship with Dylan and subsequent proximity to multi-instrumentalist David Bromberg (whom George would record with the following year). Accompanied only with the barest of backings (Klaus on bass and Keltner on drums), George augmented his acoustic guitar parts with overdubbed Dobro, a twangy instrument he'd just recently used to good effect on John's "Crippled Inside."

Production-wise, the tune marked a startlingly stark contrast to Phil Spector's approach on George's previous work. The plaintive song, sad without being self-pitying, would've made a superb addition to a timely follow-up album to ATMP—had there been one. Alas, not until summer 1973 would a full-blown set of new Harrisongs materialize (pun not intended), by which time "Deep Blue" was nearly two years old. The song had been duly issued as the flip to the topical "Bangla-Desh" but once its purpose in alerting the masses to the title crisis passed, so too did the B-side.

But the song it was not without admirers, among them Warner Brothers record producer Ted Templeman. During a pre-production meeting for what became George's 1979 self-titled release, Templeman expressed to George his admiration for the rather obscure track. Obligingly, George composed "Soft-Hearted Hana" (after Temperance Seven's 1961 recording of the 1924 hit, "Hard-Hearted Hannah") with similar musical chordings. Rather than a direct evocation of his earlier song's downbeat theme, "Hana" is a rather direct description of a "magic mushroom" trip that George had taken in Maui.

Eventually, "Deep Blue" was tacked onto the 2006 reissue of *Living In The Material World*. Oddly, its former A-side remains unissued in remastered form on CD, though a download is available.

"BLINDMAN" B-SIDE TO "BACK OFF BOOGALOO" RELEASED MARCH 20, 1972

Perhaps feeling a bit inspired by his turn in the spotlight at the Concert for Bangladesh two weeks earlier, Ringo booked time at Apple Studios, accompanied by Klaus Voormann and Badfinger's Pete Ham. With him he brought a self-penned tune that he hoped would work for the soundtrack of the film he'd just completed work on, Ferdinando Baldi's *Blindman*.

Lacking input from George, Ringo's song (also titled "Blindman") was in desperate need of some skilled hands to shape it into something memorable. While there were some rudimentary attempts at delivering the appropriate spaghetti western motifs, the lyrics, sung barely above a monotone, essentially laid out the film's plotline: "You made a promise, you would get them through. The girls to the miners, you would fix them, too."

Not for no reason was the song nixed by the film's producers, therein ending Ringo's dreams of supplying the entire soundtrack. Little more than a curiosity, the song lives on as an addition to the *Goodnight Vienna* CD.

"LITTLE WOMAN LOVE" B-SIDE TO "MARY HAD A LITTLE LAMB" RELEASED MAY 29, 1972

As Exhibit "A" in making the case that Paul was often not the best judge of his own material, consider this: subsuming a bouncy little piano-based groove in favor of a shopworn nursery rhyme, arranged in a way that would give a 5 year-old the blues. That, folks, was exactly what Paul did with Wings' second single release, a recording that must have had newly-installed guitarist Henry McCullough wondering exactly what he had gotten himself into. ("[It] wasn't the bluesiest of records," was his diplomatic take.)

Coming off the heels of the most politically incendiary song he'd ever recorded (or ever would again)—"Give Ireland Back To The Irish"—there were many that felt that "Mary Had A Little Lamb" was a deliberate poke in the eye to the Establishment that had kept the former single off the BBC's airwaves, as if to say "Ban this!" But this Paul has coyly denied, instead insisting that he was merely committing to tape something for the kids—his own as much as anyone else's (wink-wink).

"Little Woman Love"—despite the title, *not* an expression of admiration for the work of Louisa May Alcott—was yet another *Ram* leftover. Unique among the songs

Mary Had A Little Lamb
a single record from your old chums wings

release date 12 May
R 5949

Had Paul not been so intent on making a point by following his banned political screed with a children's nursery rhyme, perhaps "Little Woman Love" might've gotten its due as an A-side.

he cut at New York's Columbia Recording Studios was the appearance of a guest, jazz legend Milt "The Judge" Hinton. Mr. Hinton's career as a stand-up bassist went back to the dawn of the jazz era itself, where he played alongside the greats, notably Cab Calloway. Through lucky happenstance, he found himself pulled into the session, laying down a memorable bass break before adding an ex-Beatle to his innumerable credits.

As for the song itself, it did receive some airtime during the *James Paul McCartney* television special in 1973. But without the benefit of a slot on an LP to give it some permanency, the record all but vanished. In time, "Little Woman Love" became a bonus track on the *Red Rose Speedway* CD reissue, thereby ensuring its long term invisibility.

"THE MESS" B-SIDE TO "MY LOVE"
RELEASED APRIL 9, 1973

In August 1972, Wings resumed their tour of Europe, which had begun in France one month earlier. This second leg took them through Scandinavia as well as The Netherlands and what was known then as West Germany. Three nights before the tour concluded, the group's performance at The Hague was professionally filmed and recorded with an eye toward possible documentary or album use.

Of the live set, the only track to appear as a legitimate release was an original tune entitled "The Mess," an uncharacteristic piece of boogie (featuring a chorus that roughly resembled The Band's "The Shape I'm In"). While as a performance piece, the song worked well enough, with some superb lead work from Henry, ensemble harmonies, and even some unison riffing from the guitarists AND Linda, it really didn't rise to the level of a memorable composition, least of all coming from someone with Paul's track record.

What the recording *did* do was successfully showcase the band's progress from nowhere not that long before into a viable stage act—no small feat. In edited form, the song was issued as the flip to "My Love," giving the single release some balance. Back when *Red Rose Speedway* was being mapped out as a double album, "The Mess" would surely have made the cut. But in its single disc form, the live track was dropped, and not until the CD issue was it finally added to the package.

Like "Little Woman Love," "The Mess" was featured in Paul's TV special, airing exactly one week after the "My Love" single was released.

"MISS O'DELL" B-SIDE TO "GIVE ME LOVE"
RELEASED MAY 7, 1973

Born in Muncie, Indiana, Chris O'Dell grew up in Tucson, Arizona (of "Get Back" fame) before taking entry-level work in the record industry in Los Angeles. The time was the late sixties, and her sojourn soon put her into the orbit of Derek Taylor. As Apple was starting up, she accepted Taylor's request to relocate to London, where she settled in as A&R head Peter Asher's personal assistant, just in time to witness the Fabs at work on the "White album."

No relation to Dennis (of "You Know My Name" fame), she survived the Allen Klein takeover long enough to become close friends with Pattie Harrison before segueing into work for the Rolling Stones. (Her image can be seen in the *Exile On Main Street* album cover collage.) In any event, she made enough of an impression on George to become the springboard for this serendipitously merry yet Dylan-esque recording. Incidentally, it was not the first time she'd served as a rock star's muse: 1970's "Pisces Apple Lady," recorded by Leon Russell, was *also* inspired by her.

For the second time in his professional career, George turned the occasion of being stood up by a friend in Los Angeles into a song (1967's "Blue Jay Way" being the first). "Miss O'Dell" takes the form of a tongue-in-cheek communiqué from a jaded rock star adrift in L.A. Very much akin to a rough-hewn version of "Apple Scruffs," the acoustic guitar-and-harmonica driven tune bespeaks the weariness George's lot had become. "The smog that keeps polluting up our shores," he sings "is boring me to tears / Why don't you call me, Miss O'Dell?" Chris—expected to swing by for a visit—failed to materialize. As she would explain decades later, this was due to her drug habit at the time.

Where the recording gets *really* interesting is when George, during the second verse, mis-reads his own lyrics, substituting "rice" for "night" on the line "the night that keeps rolling on right up to my front porch." Laughter at the incongruity of such a visual ensues, as he thereupon succumbs to a fit of the giggles. He audibly struggles to maintain a straight face as he proceeds onward but to no avail. By the end of the take, levity has won; no longer in control of himself, George breaks down completely before calling out *Paul*'s Forthlin Road telephone number (Garston 6922) as the tune ends.

Another take, minus the mirth, was recorded (and has since shown up on the deluxe LITMW remaster) but it was the comic performance that George *chose* to issue. It made for a startling contrast to the earnest pleading on the single's A-side, but nonetheless exists as quite the gift to his fans. Through the advent of the CD, the song has since been rescued from oblivion—in re-mastered form—on the *Living In The Material World* reissue.

As for Chris O'Dell, her memoir (titled after the song, naturally) was published in 2009.

"I LIE AROUND" B-SIDE TO "LIVE AND LET DIE" RELEASED JUNE 18, 1973

Though he'd been a charter member of Wings from day one and

would become their mainstay until the bitter end, it wasn't until nearly two years into his employ that Denny Laine was accorded the public release of a lead vocal. (An original Laine composition, "I Would Only Smile," was recorded by Wings during the *Red Rose Speedway* sessions but sat unreleased until he put it out himself on the *Japanese Tears* album years later.)

"I Lie Around," though, was a McCartney song, and a rather unfinished sounding one at that. It begins with a field recording of idyllic outdoor fun, giving way to piano pounding out beneath a repeat of the song's title, mantra-like, shifting into something recognizable as a verse. Laine's voice is perfectly suited to the narrative, describing drifting through life at the mercy of external forces: a fairly apt summary of his Wings tenure.

That this song in particular was chosen to back the sweet bombast of "Live And Let Die" displays either complete indifference to complementing the content of the A-side or a subtle attempt at contrast. In either case, the song exists today as one of *Red Rose Speedway*'s bonus CD tracks, a curiosity worth hearing once if at all.

"DOWN AND OUT" B-SIDE TO "PHOTOGRAPH"
RELEASED SEPTEMBER 24, 1973

A song credited solely to Ringo (well, Richard Starkey actually), this brisk three-chord workout has nothing to say, but says it well. Complemented with some tasty horns and driving piano, it would've fit quite well on the *Ringo* album, but was instead dumped onto the back of Ringo's first number one hit single, "Photograph."

The track apparently features George on guitar, given his signature sound. What is intriguing is Ringo's call out of "Alright, Gary" before the break. No one named Gary is credited anywhere on the album, and while the exclamation suggests he's addressing the keyboard player, the identity is a mystery. Might it have been ex-Spooky Tooth/future "Dream Weaver" Gary Wright, whom Ringo would have known well by then, going back to their work on *All Things Must Pass*? Or could it have been Gary Brooker from Procol Harum, who likewise contributed keys to ATMP?

The likeliest answer may be "none of the above." Appearing on *Ringo* was New Orleans-born pianist James Booker. All but unknown to the public at large, Booker was a legend in his hometown and a giant to piano aficionados. Mastering every style from classical (said his friend Allen Toussaint, "At 12 years old, he could sit down and play Bach's three-part inventions…with all the sophistication that Bach would have been proud of") to boogie woogie and blues, Booker made a name for himself ghosting parts for Fats Domino and impersonating Huey "Piano" Smith (who hated touring) on the road. Additionally, he personally schooled future legends like Mac "Dr. John" Rebennack and Harry Connick Jr. (who merely stated the obvious when he called his mentor "a genius").

There was a dark side to Booker's legend. A childhood accident that nearly killed him left him with an addiction to painkillers that eventually did. (Under mysterious circumstances, he later lost an eye.) The son of a Baptist minister, Booker was a homosexual who may also have suffered from a bipolar disorder. For most of his adult years through his death at 43, he battled a heroin addiction, for which he did jail time. Still, he never lacked for work, recording with everyone from Lionel Hampton and Irma Thomas to the Doobie Brothers and Jerry Garcia.

He's officially credited on *Ringo* for one track only, Randy Newman's "Have You Seen My Baby." But it is entirely possible that when Ringo called out "Alright, Gary" on "Down and Out," he was merely playing off of the resemblance of the pianist's last name to the one that sang and played on "A Whiter Shade of Pale."

"Down and Out," an enjoyable if not earth-shattering composition, has been restored to prominence on the compact disc edition of *Ringo*.

"COUNTRY DREAMER" B-SIDE TO "HELEN WHEELS" RELEASED NOVEMBER 12, 1973

One of the *Red Rose Speedway* outtakes foolishly left in the can was this pleasing countrified pastiche, replete with charming pedal steel picking from Henry McCullough. "Country Dreamer" was a catchy little number that could very easily have been an A-side, had Macca wanted to create some "country music for people who don't like country music." That is to say, its inherent appeal makes any criticism seem callous.

Recorded in October 1972, the song was resurrected a year later to back what had been intended as a stand-alone single. In America, Capitol execs, skeptical as to Paul's as-yet undemonstrated capacity for producing a blockbuster, arm-twisted him into adding "Helen Wheels" to the *Band on the Run* album, if only in the States, as a way to boost sales.

"Country Dreamer" represented the latest in a line of pastoral airs running back at least as far as "Mother Nature's Son" and including

"Heart of the Country" from *Ram*. By now calling his Scottish farm home (in large part), the inspirational qualities of his bucolic lifestyle readily lent themselves to translation in musical terms.

The recording demonstrates that in less than a year after Henry McCullough joined, Wings had jelled into quite a solid little band, adept at straight ahead rock as they were at genre exercises like this one. It is odd that a number as solid as this one was cut from what originally had been intended as a double album in favor of often inferior material, but such was the lack of self-discernment that plagued Macca throughout his solo years. His absence of a John Lennon to act as a sounding board was evidenced over and again.

The track was duly added to the CD iteration of *Red Rose Speedway*, but escaped attention on subsequent compilations, most conspicuously on *Wingspan*, where it surely earned a place.

"ZOO GANG" B-SIDE TO "BAND ON THE RUN" (NON-U.S.) RELEASED JUNE 28, 1974

Produced by Sir Lew Grade's ATV, *The Zoo Gang* premiered on British television in April 1974. The limited run series (six episodes), somewhat akin to NBC's *The A Team* in the 1980s, featured an ensemble of "troubleshooters," known by their World War II animal code names (hence the title), out to right wrongs and settle scores in contemporary France. The series featured several familiar stars, including Brian Keith, Barry Morse, and John Mills.

Sir Lew commissioned Paul to compose and record the series' theme song. Just as *Band on the Run* was being released, Wings headed to Paris to the same Pathé Marconi studio where Paul had cut "Can't Buy Me Love" nearly ten years before. Tasked to lay down some Suzy and the Red Stripes tracks, they managed to squeeze in work on the show's two-minute opening as well.

The song's searing, hypnotic lead guitar riff came courtesy of Jimmy McCulloch: not yet an official member of Wings. For that touch of Parisian *je ne sais quoi* (not to mention *savoir-faire*), the track also featured a touch of accordion, doubtless played by Paul himself. Along for the ride was drummer Davey Lutton, who came thisclose to joining the band before accepting an offer from T. Rex.

"Zoo Gang" was issued in England as the flip to Wings' current album's title cut, nearly two months after the series had left the air. In America, where the instrumental would have meant nothing, it was passed over in favor of "Nineteen Hundred and Eighty-Five." Not until the CD issue of *Venus And Mars* in 1993 was the song given a proper airing in the States.

"SALLY G" B-SIDE TO JUNIOR'S FARM" RELEASED NOVEMBER 11, 1974

Wings Mark III (or IV) spent a productive July 1974 in Nashville, cutting a pair of tunes (as well as the requisite not-to-be-released-anytime-soon Denny Laine song, "Send Me The Heart") that would—as a single—debut the new line-up. "Junior's Farm" marked an excellent start to Jimmy McCulloch's tenure in the band, but "Sally G," the country-fried flipside, was an equally strong track, marking the most accomplished stab at the genre Macca yet mustered.

Somewhat reminiscent of the narrative style pioneered in "Rocky Raccoon," "Sally G" tells the story of an innocent who gets played by the title character "somewhere to the south of New York City." With appropriate C&W accompaniment (pedal steel, fiddle), the song displays Paul's mastery of styles beyond pop/rock. The track was catchy to boot, reaching the unexpected peak of seventeen on the Billboard Top Forty For all that, the song was only issued on CD as a bonus track to *Wings At The Speed Of Sound*, being thrice passed over for inclusion on Wings compilations; a fate not shared by the flip-side.

"I DON'T CARE ANYMORE" B-SIDE TO "DARKHORSE" RELEASED NOVEMBER 18, 1974

Perhaps the single best documentation of the "grumpy George" on record, the title of this non-album B-side said it all. Accentuating the bother that his listeners have apparently put him through in demanding a flipside to his latest album's title track, a slightly inebriated sounding George announced feeling put out at the onset: "We got a b-side to make, ladies and gentlemen. We haven't got much time now so we better get right on with it."

With that, he gruffly launched into a sordid tale of an illicit romance—something he would have been more than familiar with by this time—as he accompanied himself on a barely in tune acoustic twelve-string guitar. The pity of it is, had he committed to more than this single take, he might have crafted a somewhat more durable product. The song is a rather atypical (for George) acoustic blues, but with the usual allotment

Dark Horse	STEREO 1	C 006-05 766 U
(George Harrison)		© 1974 · EMI Records Ltd.
I Don't Care Anymore		
(George Harrison)		
GEORGE HARRISON		Cover photo: Apple
Produced by George Harrison · An Apple Record · An EMI Recording		

Die Beatles auf EMI

Walls And Bridges
Going Down On Love · Whatever
Gets You Thru The Night · Old
Dirt Road · What You Got · Bless
You · Scared · Nine Dream · Sur-
prise, Surprise · Steel And Glass ·
Beef Jerky · Nobody Loves You ·
Ya Ya
John Lennon

Band On The Run
Band On The Run · Jet · Bluebird ·
Mrs. Vandebilt · Let Me Roll It ·
Mamunia · No Words · Picasso's
Last Words · Nineteen Hundred
And Eighty Five
Paul McCartney And Wings

Goodnight Vienna
Goodnight Vienna · Occapella ·
Oo-Wee · Husbands And Wives ·
Snookeroo · All By Myself · Call
Me · No No Song · Only You · Easy
For Me · Goodnight Vienna
Ringo Starr

1C 062-05 733
Auch als MC erhältlich

1C 062-05 503
Auch als MC erhältlich

1C 062-05 782
Auch als MC erhältlich

EMI ELECTROLA
EMI Electrola GmbH, Köln. All rights reserved. Printed in Germany by Druckhaus Maack KG, 565 Lüdenscheid.

The German issue of George's "Dark Horse" single included plugs for all his ex-bandmate's most recent product.

of intriguing chord changes that were a Harrison hallmark.

For a recording that will never rate above novelty status, it's almost comical to note that a *sheet music* issue of this song was published in 1975 (bearing a 1971 photo of George). While appearing on bootleg collections, the song's only shot at a sanctioned release will only likely come when the *Dark Horse* album is remastered—if ever.

"MOVE OVER MS. L" B-SIDE TO "STAND BY ME" RELEASED MARCH 10, 1975

The epoch known in Lennon lore as "the Lost Weekend" can in actuality be seen as perhaps one of his most productive and inspired periods. Having once again found his muse, John began rebounding from the somewhat less-than-stellar output of the previous two years. When not recording with and/or writing for others (Nilsson, Ringo, Keith Moon, Elton, Jagger), he set about tackling a strong collection of original material, book-ended between bouts of oldies work.

Walls and Bridges represented a return to form, resulting in a successful marriage of production and introspection unseen since *Imagine*. Though most of the material consisted of adroit explorations of his current situation—taking stock of his life against the tableau of marital separation – he also showed that the love of wordplay that had fueled his creativity going back at least as far as adolescence was still strong.

Nowhere was that characteristic on greater display than on "Move Over Ms. L," a rollicking fifties-style rocker. Believed by many to be a slap at his estranged wife, an examination of the actual lyric shows that *that* interpretation may be a bit of stretch, at best. While one can view the song's refrain ("You know I wish you well") as a direct fare-thee-well to Yoko, it also wouldn't be the first time that John strung a

series of non-sequetic phrases together for the pure sound of them; furthermore, when communicating something personal, John famously tended toward the direct rather than the oblique.

The song was recorded in just a few takes in mid-July 1974, when his well-rehearsed band was operating at the peak of its collective powers. John had every intention of issuing the song on *Walls and Bridges*; in fact, a preliminary proof of the lyric insert placed the song on side two, between "Surprise Surprise" and "What You Got." (The latter tune was, of course, re-slotted to side one.) But at the eleventh hour, only weeks before the record was set to be pressed, the tune was dropped.

In France, "Be Bop A Lula" was pulled from Rock 'N' Roll as the single to feature "Move Over Ms. L" on the flip.

Why this occurred is a mystery. The performance captured is as good as anything else on the album and would've fit nicely alongside some of the other upbeat material. The theory that it was bumped in favor of a stronger track may hold water, for though the album consisted of eleven songs (omitting "Ya Ya," which is really just a fragment) at a time when the industry norm was twelve, *Walls and Bridges* does clock in at a hefty forty-six minutes, making it the longest single album he ever issued.

The song wouldn't remain in the can for long, though. Six months after its intended parent album was issued, "Move Over Ms. L" emerged as the flip of "Stand By Me." Though a Lennon composition and not an oldie per se, the coupling made sense, in terms of pairing a ballad with a rocker. Less explicable was passing over the song later that year when the *Shaved Fish* compilation was collated. Ostensibly an attempt to gather the stray hits and misses that had been issued on singles ("Collectible Lennon" was the album's subtitle), Lennon himself overlooked issuing the track where it might best be appreciated.

Not until the 1989 re-issue of 1982's *John Lennon Collection* on compact disc was the song finally given a proper airing, as a CD "bonus track." But as this particular compilation has twice been superseded since (by *Lennon Legend* and *Working Class Hero*), the song has again fallen through the cracks. (An alternate take was issued with superb remastering on the *Lennon Anthology* box set, but purists remain dissatisfied.)

"JUST A DREAM" B-SIDE TO "WINGS" AND "DROWNING IN THE SEA OF LOVE" RELEASED AUGUST 25, 1977 & OCTOBER 18, 1977

Possibly the most overtly "disco" track to emerge from the *Ringo the 4th* sessions—surpassing even "Drowning in the Sea of Love"—it remains somewhat surprising that "Just A Dream" was passed over for inclusion on the parent album (in favor of arguably inferior material), but was *twice* used as a B-side, for *both* singles spawned from the album. If one is able to accept the dance divo persona that permeates the album—and that's a big if—then surely this track is at least, inoffensive. That said, there are fans that understandably will wince at the track's dance floor trappings: the relentless beat, the female back-up singers, the repeated cries of "Yowsah! Yowsah! Yowsah!" (Wait—I made that last one up.) Still, it is curious that this Starkey-Poncia composition has not been added to the CD issue of RT4, if only as a curiosity. If a *Ringo Anthology* rarities

Whatever one thinks of this disco-flavored offering from Ringo, it's a sign of how disinterested those attending to his back catalog were when it could have easily been added to the CD edition of Ringo the 4th—and wasn't. (Courtesy of the Peter Pecoraro collection)

collection is one day assembled—preferably *not* by bootleggers—than perhaps this oddity will find a home alongside other artifacts of a rather singular time and place.

"GIRLS SCHOOL" B-SIDE TO "MULL OF KINTYRE" RELEASED NOVEMBER 14, 1978

The *London Town* sessions were marked by a retreat from the harder-edged sound that had largely defined Wings during their world tour. One exception to the prevailing tide was this song, a tune that would probably have fit nicely into their live sets. Given that Jimmy McCulloch was introduced to the public via a strong rocker ("Junior's Farm"), it seemed somehow fitting that he should take his leave from the band in the same style.

"Girls School" was written in Hawaii during some downtime from the 1975 Australian tour. Having stumbled across a local newspaper, Paul was intrigued to discover the listings for "adult" movie fare in the paper's back pages. The song grew out of an attempt to string together as many titles as he could, resulting in lyrics citing "Kid Sister," "Spanish Doll," "Oriental Princess," and—most intriguingly—"The Woman Trainer."

To anyone who'd witnessed their live shows, the recording represented a promising return to form. The drums thunder along, and some fine slide guitar interplay provides support for a typically superlative McCartney rock vocal. But the song had the singular misfortune of being issued on the flip of what in Britain proved to be a phenomenon; "Mull Of Kintyre" was a monster, shattering singles sales records in the U.K. held since 1963. Alongside such a uniquely British tune, the rather conventional rocker didn't stand a chance, no matter what its merits.

In the States, the path to airplay was clear with Capitol not even attempting to promote the rather sketchy bagpipe-ladenside. Instead, the virtues of "something for everyone" were played up, with radio stations encouraged to make "Girls School" the plug side (with a specially edited DJ version). Notwithstanding the qualities of either side of Wings' latest offering, the public wasn't biting. As the more commercial (at least to American ears) side, "Girls School" just wasn't finding its groove with record buyers, stalling at thirty-three.

Had it been issued without the burden of "Mull of Kintyre" strapped to its back, "Girls School" might have done better. But coming in the shadow of a song destined to remain little more than a novelty in the former colonies, the track was doomed. Its relative American failure, conspicuously in the face of such success elsewhere, did not sit well with its creator. Feeling Capitol had let him down made the decision to sign with Columbia in 1979 that much easier.

"DAYTIME NIGHTIME SUFFERING" B-SIDE TO "GOODNIGHT TONIGHT" RELEASED MARCH 15, 1979

"Goodnight Tonight," as packaged in other markets; in this instance, Sweden.

The genesis of this inexplicably overlooked track came from a challenge Macca issued to his Wingmates one day. Whoever wrote the best song over the weekend would reap the financial reward of having the tune accorded the B-side of the sure-fire hit, "Goodnight Tonight." Each member of the band therefore set to work on composing material, but come Monday, Paul announced—surprise!—that his own composition, "Daytime Nighttime

174

Suffering," was the winner.

Characteristic immodesty aside, for once Paul's conceit was justified. This perfect pop creation was a stunner, from its harmonized vocal opening to the adroit instrumental arrangement and performance. What *is* interesting is the moral quandary Paul found himself in when he recognized that he now had *two* suitable candidates for the A-side. A prolonged period of deliberation ensued, as the tracks sat in the can while Macca dilly-dallied over a final decision (given that the day of the double-A side single had come and gone, or so Paul believed after "Girls School" stiffed).

Ultimately, he went with his original choice, therein losing the chance at giving "Nighttime" its day. While "Goodnight Tonight" performed respectably enough upon release, peaking at number five, the dance track hasn't exactly been embraced by latter-day radio programmers; when was the last time *you* heard it on the radio? Meanwhile, other Macca pop offerings like "Listen To What The Man Said" and "Another Day" have never gone out of fashion. Had it been issued separately or as a track on the *Back To The Egg* album, perhaps "Daytime Nighttime Suffering" might've been spared the obscurity it now resides in. (Though included on the *Wingspan* set, it is almost never given airplay.)

"LUNCHBOX/ODD SOX" B-SIDE TO "COMING UP" RELEASED APRIL 15, 1980

This non-album B-side was five years old by the time the public first got to hear it. Recorded at the start of the New Orleans sessions in January 1975, the instrumental "Lunch Box/Odd Sox" was among Geoff Britton's final tracks with Wings. It's basically a signature McCartney-esque piano lick, graced with an overlay of synthesizer.

Like far too many Macca recordings, the track contains some marvelously inventive passages that simply go undeveloped. Had he access to another songwriter who might have been able to contribute something of value, or had he himself taken it a little more seriously, the track could have made for something that merited repeat listenings. As it is, it's little more than a structured jam, bereft of even some guitar to keep it interesting.

Such is the price of undervaluing your own gifts; if musical ideas keep pouring out of you, it's challenging to properly channel one when ten more are queuing up. "Lunch Box/Odd Sox" currently resides alongside the heretofore unreleased "My Carnival" (cut during the same sessions) on the *Venus and Mars* CD.

"CHECK MY MACHINE" B-SIDE TO "WATERFALLS" RELEASED JULY 22, 1980

We close here with the last non-album B-side issued within the scope of this book, and beyond a doubt, the strangest. Granted, much of what emerged from the *McCartney II* sessions transcended the established Beatle/McCartney paradigms anyway (this *was* pre-Fireman, after all). But even by the loose compositional standards of the parent album, "Check My Machine" is a real outlier: pointing the way toward the electronica experiments that Paul would increasingly become comfortable with issuing, albeit under the aforementioned pseudonym. Significantly, he made the decision to make this electronic doodling public, on the B-side of a single he had high commercial hopes for: the melancholy "Waterfalls." But that release sold poorly, ensuring that most fans never heard it.

"Check My Machine" was, as the name suggests, his try-out for the new recording gear he'd leased: a made-up-on-the-spot piece of sound, conceived with no deeper intentions than to put the equipment through its paces and familiarize himself with what it could do. At the same time, he was also re-calibrating his approach to recording: singing in a high falsetto throughout, a repetitious vamping never intended to be heard by ears beyond his own. That he found the results pleasing enough to share speaks well of his desire to offer music outside the commercial pop box he'd so successfully created during the past near-two decades.

It therefore takes a recalibration of one's listening expectations to "get" what he was offering with this. It is not meant to be judged by the standards of his usual commercial output: there are no real lyrics, it isn't meant to be particularly melodious and the amount of listening pleasure derived from this recording really depends on one's taste for groove-driven electronica. In comparison to the work of artists steeped in the genre full-time, Paul's efforts might be seen as amateurish; even laughable. But that's beside the point: Paul was a newbie, and he chose precisely the right outlet for bringing this rough-hewn experiment to the public: not as part of the, by comparison, listener-friendly parent album, but in the ephemeral media of the non-album B-side.

"Check My Machine" was issued on CD in 2011 as part of the *McCartney II* remaster package: the original 5:50 single edit and the full-length 8:58 version.

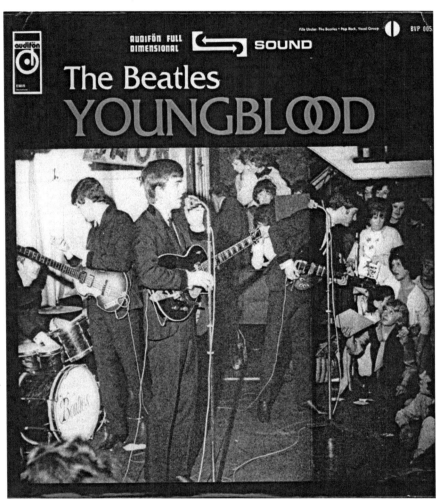

AUDIFÖN FULL DIMENSIONAL ←⟶ SOUND

File Under: The Beatles • Pop Rock, Vocal Group

BVP 005

audifön

The Beatles
YOUNGBL**OO**D

Issued by Audifön, this collection of BBC radio broadcasts came in packaging taken straight from Nicholas Schaffner's 1977 book, The Beatles Forever. Note the top to bottom "gutter" between pages running through John.

CHAPTER 10

YOU WERE STANDING WITH A BOOTLEG IN YOUR HAND: SOME UNDERGROUND RELEASES

T he unceasing public clamor for a Beatle reunion in the wake of their break-up was matched only by the demand for new Fab product—*any* product. During the 1970s, there were only two officially sanctioned releases of heretofore unheard-in-public Beatle recordings: the *Live! At The Star-Club* set in 1977, and *Hollywood Bowl* concert, issued that same year. Though EMI was game for repackaging already-issued material in as many ways as possible, fans throughout the decade had to look elsewhere to find the good stuff in this pre-*Anthology* era.

Enter the bootleggers. Underground entrepreneurs did a brisk business among the fan base with a series of records that became increasingly more polished over time. Featuring both desirable material as well as an increased sophistication in packaging, labels such as "Tobe Milo," "Ruthless Rhymes," and "Melvin" fed the ever-increasing demand. Given the lawless nature of the bootleg industry, some albums came disguised as "imported" product, bearing all the earmarks of legitimate overseas issues (while featuring false addresses to thwart any nosy law enforcers that might be probing too deeply). So it was—then as now—that the hardcore aficionados were satiated in their pursuit of anything of value caught on tape concerning the Fabs that was impossible to obtain through lawful channels.

Most of this material falls into five categories:

1. Live recordings: Given the relatively narrow window within which the Beatles toured (1964-1966), most of what turned up was of dreadful sound, with only a few exceptions.
2. Studio out-takes: These were among the most desirable recordings, usually being unheard alternates of songs officially issued. During the seventies, completely unreleased songs such as "Not Guilty" rarely turned up.
3. BBC recordings: Decades before an authorized package appeared in 1994, the hundreds of broadcasts of mostly otherwise unrecorded

material were highly prized.

4. *Let It Be* sessions: With hundreds of hours of music, tomfoolery, and lethargy committed to tape in January 1969, enterprising bootleggers were able to present the material in myriad ways.

5. Broadcasts: Anything gathered from radio or television—whether as a group or individually—was considered fair game for underground issue.

It should be noted that an awful lot of what made it to vinyl was simply that—awful. With authentic rarities scarce, bootleggers frequently issued the odd gem among much dross in terrible sound, or even recordings that had nothing to do with the Beatles, under their name. But fans lapped it up, absent any choice. The seventies were a heyday for this illicit activity, with anything Beatle-related occupying a dominant position within the shadow industry. While entire books have been written detailing nearly every release, we'll limit the discussion to some of the more significant ones.

Note: All dates approximate, due to the inexact record keeping.

GET BACK TO TORONTO – 1971

Hitting the stores in late 1969, *Kum Back* is widely regarded as the earliest Beatle bootleg, coming off the heels of the Bob Dylan *Great White Wonder* and Rolling Stones' *Liver Than You'll Ever Be*. It marked the first public appearance of anything from the "Get Back" project (beyond both sides of the single of the same name issued in May 1969), and was sourced from a Glyn Johns compilation put together at the Fabs' request. It was a spartan affair: a plain white sleeve with the title stamped on it, and no artist credit given. Inside were eight *Let It Be* selections in pre-Spectorized form, with the inclusion of "Teddy Boy," plus a half-assed version of Jimmy McCracklin's 1958 hit, "The Walk."

As the authorized *Let It Be* album had not yet seen release, some creative titling went on with the songs enclosed: "Dig A Pony" became "All I Want Is You," while "Two of Us" was dubbed "On Our Way Home"—as it happened, its actual working title. From ads placed in the back of rock journals and under-the-counter distribution, *Kum Back* generated quite a buzz among fanatics, hinting at the potential goldmine of unheard material that lay in EMI's vaults. In actuality, such "gems" as "What's The New Mary Jane" took some years to surface; therefore, most of the same material was endlessly recycled. In this instance, once the original *Kum Back* pressing sold out, other enterprising folk moved in, augmenting the existing issue with a pair of Lennon "peace" interviews and a Beatles "Christmas message," titling the result *Get Back To Toronto.*

Once the Fabs' final LP saw issue, the novelty value of *GBTT* became clear, as an alternate to the official version, being much more representative of the *Let It Be* film than the purported soundtrack actually was. (Years later, of course, the McCartney-driven *Let It Be...Naked* project became the more or less official iteration of the bootleg—not the only time that underground releases actually influenced the issue of authorized product.)

YELLOW MATTER CUSTARD – 1971

Alongside the trove of what would soon emerge as the *Let It Be* sessions was the seemingly bottomless bounty of recordings the Beatles had recorded for broadcast on BBC radio between 1962 and 1965. What made these tracks so intriguing to collectors was the wide range of cover songs performed, most of which never made it to "official" issue on a Parlophone album. The body of material recorded was the closest most fans would ever get to experiencing the nascent Fabs' club sets—at least until the *Star-Club* tapes finally surfaced.

Yellow Matter Custard (sometimes issued under the name *As Sweet As You Are* and by Berkeley in 1975 as—erroneously—*The Decca Audition Tapes*; a description that no less than John Lennon himself believed to be accurate) was apparently sourced from a fan in Britain who'd taped their performances off the radio in 1963. Apart from Larry Williams' "Slow Down," all fourteen of the performances were fresh to American ears and revealed an astonishing range: from Ray Charles, by way of Elvis ("I Got A Woman") to Ann-Margret ("I Just Don't Understand"). George's Carl Perkins fixation was amply displayed on the marvelous "Glad All Over" (nope, not the far cruder Dave Clark Five song of the same name), as well as on "Nothing Shakin' (But The Leaves On The Tree)." This latter song would later be heard live on the *Star-Club* set.

Paul was represented with a Perkins cover of his own, "Sure To Fall" (later recorded by Ringo) and "The Honeymoon Song," the title tune of a 1959 film. Not exactly rock and roll, this pop confection wasn't much appreciated by his fellow Fabs and was therefore only taped once (on July 16, 1963). Still, it was a pleasant performance; years later, Paul resurrected the tune for Mary Hopkin's Apple debut LP. While Ringo didn't take any lead vocals, the other three's ensemble harmonies were shown to good effect on "To Know Her Is To Love Her," Buddy Holly's posthumously released "Crying, Waiting, Hoping," the Holly-less Crickets' recording of "Don't Ever Change," and "So How Come (Nobody Loves Me)," a hit by the Everly Brothers.

John took the lion's share of the lead vocals, including on "I'm Gonna Sit Right Down And Cry (Over You)," a powerhouse rocker featuring a stellar performance from their newly-seated drummer, bested only by the *Star-Club* recording. Lennon's affinity for American R&B was demonstrated with his reading of Arthur Alexander's "A Shot of Rhythm and Blues," while his rockabilly fixation took the form of "Lonesome Tears In My Eyes," originally recorded by the Johnny Burnette Trio. (Elements of this song were deftly woven into "The Ballad of John and Yoko" six years later.)

What's amazing about this release is how well it hung together as an album. In a parallel universe where the Beatles existed as a club band without their in-house songwriting skills, *Yellow Matter Custard*—preferably under a different title—would've made an impressive debut album. While all of these tracks have long since been made available legitimately as part of 1994's *The Beatles at the BBC* set, spreading them over two discs diluted their power, especially alongside familiar EMI recordings. Here's an instance where the bootleggers got it right: pared to a single record, these recordings still pack a punch.

L.S. BUMBLE BEE – 1973 / *HAVE YOU HEARD THE WORD* – 1975

Given the demand for more unreleased Beatle product and an increasingly discerning audience for it, bootleggers became hard - pressed for new material when it simply wasn't available. Recycling the same tracks over and over again wasn't going to cut it, nor would simply upgrading the packaging. (Most underground releases consisted of plain white covers with paper inserts detailing the contents.) So began the practice of adding material that wasn't the Fabs at all, but to unsophisticated ears possessing a need for wish fulfillment, a well-chosen non-Beatle tune could sometimes suffice as at least a drawing card. Such was the case with this release, which lured buyers with the promise of a 1967 recording, which it was. Only trouble was, the performance wasn't by the Beatles—it was from the English comedy duo of Peter Cook and Dudley Moore.

"L.S. Bumble Bee," the song, was a not-bad send-up of the psychedelic phenomenon sweeping the world's youth culture, but as

Dudley Moore explained years later in response to the song's resurrection as a newfound Beatle track, it was actually intended more as a Beach Boys homage. The remainder of the release was comprised of audio excerpts from the *Let It Be* film, an *Ed Sullivan Show* performance from 1965 ("Yesterday"), and—making its bootleg debut—a cut from the legendary 1962 Decca audition tape, with Pete Best: "Love of the Loved" (more on the Decca tape below).

Two years after this nonsense, the formula was repeated with the issue of *Have You Heard The Word*. Like *L.S. Bumble Bee*, it too featured one "newly discovered Beatle track" and an assortment of already-heard rubbish, again mostly from the *Let It Be* film and assorted BBC performances. As before, the selling point was fraudulent: "Have You Heard The Word" was an undeniably Beatlesque recording, but no more so than other material recorded by Badfinger, Marmalade, or the Bee Gees circa 1970. What may have made it more believable as coming from the Fabs, or at least Lennon (given the background screams, reminiscent of his wife's work—or Macca's), was the evident lack of sincerity, reminiscent of "You Know My Name," or "What's The New Mary Jane."

"Have You Heard The Word" was released on Beacon records in England as a single in 1970. Credited to "The Fut" (performer, writer, and producer credits), it was in fact a one-off collaboration between Australian ex-pats Tin Tin and their producer, Bee Gee Maurice Gibb. Tin Tin scored a belated hit in 1971 with their classic "Toast and Marmalade For Tea," a pop gem that many undoubtedly mistook for the Brothers Gibb themselves. According to legend, a 1969 Tin Tin session featuring a little too much high spirits and Maurice at the mic, doing his best Lennon impression, resulted in an inside-joke never intended for public ears. Of course, buyers of this bootleg were not aware of this.

The frequent interjections of "all together now!" certainly would've fooled those prepared to believe the Fabs capable of anything, even a mess like this. (In fact, Yoko tried to copyright the tune as a Lennon composition in 1985.) Had it come along a little later in the decade, it might even have made an entirely acceptable Rutles out-take, but by the time Neil Innes began perfecting his Lennon impression, his "Cheese and Onions" was being bootlegged as a "solo John L. outtake" on 1978's *Indian Rope Trick*.

At least these were recordings that actually existed. But much effort in seeking some elusive tracks was expended by fans during the seventies when a 1971 report on bootlegs in *Disc* magazine listed four heretofore unheard of songs: "Pink Litmus Paper Shirt," described as *Revolver*-era George; a pair of Lennon compositions, "Colliding Circles" and "Left Is Right (Right Is Wrong)," the latter a political diatribe; and "Deck Chair," a vaudeville-type tune from Paul. True, these were odd titles, but no more so than "Dig A Pony" or "Old Brown Shoe." Soon, the list began turning up in scholarly works on unreleased Beatles recordings, taking on the air of a Holy Grail among fanatics. Only trouble was, it was all a hoax, dreamed up by 19 year-old Martin Lewis, future professional Beatle fan and then a freelance music writer. Lewis confessed the deception thirty years later, but the myth had so taken root that few took him at his word.

This bootleg release scooped up material from each ex-Beatle's solo efforts and presented it as a single entity. Note the Lifting Material from the World artwork, lifted from the October 1977 issue of National Lampoon. (Courtesy of the Mike Eder collection)

TELECASTS – 1973

As individuals, the former Fab foursome also drew attention from bootleggers. During the seventies, as their separate careers took off, the material to work with was of course limited, but underground entrepreneurs made the best of what was available. Live material was very much in demand, though the quality of such material varied according to venue and conditions. For example, bootleg recordings of the *Concert for Bangla Desh* hit the street well in advance of the authorized collection, taped on the floor by attendees. The legal issue of the show in December 1971 may have dried up much of the audience for the illicit recordings, but hardcores recognized the differences between the afternoon and evening shows and therefore needed *both*.

Another source of material for bootleggers was any stray material that hadn't been issued on an album. Given Paul's prolific tendencies, and his chronic inability to collate them officially, despite threats of releasing *Cold Cuts* year after year, shrewd collectors gathered up his non-album single sides and delivered their own packages. One of the most creative was issued in 1975; it was called *Wings On The Radio* and featured ten pre-*Band on the Run* singles, plus "My Love" for some reason (perhaps to spare listeners any reason to buy *Red Rose Speedway*). What made the LP interesting was its lack of dead groove space: the sound of a tuner seeking out a station, along with recognizable excerpts from radio and TV broadcasts, circa 1974, filled the space between songs, making for a priceless listening experience, as well as an enjoyable time capsule.

Around 1973, someone gathered together some eight John Lennon live performances, culled from appearances on the *David Frost Show* in 1971, as well as *Mike Douglas, Dick Cavett*, and the *Jerry Lewis Telethon* in 1972, threw in two Yoko songs for good measure, and called the package *Telecasts*. Featuring a deluxe full color cover shot (taken from his 1970 "Instant Karma" appearance on *Top Of The Pops*, which, with his live vocal, would've made a nice addition) and a title design that mimicked the one on *Imagine*, it was an excellent concept, featuring fair to decent sound.

The other ex-Fabs were also well-represented throughout the seventies on bootleg vinyl. George's *Dark Horse* tour begat several live packagings of various dates, as well as some recordings he'd done with Dylan. Paul's constant touring naturally produced a lot to work with, as did his *James Paul McCartney* television special. The music from Ringo's 1978 *Ognir Rrats* broadcast was presented as side two of *Ognir*

185

Rrats Greatest Hits (actually duplicating the album cover artwork seen in the show) while the first side collected his non-album B-sides, plus rarities like the extended version of "Six O'Clock."

SWEET APPLE TRAX – 1974

Thus far with the *Let It Be* session tapes, material had been parceled out song by song, except where excerpts lifted straight from the film appeared. This changed in 1974 with the first issue of an LP that presented sessions from Twickenham more or less unspooled in real time. Release by CBM (for "Contra Band Music), *Sweet Apple Trax Vol. 1* and *II* presented material dating from January 8-10, 1969; the "intimate microscopic experience" promised in posters to the *Let It Be* film was actually presented within the grooves of this release, truly placing listeners inside the room.

The material was culled from ¼" monaural tapes recorded during the sessions for the benefit of the film crew, as opposed to the recording engineers. They ran continuously at about sixteen minutes a reel on Nagra tape decks (hence the term "Nagra reels") and were in no way ever intended to be used on a record. The tapes were designated either 'A' or 'B' rolls; the 'A' roll ran as long as there was tape, while the 'B' roll kicked in just before the 'A' spool ended to maintain continuity as the first tape operator changed reels. In order to synch the sound with the film, the tapes are punctuated with an occasional electronic "beep," adding to the ambiance.

Sweet Apple Trax was reissued in 1975 by Newsound as a double album in a deluxe gatefold sleeve, bearing a cover photo taken during filming of the "Revolution" promo back in September 1968. Song listings were approximate, as the cuts contained much dialogue, asides, false starts, re-takes, and unclassifiable noodling. What is obvious to anyone listening to this record is how incredibly lighthearted the proceedings could be, especially when contrasted with the dreary tone of the finished film. The band is in rare form, delivering improvised satires such as the infamous "White Power" ("get off!") and "Commonwealth" jams. Had George's resignation not occurred the next day (unheard here), it might've been remembered as one of the highlights of the project.

The collection abounds with fascinating moments, such as Paul's debut of "Let It Be," the song. The lyrics are only half-finished, but already he has an arrangement in his head, as he vocalizes the hi-hat percussion to Ringo and calls out the chords and sings the harmonies to John and George. Meanwhile, George's attempt to steer the band back into a rehearsal of the newly-minted "I Me Mine" is doomed after John hijacks the proceedings, imposing a grotesque take on "House of the Rising Sun" over Ringo's waltz rhythm. (Though George was likely furious at the disruption, elsewhere John can be heard mocking his own "Across The Universe," delivering a verse in a thick Scottish burr.)

Apart from the evident disrespect of each other's material throughout, some really fine moments were captured. A rocking, sped up version of "Get Back" with John taking the lead vocal (to the extent that he knew any of the words) featured a wah-wah solo from George and a breathtaking drum break from Ringo. George, meanwhile, delivered a stunning medley of Dylan songs: "Ramblin' Woman," "I Threw It All Away," and "Mama, You've Been On My Mind" on acoustic, momentarily silencing his bandmates as they stopped to listen. Elsewhere, the complete performance of "Suzy's Parlour" (aka "Suzy Parker"), as seen in the film, can be heard.

Though appearing in less than stellar sound and representing only the tip of the iceberg of the entire *Let It Be* session tapes, *Sweet Apple Trax* profoundly shaped the expectations Fab collectors had toward underground releases. Suddenly, a tantalizing taste of the Beatles' rough notes had appeared, complete with all of the peripheral non-musical elements that made up their world. Fans were at last embracing what had been the Fabs' intent for a "warts and all" listening experience all along.

FIVE NIGHTS IN A JUDO ARENA – 1975

Ever since they first hit stardom, Beatle concert recordings were a highly sought-after item. While three shows were recorded professionally for potential release at the Hollywood Bowl in 1964 and 1965, other venues and shows went largely undocumented. Most recordings known to exist were of poor fidelity, due both to technical limitations and the inherent noise present at such events. Therefore, whenever something that was actually listenable surfaced, it was a big deal.

Around 1971, when Apple had made the effort to see if Phil Spector could salvage the 1964 Hollywood Bowl show, a copy leaked out and soon began making the rounds as *Shea, The Good Old Days*. Given the high-profile nature of this particular gig, it probably made for a good selling point to anyone that hadn't seen the TV special, notwithstanding a substantial difference in the set list. Within a year or two, the actual Shea soundtrack, lifted from the TV film, began appearing on the underground market as *Last Live Show*. Again, this was not the case, but

BEATLES' 66

INTRO· ROCK AND ROLL MUSIC·SHE'S A WOMAN
DAY TRIPPER· IF I NEEDED SOMEONE · BABY'S
IN BLACK· I FEEL FINE· I WANNA BE YOUR MAN
YESTERDAY· NOWHERE MAN · A PAPERBACK
WRITER · I'M DOWN· OUTRO ··· INTERVIEW

LIMITED EDITION 2 RECORD SET

This Tobe Milo limited edition presentation of the June 30 Tokyo show came in the rare form of a double 33& 1/3rpm double EP.

the mystique of their Candlestick Park swan song was reason enough for many to take a chance on the record.

Buyers of these releases were therefore doubtless pleased when another quite listenable concert recording surfaced, this one titled *Live In Atlanta Whiskey Flat.* Exactly *why* the bootleggers responsible for this product felt the need to invent a fictitious venue is anyone's guess; inside joke perhaps. In actuality, the September 2, 1964 show was sourced from a reel-to-reel tape recorded by a Philadelphia radio station. While these shows adequately filled the demand for something covering the first two of three tours, 1966 was still unrepresented; as the year that the band segued into a full-time studio entity, their final tour therefore piqued much interest.

The issue of *Five Nights In A Judo Arena* was therefore much anticipated. Professionally recorded *and* filmed, the *three* (not five) performances at Tokyo's Budokan Martial Arts Arena preceded the North American swing, as well as the Philippines debacle. The set this year was largely new, dropping six of eleven songs played in 1965 in favor of fresher material like "Paperback Writer," "Nowhere Man," and George's "If I Needed Someone." Therefore, the fans that snapped up copies of the release could be expected to be thrilled by the latest addition to their live Beatles stash.

Instead, the music within was something of a letdown. The fact was, *Five Nights In A Judo Arena* (sic) captured nothing less than a band going through the motions and marking time as their touring clock wound down. The performances were lackluster; the band seemingly distracted. George's vocal spotlight was a train wreck, with indifferent singing and a couldn't-care-less attitude projecting through. John and Paul, true to form, mixed their pronouns on "Baby's In Black," while

"Yesterday," performed electrically as a four-piece, demonstrated graphically the cross-purposes with which their newer material and their stage act conflicted.

THE DECCAGONE SINGLES – 1977

For as long as Beatle books were being published, the legend of their Decca audition on January 1, 1962, had haunted fans. Though they were famously turned down, curiosity about how bad it could have been was an open question. While Pete Best's drumming was never stellar, the inference was that the group as a whole simply performed badly and that their choice of material did not help. It was therefore high on everyone's list to one day hear the mysterious tapes that captured the up-and-comers during their career crossroads.

Although it's long been alleged that Decca execs would trot out

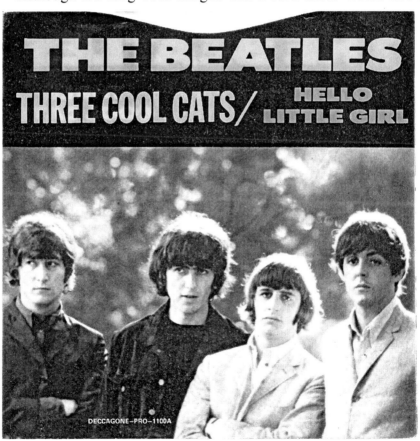

For those that might have missed those beautiful issues of Joe Pope's Deccagone single series, Smilin' Ears re-bootlegged them in LP form by (while also ripping off the cover of Ron Schaumburg's Growing Up With the Beatles for its artwork).

the tape to play at parties after the Fabs became successful, the actual recording never aired publicly until 1973, when one track, Paul's "Love of the Loved," somehow escaped whatever vault had contained it and was booted on *L.S. Bumble Bee*. It was a tantalizing piece of the puzzle, demonstrating a sophistication largely absent on the rest of the tape. But not until four years later would the rest of the picture emerge, offering a rounded out view of what, to the Fabs, must've been a major humiliation.

Joe Pope, the Boston Beatlemaniac who'd founded the *Strawberry Fields Forever* fanzine some years earlier, bought a copy of the Decca audition tape from a contact in England, reportedly for $5,000. With Joe, presentation was everything: rather than simply press up an LP and reap the rewards of issuing material that was to die for, he took it a step further. The fourteen songs were parceled out as *singles*, pressed on colored vinyl and contained in beautiful full color picture sleeves. The Deccagone series, as it was called, were issued at the regal pace of two singles (or four songs) a year. At $6 a pop, they were not cheap, but still, in studio quality and containing long-sought performances, the 45s quickly sold out. (At which time, the bootlegs were counterfeited by others on inferior vinyl.)

The material itself was literally the stuff of novelty. It's hard to see how a band angling for a recording contract could expect to be taken seriously when performing songs like "Sheik of Araby" and "Three Cool Cats," but at least the three original tunes were worth hearing. Though "Hello Little Girl" and "Like Dreamers Do" would one day be released legitimately on *Anthology 1*, "Love of the Loved" *still* hasn't. "Till There Was You" (boasting *two* guitar breaks here) and "Money (That's What I Want)" would be re-made for issue on EMI in due course but the remainder of the fourteen songs only existed by the Fabs in BBC recordings or as performed at the *Star-Club*, though only the versions cut on this day featured Pete Best.

In 1979, a *fifteenth* song surfaced: Bobby Vee's "Take Good Care of My Baby," with a lead vocal by George. It appeared on an LP of dubious legality issued on Circuit Records as *The Decca Tapes*. (The album came complete with a fictitious Beatle history in the liner notes.) Pope was not pleased to see his exclusive blown; apparently his English friend had *two* copies to sell. But by the early 1980s, the material was being issued nearly everywhere as gray market budget releases until Apple at last put a stop to it by 1983.

Worth noting was a bootleg single issued around 1978. Not part of Pope's series but issued in the same format—colored vinyl and a picture sleeve—was yet another much-fabled recording: the George Martin-produced take of Mitch Murray's "How Do You Do It," backed with the "live" performance of "Revolution" seen in the promo clip: fast but with the "shooby doo-wops." By decade's end, being a bootleg collector was finally starting to pay off.

NO. 3 ABBEY ROAD NW8 – 1977

Fans hoping for some insight into the recording process for one the Beatles' most acclaimed albums were at last rewarded with this release, comprised of one album side's worth of unadorned session tapes. Though incomplete of course, *No. 3 Abbey Road NW8* still stands as a fascinating glimpse into the Beatles' final project as a foursome, especially in contrast to the finished product.

The album opens with "Golden Slumbers/Carry That Weight." Recorded initially as a three-piece (due to John's road accident in Scotland), it features Paul's solo vocal throughout, and ends cold, before "The End" would normally kick in. "Her Majesty" follows, featuring the "missing" final chord and minus the opening cymbal crash. While on paper, this variation doesn't amount to much, to Beatle fans, it functioned as the same sort of intoxicant that catnip does to felines.

Even more interesting was the take of "You Never Give Me Your Money" that followed. Featuring the same basic track that ended up on the finished master, the performance continued well past the cross fade into "Sun King" on *Abbey Road*, depicting the band launching into a double-time jam on a I-IV-V chord pattern (akin to "At The Hop"). To fans, it was revelatory that the Fabs were still having a blast in the studio, given every other stress then going on in their lives.

Other cuts included "Oh! Darling" and "Maxwell's Silver Hammer," both minus the production gloss. But the side-concluding "Something" was also worth hearing. Running over five and a half minutes length, it featured the piano-based coda, played by John and utilizing a chord sequence that later surfaced as *Plastic Ono Band*'s "Remember."

While fans would have been ecstatic to hear more material from these final Fab sessions in such presentable sound quality, they would have to wait almost two more decades for further outtakes to surface. The collection was rounded out on side two with a song swap taped during sessions for Mary Hopkin's *Postcard* album, featuring Paul and Donovan. While eminently listenable, it's strictly for fans of the two featured individuals.

LIVE FROM THE SAM HOUSTON
COLOSSEUM – 1978

By the time this *double* album release happened along, one might

have expected the demand for live Beatle concerts to be played out, what with the long-awaited official issue of the *Hollywood Bowl* set, as well as other concert bootlegs. But *Live from the Sam Houston Colosseum* (sic) was in a class by itself, being not one, but two complete shows—afternoon and evening—performed in Texas on Thursday, August 19, 1965. Just four days after their American tour was launched before 55,000

Outside the Hollywood Bowl live set, no bootleg quite captured the ambience of the Beatles in concert in America in 1965 like this collection.

fans at Shea Stadium in New York and a week before they would meet Elvis in Los Angeles, the band found themselves thoroughly enmeshed in the two-shows-a-day grind. *LFTSHC* is a singular snapshot of a long gone time when rock stars were compelled to work their game amidst the insanity surrounding them.

Apparently recorded by KILT for broadcast, the tapes documented the buildup before they took the stage. Emceeing the shows was KILT radio DJ Russ "Weird Beard" Knight, in between stints at KLIF in 1965. The beefy Knight comes off as a bit overbearing to unfamiliar ears, but granted, the man was required to fill air time until things were in place for the Beatles to take the stage. Seemingly, he is charged with keeping the crowd's emotions in check, as he berates them at every outburst. "They're just moving the drum!" he chastises them after one such eruption. "That's a Ludwig...I'd like to play that drum...."

At last, the Fabs begin their set and it is immediately apparent the toll that playing twice daily has been taking on their voices, especially John's. Typically bearing a bit of a rasp under normal strains, it threatens to fragment on the opener, "Twist and Shout"; during the same song in the second show, it disintegrates completely, eliciting laughter from Paul and George. What's particularly worthwhile about this set is how clear the vocals are. One can practically hear every intake of breath; consequently, it's easy to pick up on the group's high spirits as they entertain each other as much as their audience. (After one particularly unctuous bit of stage patter too many from the bassist, John, in a tone of faux enthusiasm, chimed in, "Thanks very much, Uncle Paul!," to which Macca responded in a deliberately hammy voice, "Is everybody happy?")

The technical limitations of the time are well documented, as the inevitable pause in the proceedings comes when Ringo's microphone is swung over so he can sing "I Wanna Be Your Man." (For all that, in the evening show it's not even working.) Also conveyed throughout is the rising tide of hysteria. At this distance from history, it may be hard for contemporary fans to understand the behavior of all those screaming girls seen in black and white film clips. Not here: instead, there is an adrenalin-raising immediacy felt when the show was stopped about three-quarters into the afternoon performance, just after "A Hard Day's Night" ended. Weird Beard commandeered the microphone and yelled, "QUIET! Quiet please! People are getting hurt on the front two rows... This is the Houston Security Beatle Division—move back PLEASE!... OK, go on..." Unimpressed, John thanked him sardonically: "That was wonderful!"

The cover artwork to this release featured the added attraction of a "butcher cover" outtake, further making the set irresistible to would-be buyers. What *Live from the Sam Houston Colosseum* preserved was the greatest rock band in history on a hot summer day at the peak of their powers in front of an audience. Greater triumphs lie ahead, but for that moment, the sheer exuberance of having so much devotion thrown your way on a level that was becoming routine was all that mattered.

WATCHING RAINBOWS – 1978

Yet another serving of Twickenham recordings surfaced just a few years after *Sweet Apple Trax* but before the floodgates opened in the 1980s. This release was significant in that it represented a sort of one-disc "greatest hits" of both the *No. 3 Abbey Road NW8* and *Sweet Apple Trax* LPs, while adding a few significant attractions. Beyond cuts reiterated on the earlier releases was a pair of Lennon songs recorded on the Tuesday following George's Friday walk-out. "Madman" was a stream-of-consciousness work out with a fully-realized vocal line and chord changes; everything but a point. John was loath to throw away any musical ideas, sometimes reworking tunes years after their first conception, but this one seems to have been completely abandoned ever after.

"Madman" segued seamlessly into a first draft of "Mean Mr. Mustard." The performance here featured John on electric piano, Ringo on drums, and Paul on

As the seventies wound down, the packaging bootlegs were presented in grew increasingly sophisticated; tasteful even. The shot from the 1968 Mad Day Out shoot gracing Watching Rainbows made a striking visual, albeit on content originating from the Let It Be sessions, six months later.

lead guitar in George's absence. Unlike the version eventually stitched into the *Abbey Road* side two medley, this "Mustard" featured a bridge that was later dropped. The other Lennon composition heard here is the title cut. "Watching Rainbows," featuring the same instrumental lineup, sounded much more like an improvisation, or at least the germ of a song that hadn't yet been developed. Slower of tempo than the other track, lyrically it seemed to draw inspiration from the middle-eight of "I am the Walrus" ("Sitting in an English garden...") while musically resembling Paul's far more finished "I've Got A Feeling." Suffice to say, these tracks are interesting simply because they seem to be serious efforts that were put aside and never returned to.

Also of interest on *Watching Rainbows* was the snippet of The Who's "A Quick One While He's Away." Just a month earlier, John had been on hand as the group performed a stunning version of this live on the set of the Rolling Stones' aborted *Rock and Roll Circus* television special. The Who's mini-set was beyond a doubt the highlight of the show, even alongside Lennon's all-star "Yer Blues." Its parodic "performance" led by John seems to have been initiated for no other reason than to comment on what had happened just moments earlier: George's walkout after announcing that he was quitting the group.

194

Watching Rainbows came in a beautiful full color sleeve, adorned front and back by images from the "Mad Day Out" photo shoot of July 1968. The annotation, however, was uniformly wrong, giving erroneous dates and context for virtually everything heard on the record. (March 1969 in Apple studios for the title recording? Really?)

Along with *Sweet Apple Trax*, this album was reissued in 1981 as a *three*-record set known as "The Black Album." While the sound quality was nothing to write home about, the packaging was a wonder. It came in a *black* gatefold sleeve with "The Beatles" embossed in front; inside was a pitch-perfect alternate collage poster, sporting—in place of lyrics—a dialogue transcription on the reverse. In ten years' time, bootlegs had come a *long* way.

A rare bootleg issue of a bona fide unreleased Beatles recording came with the arrival of this "White Album" outtake, later issued on Anthology 3.

Jeff Lynne's Electric Light Orchestra invited Beatles comparisons. Their take on Chuck Berry's "Roll Over Beethoven" showed what it might have sounded like, had the Beatles recorded it in 1967 instead of 1963.

CHAPTER 11

YOU MADE ME SUCH A BIG STAR: THEY TOO WEREN'T THE BEATLES

A s early as 1964, newly-minted bands bursting upon the scene were being touted as "the new Beatles," praise that—as often as not—proved to be the kiss of death. (Similarly, among the countless artists praised as "the new Dylan" through the years, exactly one—Bruce Springsteen—managed to transcend the hype while spawning a nomenclature for others that followed: "the new Springsteen.")

When the Beatles segued from being cuddly mop-tops cranking out simple, catchy pop tunes into a successful collective pushing the boundaries of their individual artistry (within a group setting), a large segment of their audience was left behind. It is not for no reason that the most successful Beatle tribute bands are the ones that wear matching suits and tend to stop short of 1967: that joyous earlier era simply makes for an uncomplicated listening experience to those wishing for a simple escape from the complexities of life.

That and *other* constituencies were served throughout the following decade by a number of acts that seemed to pick up on one aspect or another of the Beatles' fabness and retooled it to fit the new paradigm. Some, like The Raspberries or The Knack, tailored their presentation to fit the *Meet The Beatles!* mold. Others, like Electric Light Orchestra, Stackridge, or Klaatu, took up the *Pepper/Magical Mystery Tour* mantle and proceeded as though the Beatles hadn't retreated back to where they once belonged with the "White album." Still others eschewed the blatantly Fab packaging and simply went for the pop craftsmanship, like Big Star and Squeeze. (The latter act's Difford-Tilbrook songwriting team frequently bore the appellation "the new Lennon-McCartney" for their trouble.)

The following groups, for better or worse, labored under the burden of comparisons to the fabulous foursome phenomenon that the Beatles were. That so much classic material within this genre was produced is a testament to the fact that, regardless of how consciously they absorbed the Fabs' influence, other artists were able to take that inspiration and create something of their own—a fitting tribute to the Beatles' everlasting legacy.

THE RASPBERRIES

The Raspberries presented themselves musically and visually as if the Summer of Love, psychedelia and hard rock had never happened.

This Cleveland quartet was spawned from the ashes of two mid-sixties garage bands, The Choir ("It's Cold Outside") and Cyrus Erie, the latter featuring singer/songwriter Eric Carmen. In 1970, Carmen joined with three former Choir boys: Dave Smalley, Jim Bonfanti and Wally Bryson to form The Raspberries. Between the four of them, their collective appreciation for all things British Invasion placed them out of step with the prevailing sounds of the day, be it Led Zeppelin or Sly Stone. (Their insistence on bouffant hair-dos and matching suits further set them apart, but as Carmen pointed out, the presentation simply complemented the music.)

The Raspberries signed with Capitol (which given their roots, must've pleased them to no end) and released their first self-titled album in 1972. Carmen's "Go All The Way"—the spiritual son of "Please Please Me"—rocketed up the charts, peaking at number five. The song was an artful amalgamation of gritty guitar, sweet crooning verses, and a ballsy lead vocal, complete with a "come on, come on" ascending climax. (Years later, one of Carmen's bandmates on a Ringo All-Starr tour, noted—with a mixture of amazement and frustration—that the song virtually had a chord change for every word of the lyrics.)

Bouffants and all, the band toured relentlessly, on at least one occasion sharing a bill with an act similarly hamstrung by Beatle comparisons, Badfinger. (The latter's stage act couldn't have been more different, however; featuring blazing twin leads and perhaps a little too much jamming for their own good.) Rather than advance to "From Me

To You" or "She Loves You" for their next hit, Carmen and company offered a re-tool of "Go All The Way" with "I Wanna Be With You," which made the top twenty.

Carmen traded musical roles with Smalley, switching from bass to rhythm guitar, in order to better fulfill frontman duties, but egos and "creative differences" began creeping in. As other bands featuring one great talent among several good ones discovered, true democracy does not work. Not long after their third album, *Side Three*, was released in 1973, Smalley and Bonfanti departed to form Dynamite (anticipating comedian Jimmy Walker's similar catchphrase by a year or two). A re-tooled Raspberries issued the aptly named *Starting Over* in 1974, which produced their final top twenty hit, "Overnight Sensation (Hit Record)."

Though the Raspberries never really achieved the stability or consistent success that their talent warranted, they were not without their admirers. Critics at *Rolling Stone* were, somewhat surprisingly, quite enamored of their throwback sound, going so far as to rank their final long-player as one the top albums of the year (alongside the Rolling Stones and Steely Dan). John Lennon was photographed wearing a "Raspberries" sweatshirt, while Keith Moon joined the band onstage at The Whiskey for a cover of Free's "All Right Now."

The group disbanded on April 19, 1975 (just days before Pete Ham's suicide, as it happened). Carmen went on to a successful solo career that same year with a pair of power ballads, "All By Myself" and "Never Gonna Fall In Love Again,"—both with melodies lifted from Sergei Rachmaninoff. (Carmen thought the tunes were in public domain but found out otherwise when Sergie's relations came a-knockin.') In the eighties, he struck chart gold again with "Hungry Eyes" from the *Dirty Dancing* soundtrack and "Make Me Lose Control." In 2000, Carmen went on tour as part of Ringo's sixth All-Starr band, bringing a lifelong Beatle fixation full circle.

ELECTRIC LIGHT ORCHESTRA

The Move was an English pop band, fronted by multi-instrumentalist and singer, Roy Wood. Though they scored a succession of hit singles in their native country (including 1967's "Night of Fear" and the 1969 number one, "Blackberry Way"—a sardonic "response" to "Penny Lane"), the band failed to stir any ripples in the states. Wood and drummer Bev Bevan would be the only constants within a shifting line-up, but the addition of guitarist/singer/songwriter Jeff Lynne from

Idle Race provided the impetus to wind The Move down and begin anew in a fresh direction. (Lynne had briefly met the Beatles during the "White album" sessions and made no bones about his admiration.)

Heavily influenced by the orchestration used on some of the Beatles' mid-career recordings, Wood and Lynne began recording the debut of their Electric Light Orchestra in 1971, simultaneously with the final Move release. (Ironically, the latter band's final single, Lynne's "Do Ya" backed with Wood's "California Man"—later recorded by Cheap Trick—proved to be their only charting U.S. single.) Their resulting debut was asserted to "pick up where the Beatles left off"—assuming that the Fabs ceased recording in 1967. Though the potential for pretension was ample with such ingredients, their artful implementation and pop sensibilities ensured that competing with the loftier aspirations of say, the Moody Blues, was never likely to occur.

The "baroque and roll" sound was certainly unique, with strings and woodwinds slathered over the rock rhythm section with abandon. But their first outing was not a commercial success, and in a dispute over their next move (so to speak), Wood left to form Wizzard, leaving Lynne and Bevan to soldier on. The two would become the mainstays over the next decade as an assortment of string players came and went. 1973's *Electric Light Orchestra II* spawned the group's first U.S. hit single, an eight-minute re-working of Chuck Berry's "Roll Over Beethoven" that quoted liberally from Beethoven's Fifth Symphony.

Their next album, 1973's *On The Third Day*, contained a minor hit, "Showdown." Given Jeff Lynne's Fab fixation, it must have pleased him to no end when John Lennon, in a radio interview, remarked how much he enjoyed ELO's latest single. (John's arms-length admiration was expressed repeatedly during his remaining years, including during his 1980 *Newsweek* interview and the lengthy one given to *Playboy* around the same time.)

Not until 1974 and the *Eldorado* album (with a jacket designed by the future Mrs. Ozzy Osbourne, the daughter of ELO's manager) did the band finally break big in America. "Can't Get It Out Of My Head" was issued as a single in the eventful month of November 1974; the song's opening minute sounded to some listeners as though it were the latest offering from Ringo before turning in a direction that tended to preclude that possibility. In early 1975, the song peaked in America at—wait for it—number nine.

The hits continued over the course their next several albums, including *Face The Music*, *A New World Record*, and *Out Of The Blue*. Lynne had perfected his craft to the point that ELO's hit singles sounded Beatle-esque without being overtly so. "Evil Woman," "Strange Magic," a re-recording of The Move's "Do Ya" (the latter featuring a Harrisonian slide guitar lead): all had their elements of Fabness but stopped well short of the sort of slavish copyage that would become Oasis' trademark in another decade.

Interestingly, for all of the intertwining of Jeff Lynne with first George, and then the "Threetles" in the years to come, during the seventies the only contact between them was on the charts. George would formally meet his future producer and fellow Wilbury in the 1980s after being introduced by Dave Edmunds. (Edmunds had scored in 1970 with a recasting of Smiley Lewis' "I Hear You Knocking"—a favorite single of John Lennon's. The Welsh-born roots rocker would successfully pair up later in the seventies with Nick Lowe in Rockpile. Lowe, in turn, had been a member of pub-rockers Brinsley Schwarz, an act that had toured with Paul as Wings' support act in the U.K. Six degrees of Beatleness at work, folks.)

BIG STAR

At the age of 16, Memphis native Alex Chilton's rough-edged voice could be heard on AM radios all over the country as The Box Tops' hit, "The Letter," sat at number one for four weeks in the fall of 1967. Something of a prodigy, the young singer fronted the band until their 1970 break-up. With a run of hits that included "Cry Like A Baby" and "Soul Deep," indifferent management that treated the teens as a resource to be exploited undermined the band's success, leading to their early dissolution.

In 1971, Chilton was invited to join a quartet formed in Memphis by musician/recording engineer Chris Bell. Having spent the last year or so in New York recording demos and honing his guitar chops, Chilton happily agreed. The band settled on the name Big Star (after a local grocery store) and released their debut album, *#1 Record*, in 1972. The band's overt sixties British Invasion influence, shown in tightly composed melodies and soaring harmonies, cut against the current grain of extended tracks and heavier sounds.

Though unlike the Raspberries, they didn't exactly dress the part, Big Star certainly possessed all of the musical values common to the Beatles' heyday. Indeed, their muscular guitar sound coupled with catchy melodies laid the blueprint for what would flower later in the decade as "power pop." Clearly, there was still an audience for what the Beatles had provided; in their absence, bands like Badfinger, Big

Star, The Raspberries, and so forth filled that niche, though their long - term viability was shaky, if for no other reason than their being slightly ahead of mainstream tastes.

Compounding their bad timing issues were distribution troubles, leading to *#1 Record*'s commercial failure, despite two singles issued. (Another track from the album, "In The Street," was resurrected in 1998 for use as the theme song to television's *That '70s Show*. A year later, the song was re-recorded by Cheap Trick and re-titled "That '70s Song.") So soured was Bell on the album's failure that by the end of 1972 he quit the band he'd started and went solo (though he did make uncredited contributions to their next album). Struggles with drugs and personal issues plagued him until his death in a one car accident in 1978—one day before Chilton's 28th birthday.

Big Star effectively ceased to exist after Bell's departure, but a one-off reunion at an industry convention (minus Bell) in 1973 made Chilton and company rethink their dissolution. Facing some unexpected adulation, the band decided to give it another go. *Radio City*, released in 1974, built upon the paradigm created with their first long-player while transcending it, featuring less of a Beatley pop sheen (Bell's primary influence) in favor of a rawer and more emotionally intense presentation. "September Gurls" was a pop gem; replete with ringing Byrd-like guitars and an insidiously captivating refrain, it was a stand-out track among many. "Back Of A Car" was another classic, featuring Chilton's jagged vocals and churning riffing. (To anyone who's never heard these tracks or this band: it's absolutely astonishing how contemporary these recordings sound, as though they were laid down last week.)

Lightning struck twice and *Radio City*, despite uniformly positive reviews, again stiffed in the marketplace, largely due to label troubles. Despite the criminal neglect accorded this sterling release, copies of it fell into the right hands. During the 1980s, a host of bands sprang up, among them R.E.M., The Replacements, The Bangles, The dBs, The Posies, and many more: to a man (and woman), all of these groups worshipped at the altar of Chilton and *Radio City*.

Their second straight commercial failure led to predictable self-doubt and turmoil. Big Star suffered another defection, and their next recording, a comparatively less focused affair (titled variously *Third*, *Sister Lovers*, and *Beale Street Blue*) was deemed unsalable at Ardent Records and went unreleased until 1978, by which time the band had long since dissolved. By far the most experimental (if anti-commercial) of their releases, the album was a challenging mix of brutally frank confessionals (comparisons to John's *Plastic Ono Band* are not unwarranted, especially on the song "Holocaust") and covers (Velvet Underground's "Femme Fatale," later recorded by R.E.M., quite likely after the Big Star version). Recordings for what had been intended as a two-record set featuring assorted "guests" came replete with synthesizers, liberal use of echo, feedback; in short, Big Star went straight from *With The Beatles* to *Rubber Soul* to *The Beatles*.

Today, Big Star is regarded as the missing link between the original sixties British Invasion bands and the aforementioned "alternative" acts of a later era. All three of their releases made *Rolling Stone* magazine's list of the 500 greatest albums of all time. (The Beatles themselves, whose output was four times that of Big Star's, placed a mere four albums in the 500.) Their work holds up as fresh and engaging; that they remain all but unknown to the public today is a minor tragedy. A revamped group featuring Chilton, drummer Jody Stephens, and The Posies' Jon Auer and Ken Stringfellow recorded a new album, 2005's *In Space*, and performed live sporadically until Chilton's death at 59 in 2010. 2013 saw the issue of a career-encompassing box set, *Keep an Eye on the Sky*, as well as a documentary film, *Big Star: Nothing Can Hurt Me*.

STACKRIDGE

Picking up at around the same time the Beatles were winding down, Stackridge was an English prog/pop band, though in truth their music defied classification. Over the course of five albums during their initial run, their albums blended elements of folk, psychedelia, classical, English music hall, and old time jazz. Among their contemporaries, they were poppier than Yes, but quirkier than Supertramp.

Their self-titled debut was released in 1971; their final long-player prior to their break-up, *Mr. Mick*, was issued in early 1976. During that career span, they qualified as a cult act, for though they toured relentlessly and appeared on *The Old Grey Whistle Test* in their homeland, they never really sustained any commercial success. In America, they really couldn't get arrested. Part of this was due to a chronic instability, with members coming and going (and sometimes returning). Another was simply that their music didn't really qualify as overtly commercial; a hit single was beyond both their talents *and* interests.

To some, Stackridge was known as "the West Country Beatles." This handle probably didn't help them connect with an audience at all, especially in England, where at that time, the public tended to disdain any perceived Fab pretenders. Stackridge didn't shy away from the comparisons—indeed, they covered "Norwegian Wood" on the very public John Peel BBC radio program, while their albums were steeped in little details and sounds that evoked the Fabs indirectly.

Their debut, *Stackridge*, is notable today for containing a song entitled "Dora The Female Explorer" that was intended to be the basis for a series of

Released in the UK as The Man in the Bowler Hat, Pinafore Days (as Stackridge's third album was retitled here) was produced by George Martin. It was their highest charting album in Britain, and only charting release, stateside.

children's books. Doubtless most people reading this will have some familiarity with the similarly-named television cartoon character (and/or the host of spin-off products) but as far as anyone can tell, the spunky Latina and Stackridge's creation are related only by coincidence. In 1973, the band scored a coup by securing George Martin to produce their third LP, *The Man In The Bowler Hat* (released in America as *Pinafore Days*). It was their highest-charting U.K. release, while barely scraping into the Top Two Hundred in the states. (In between, guitarist Andy Creswell-Davis guested on John's *Imagine* album.)

After a major re-tooling that saw only two (of six) original members left, Stackridge signed with Elton John's Rocket Records and released *Extravaganza*, possibly their most satisfying album, in 1974. Despite the boost of such big-name sponsorship, it too failed to find its commercial niche. A year later, *Mr. Mick*, a concept album on aging, marked their swan song—for a time. Their rampant Beatle-isms on this release took the form of a reggaefied version of "Hold Me Tight"—one the Fabs' most undervalued tunes.

Their break-up was announced in 1977. James Warren and Andy Cresswell-Davis soon after formed The Korgis, who in 1980, achieved something Stackridge never did: a U.S. hit single, "Everybody's Got to Learn Sometime." By the late 1990s, with the Korgis dissolved and

Stackridge history, various groupings of the musicians who'd passed through both bands began reconvening, with a Stackridge live album resulting. In 2006, a CD single appeared under the Korgis' name entitled "Something About The Beatles." It's an apt nod to their collective past and well worth seeking out. Do it now.

THE HUDSON BROTHERS

It is entirely likely that, had they not diverted their career path into a stint or two on television, the Hudsons would be regarded today for what they were: a serious trio of pop craftsmen, steeped in Beatleisms, to be sure, but possessing an energy and tunefulness that stands alongside the best of Badfinger or The Raspberries. Instead, they are likely remembered by most as a bubblegum act that had a kid's TV show. It's the same sort of taint that plagues the Monkees, notwithstanding the fact they were equally talented at both media.

The brothers Hudson discovered music in their native Portland, Oregon in 1964—the same year that the world and its possibilities were changed for an entire generation. Fourteen year-old Bill, the oldest brother (the family name was actually Salerno) and a friend took up guitar and practiced singing harmony together. Already thoroughly enamored of the Beatles, the two were soon joined by thirteen year-old Mark, who himself possessed a wonderful voice and played a mean tambourine. As a trio, the ensemble entertained at parties during high school, calling themselves My Sirs.

Not long after, baby brother Brett conned his way into the group and took up bass, completing the foursome. (He'd been sick and, after they promised him they'd let him play with them if he got better, a miracle cure occurred.) By 1966, My Sirs were one of the Pacific Northwest's top-ranked groups, winning a battle of the bands and drawing notice. An advertising exec employed by Chrysler liked what he saw and took them on as clients, booking them to perform at dealerships and company events around the country. The catch was: they had to change their name to a Chrysler product. For this reason, My Sirs became The New Yorkers.

Already penning their own material by this time, the group released a trio of singles on Scepter Records. The first, "When I'm Gone," made it to *number nine* on the regional charts. The brothers would soon learne a hard lesson about the ways of the music industry after discovering that their manager, having placed all their assets in his name, had robbed them blind to the tune of six figures. The devastating revelation knocked them for a loop, causing the brothers to reconsider their future as they took a year off.

After a change in personnel (Kent Fillmore, the one non-Hudson, was replaced by Bob Haworth), the New Yorkers decided to give it another shot and recorded Harry Nilsson's "I Guess The Lord Must Be In New York City." Decca picked it up, but soon after lost interest, leaving the boys stranded on the East Coast. The boys made it back home, took stock, and decided that a move to Los Angeles would best serve their future. In 1972, they

Trying to balance a comedic TV presence with a respectable pop-rock output would have been a daunting challenge for any act, but in 1974, the Hudson Brothers pulled it off—for a time—as well as anybody could have.

issued an album on Playboy Records entitled *Hudson*. Though not exactly a hit, their well-honed stage act began drawing notice.

In 1973, their manager introduced them to Bernie Taupin, Elton John's lyricist. Both Elton and Bernie were blown away by their music and their charisma, leading to their signing to Elton's Rocket Records (making them label-mates with Stackridge). Taupin himself assumed the production chores on *Totally Out Of Control*, recorded in England and issued that same year. The album was a wonderfully realized pop/rock showcase, displaying their Beatle devotion without being slavish. (The second side even featured an *Abbey Road*-like medley.) A single, the marvelously Brit-pop-ish "If You Really Need Me," fully showcased the Hudson's musical talents but went completely overlooked by radio programmers.

The Hudsons arrived back in the states to discover that television producer Chris Bearde, whom they'd met at a party months before, was interested in securing them for a short-run summer replacement series for the immensely popular *Sonny and Cher Comedy Hour*. After the formality of an audition, *The Hudson Brothers Show* premiered on July 31, 1974. Implementing the same production team as S&C, the show followed the same successful formula, substituting the innately zany personas of the brothers. Like the Beatles in their day, the Hudson's comic interactions also elicited comparisons to the Marx Brothers, making both acts renowned for their humor as much as for their music.

A certified hit, the Hudsons segued seamlessly from the summer stint straight into their own series aimed at younger viewers on Saturday mornings. *The Hudson Brothers Razzle Dazzle Show* commenced on CBS on September 7 (the same day as the first Beatlefest, with which brother Mark would one day be inextricably associated). Featuring an array of shtick and cast regulars (Fabulous Freddie; Rod Hull and Emu; The Bear; announcer Gary Owens), the show was nothing less than an adolescent version of *Laugh-In*, with a dose of music thrown in.

In the minds of the public, the perceived *Laugh-In* connection gave them their most enduring musical hit. Bill was dating one of *that* show's cast members, the relentlessly bubbly Goldie Hawn. But it was Mark that would pen and sing lead on a song believed by many to have been inspired by her, "So You Are A Star." (This has been disputed through the years.) Released as a single (from the album *Hollywood Situation*), the eerily Lennon-esque piano ballad peaked at twenty-one, making them a genuine national chart success at last. As for Bill and Goldie, they would marry in 1976, producing actress Kate Hudson and actor Oliver Hudson, before splitting in 1980.

The Hudson Brothers scored a couple more hits (1975's "Rendezvous," co-written with Beach Boy Bruce Johnston) and "Lonely School Year" before their charting career faded. As for *Razzle Dazzle*, it lasted seventeen episodes in all, but continued airing in repeats for another three years. (In 2008, the much-loved series was at last released on DVD.)

The Hudsons parlayed their hard-earned connections into the ex-Fab's inner circle. They met all four during the seventies and indeed, hung out with their hero John Lennon (who dubbed them "the Kings of Saturday morning") during the Los Angeles epoch. They were present on the night of the infamous Smothers Brothers/Troubadour incident; a fonder memory came one time at Harry Nilsson's house when John serenaded them with an impromptu 5AM performance of "In My Life," played on a battery-powered piano.

In later years, Mark—the most high-profiled of the group—spearheaded Ringo's latter-day recording renaissance as his producer/

collaborator, revitalizing the drummer's gifts and giving him the confidence to generate a string of really fine releases. (Unfortunately, a business conflict derailed the friendship in 2006.) He also co-wrote Aerosmith's Grammy-winning smash, "Livin' On The Edge," and remains a popular guest at The Fest For Beatles Fans.

Brett stayed busy with Frozen Pictures, a production company. In 2008, his documentary on the life and times of Bonzo Rutle Neil Innes debuted, entitled *The Seventh Python*; a similar project on one-time Beatles tour mate Chris Montez is likewise in the works. The oldest Hudson, Bill, penned a memoir entitled *Two Versions: The Other Side of Fame and Family* in 2011, detailing his failed first marriage and disappointment with his children.

KLAATU

No, of course they weren't the Beatles. But that didn't stop the spread of the most widespread Beatle conspiracy theory since Paul had died. Just as *that* rumor got going courtesy of DJ Russ Gibbs, the suggestion that—once again—clues were being planted to convey something important through an album got started by a journalist with the *Providence Journal*. And as before, Capitol Records did exactly nothing to stop it.

Klaatu's story begins in the early seventies. Musicians John Woloschuk and Dee Long made an arrangement with producer Terry Brown at Toronto Sound recording studios, where Woloschuk worked, wherein the duo was given a blank check to use the facilities during any downtime between paying clients. Dubbed Klaatu (after Michael Rennie's character—an interplanetary visitor—in the sci-fi classic, *The Day The Earth Stood Still*), they released their first single, "Hanus of Uranus," backed with "Sub-Rosa Subway" on the now-defunct GRT Records in 1973. A second single, "Dr. Marvello" followed, but neither release drew much attention.

Drummer Terry Draper joined in 1974 as the singles continued to flow. Meanwhile, their manager was actively working on securing a major record deal. By the time he'd made his breakthrough, Klaatu made the fateful decision to, in the name of letting the music do the talking, maintain anonymity. No interviews, no touring, not even the public release of their identities. Of all the labels to have cut a deal with them it was Capitol—the *Beatles'* label—that agreed to those terms and inked a contract with Klaatu.

Klaatu was released in August 1976—hitting the streets almost exactly between the in-store dates of Capitol's *Rock 'n' Roll Music* compilation and *Ringo's Rotogravure* on Atlantic (in Canada and elsewhere, Klaatu's LP debut was titled *3:47 EST*). The album was comprised of remixes of their singles-issued material (although their debut was now re-titled "Anus of Uranus"—nice), plus some new recordings, among them the opening cut, "Calling Occupants" (covered a year later by, of all people, The Carpenters). The album itself was a pleasing mix of psychedelic/progressive pop, featuring layered effects, adroit production, and unmistakable traces of the 1967 Beatles influence. (So too did ELO, though the two bands sounded nothing like each other.)

Lacking anything in the way of a promotional effort from the unnamed individuals comprising the band, *Klaatu* sank, generating little notice from anyone. The trio flew to England to begin work on their follow-up, entitled *Hope*, that autumn. But in February the following year—out of nowhere—the album suddenly exploded. Steven Smith, a reporter with the *Providence Journal* by-lined an article entitled "Could Klaatu Be The Beatles? Mystery is a Magical Mystery Tour." By releasing an album that lacked explicit songwriting and production credits, as well as the conspicuous absence of any individual names anywhere in the packaging, the band had unwittingly enabled the imaginations of Beatle-starved conspiracy-minded folks to run wild.

On the basis of Smith's article, plus similar chatter on Hartford, Connecticut radio station WDRC, the rumor that the Beatles had reunited and were calling themselves Klaatu took root and spread like wildfire. Inquiries to Capitol and Klaatu's management were met with open-ended non-denials that stopped just short of lying. But those attempting to bolster their case were armed with an array of "clues," each more asinine than the one before it; among them:

1. The album was issued on Capitol, the Beatles' once and future label.
2. On the cover of Ringo's *Goodnight Vienna* album, his face is superimposed over actor Michael Rennie's in a still from *The Day The Earth Stood Still*. Rennie, of course, played the character whose extraterrestrial name was Klaatu.
3. The first album (and all that followed) featured an image of the sun on the cover, as if it were Klaatu's logo. The Egyptian sun god's name was Ra; reverse the two letters and one is left with A R – the initials of the Fabs' last recorded album.
4. *Abbey Road*, of course, featured "Here Comes The Sun" and "Sun

King," so Klaatu's use would be merely reinforcing an existing motif. The latter tune began with the sound of crickets chirping, as does the *Klaatu* album—picking up where they left off?

5. Side one's closing track, "Sub-Rosa Subway" features the most overtly McCartney-sounding lead vocal. Was the song's title a play on Paul's *Red Rose Speedway*?

6. That same song mentions New York City and Washington D.C., in that order. These were the first two cities that the Beatles had played on American soil—in that order.

7. As the above named track's final seconds play out, a Morse code-like beeping is heard, said by some to translate to *some* relevant message (along the lines of "It's us!").

Fueling the nonsense, some radio stations began dedicating weekends to airing the Klaatu album alongside Beatle material, encouraging listeners to chime in with their opinions, one way or another. Recognizing a good thing when they saw it, Capitol stepped up production of the dead-in-the-water release (while postponing the issue of *Hope*). They also made a point of disseminating Smith's article. Within a year of its release, Klaatu had gone from nowhere to selling anywhere between a quarter and half a million copies, all on the strength of a rumor.

The band itself, just returned from England in early 1977, had heard nothing of the ongoing mythmaking (although *New Musical Express* had headlined a story on the phenomenon: "Deaf idiot journalist starts Beatle rumour"). Given their bent toward privacy and the desires of their label—having seen their debut resurrected from the dead—Klaatu went about their business and let the story play itself out. This it did, once some enterprising soul went to the trouble of looking up Klaatu's compositional copyrights at the Library of Congress and saw the names associated with the group, thus bringing the buzz to an end. The whole tawdry tale was summed up by *Rolling Stone* as "Hype of the Year."

All drummed-up hysteria aside, the music itself was hardly an embarrassment. To anyone listening objectively, the Beatleisms were no more than those of any other act that developed in their wake. Possibly the debut's strongest track, "California Jam," bore no obvious Fabness whatsoever. But by the time *Hope* was issued in the fall of 1977, the brand had been damaged. Despite near-universal glowing reviews, a backlash against the band resulted in poor sales.

Klaatu went on to issue two more Capitol albums: *Sir Army Suit* in 1978, followed by *Endangered Species* in 1980. Their swan song, *Magentalane*, was released in Canada in 1981. For their final LP, their images were at last included on the jacket; also, the band followed its release with their first ever tour. By now, Klaatu was solidly a niche act—perhaps where they should have been in the first place. Their shows received positive reviews, but perhaps weary of the ups and downs, they called it quits not long after. As a final footnote, a one-off reunion in 1988 generated one new tune: utilizing a title already used by both Paul (in 1966) and John (in 1980), the song was called "Woman."

BAY CITY ROLLERS

For a time around 1976, there were those who should have known better that went around stirring up what became known as "Rollermania," further asserting that this Scottish quintet was nothing less than the "New Beatles." At this late a date, it's probably hard for readers who weren't of age in the mid-seventies to understand all the fuss about an unremarkable group of popsters whose recorded output was nothing special, much less in the Fabs' league. But if "mania" is measured in the mass of pre-pubescent screamers, then the Bay City Rollers did indeed give the Beatles a run for their money.

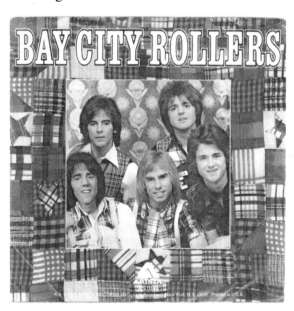

Formed in 1967 as The Saxons, the band's rhythm section was comprised of brothers Alan (bass) and Derek (drums) Longmuir. One Nobby Clark was on vocals, while the other two slots were filled by a series of transitional members who came and went. (Among them were David Paton and Billy Lyall, both of whom— as members of Pilot—

Like many a bubblegum phenomenon, the long term effects of "Rollermania" are non-existent. Even their few halfway decent tracks have been completely shut out of contemporary oldies radio play lists.

scored a hit in 1975 with "Magic" before joining the Alan Parsons Project.) Early on, the band recognized that their name might be too limiting, being so English sounding, so, as the famous story goes, they arbitrarily stuck a pin in a map of the U.S., coming up with Bay City, Michigan on their second try and then adding "Rollers." (The first shot yielded Arkansas, a place name that they divined would do them little good.)

Under the management auspices of Tom Paton, the band began generating a buzz around Edinburgh as the new decade began. Apparent already was that, irrespective of the music, BCR were drawing loads of screaming girls to their gigs. Indeed, Bell Records exec Dick Leahy signed them not because of their sound, which he deemed irrelevant, but because of the reaction their appearances drew. English pop impresario Jonathan "Everyone's Gone To The Moon" King, who'd produced the first Genesis album, was teamed with the band in the studio for the recording of their debut single, a remake of The Gentrys' "Keep on Dancing," which peaked at nine in the U.K. in late 1971.

Over the next couple of years, their hit-making abilities proved rather inconsistent. After adding Eric Faulkner and Stuart "Woody" Wood, the band released the anthemic "Saturday Night" as a U.K. single—it did not chart. Nobby Clark quit in frustration at their inability to sustain their success, to be succeeded by Les McKeown. The changeover actually resulted in several more Top Ten singles in the U.K., and by 1975, BCR were among the top-selling acts of Britain.

Privately, the band had been chafing at both the material they'd had foisted upon them and the marketing that brought them sales at the cost of respect. Most of their recordings had been cut with session musicians, and at long last, as things were peaking career-wise, BCR pulled a Monkees: chucking the production team that had brought them so much success and assuming all recording duties themselves. One of the first results of their newfound autonomy was the edgier "Money Honey," which became their second American hit.

Clive Davis, head of Arista (their American label), decided that breaking the band in the U.S. would be a top priority. He began laying the groundwork for recreating the same brainless adulation that accompanied their every move on their native continent. Soon, tartan patterns and the band's five well-scrubbed faces began appearing regularly in the teen magazines on this side of the pond. By the time their debut Arista single was launched in the U.S. in the fall of 1975, the audience for BCR had been primed. The two-year old "Saturday Night" was dusted off and, with a live remote performance airing on Howard Cosell's short-lived *Saturday Night Live* show (no relation to the concurrent NBC *Saturday Night*, as it was then called), Rollermania was ignited in the states. By January 1976, "Saturday Night" had hit number one.

Though they never again reached the top slot in America, they did manage to sustain a respectable string of Top Forty singles, including a remake of Dusty Springfield's "I Only Want To Be With You," "Rock N Roll Love Letter," and lastly, 1977's "You Made Me Believe In Magic." Alan Longmuir departed, leaving the band a four-piece by the time they followed the path of so many fancies of the moment and got their own brief television series, which bizarrely paired them with renowned little person, Billy Barty. 'Twas the seventies, folks.

The overwork and general stress associated with being a teen idol took its toll on the individual members. Both Alan Longmuir and Eric Faulkner attempted suicide at the height of Rollermania (though the latter insists that his incident was merely an accidental overdose). While onstage in Japan in 1979, McKeown and Faulkner got into a fistfight that resulted in the singer's departure from the group. In recent years, McKeown was acquitted on charges of drug trafficking, while drummer Derek Longmuir was found guilty of possession of child pornography. Most recently the members of the band's most successful iteration were in court, suing their management and record companies, alleging that they'd been cheated out of millions.

SQUEEZE

Perhaps the second best known English songwriting team in rock (does anyone really think of Jagger-Richards in those terms?), Chris Difford and Glen Tilbrook of Squeeze were/are widely-regarded as the natural successors to Lennon-McCartney. In point of fact, theirs was a truer collaboration than John and Paul's typically was, with Tilbrook supplying the melodies (and nearly always, the lead vocals) to Difford's witty, dry, and inescapably British prose. The two, along with keyboardist Jools Holland, formed the backbone of Squeeze in 1974.

The band chose their name (in a bit of irony) as a "tribute" to the album of the same name released by New York's legendary Velvet Underground in 1973; with all the group's mainstays departed by the time of the recording, celebrating their most unrepresentative album would be the equivalent of someone paying similar homage to The Doors' *Other Voices* or CCR's *Mardi Gras*. The VU association with Squeeze continued when the band hired the Velvets' co-founder John Cale to produce their self-titled debut in 1978. (In the U.S., the album was dubbed *U.K. Squeeze* to avoid a conflict with the now-forgotten band, Tight Squeeze.)

Their debut contained the rather unique sounding "Take Me I'm Yours," which featured Tilbrook's sharp tenor paired with Difford's baritone growl to create a third voice (much like the fusion of Lindsey Buckingham's and Christine McVie's singing). The song

Squeeze's 1980 single, "Another Nail in My Heart" was a great example of their spot-on pop instincts, presented with a suitably cynical modern sensibility.

landed them firmly in the U.K.'s Top Twenty while doing nothing at all in the states. At this stage of their career, Squeeze—like labelmates The Police around the same time—were not shy about exploiting the dying embers of punk, taking to presenting themselves as one with their audience via safety pins and other punk trappings. (They later would profess a complete disdain for the genre.)

Indeed, what Squeeze did best in the best post-Beatles tradition was offer up meticulously crafted pop, welding a love of observational wordplay with hooks that were sure to make Paul jealous. The endlessly inventive Jools Holland helped color their instrumental texture, while onstage, drummer Gilson Lavis drove the band with an energy that certainly emulated the punks in spirit. Their hit singles streak continued in England with the title track to their follow-up, "Cool for Cats" (croaked by Difford) and "Up the Junction" (a soap opera set to music).

Following relentless touring, 1980 saw the release of their most fully realized album to date, *Argybargy*. It featured the hits "Another Nail In My Heart" and "Pulling Mussels (From The Shell)," songs that actually received some airplay on the more cutting-edge radio stations in America. Despite the upward trending career-wise, Holland quit around this time to start a band built around his boogie-woogie piano stylings, The Millionaires.

Despite the Lennon-McCartney handle, Difford and Tilbrook soldiered on, recruiting former Ace ("How Long") keyboardist/vocalist Paul

214

Carrack for their 1981 album, *East Side Story*. (It's Carrack's voice heard handling most of the vocals on their U.S. breakthrough single, "Tempted." He would soon depart for a solo career and vocal duty with Genesis' Mike Rutherford's side band, Mike + The Mechanics.) As originally conceived, *East* was to be a double album, with each side featuring a different producer: Elvis Costello; Dave Edmunds; Nick Lowe: and Paul McCartney. Suffice to say, this did not happen.

After dissolving in 1982 following a *Saturday Night Live* "farewell" appearance, the band went their separate ways until a 1985 reformation, which featured Holland. Since then, the "Squeeze" brand has been applied to whomever Difford and Tilbrook play with. As a final Beatle note, Holland—by the 1990s a well-established fixture on the tube in Britain—was chosen to act as unseen interviewer for much of the Beatles *Anthology* documentary. In 2002, he turned in a well-received performance, backing singer Sam Brown at the *Concert For George* event with a rendition of George's final recording, "Horse To The Water" (which appeared on Holland's *Small World Big Band* release).

THE KNACK

In 1970, a trio of Detroit teenagers calling themselves Sky recorded an album for RCA entitled *Don't Hold Back*. Their sound was very T. Rex-ish, almost glam. What was remarkable about the otherwise none too impressive debut was its pedigree: Sky was signed to Rolling Stone producer Jimmy Miller's production company, though Miller himself did not handle the chores, due to a scheduling conflict. Instead, Gary Wright manned the board at the London sessions, which included contributions from horn players Bobby Keys and Jim Price. Despite the big names supporting the group of unknowns, the album bombed—reviews and all. (It couldn't have helped that a song was cited on the jacket as "unsuitable for broadcast purposes"—the portentously titled "How's That Treatin' Your Mouth, Babe?")

Another album, *Sailor's Delight*, followed in 1971, but it too failed to make an impression. (This release featured drummer Rob Stawinski—a year later, he would sit in for Badfinger's Mike Gibbins on their American tour.) The trio split and their lead singer/songwriter, Doug Fieger, eventually made his way to L.A. When next heard from, he was frontman/bassist with an outfit called Sunset Bombers. They released one album for Ariola in 1978 before dissolving, laying the groundwork for his successful shot at the brass ring, The Knack.

Though Doug Fieger's much better known Knack elicited endless (and groundless) Beatle comparisons, his earlier act had a direct connection to the Rolling Stones, via producer Jimmy Miller.

Supported by lead guitarist Berton Averre, bassist Prescott Niles, and seasoned pro drummer Bruce Gary, Fieger's Knack represented the most successful attempt yet at encapsulating the freshness and energy of the Beatles initial launch in America. Embodying the so-called New Wave "skinny tie" ethos, the group signed with Capitol, opting to use the exact same label configuration employed in the mid-sixties. Further, their 1979 debut, *Get The Knack*, featured on the front cover a black and white group portrait, recalling the look of *With The Beatles*, while the rear jacket sported a shot of the group in performance mode on a television soundstage, evoking *A Hard Day's Night*. (The irony was that the only Beatles resemblances were purely external; musically, The Knack had far more in common with early Who or Kinks than they did the Fabs.)

Among American rock journalists at least, such blatant Beatle aping rubbed many the wrong way. (No such problem in England, where in the 1990s Oasis made a career of it.) The group's policy of not giving interviews to the press, dictated by their management, proved disastrous. Instead of a mystique, it generated antipathy, directed at the band generally and leader Doug Fieger particularly. (As Dave Marsh characterized him in *Rolling Stone*: "...in every photo I've ever seen of him, he's either smirking or about to.")

Most of this critical animosity mattered not to the masses who flocked to buy the group's first single, "My Sharona." Powered by Gary's cracking drums and Averre's muscular riffing, the song came like a bolt out of the blue to rock fans longing for something—*anything*— that wasn't disco and wasn't powered by synthesizers. "Sharona" was a throwback to the sixties (indeed, buoyed by a lick that stopped short of completely boosting the Spencer Davis Group's "Gimme Some Lovin'") while sounding not the least bit dated. It made number one in late summer of '79, staying atop the charts for six weeks before the market reverted to form with Robert John's tepid ballad, "Sad Eyes."

The follow-up single, "Good Girls Don't," generated attention and airplay too (that is, in the cleaned-up version that removed some unsavory lyrics), but it was here that the pushback began, with charges of misogyny. That Fieger's lyrics were unmistakably lascivious (if not downright puerile) was undeniable, but the very critics who fell over themselves in praise of the Rolling Stones' *Some Girls* a year earlier now had the knives out for Fieger and crew. While the band had been the kings of L.A.'s Sunset Strip, an artist up in San Francisco launched the "Knuke the Knack" movement, selling "kits" complete with a t-shirt and button. The backlash had begun.

Less than a year after *Get The Knack* dropped, a second album appeared in early 1980. Clearly responding to the growing ill will, the LP was defensively titled *"...but the little girls understand"* and featured a star-struck female fan gazing adoringly up at an unseen onstage performer. Defiantly, the lead-off single, a "Sharona" re-write entitled "Baby Talks Dirty" encapsulated beautifully every tendency that drove critics up the wall: their juvenile view of sexuality; the bombastic lack of subtlety; and Fieger's grating panting. The album was soon cut-out bound, despite bearing a few pleasing cuts like "I

Want Ya" that almost no one heard.

After so many years of toiling, it seemed that Fieger's meteoric career with the Knack was ready to come crashing down. (Or as The Clash had asserted on the title track of *London Calling*, their remarkable two-record set the year before: phony Beatlemania *had* bitten the dust.) But the group had sold a few records, so their Capitol two-album deal was extended by one. The writing on the wall and his career on the line, Fieger's writing for their third album, the prophetically named *Round Trip*, displayed a posture never before heard on a Knack record: humility. Realizing perhaps that the joyride was about over and their heyday was slipping away, some songs reflected upon the capriciousness of fame, especially "Another Lousy Day In Paradise." Others seemed to ask for their detractors to suspend judgment and give them another chance.

It's a shame that 1981's *Round Trip* bombed so badly, for it contained far and away the most ambitious material the group would ever record. From the horn-driven verve of "Lil' Cal's Big Mistake" to the psychedelia of "We Are Waiting," the album rewarded repeated listenings. Also notable was the band's forgoing the services of producer Mike Chapman (The Sweet, Blondie), who possibly didn't endear himself to his charges with his liner notes to their second release, describing the contents as "an assortment of feelings expressed redundantly as only The Knack can".

Instead, Jack Douglas, fresh off the comeback triumph of *Double Fantasy*, did the honors. (Early on in the sessions, he pulled Fieger aside to let him know how much John was a fan of *Get The Knack*.) Not long before the recording began, both men's worlds were shattered— Douglas's irrevocably—by the murder of Lennon. By way of catharsis, he plunged into the work, resulting in his most layered and nuanced project to date. As for Fieger, he channeled his grief and bewilderment into a lyrical elegy: "Sweet Dreams," a sort of son of "I'm Only Sleeping" that paid tribute while attempting to come to grips with the insanity of what had transpired.

The album's poor reception, internal battles between Fieger and Bruce, and the standard chemical abuse issues fragmented the band, as they called it quits on New Years Day 1982. Twelve years later, the group experienced a second career wind, due to "My Sharona" re-entering the charts unexpectedly (following its use in the film *Reality Bites*). A re-tooled Knack re-formed—minus Gary (who had since died)—and went on to record several more well-received albums. While nowhere near the wild success enjoyed in 1979, apparently all was forgiven at last. Their last new collection of tunes, *Normal as the Next Guy*, was released in September 2001; Fieger died of cancer at 57 on Valentine's Day 2010.

WINGS

For a while in the 1970s, especially after Paul's triumphant *Wings Over America* tour, the joke going around was: "Did you know that Paul McCartney was in a band *before* Wings?" (Another less savory witticism went: "What do you call a pig with wings? Linda.") Beneath the feeble attempt at irony was the greater point that as his Fab Four past was receding into history, Wings had become one of the hottest-selling bands around, and maybe some of Wings' fans were unaware of his past. Though Paul certainly expressed his belief that his current band would never outshine his past one, he just as surely must have recognized that perversely, for some Beatle fans, Wings' high profile successes filled the void created by their collective absence.

Paul certainly avoided direct comparisons with his old band as Wings prepared for launch, purposely steering clear of performing any Beatle material in their sets for as long as possible, despite the inevitable clamor for it. (Not until 1975, after three years of performing live, did five Beatle songs—Paul songs, to be sure—creep into the set.) He *did* regularly perform "Long Tall Sally," a cover long associated with him during the Beatle years—and in fact the last song the group ever played to a paying audience. (Had John been as proactive about entertaining in concert as Paul, would he would have similarly performed "Twist and Shout"? George *did* resurrect "Roll Over Beethoven" during his Japanese sojourn with Eric Clapton.)

But try as Paul might to avoid apples and oranges comparisons to the Fabs, his ex-bandmates did not. When asked about the fans flocking to his shows in 1974, wanting a taste of "Beatle George," Hari Georgeson snapped "If they want to do that, they can go and see Wings. Why live in the past?" In so responding, George was explicitly making the case that anyone nostalgic for his previous incarnation would be satisfied by Paul's latest offerings.

John was even more blunt. In his 1980 *Playboy* interview, he derided the fans, Paul, and the Rolling Stones in one fell swoop: "They want to hold on to something they never had in the first place…They're just jacking off to—it could be anybody: Mick Jagger or somebody else. Let them go jack off to Mick Jagger, okay?…Let them chase Wings… Go play with Rolling Wings."

All snark aside, Paul himself was quite willing to re-write his past when it suited him. For all of the uproar in 2002 when he reversed the Lennon-McCartney credits on his live album, *Back In The U.S.*, most people overlooked the fact that he had already done this before—in 1977. For the *Wings Over America* release, all McCartney-penned Beatle material was credited as McCartney-Lennon—in John Lennon's lifetime (though it's doubtful that the self-proclaimed househusband would have paid it any mind at all).

Despite their overall popularity, Wings' ups and downs in public favor never successfully made Beatle fans stop wishing for a reunion. For his part, Paul would increasingly attempt to placate them by shuffling the set-list to include fresh Fab material. Though he could never escape the shadow of "Yesterday" (he dared not drop that song), he did keep things interesting by performing at Wings' final tour "Got To Get You Into My Life" (a smart move, given Earth, Wind, and Fire's recent hit version); and "Let It Be" (which made sense in that both he and Linda performed on the original).

The late Barry Feinstein's photography was the perfect fit for the mood and music George Harrison presented his first time out.

CHAPTER 12

YOU THINK YOU'RE A GROOVE: ALBUM PACKAGING

A s the CD era gives way to the download years, memories of what were the glory days of album packaging recede further into the past. As usual, it was the Beatles during the 1960s who led the way in elevating the pop/rock album jacket design to art, with groundbreaking images such as the ones that graced *With The Beatles*, *Rubber Soul*, *Revolver*, and of course, *Sgt. Pepper's* expanding the ways that the physical wrapping of one's music was approached.

By the following decade, presentation had developed into big business as far as LPs were concerned, and with a 12" square template to work from, artists ranging from Andy Warhol (the Velvet Underground's first long player; *Sticky Fingers* by the Rolling Stones) to Roger Dean (almost every Yes album) explored the medium, issuing graphic statements that sometimes drew as much notice as the musical contents housed within. Any number of iconic images released on LP jackets during those glory years (such as Pink Floyd's *Dark Side of the Moon* or Supertramp's *Breakfast In America*) exist today in our collective memory as indelible evocations of the era.

While no albums issued by the ex-Beatles during the seventies rise to the level in design of say, *Sgt. Pepper's* as cultural touchstones per se, the four of them nonetheless put much care into their packaging. Long past the point where a simple Robert Freeman image would do the trick, their individual choices graphically reflect the ways in which they saw themselves – and how they wished the public to see them.

MCCARTNEY (1970)

The former Linda Eastman made a name for herself with her camera, documenting famous musicians of the late sixties at work and play. Despite the assertion of many that it was a role she should have stayed in, she did of course largely abandon her work in the name of providing musical moral support to her husband in his post-Beatles career. But a final dose of her indisputable talents before reinvention as a keyboardist came with the arrival of Paul's solo debut, in effect providing the sugarcoating to what was undoubtedly a bitter pill for millions of fans

223

to swallow: the disintegration of the Fab Four.

McCartney arrived graced with a stark cover photo depicting some scattered cherries and a bowl (containing some red juice, suggesting that the cherries had spilt), framed by blackness on either side. Given the context of the release—the break-up of the Beatles, apparently McCartney-instigated—fans looked for symbolism, as they'd long been conditioned to do. The best anyone could make of it was: life is just a bowl of cherries (as the old song went), and now the bowl had been upset. Whether or not that had been the intent is unknown; it's just as likely that Linda and her ever-aware eye simply captured what she conceived as a striking visual and nothing more.

It would be the last album released by Paul (or Wings) for five years *not* to feature his image on the front. On the back, however, was the well-known shot taken of a smiling, bearded Macca, an ex-Beatle in all but public declaration, cradling his infant daughter Mary within his jacket. The image spoke volumes about where his priorities now lie: if his last released album of newly-recorded material featured him walking away from his place of work—eyes closed—into an unknown future, *McCartney* showed him firmly and happily immersed in what has frequently been termed "cozy domesticity."

Lest anyone miss the point, the inner spread featured an array of Linda's pictures depicting home and family in a variety of settings. (One shot was re-used in 1997 on the cover of his classical *Standing Stone* release, just months before she succumbed to cancer. It's a minor irony that the same photo bookended her husband's solo work for the duration of her lifetime.) Both daughters, Heather and Mary are shown, as well as Linda and Martha, the sheepdog. Only one shot actually depicts Paul as a musician.

ALL THINGS MUST PASS (1970)

If there were a single word to characterize the issue of George Harrison's debut as an artist in his own right, it could be "gravitas." *All Things Must Pass* was a serious statement, with very nearly every song a sermon on one topic or another. The weighty contents of the staggering collection of eighteen new Harrisongs (plus a bonus disc of superstar jamming) warranted the elaborate yet dignified packaging that fans received, echoing the deluxe treatment accorded (in the U.K. at least) the *Let It Be* release earlier that year.

The late photographer Barry Feinstein was recruited to shoot the cover image. While he's esteemed for his close association with Bob

Dylan, having shot the cover to 1963's *The Times They Are a-Changin'* as well as documentary photos of Dylan's historic 1966 British tour, his list of credits is long and impressive. The original graffiti-slopped lavatory photo for the Rolling Stones' *Beggar's Banquet* was his; Feinstein also shot the cover of Janis Joplin's *Pearl* one day before she overdosed.

Feinstein spent several days at Friar Park as George's guest. He would later describe him as a "nice, easy human being…very giving, very honest." As was frequently the case where a Beatle was concerned, serendipity placed everyone in the right place at the right time: during Feinstein's stay, George received a phone call from someone who had located gnomes that had been stolen from the estate a hundred years earlier, asking if he wanted to buy them back. George agreed, and when the two men saw them where they'd been dropped on the lawn, Feinstein exclaimed, "There's your cover!" Without moving a thing, he simply placed George on a stool within the grouping of statuary, clad in his gardening gear, and snapped a few frames. Said Feinstein later: "It was spontaneous."

Other photos taken at Friar Park included some of George through a window; one of these was used on the picture sleeve to "My Sweet Lord." Another showed him playing guitar, high up in Friar Park's highest tower—this was issued in the U.S. for the "What Is Life" sleeve (as well as part of an elaborate poster commissioned but not used). The most haunting of the images Feinstein captured was a rather shadowy shot of George, backlit against a window in a narrow stairway, wearing a hat (the same one he's *not* wearing on the *Hey Jude* album jacket). This one was included in the *All Things Must Pass* package as a poster.

All of the album's lyrics were presented on the inner sleeves, while the two records of song were pressed on vinyl sporting an *orange* apple. (The "Apple Jam" disc came with a label designed by Tom Wilkes, Feinstein's partner in Camouflage Productions.) Despite the nearly overwhelming scale of the release and the almost dauntingly dignified impression conveyed to record buyers by the packaging, *All Things Must Pass* became a runaway success upon its release.

Less than impressed—at least outwardly—by the magnitude of George's achievement was John. He happened upon it during a visit to Friar Park (to see Klaus Voormann while George was out, as it happened). Revealing a resentment that went back at least as far as the *Let It Be* sessions (wherein George was presenting high-quality compositions almost daily while John struggled through writer's block), he reportedly told Klaus "He (George) must be fucking mad, putting

225

three records out. And look at the picture on the front, he looks like an asthmatic Leon Russell." Seeing his ex-bandmate grouped among the *four* gnomes, Lennon was convinced that some sort of statement was being made—and he didn't like it. Observed George: "There was a lot of negativity going down."

Thirty years after its issue, as his final public act before succumbing to cancer, George released a remastered edition of the set on compact disc (while noting his struggle against the impulse to re-mix the entire release). For the re-presentation of his most acclaimed work, he offered an alternate cover shot, newly colorized. As a biting commentary on how the world had changed since 1970, he had a pair of artists from a contemporary design group (Wherefore Art?) add the fixtures of modern-day encroachment to the background: skyscrapers, smoke belching nuclear power plant towers, a highway ramp, jets, and so forth.

JOHN LENNON/PLASTIC ONO BAND (1970)

After four collaborative solo albums with his wife, John was at last ready to properly launch his solo career by late 1970. With inspiration drawn from Yoko, his group's break-up, "primal scream" therapy, and his relationship with the world, *John Lennon/Plastic Ono Band* was the edgiest musical statement John would ever make, marrying his rock sensibility to raw emotions and deeply personal observations. As a result, while it took him far past what was regarded as the outer edge of commerciality, it also gave him deep satisfaction as the most artistically truthful work he'd ever produced.

Issued alongside it was Yoko's concurrently recorded solo LP debut. As companion volumes, the couple wanted the two releases to be regarded as a matching set. This was achieved with near-identical jacket images, photographed (on a Kodak Instamatic) by Dan Richter, a friend of the Lennons. Taken on the grounds of their Tittenhurst Park estate, John's cover shot depicts him reclining on Yoko against a large tree, while Yoko's album features the pose reversed, with her leaning against John. (Unless examined closely by would-be record buyers, it was quite possible to purchase the opposite release by mistake, despite the childhood images on the back cover—this may have been their intent.)

Richter is a most interesting fellow in his own right. For four years, he worked alongside the Lennons, mostly assisting in the production of their various film projects, notably *Imagine* (the video album) While fans may know him from his appearance in the 1988 documentary

Imagine: John Lennon (Richter is seen when the bewildered American fan shows up at their home), or 2006's *The U.S. vs. John Lennon*, he is—in the words of author Arthur C. Clark—"the most famous unknown actor in the world." A mime by trade during the 1960s, Richter was hired by director Stanley Kubrick to choreograph the opening "Dawn of Man" sequence in *2001: A Space Odyssey*. He ended up (uncredited) as the lead primate, "Moonwatcher," who hurls the bone skyward in a cinematic moment known to millions. Dan's memoir, *The Dream is Over*, was published in 2010.

JL/POB came with a stark inner sleeve containing the lyrics to the songs, along with some sparse credits ("Yoko: wind"). The two F-bombs in "Working Class Hero" were replaced with asterisks tartly noting "Omitted at the insistence of E.M.I." A dedication (to Yoko) was also inscribed, dated October 9, 1970—John's thirtieth birthday (and the day he saw his father for the last time). For the first time on a Lennon release, John departed from custom by issuing a plain white apple on the label.

RAM (1971)

The rather home-made looking sleeve design of *McCartney*'s follow-up belied the magnificently produced music found within. *Ram* represented a return to the full studio sheen realized on *Abbey Road*. If the critics were underwhelmed by his debut's rough-hewn sound, perhaps

If anything, the outward presentation of Ram was even more homemade-looking (which it was) than that for the McCartney album. The music inside was anything but: despite the mixed signals, the album spawned a number one single, while stopping just shy of the top on the LP chart.

they could get behind his doing what he did best, Macca must have reasoned. Unfortunately, the Fabs' errant bassist seemed to be getting judged by rock journalists more for his courtroom actions than by his musical output in 1971.

Reinforcing the homespun country life meme planted with his previous release, Paul was shown on the cover of his second album taking the sheep by the horns—literally. Though heretofore not yet the activist vegetarian he would one day become, the cover image certainly planted the seeds for the public's eventual identification of Macca with animal rights issues—a theme amplified in the title tune to his next release.

The *Ram* cover was a joint Paul-Linda effort, as was the album itself so credited. Using Linda's photo of him as a starting point, Paul then embellished it with markers (primarily yellow), creating patterned doodles around the borders and a couple of childlike sketches apropos of nothing. Less random were the initials "L.I.L.Y." subtly inked in within the right-hand border, standing for (wait for it!) "Linda I love you."

Subtlety was cast to the winds with the selection of two photos affixed to the rear cover. Alongside the expected McCartney family portrait was a close-up of one beetle performing actual buggery upon another. (It didn't take an entomologist to figure out what the couple was signaling here.) Never one to let a slight pass—real or imagined—Lennon took the visual cue, along with the lyrics of several cuts, as the provocation they were doubtlessly intended as. As the late Nicholas Schaffner once noted: "Give Peace A Chance" notwithstanding, one tangled with John Lennon at one's own risk—something Paul had apparently forgotten.

IMAGINE (1971)

After getting some personal issues off his chest, John was at last ready to produce a more audience-friendly follow-up to his official debut. *Imagine* ran the gamut from gentle, string-laden ballads to gritty guitar-driven rock. Though its title tune stalled at number three, it still proved to be his best-performing single in over a year, while the album itself ended up topping the charts.

The packaging continued, in a fashion, the pastoral mood established with its predecessor. Designed by Yoko, the front echoed Iain MacMillan's *Live Peace In Toronto* cloud motif, this time overlaying a ghostly Polaroid image of John (purportedly taken by Andy Warhol and uncredited) upon it. Clouds seemed to be an ongoing theme with the Lennons: the back cover bore a 1963 Yoko quote ("Imagine the clouds are dripping—dig a hole in your garden to put them in"), while John himself evoked like imagery ("In the middle of a cloud I call your name") lyrically.

The same cloud shot on the front cover was reprised on the back, this time with a profile image of John placed backside down on the bottom edge, as though he were lying on the ground and gazing skyward ("Above us only sky"). Nine years later, in the wake of her husband's murder, Yoko used this image in the video produced for "Woman," juxtaposing it with the infamous post-mortem shot of John published on the cover of the *National Enquirer* (horrifying Beatle fans everywhere).

While the inner sleeve contained lyrics and personnel information (some of which was inaccurate), the real value came with a beautiful 22" by 33" black & white poster of John at his piano, shot by Peter Fordham, who documented the sessions extensively. Dan Richter did the honors for the custom Apple label featuring John's face. (A glimpse of the shoot is shown in the *Imagine: John Lennon* film.)

While John was able to channel some of his ongoing animus toward Paul into a wickedly acerbic track on the album, he wasn't quite through responding to *Ram*'s numerous insults. Included in the packaging was a postcard unmistakably mocking Paul's album cover, depicting John with a rather grotesque looking pig (standing in for the sheep). The idea that he would actually go through the trouble of arranging such a shoot speaks far more for Lennon's sense of humor than it does about the level of enmity between the two former partners. (To his credit, John chose the rather ephemeral media of a postcard to pull his stunt; once he'd gotten the McCartney-bashing out of his system, a different image—portraying himself as a satyr with a pan pipe and Yoko as a wood nymph—was substituted.)

THE CONCERT FOR BANGLA DESH (1971)

In his effort to draw attention to the plight of the millions of refugee lives being claimed by disease and starvation, George pulled no punches. With the "Bangla Desh" single publicly signaling George's involvement, Tom Wilkes was commissioned to produce a single sleeve that conveyed the despair brought on by the war and catastrophic flooding. His design depicted a collage of headlines on one side and a single, heart-rending image of a mother and her dying child on the other. Though not exactly the stuff that hit singles were made of, the imagery helped underscore the need to act quickly to alleviate the suffering.

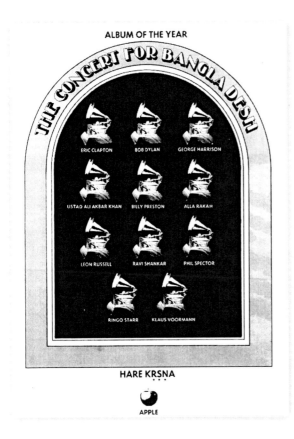

ALBUM OF THE YEAR

THE CONCERT FOR BANGLA DESH

ERIC CLAPTON BOB DYLAN GEORGE HARRISON

USTAD ALI AKBAR KHAN BILLY PRESTON ALLA RAKAH

LEON RUSSELL RAVI SHANKAR PHIL SPECTOR

RINGO STARR KLAUS VOORMANN

HARE KRṢNA

APPLE

Though the original cover art of the Bangladesh concert recording album wasn't exactly designed for aesthetic enjoyment, it got the point across. Still, EMI managed to dodge every opportunity to remind people of it, even when celebrating multiple Grammy wins.

Immediately following the concert on August 1st, George and Phil Spector got down to business to produce a marketable three-LP set documenting the event. The gravity of the crisis mandated getting the release into stores as quickly as possible in order to begin generating a much-needed flow of cash. Camouflage Productions was tasked with designing the package, something that expressed the magnitude of the cause, and not simply a photo showing a bunch of rock stars on a stage.

Wilkes did extensive photo research through wire service documentation of the disaster before collecting a handful of suitable images. What was needed was an arresting single frame that said all that needed saying, instantly. He soon found it in the form of a starving refugee boy, sitting beside an empty bowl. It was a powerful image, made all the more compelling once Wilkes removed all unnecessary background distractions. Without being unduly graphic, the photo certainly elicited sympathy.

George approved it at once, but what neither he nor Wilkes counted on was the intransigence of Capitol records, or more specifically, their marketing department. Everything they had ever been conditioned to believe about selling the public on their product in a very competitive market suggested that placing a photo as unsavory as a starving child on an album cover was a definite downer. But George wasn't about to back down on principle. Such was his hard-earned Beatle/*All Things*

Must Pass clout that Capitol had no choice but to adhere to his wishes. (Thirty-five years later and come the reissue, things were a little different; George was gone, the starving masses of Bangladesh were no longer a hot concern, and so the image was replaced with an onstage photo of the concert's prime mover.)

As it happened, the public was very much in tune with Harrison's intentions and gamely bought the charitable set, buzz-killing image and all. *The Concert For Bangla Desh* went to number one while becoming the first triple-record set to be awarded a Grammy for Album of the Year in 1972. That same year, UNICEF presented George and Ravi Shankar with "Child Is Father To The Man" honors.

Barry Feinstein, Tom Wilkes, and Alan Parise thoroughly documented the show in photographs. The results of their labors were presented in a 64-page souvenir booklet within the package, affording the millions who did not attend either of the two concerts the closest thing to experiencing the shows up-close. One photo, taken by Feinstein, found use as the cover of *Bob Dylan's Greatest Hits Volume II* three months after the event. Another striking visual was run on the back cover of the book: in addition to displaying a check made out to UNICEF for the quarter-million dollars of box office receipts, it showed an open guitar case filled with canned goods, medical supplies, and sacks of foodstuffs stenciled "Bangla Desh."

Like all of the musicians recruited by George, Feinstein, Wilkes, and company donated their time and services to the project, accepting payment only for expenses. In recognition of their contribution, George presented them with commemorative pewter medallions, struck with the album's cover image.

MIND GAMES (1973)

Within the John Lennon oeuvre, *Mind Games* is regarded as a transitional album at best, as he shook off the heavy politics of *Some Time in New York City* and consciously returned to the *Imagine* formula. Here too he produced a title track with universal appeal (in this case, originally conceived as "Make Love, Not War"); a mea culpa to his missus ("Aisumasen" in place of "Jealous Guy"); a rabble rousing rant (the tongue-in-cheek "Bring On The Lucie" as the new "Gimme Some Truth") a genre exercise (the Tex-Mex "Tight A$" replacing the straight blues of "It's So Hard"); a gentle love ballad ("Out The Blue" for "Oh My Love"); and, to quote Roy Carr and Tony Tyler, a "noise" ("Meat City" for "I Don't Wanna Be A Soldier").

231

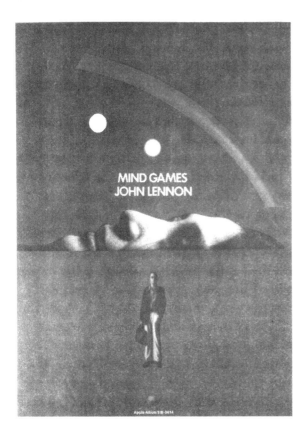

The rendering of John's Mind Games artwork used in print ads combined elements of the front and back cover: the rainbow and the two celestial orbs.

Unfortunately, the results were mixed. Eschewing the talents of Phil Spector and employing studio pros rather than his crew of stalwarts (save Keltner), *Mind Games* lacked the cohesion of *Imagine* and the fire of his best work. Though John would one day dismiss *Walls and Bridges* as the work of a "semi-sick craftsman," *that* self-assessment is a far better fit for *this* release than it is for the one that followed.

In addition to seizing the production reigns from Spector, John also designed the cover himself. Original pencil sketches (shown in the booklet to the CD reissue) reveal a preoccupation with eyes; also, he'd intended from the start to include Yoko in some way, though their relationship had been unraveling for some time. (*Mind Games* marked the first album since they'd been together where they weren't living in each other's pockets during its production.) What he eventually conceived was a landscape. John was shown full-length (in a Polaroid image taken by Yoko) standing in a field as a looming mountain—Yoko's profile—dominated the scene. There are two spherical objects in the sky—whether moons, stars or suns is in the eye of the beholder. Also present, in the lower right corner, is a Japanese "chop," connoting John's signature.

For those looking for meaning in the packaging, it is the contrast of the rear cover with the front that provides some fodder. The image is essentially the same, but for two major changes. First, John's image is now roughly twice the size as it appears on the front, as though he is "approaching" the viewer—everything else is the same size as before.

Second, a rainbow has replaced the two objects in the sky.

When discussing the design with May Pang much later, John said that only in hindsight did he realize that the rear cover image denoted him "walking away" from Yoko, though her influence is still mountainous. Second, the rainbow itself could be connoting "hope" for a brighter future as he left his past behind. (The artwork for the single sleeve melded the Yoko profile to the top of his head, as if to say that she was "on his mind.")

RINGO (1973)

As a concept, the *Ringo* release offered something that none of his fellow ex-Fabs had heretofore enacted: a celebration of their glorious past. John's "I'm The Greatest," tricked out with references to the Beatle days ("Yes, my name is Billy Shears"), punctuated by *Pepper*–like bursts of applause, started things off. But as celebratorially atmospheric as the song was, it was only amplifying what was already on the LP's cover.

Artist Tim Bruckner, under the art direction of our Barry Feinstein, created a painting depicting the Starr of the show onstage before an audience made up of known and unknown personages (just like *Pepper*). Accompanied by a rather devilish-looking cherub, Ringo is seen, in place of the letter I, spelling out his own name in lights. Above the stage of the old-time theatre is a sign bearing a green apple (of course!), the standard comedy-drama stage masks, and an apparent French slogan, "Duit On Mon Dei."

The phrase was in fact a joke, an utterly English play on the royal motto, "Dieu et mon droit." Adapted by King Richard I (get it?) in 1198, it's French for "God and my right." As twisted in Ringo's hands, "Duit on Mon Dei" translates to "Do it on Monday"—in other words, worry about it later. The slogan was a pet phrase among their English-American party axis; in 1975, Harry Nilsson used it as an album title.

Equally notable about Bruckner's cover art were the members of the audience. Virtually everyone who participated in the recording of the album was depicted: John (with Yoko beside him, in a bag); George (holding a balloon with an 'Om' symbol); Paul, with Linda (worth noting: all the ex-Fabs are seen wearing bib overalls, matching Ringo); producer Richard Perry (talking on two phones at once) and engineer Bill Schnee ("ever smiling"); Klaus Voormann (sketching away), as well as Billy Preston, Marc Bolan, The Band, Nilsson, Mal Evans, Nicky Hopkins, and so on. (At the very back can be seen a rendering of

Ringo as Merlin in *Son of Dracula*, holding a hand puppet of—himself.)

An unspared extravagance came with the inclusion of a twenty-four page booklet containing all the lyrics and some beautifully rendered Klaus Voormann lithographs. Each song on the album was accompanied by an appropriately imaginative graphic: "I'm The Greatest," for example, depicted

Klaus Voormann's lithographs illustrating each song on the Ringo album showed the great care with presentation that was taken for this top drawer release.

a statue of Ringo, fist raised, atop a column in a public square, while "Oh My My" showed The Ringed One (as a hospital patient) boogieing out of bed in a sick ward, surrounded by medical staff.

The whole package was a fitting investment for an album that burst all expectations with its sheer charm, tunefulness, and exuberance. In so doing, the *Ringo* album recalled what a joyous *event* the issue of a new Beatles album was like during the sixties: no small feat.

BAND ON THE RUN (1973)

For what would turn out to be the most acclaimed album of his entire solo career, Paul instinctively sought to put something special on the cover. Having the entire album already in the can by the time the image was shot gave him the luxury of conceptualizing something sure to tie in with the music in one fashion or another. As discussed in *Fab Four FAQ 2.0*, there was no explicit overarching theme within the songs per se, only a vague notion of escape and identification with the "outsider." Added together and given Paul's occasionally literal visualization process, this added up to one thing: an escape by outlaws for the album's cover.

There were any number of ways to effect this notion but, like Ringo before him, Paul was not averse to playing the *Pepper* card by populating his milieu with well-known personas. Unlike the Beatle album, however, the notables included on *Band on the Run* would be living breathing celebrities, expected to actually show up for the shoot. A short list was drawn up, with most selections coming about simply by the proximity of the people involved.

Chosen were a mix of faces familiar to Brits at that time, but less so to Americans (with a couple of exceptions). From left to right (as shown on the cover), we begin with Michael Parkinson, a popular English chat show host and a McCartney favorite. Just behind Paul was singer Kenny Lynch, self-described as "one of Britain's best-loved entertainers." Lynch, an old showbiz pro by the time he toured with the Beatles in 1963 in support of Helen Shapiro, scored the first successful cover of a Beatles song, "Misery," after Helen's management turned it down.

Flat against the wall behind the "prisoners" was possibly the best-known face to us Yanks, actor James Coburn. (He was in Britain filming *The Internecine Project* at the time). Just behind Linda was Clement Freud, grandson of the famed psychologist. He had just been elected to a seat in Parliament in 1973, after having gained notoriety in Britain as a chef, columnist, and dog food shill. Looking characteristically sinister, Christopher Lee was next. The actor gained renown around the world for a series of Hammer horror films; his most recent appearances at the time of the *BOTR* shoot were in Richard Lester's *The Three Musketeers* and in the cult classic, *The Wicker Man*.

Last was John Conteh, a Liverpool-born boxer who, in his mid-seventies prime, was touted as a potential challenger to Muhammad Ali (an aspiration Ali himself discouraged, as he felt Conteh was too small). Paul and Linda were a key part of a ruse to "entrap" Conteh at the Abbey Road studio a year later for an episode of *This Is Your Life*.

The group of six were invited to meet up with the McCartneys on October 28 at Osterley Park, Brentford, London. There, a wall deemed suitable for simulating a prison yard was selected, and the nine would-be escapees, garbed in prison attire, were put through their paces beneath the glare of a "guard tower" spotlight under the direction of fashion photographer Clive Arrowsmith. (The proceedings were also captured on 16-millimeter film; during performances of "Band on the Run" during Wings' 1975-76 world tour, the footage would be projected on a screen above the stage.)

Band on the Run came packaged with a poster comprised of Polaroid photos taken during the sessions in Lagos. The back cover of the album played up the exotic travel aspect of the production, depicting stamped (faked) passport photos of Paul, Linda, and Denny. (Oddly, Denny and Linda's photos were switched in order between the U.S. and U.K. pressings.)

WALLS AND BRIDGES (1974)

As originally conceived, 1973 called for John to reunite with Phil Spector after *Mind Games* to commence the oldies project in Los Angeles. For roughly three months—largely to diminishing returns—work did indeed proceed. As the two musical giants waged battle in the studio, Capitol was on the case, at work on putting together the appropriate package for what might have ended up being called *Mouldies...But Goldies*, *Old Hat*, or any of the other titles Lennon was kicking around for the project.

John's input on the packaging was to provide some childhood drawings he'd preserved, made during the fifties in his pre-teen years. Clearly, the concept as originally intended was to present a look back at his roots; the drawings represented his oldest surviving artistic expressions while the music within represented an opportunity to revisit his earliest musical influences, ones that placed him on the path to one day create an "I Am The Walrus" or a "Cold Turkey."

Under the art direction of Capitol's Roy Kohara (who had also worked on a host of ex-Fab album designs, including *Goodnight Vienna*, *Extra Texture*, *Blast From Your Past*, *The Best Of George Harrison*, and *Rock 'n' Roll Music*), a sleeve was put together featuring a painting of a soccer match, dated June 1952, on the front cover. (Years later, when the illustration entered public consciousness, Lennon noted that the number he drew on the player's back at age eleven was—what else?—nine.)

But once the Spector project was abandoned, the artwork became orphaned. Not to worry, John felt—he'd simply use the design in progress for his next up release, *Walls and Bridges*. This collection of deeply personal compositions offered a view of his life since the time he'd last addressed the public. The material was comprised largely of compositions detailing his separation from Yoko; his new love, May; the toll that the hard-partying life was taking on him; and musings on assorted inner demons.

While nothing in the album's lyrical content explicitly suggested a look back at his childhood per se, the packaging nonetheless was declared suitable. To raise the commercial appeal, however, the existing

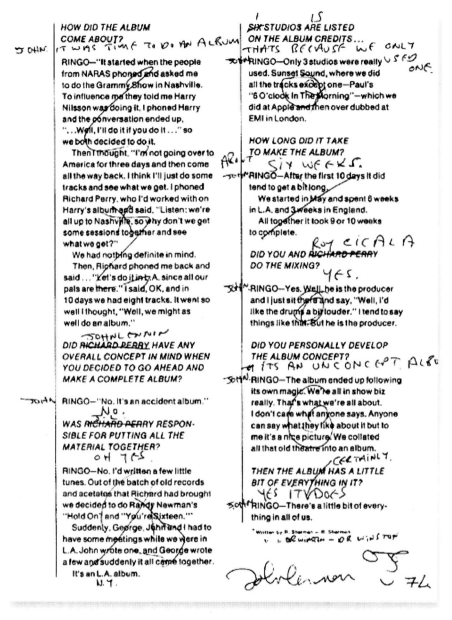

[handwritten: JOHN — IT WAS TIME TO DO AN ALBUM]

RINGO—"It started when the people from NARAS phoned and asked me to do the Grammy Show in Nashville. To influence me they told me Harry Nilsson was doing it. I phoned Harry and the conversation ended up, "...Well, I'll do it if you do it ..." so we both decided to do it.

Then I thought, "I'm not going over to America for three days and then come all the way back. I think I'll just do some tracks and see what we get. I phoned Richard Perry, who I'd worked with on Harry's album and said, "Listen: we're all up to Nashville, so why don't we get some sessions together and see what we get?"

We had nothing definite in mind.

Then, Richard phoned me back and said ..."Let's do it in L.A. since all our pals are there." I said, OK, and in 10 days we had eight tracks. It went so well I thought, "Well, we might as well do an album."

[handwritten: JOHN LENNIN]
DID RICHARD PERRY HAVE ANY OVERALL CONCEPT IN MIND WHEN YOU DECIDED TO GO AHEAD AND MAKE A COMPLETE ALBUM?

[handwritten: JOHN]
RINGO—"No. It's an accident album."
[handwritten: No.]

WAS RICHARD PERRY RESPONSIBLE FOR PUTTING ALL THE MATERIAL TOGETHER?
[handwritten: OH YES.]

RINGO—No. I'd written a few little tunes. Out of the batch of old records and acetates that Richard had brought we decided to do Randy Newman's "Hold On" and "You're Sixteen.'"

Suddenly, George, John and I had to have some meetings while we were in L.A. John wrote one, and George wrote a few and suddenly it all came together.

It's an L.A. album.
[handwritten: N.Y.]

[handwritten: 1 / IS]
SIX STUDIOS ARE LISTED ON THE ALBUM CREDITS...
[handwritten: THATS BECAUSE WE ONLY USED ONE]

RINGO—Only 3 studios were really used. Sunset Sound, where we did all the tracks except one—Paul's "6 O'clock In The Morning"—which we did at Apple and then over dubbed at EMI in London.

HOW LONG DID IT TAKE TO MAKE THE ALBUM?
[handwritten: ABOUT SIX WEEKS.]

RINGO—After the first 10 days it did tend to get a bit long.

We started in May and spent 6 weeks in L.A. and 3 weeks in England.

All together it took 9 or 10 weeks to complete.

[handwritten: ROY CICALA]
DID YOU AND RICHARD PERRY DO THE MIXING?
[handwritten: YES.]

RINGO—Yes. Well, he is the producer and I just sit there and say, "Well, I'd like the drums a bit louder." I tend to say things like that. But he is the producer.

DID YOU PERSONALLY DEVELOP THE ALBUM CONCEPT?
[handwritten: ITS AN UNCONCEPT ALBU]

RINGO—The album ended up following its own magic. We're all in show biz really. That's what we're all about. I don't care what anyone says. Anyone can say what they like about it but to me it's a nice picture. We collated all that old theatre into an album.

[handwritten: CERTAINLY.]
THEN THE ALBUM HAS A LITTLE BIT OF EVERYTHING IN IT?
[handwritten: YES IT DOES]

RINGO—There's a little bit of everything in all of us.

* Written by R. Sherman – R. Sherman
[handwritten: R. WILSON – OR WINSTON]

[signature: John Lennon '74]

As part of the Walls and Bridges promotion, John re-purposed an interview Ringo had given for his self-titled 1973 release, adjusting the answers accordingly.

concept was then melded to a series of contemporary images of John in a long-unseen playful mood. Bob Gruen, John's local photographer of choice, took a series of facial shots in a variety of expressions: smiling, jeering, wearing five pairs of glasses at once, sticking out his tongue.

Kohara then used the photo series to create an "interactive" experience for buyers of the LP: the three-flap mechanism enabled purchasers to custom-craft their own Lennon images by switching facial components at will. Given the inherent intensity captured within the grooves, John could very easily have packaged his wares in something heavier, but the lighthearted presentation demonstrated that, no matter what personal struggles (and bad press) he faced, there was always a good reason to play the fool.

Also included was a handsome eight-page booklet, containing lyrics, more childhood drawings, and more Gruen shots. Underscoring the jocularity of the proceedings are the pseudonyms that John used throughout. On "What You Got," he's billed as "Kaptain Kundalini"; for "Surprise, Surprise (Sweet Bird of Paradox)," he's "Dr. Winston O'Ghurkin"; on "Scared," he's billed as "Mel Torment," while on "Nobody Loves You (When You're Down and Out)," he credits himself as "Dwarf McDougal." This latter nomenclature comes as something of an inside joke, as Bob Dylan's music publisher is Dwarf Music, while he established himself professionally at the coffeehouse, Café Wha?, located on McDougal Street in New York's Greenwich Village.

In 2005, devotees of *Walls and Bridges* awaiting its re-mastered reissue on CD were outraged at the rampant revisionism that the collection had undergone. *WAB* was the only LP of Lennon originals that did *not* feature Yoko in any capacity during its production, being recorded during their 1974 estrangement. However, her fingerprints were all over the re-master, starting with the cover. Gone from the exterior packaging were his childhood drawings, in favor of a single Gruen shot used earlier for the back cover.

Also dropped was the Apple label (a generic Parlophone label had been used in the first CD iteration); in its place, the series of shots used on the *Some Time In New York City* LP label (wherein John morphs into Yoko) were substituted—*in reverse*—with Yoko morphing into John. Lastly, the original production credit ("Produced and Arranged by John Lennon With the Plastic Ono Nuclear Band/Little Big Horns and the Philharmanic Orchestrange") was replaced by (in caps) "PRODUCED BY YOKO ONO." Most galling of all was the apparent addition of a drop-in to the fadeout of "Surprise, Surprise (Sweet Bird of Paradox)." This musical valentine to May Pang appeared to have been sonically altered, as a previously unheard vocal sounding an awful lot like someone yelling "Yoko!" was dropped into the fading refrain, "Sweet sweet, sweet sweet love."

They say that history is written by survivors. By *re*-writing history, John's widow took it upon herself to erase the choices John himself had made over thirty years earlier. Whatever one thinks of Yoko, the blatant propagandizing is nothing less than disturbing.

GOODNIGHT VIENNA (1974)

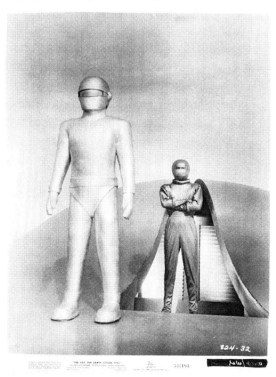

Here's an alternate of the production still from 1951's The Day the Earth Stood Still that Ringo modeled his Goodnight Vienna album cover after.

Ringo had long been a fan of science fiction and therefore was quite likely well-familiar with the 1951 classic, *The Day The Earth Stood Still.* Starring Michael Rennie and directed by Robert Wise, the film was a cautionary tale, warning mankind to quit their warring ways or face annihilation. Released at the height of Cold War paranoia, the film packed a powerful yet thoughtful message.

Harry Nilsson was also a fan and it was while visiting one day that Ringo noticed Harry's stash of lobby cards from the film. Rifling through them, the shot of Michael Rennie (as Klaatu), with hand upraised as if saying "farewell" caught his eye. It was a striking image, with Klaatu's saucer behind him and Gort, the gigantic enforcer robot beside him. (Though the film is in black & white, this particular lobby card was in color.) In addition to being an arresting visual, in Ringo's mind it worked well with the *Goodnight Vienna* (Northern slang for "Let's get out of here") theme. As he explained: "(When) you finish an album…you want to take a trip to Mars just to get away."

The album's front cover necessarily replaced Michael Rennie's head with the drummer's; also, a star was emblazoned onto his chest. (The actual space suit he wore while promoting the album was designed by rock costumer Ola Hudson; her son Saul is better known to the masses as the guitarist, Slash.) To enhance the already pleasing aesthetics, a heavenly body was added to the sky as well as a New York City skyline.

For the back cover, a color photo of deep space was used, resulting in a simple but effective design. (This same imagery was also used in place of the regular Apple label on the album and singles.)

Given such spectacular imagery to work with, Capitol—on behalf of the fading Apple label—pulled out all the promotional stops for the album. A video for "Only You" was produced, depicting Ringo's "spaceman" landing in Hollywood at the Capitol tower. In lieu of the usual Sunset Boulevard billboard, the label went through the time and expense to actually replicate, in three-dimensional form, the album's cover for display atop the tower. A thirty-foot Gort was created, along with a twenty-three foot Ringo (actually modified from a display bought from a car dealer). For the final touch, a "flying" saucer was constructed and placed atop the already-"Space Age-y" looking building.

The album's inner sleeve contained the lyrics on one side and a collage of production photos on the other (taken by recording engineer Larry Emerine). These latter images are fascinating, documenting a camaraderie between John and Ringo unseen publicly since the Beatle days. Among the other players depicted are Elton John, Billy Preston, Klaus, Nilsson, Keltner, Jesse Ed Davis, and May Pang.

ROCK 'N' ROLL (1975)

It may not be an overstatement to suggest that the eventual album cover for John's long-delayed oldies project was facilitated by Mark Lapidos and the first Beatlefest. While attending the September 1974 event in New York City, May Pang happened to run into Jurgen Vollmer, John's photographer friend from Hamburg, many years before. Her purchase of the iconic 1961 photo and John's subsequent re-connection with his long lost mate paved the way for bringing Vollmer's utterly fitting archival images into the project.

The young German "exi" made up one third of the Fabs' closest friends during their initial forays onto the continent in 1960. Like Astrid Kirchherr, Vollmer first befriended, then photographed the band, offstage and on. The photo selected for the *Rock 'N' Roll* cover was taken in the spring of 1961, at Hamburg's Jäger-Passage, Wohlwillstraße 22. All but Pete Best were present for the shoot, which followed a staged "performance" at the Top Ten Club in St. Pauli. (Interestingly, it's John and George whom Jurgen seemed most intent on focusing on.)

Jurgen shot at least a dozen images; all composed by having three Beatles (in order, l-r: George, Stu, and Paul) stroll past John, who remained frozen in the doorway. What's interesting is that, of all the

images to select, John chose the one where his former bandmates are *closest* to him, rather than the other shots where they are farther away (and therefore, easier to remove). The inclusion of those three on John's album of oldies was a *deliberate* choice.

While John Uotomo created the period-authentic neon light fixture proclaiming the album's title, Vollmer began conceptualizing what was intended to be a gatefold sleeve containing more appropriate imagery, perhaps including some of the exquisite photos he would include in his forthcoming book, *Rock and Roll Times* (with a Foreword by John). Unfortunately, the unexpected issue of Morris Levy's unauthorized version of the project forced Apple/Capitol to rush theirs into stores before the concept could be fully realized.

No once could have known in 1961 how incredibly handy the photos being taken of the Beatles in Hamburg would one day come to be as album cover art. Jurgen Vollmer's evocative street photography perfectly suited the "You shoulda been there" vibe John was putting across.

VENUS AND MARS (1975)

Unless she happened to be in the photo, Linda was often responsible for shooting Wings' album cover images. (The first one she took a pass on was for the group's debut album, shot by Barry Lategan, who was known for his iconic images of Twiggy as well as a plethora of nude studies.) Perhaps the most striking shot that she ever offered up was the one, which graced the *Venus and Mars* album. Two billiard balls—one red, one yellow—simply and fittingly summed up the title concept perfectly.

Paul later indicated that he'd forgotten that, in Roman mythology, Venus was the goddess of love, Mars the god of war. As was often the case in his songwriting, he'd simply conjured up a character ("waiting for the show to begin") that had an astrologer friend. Said friend advised him that, astrologically, it was a good evening for a rock concert (as opposed to the night of Altamont, which apparently wasn't); the two heavenly bodies that Macca chose to denote this simply scanned well, with no further significance whatsoever. (Imagine then the mortification both McCartney's felt when, at the party launching the album, an acquaintance greeted them by saying, "Hello Venus, hello Mars.")

The album's cover was replicated with a round sticker (bearing the caption "Venus and Mars Are Alright Tonight—Wings") packaged within the gatefold album. Also included (for the edification of Wings fans) was another sticker laying out our solar system, with the planets depicted to scale. *Venus and Mars* outstripped other ex-Fab releases by enclosing *two* full-sized posters: one being a series of images (shot in Northern California) of the band pantomiming with two appropriately colored spheres painted in; the other showed the McCartneys at Mardi Gras earlier that year. Lyrics were included on the back cover, *Sgt. Pepper's*-style.

The album represented the first Wings package designed by rock's premier LP art-crafters, Hipgnosis. This English outfit utterly dominated the seventies, creating memorable, often surreal sleeves. Some that most rock fans are familiar with include Led Zeppelin's *Houses of the Holy*; Pink Floyd's *Wish You Were Here*; and the often-censored *Lovedrive* by The Scorpions. Hipgnosis would go on to design the next two Wings LPs before the band resumed designing their own releases, albeit with input from Hipgnosis' George Hardie and Aubrey Powell.

An interesting aspect to *Venus and Mars'* packaging concerned Paul's abandonment of the Apple label. The LP was issued using the 1940s Capitol label design, at his request. Though all four ex-Fabs' contract with EMI did not end until January 1976, Capitol made a special point of wooing Paul, offering him a larger cut of royalties than his band mates were getting on Beatle product (something that they would take him to court for in the 1980s after they learned of it). Though *Venus and Mars* could have been released with an Apple label (and in some overseas markets, it was), Paul was eager to distance himself from what had become an ongoing nightmare virtually from the advent of Allen Klein on.

It was no accident that *Ram* was the last album Paul issued with the corporate Apple label. Ever after, his labels were custom-crafted: on

Wild Life, the label bore an image of Linda on one side and himself on the other; *Red Rose Speedway* bore a plain black label bearing specially designed logos for both the title and the group (which, in the wake of *Wild Life*'s lackluster sales, was now called "Paul McCartney and Wings," lest anyone miss the point). *Band on the Run* also came on a black label, this time bearing simulated passport photos of Paul, Linda, and Denny, though for some reason, the order of the last two personages was switched for side two. (This echoed the arrangement shift noted above on the LP's back cover.)

The practice also manifested itself on the singles he issued. Beginning in 1972, "Give Ireland Back To The Irish," "Mary Had A Little Lamb," "Hi Hi Hi," and "My Love" all had custom labels until Macca, perhaps feeling his point had been made (since the contract with Allen Klein had expired), reverted back to the standard Apple on "Live And Let Die," continuing through his next five singles. (John had used *his* own custom Apple labels on three singles: "Imagine," "Happy Xmas," and "Woman Is The Nigger Of The World"; George, likewise three times: "Ding Dong; Ding Dong," "Dark Horse," and "You," while Ringo followed suit by issuing *all six* singles from *Ringo* and *Goodnight Vienna* combined with custom labels, although most of these songs could *also* be found in the standard Apple iteration as well, curiously enough.)

EXTRA TEXTURE (READ ALL ABOUT IT) (1975)

With uncharacteristic lack of preparation, George was compelled to rush into the studio in the spring of 1975, intent on realizing the twin goals of 1) salvaging studio time bought and paid for on behalf of Splinter, Dark Horse's most promising signing, and 2) rehabilitating his image in the wake of the Dark Horse tour's bad vibes. Part and parcel of the latter end was to bring back a long absent sense of lightness to the Harrison brand. (*Dark Horse*, the album, contained a few dry splashes of humor, but his most notorious attempt at drawing smiles—crediting his cuckolding wife and her paramour as performers on "Bye Bye Love"—was an effort that elicited more discomfort than mirth.)

It couldn't have helped that almost every song on the record was rather downbeat in tone. This isn't intended as a criticism, but just as an observation: the one up-tempo, catchy tune on the album was four years old—a song that George in fact tried to give away ("You," to Ronnie Spector). Therefore, by any measure, Jai Raj Harisein knew that the goods he had to offer might be a tough sell, irrespective of their merit.

For this reason, he felt that presentation would be key to the album's success. The Hare Krishna hoopla that accompanied his last two releases would be drastically toned down; only a single, tasteful "Om' symbol would be allowed to grace the front cover. (Curiously, the glyph was relocated to the *back* cover of the U.K. issue.) The album's title, *Extra Texture*, had been offered up by session bassist Paul Stallworth, by way of commenting on George's habit of layering on assorted

The lighthearted "OHNOTHIMAGEN" theme to George's Extra Texture promotion represented a step in the right direction, though listeners no doubt may have felt a bit disappointed that the collection's overall mood was one of bluesy soul rather than upbeat cheer.

instruments during recording *ala* Spector. (That George didn't already have an idea as to what to call his creation reinforces how truly low on inspiration he was at this time.)

Still, Roy Kohara duly worked his magic, creating a lively sleeve design that actually offered a sensorial dimension to the proceedings (in that the cardboard used really was textured). The album's title was die-cut in the front, allowing the blue-tinted inner sleeve photo (of George sporting a disarming grin) to show through. In probably the most self-deprecating gesture from one of rock's most self-effacing men, the photo bears the caption (in bold letters): OHNOTHIMAGEN. (Translation: "Oh, not him again!")

Interestingly, *Extra Texture* would be the first of only three Harrison albums *not* to include the lyrics inside. (*Cloud Nine* and *Brainwashed* were the other two.) Instead, the inner sleeve's reverse side featured another photo of George, this one taken on the Dark Horse tour. Both were shot by long-time Beatle photographer Henry Grossman, who'd also captured the famous Fab series of early 1967, one shot of which graced the picture sleeve to "Hello Goodbye." (A limited edition book of

Grossman photos taken during the *Sgt. Pepper's* sessions, *Kaleidoscope Eyes*, was published in 2008.)

Further attempts at levity came with the sleeve notes; after duly listing the personnel on each of the album's ten (plus one snippet) songs, listeners were told: "Danny Kootch doesn't appear on this record. Also not appearing on this record : Derek Taylor, Peter Sellers, Chuck Trammell, Dino Airali, Eric Idle, Dennis Killeen and Emil Richards." Kootch was, of course, session guitarist Danny Kortchmar and one quarter of Attitudes, another Dark Horse signing. Trammell was a legendary Los Angeles DJ of the 1950s and 60s, while Airali was president of Dark Horse. Dennis Killeen was with Capitol, while world famous percussionist Emil Richards played on the Dark Horse tour (he would also appear at 2002's Concert for George).

Perhaps the most striking statement issued on the jacket and label was the reduced-to-a-core apple, denoting what was the final album of new material issued by the Beatles' once-exalted foray into capitalism (Capitolism?). George would later note that his own *Wonderwall Music* was Apple's first long player and now, seven years later, *Extra Texture* was the last (not counting Ringo's *Blast From Your Past*, which was a compilation). "I feel a bit of sentiment about it because Apple did a few good things, you know...But it went crazy at the end and that's why I'm here now with Dark Horse Records. Good musicians are really worth encouraging."

RINGO THE 4TH (1977)

For his second Atlantic release, Ringo departed from custom and recorded (mostly) away from L.A., at the label's New York City studios under the direction of Arif Mardin. (Seeing *Sentimental Journey* and *Beaucoups of Blues* as special one-off projects, Ringo called this new production *Ringo the 4th*—as opposed to the "6th"—which it technically was.) While discussing the name with Nancy Andrews at their Plaza Hotel suite, he riffed on how "medieval" sounding it was: "I want a sword." That off-hand comment provided the spark of inspiration needed for conceptualizing the album's rather unique cover.

The New York Blizzard at the end of January, 1977 had left them holed up in their room. With the idea of shooting the cover themselves developing for some time, Nancy—already a little stir-crazy—was ready to act on their plan once she noted from their window that people on the ground were getting around on skis. A friend, model Rita Wolf, had popped into town for a visit before the storm had hit. Together, the two women ventured out to hit a prop rental shop in the city, returning with an assortment of items, including a heavy, period-appropriate sword ("to represent him slaying his demons").

Ever the shutterbug, Nancy had discovered that the palatial closets in their Plaza suite made for, with the use of a flash, "the perfect light box." While in said closet, Ringo was placed in a series poses for his cover. At some point during the shoot, Rita—at Nancy's suggestion—donned red heels, stockings, and a teddy before mounting her beau's shoulders, as he sat upon his "throne"—a pillow atop an overturned wastepaper basket. Though possibly not the artiest of concepts, the visual worked; for the back cover, Nancy simply photographed his backside (with Rita still aboard), completing the package.

Ringo The 4th ended up being not one of his highest regarded albums, to put it charitably. Some fans were outraged at the *au courant* disco trappings; others disappointed at the complete lack of ex-Fab input; still others at what they saw as his increasingly disengaged efforts, as though he believed his name alone would guarantee surefire success for any old dreck he cared to release. In fact, the album was not without some fine moments, but detractors saw the cover art as evidence that the high life had gone to his head, rather than read it as the cheeky inside joke it had been intended as.

As for Nancy, she shot his next album cover as well. It showed his famously ringed hand resting on one arm of a chair; a glass in the other, with the beautiful Mediterranean serving as backdrop. The *Bad Boy* cover was taken on the balcony of their place in Monte Carlo; perhaps unwittingly, she'd captured the symbols of what many saw as an empty, jet-setting lifestyle that, musically at least, was at odds with the values of gritty rock and roll pounded out in a sweaty basement, all those years ago.

BACK TO THE EGG (1979)

Having once again rebuilt Wings from its core threesome (for the second time in five years) while at the same time leaving EMI to ink a record deal with CBS, Paul was of the mindset that a new beginning was in the offing. What better to underscore a fresh start than with the album's title, *Back To The Egg*? Big plans were in the offing, encompassing a world tour, videos, and—doubtlessly in response to the rise of punk sweeping England—a musical return to a rawer sound than had typified *London Town*. Wings was about to take a step into what promised to be a brighter future, and so the new album's packaging

John Shaw's futuristic sci-fi design for Back to the Egg, shown here on the cover of Song Hits magazine, was presented in live action form as part of the syndicated video package shown on television.

needed to reflect that.

Someone—possibly one of the McCartneys, a Wings member, or somebody else within their orbit—saw the artwork on Status Quo's recently released album, *If You Can't Stand The Heat*. The cover, depicting a tone-arm "playing" the round heat element on an electric range, was shot by a former advertising photographer named John Shaw, who had branched out into album cover art. He received a call from Paul's MPL office to come down and meet at Abbey Road studios. (Wishing privacy for a discussion, Macca blithely entered the women's loo without first bothering to make sure it was empty. It wasn't, but the McCartney charm saved the day.)

Paul was keen on Shaw's surrealistic style, as typified by the cover of Manfred Mann's *Angel Station* album, released in early 1979. Shaw obliged by conceptualizing an image inspired by Douglas Adams' *The Hitchhiker's Guide To The Universe*. The band was shown in what appeared to be a well-appointed drawing room. (At the rear, upon the mantle, sharp-eyed observers may see the art deco statuette shown on *Wings Greatest*.)

At first glance, many thought that the band members were standing around a billiards table with a rather unique surface. In fact, they are on the floor, gathered around what Shaw described as a "portal to another dimension." Earth is seen in the distance, as the individual band members gaze into the opening, their faces lit by the celestial glow. It is possibly the most enthralling image ever to grace a Wings album, though in the opinion of some, the pity was that the musical contents within didn't live up to the promise of its packaging.

The back cover was *not* provided by Shaw, being of a more pedestrian (though more contemporary-feeling and therefore less timeless) design than the front. Inside, the poultry ovum theme was underscored by the platter's labels, one being tagged "sunny side up," the other "over easy." No lyrics were provided on the inner sleeve.

Sadly for Wings, what had been hoped to be the start of a new chapter ended up being an Epilogue. Dissed by critics and largely unloved by the public (not unlike Wings' debut), *Back To The Egg* was the final album from Paul's nearly decade-long post-Beatles act.

SOMEWHERE IN ENGLAND
(SCHEDULED OCTOBER 1980)

A year after his last hit, George prepared his third Dark Horse/Warner Brothers product for release. In the time since *George Harrison* had spawned one successful single and one stiff, the record industry had been hit hard by a recession. The signing frenzy of the mid-seventies was over, as record companies looked to their heaviest hitters to save them from the rising flood of red ink. Layoffs were taking their toll at all labels; hit especially hard was Warner Brothers, which had high hopes for Fleetwood Mac's follow-up to *Rumours*. But instead of being Mo Ostin's salvation, 1979's *Tusk* sold "only" about two million copies, a mere fraction of its predecessor.

It was therefore with considerable anticipation that Ostin looked to George to give him another "My Sweet Lord." What he received instead was a collection so singular and lacking the qualities that blockbusters are made of that he sent its creator back to the drawing board. *Somewhere In England*, as delivered, was—like the album before it—a mostly mellow excursion into Hari's earthly concerns: meditation; Krishna; love; the environment; death; plus a couple of Hoagy Carmichael standards thrown in for good measure. To a record exec in bleak times looking for a lifeline, this exquisitely crafted offering was more suited to a sub-genre of the adult contemporary market than anything else.

Thus it was that despite ostensibly being master of his own label, George was utterly at cross-purposes with the parent company's needs. (For a discussion of the "problematic" material dropped from the release, see *Fab Four FAQ 2.0*.) Beyond the content of the grooves, however, the presentation irked Ostin. To him, the monochromatic artwork simply didn't "pop." *Somewhere In England* featured a black & white image that fused George's profile to a satellite photo of the U.K.'s west coast. As art, it was an effective and reasonably eye-catching cover. (The rear jacket featured an unaltered aerial shot.)

But Warner already had John Lennon's comeback album (on Geffen) likewise penciled in for a late autumn release; it too sported a black & white cover shot, taken by Japanese photographer Kishin Shinoyama. As *Double Fantasy* arrived with its own built-in hype, its photo was fine as-is. Warner only had room on the roster for one ex-Fab bearing a black and white album cover and so George's would have to go.

Somewhere In England's album jacket had been designed by photographer/graphic designer Ho-Yun, better known in the west as Basil Pao. Born in Hong Kong, he came to work at the Warner Brothers art department in the late seventies; his work there encompassed artists ranging from SNL comedienne Gilda Radner to The Rutles' soundtrack (and accompanying booklet). It was perhaps Pao's work with the Monty Python alumnae that brought him into George's orbit; he eventually became the photographer accompanying Michael Palin on his world travels.

Before being scrapped, Pao's *Somewhere In England* design was depicted in both promotional literature heralding new releases from Warner-Elektra-Atlantic, as well as on the obi strip found on Japanese copies of *Double Fantasy*. But Ostin and the label wanted a fresh start and so the Pao design was relegated to history, surfacing occasionally as an unused album slick or on bootleg copies of the original *SIE* non-release. When the re-tooled album finally dropped in June 1981, it came in a more colorful design based on a concept originating with percussionist/co-producer Ray Cooper. It consisted of an image taken of George, apparently lying flat on his back on a city sidewalk. In fact, as revealed by the back cover image, he is posed before Mark Boyle's 1967 painting, *Holland Park Avenue Study,* displayed in London's Tate Gallery.

In slightly modified form, Bail Pao's original Somewhere in England artwork was used for the CD remastered edition, while a perfectly good opportunity to restore the four dropped tracks was squandered.

With the arrival of the Dark Horse remastered re-issues on CD in 2004, *Somewhere In England* at last appeared with the original, George-sanctioned design restored, more or less (the title print was altered slightly). Unfortunately for fans, the original track selection was not.

The Beatles were always quick to zero in on the non-hit side of American singles – in this case, a song that would stay with John for years afterward. For their last single of note, The Olympics recorded "Good Lovin'" in 1965. Felix Cavaliere heard it on a New York radio station and the version recorded by his band, The Young Rascals, went to #1 in 1966.

CHAPTER 13

THIS SONG WE'LL LET BE: TRACKS LEFT IN THE CAN

T hroughout the seventies, while the ex-Fabs recorded prolifically, not everything produced saw issue. Though some may argue that certain songs should have *stayed* unreleased, for the most part the quality level of the unheard tunes remained on par with everything that *was* released. Traditionally, Paul was the one out of the four most likely to record more songs than he could use on a given project, though if a particular recording passed muster (at least in his own head), it would find a home on a subsequent album. (Material cut during the *Ram* sessions found issue on his next *two* LPs.)

Still, even after implementing the convenient outlet of the non-album B-side, there remained some tracks that never saw release on vinyl. The compact disc era would prove a boon to fans as artists offered bonus tracks of leftover material on reissues of their albums, or as part of "anthologies" that served to present all kinds of recordings in a setting not necessarily geared toward overall greatness. Deluxe remaster packagings gave further outlet to vault holdings, at last providing fans with the opportunity to hear and own recordings that might only have read about.

There were far more tracks left high and dry than there's space in this book to itemize; many of them have slowly started trickling out via the aforementioned avenues. Nonetheless, here's a rundown of some of the more notable recordings that were deemed lacking in some way at the time they were committed to tape. Of them, a few have since seen authorized release while most of the remainder have thankfully (for us fans) been made available through less legitimate channels (Hello, torrents!).

"STORMY WEATHER" – 1969 or 1970

Ringo's album of Big Band-era standards surprised a lot of people, not least because the genre is a singer's medium, something that his particular set of pipes didn't readily lend itself to (to put it one way). Still, the concept of having each song arranged by a different musician was an intriguing one. The resulting release was an eclectic stylistic blend, given uniformity by George Martin's orchestra (under his production) and the Starr singer.

Only one documented leftover has surfaced: a jazzy up-tempo reworking of "Stormy Weather." At this late a date, it is unknown who arranged it. Possibilities included Frank Sinatra associates Nelson Riddle and Billy May, who were mentioned in an industry article on the project and are otherwise unrepresented on the release. Considering the quality of the recording and the otherwise complete absence of bonus material on the CD issue, it is surprising that the track wasn't included.

THE DYLAN SESSION – 1970

George was a very busy man in the winter and spring of 1970. He began the year laying the Beatles to rest, recording his own "I Me Mine" for the band's swan song. Not long after, he assisted John on "Instant Karma" and Ringo on "It Don't Come Easy." In between, he maintained his studio tan with Apple projects centering on Doris Troy, Billy, and Jackie. In April, two weeks after Paul broke it to the world— roughly—that the Fabs were history, George headed to New York City, visiting Allen Klein's digs on Broadway. While in town, he took the opportunity to drop in on buddy Bob Dylan, who was preparing to work on what became *New Morning* (which itself followed closely on the heels of the soon-to-be-issued *Self-Portrait*, a double album of covers commonly judged to be his worst album *ever*).

The two met up at the end of the month and jammed a bit; on Friday, May 1, 1970, they convened at Columbia Studio B. There, with country legend-to-be Charlie Daniels on bass, Russ Kunkel on drums, and Bob Johnston producing (and occasionally playing piano), the ensemble set about lying down tracks. George and Bob had already collaborated on the writing of "I'd Have You Anytime," the eventual lead-off track to *All Things Must Pass* (which would commence recording later that month in London); further, Bob's "If Not For You" would also end up on both men's next LP releases.

But on this day, only the latter song was attempted: it marks the earliest documented example of George playing what quickly became his trademark, slide guitar. Though Bob would re-record the track later for release on *New Morning* (replicating George's part in the arrangement), this day's take was eventually released on *The Bootleg Series Volumes 1-3* in 1991. In 2013, the tenth volume of Bob Dylan's *Bootleg* series of vault material arrived: *Another Self Portrait*. It included two cuts taped this day: "Time Passes Slowly" and "Working On A Guru."

The sessions were broken into two parts: the first being something of a hootenanny, with a variety of songs tried on, if just for a laugh, before the evening session's more serious efforts. (According to the engineers working that day, the musicians were killing time while awaiting the expected arrival of Elvis.) A rich assortment of tunes were attempted, several of which ended up on *New Morning*, though nearly all were re-recorded later. (One that *wasn't* was the day's take of "Went To See The Gypsy"—though uncredited, George's lead guitar at the song's finish is unmistakable.) Some familiar Dylan compositions were run through also, including "Don't Think Twice, It's Alright," "Just Like Tom Thumb's Blues," and "Mama, You Been On My Mind"—that last song is notable to Beatle fans for George's stirring, much-bootlegged performance of it during the *Let It Be* sessions over a year before.

Both Britain's *New Musical Express* and *Rolling Stone* reported on the session, though their coverage was not entirely accurate. It suggested that the two were making an album together, further claiming that several Beatle songs were performed; actually, only "Yesterday" was and only as something of a joke (George facetiously suggested adding cellos after the performance ended). But some early rock and roll cuts were, including "Da Doo Ron Ron," "All I Have To Do Is Dream," and Carl Perkins' "Your True Love."

While few of these recordings rise to the level of what's typically considered releasable quality (think *Let It Be* sessions in pristine sound), it is for their historic value that a full-length album issue would be fascinating. They show a comfort level and camaraderie unimaginable in a Beatle setting. The atmosphere is lighthearted (Charlie Daniels later noted that Dylan "was in a good mood that day") and loose; on the eve of recording his magnum opus, George is heard as confident and firing on all cylinders in a relaxed setting. Given the rapport displayed on this day, the real wonder isn't that the Traveling Wilburys happened so much as that they didn't happen sooner.

"THE WISHING BOOK" – 1970

Believed to be penned by Nashville guitarist Chuck Howard (who also wrote "Love Don't Last Long" and "Waiting"), this *Beaucoups of Blues* outtake somehow also managed to escape issue on the CD release. It's a fine, melodic ballad, though it clocks in at less than a minute and a half. Given its brevity, it's all the more odd that it wasn't simply tacked on.

"WELL (BABY PLEASE DON'T GO)" – 1971

The Olympics were a west coast doo-wop band led by singer Walter Ward. If remembered at all today, it is for their 1958 hit, "Western Movies," a comic novelty tune complete with gunshots and ricochet sounds. But it was the single's deadly serious B-side that caught the ears of the young Beatles: an edgy blues number entitled "Well!" According to John Lennon, the Fabs used to perform it during their Cavern days, although it must have been dropped from their set by the time things became fully documented.

In the early morning hours of June 5, 1971, John and Yoko joined Frank Zappa and the Mothers onstage at the Fillmore East in New York. Of the rather freeform set that ensued, the most straightforward song was this one, resurrected out of the blue a decade after he'd last publicly performed it. The song must've stuck in Lennon's head though, because early on in the *Imagine* sessions commencing a few weeks later at Ascot Sound Studios, the song was trotted out again for no obvious reason. John and Phil Spector took the song seriously enough to lay down a recording featuring Jim Gordon on drums, Klaus, and Bobby Keys on sax. Lennon laid down an impassioned vocal, as committed as any on *Plastic Ono Band*.

It's not known what the point of the recording was, as it doesn't seem to have been destined for *Imagine*, although it certainly qualified as high quality B-side material. This did not happen, and the track was apparently archived and forgotten. (Meanwhile, the Zappa collaboration was issued a year later as a bonus to the *Some Time In New York City* set.) Only in 1998 was the song at last dusted off and issued, as part of the Lennon *Anthology* box set (under the title "Baby Please Don't Go").

"HEAR ME LORD" (live) – 1971

All Things Must Pass came to a grand, majestic finish with this impassioned entreaty to the Almighty. Arranged with panache, the song certainly would've seemed to be a sure bet to translate well live, given the platoon of backup singers, musicians, and horn section present at the Concert for Bangladesh. And so it was that the song was performed at the afternoon show, signaling the home stretch after Bob Dylan's set.

For the evening performance however—with the band now thoroughly warmed up—the set list was reconfigured slightly: "Something," which had been at the top of the set just after "Wah-Wah," was now slotted just before the end of the show. Dylan's "Love Minus Zero/No Limit" was dropped completely for the second performance, replaced with "Mr. Tambourine Man." George's "Hear Me Lord" was also cut, but without

Given the demands on George's time with the Bangladesh benefit, including duties that would occupy him well into the next year, it was fortunate that "Deep Blue" was in the can, sparing him to come up with another new song to back the "Bangla Desh" single.

replacement. It is not known with any certainty why the changes were made; indeed, except for a low-fidelity audience recording, we wouldn't know that the song was performed at all.

In 2005, after being out of circulation for a time, the film of the event, with an accompanying CD soundtrack, was remastered and reissued. As bonus material, Dylan's missing performance was restored in both iterations, but "Hear Me Lord" was not. This naturally begs the question: why? Was the song so sloppily performed that it would have been too embarrassing? Or were there perhaps technical issues beyond fixing that precluded its inclusion (i.e. damage to the master tape, dead mic issues on vocals, etc.)? There's never been a public explanation for the exclusion, adding one more mystery to the ex-Fabs' well of obscurity.

"1882" – 1972

Unquestionably, one of the strangest songs Paul McCartney ever wrote was this one, a lilting waltz that tells the story of an impoverished 19th century lad. Taking a page from the literature of that era, wherein crime was punished, no matter what the mitigating circumstance (especially if one was poor—then as now), the song's subject finds himself facing the prospect of being "hung like a ham" for stealing bread. Though the song's arpeggioed chords recall "I Want You (She's So Heavy)," in general, "1882" resembles nothing ever associated with Macca.

Written and demoed in 1970, the song became a staple of Wings' earliest live shows. It is believed that a studio recording was laid down in early 1972 after Henry McCullough joined Wings, during the sessions for their debut single, "Give Ireland Back To The Irish." "1882" was introduced onstage as "from our next album" and indeed, had *Red Rose Speedway* been issued as the double album it was intended to be, it is likely the song would have ended up there instead of all but unknown to the general public today.

"ROCK 'N' ROLL PEOPLE" – 1973

Of the four ex-Fabs, John was the least likely to generate leftover material. For better or worse, once he committed to the recording of a song, he very seldom let anything completed go to waste. In the case of this composition, given the demonstrable lack of confidence he was experiencing in 1973, his judgment in shelving the track was spot-on.

The tune bore all the earmarks of going through the motions: a so-so melody, lyrics that aspired to the clever wordplay of his best work but fell severely short, and a vocal that tried to generate some sparks but comes off as forced. While John was content to regard the effort as a misfire, engineer Shelly Yakus thought enough of the throwaway to solicit it for his debut as producer on behalf of Texas bluesman Johnny Winter. The song duly appeared on *John Dawson Winter III* in 1974. (Contrary to repeated misinfo, it was not written *for* Winter.)

As for Lennon's version, it finally debuted in public not as a bonus track for a CD issue of *Mind Games*, as would have made sense, but earlier still, in 1986 as a track on the rather pointless posthumous release, *Menlove Avenue*.

"TOO MANY COOKS" – 1974

When not making trouble in nightclubs during the so-called "Lost Weekend," John logged an awful lot of studio hours. Perhaps recognizing that the path to salvation lie in work, he kept up the pace, moving quickly from one project to another. Not long after completing work on *Pussy Cats* with Harry Nilsson, what was intended as nothing more than a freeform jam night (featuring the "Jim Keltner Orchestra": as named by Lennon, an ensemble featuring Keltner, Nilsson, Al Kooper, Jesse Ed Davis, Jack Bruce, Bobby Keys and Trevor Lawrence on sax) actually resulted in a viable recording, featuring none other than Mick Jagger on lead vocals.

"Too Many Cooks (Spoil The Soup)" was, all Willie Dixon speculation notwithstanding, the debut single of Motown's Holland-Dozier-Holland protégés, 100 Proof Aged In Soul. Issued in 1969, it peaked at twenty-four on the soul charts while most white record buyers remained blissfully unaware of its existence. Not so Jagger and company; with Lennon producing (or as he self-deprecatingly described his production efforts, "sitting behind the desk"), a suitably funky take was captured, replete with horns and an outstanding Jagger vocal. Given the typical chemical state of some participants during that time, it's a minor miracle that something of value was captured at all.

It's impossible to hear this song without recognizing the apparent care that was put into producing and arranging the recording; this wasn't simply a tossed-off jam. Indeed, speculation at the time held that it would be issued as a single on Apple. But instead, extra-musical issues, largely involving record labels and securing the necessary permissions for all involved, led to the track's abandonment.

By the time the session was recalled by Jagger decades later, no one knew if a releasable tape even survived. According to Mick, one master known to have existed was destroyed in a fire; another was unceremoniously trashed by an ex-wife (he didn't say which one). But still another was found in the possession of May Pang, who kept it underneath her bed. She lent it to Jagger, who then released it to near universal acclaim on his 2007 solo compilation.

Prior to its resurfacing, "Too Many Cooks" was the object of much speculation, some calling it a Jagger-Lennon duet (which would've been fascinating); others suggesting that Ringo was on drums. That neither canard was true doesn't much matter, for the recording's quality is itself enough reason to justify all the interest.

"SOILY" – 1974

Another song cut at the early 1972 sessions was a rollicking rocker entitled "Soily." Like "1882," this Macca composition was also a regular feature of the early Wings set. While the song took a few years

George's bringing Dark Horse to Warner Brothers was widely touted in the industry, with print ads depicting him with Mo Ostin and his "big button"—one that presumably pushed sales. Noted George: "Did you know that MO spelled backwards is OM?"

of performing to truly rise to its thundering sonic potential, the lyrics remain as inscrutable as ever, being one of the better examples of Paul's penchant for stringing a series of words together that roll off the tongue nicely, while possessing not an ounce of clear meaning. This early version has not been widely booted.

In August 1974, the Jimmy McCulloch/Geoff Britton version of Wings gathered at the Fabs' former stomping grounds at EMI's number two studio in St. John's Wood. Their purpose was to lay down some tracks and produce a film entitled *One Hand Clapping*. The project, combining new and old material, was conceived as a sort of refinement of *Let It Be*, showing the band at work in the studio. Perhaps feeling that his current group possessed a better grasp of where he wanted to go, Paul revisited "Soily."

With McCulloch aboard, the band now possessed a firepower that, with all due respect to Henry McCullough, took the song to another level. The 1974 studio version virtually out-rocked anything the band ever recorded in the studio, though "Junior's Farm" comes close. (Interestingly—and apropos of nothing—Paul can be heard saying just before the take began, "Terrible, I'm in a band full of queers, honest... alright!")

The track—and the film—did not make it to a public release during the group's lifetime. Instead, *Venus And Mars* was issued the following year; the band went on tour; they recorded *At The Speed Of Sound*, and went on tour again. Bolstered by a full horn section, a smoke and laser show, and wah-wah pedals, "Soily" made the ultimate encore, following two hours' worth of sheer Macca bliss. It is this version that most people are familiar with, released in 1977 on the *Wings Over America* set and as the B-side to the "Maybe I'm Amazed" single. As noted in chapter 1, *One Hand Clapping* at last was issued as a part of 2010's *Band on the Run* deluxe remaster set.

"MO" – 1977

When George moved Dark Horse's distribution from A&M to Warner Brothers in 1976, one of the factors in making his choice was that label's president, veteran exec Mo Ostin. In 1963, Ostin—an accountant by training—was enticed over to Frank Sinatra's Reprise Records from Verve by none other than the chairman of the board himself. There, he quickly gained a reputation as an executive devoted to the artist rather than the bottom line. Spotting and nurturing talent, Ostin was responsible for signing Jimi Hendrix, Joni Mitchell, Van Morrison,

Frank Zappa, and many other era-defining artists.

As part of a fiftieth birthday celebration for Ostin in March 1977, George performed an original composition saluting the label head, entitled (fittingly enough) "Mo." The gently teasing lyric expresses love and thanks for all the success experienced by his labelmates. The song was also recorded, but despite George's desire to include it on first *George Harrison* in 1979, then *Somewhere In England* a year later, the song went unissued both times, at Ostin's request. (Musically, the arrangement bore a slight resemblance to "Faster" (being a mid-tempo Harrisong featuring his trademark slide over a bed of 12-string acoustics) while recalling *Dark Horse*'s "So Sad" melodically.

Eventually, it was issued—after a fashion—on an employee-only six-CD set entitled *Mo's Songs*. The beautifully packaged collection, containing virtually every great hit produced during Warner's glory years, was distributed at Ostin's retirement party in December 1994. Limited to six hundred copies, it trades for high figures today.

Ostin would say with great profundity that "Warner Brothers Records has never been run from the perspective of financial people," something that George might've taken issue with after having *Somewhere In England* handed back to him in 1980 by Ostin himself for not being commercial enough. Perhaps by then, George may have been rethinking the sentiments expressed toward the label head in one of his finer recordings.

"DID WE MEET SOMEWHERE BEFORE" – 1978

A reincarnation theme was explored in this soft but elegant Macca ballad; fittingly, for it was written expressly for *Heaven Can Wait*, Warren Beatty's remake of Alexander Hall's 1941 film *Here Comes Mr. Jordan*. Alas, the song was not included in the movie—Beatty's, anyway. Instead, it was used over the opening credits of (and reprised within) an utterly inappropriate vehicle: Allan Arkush's *Rock 'n' Roll High School*. This adolescent star vehicle for actress P.J. Soles was built upon a plotline centering on The Ramones, the leather-clad three-chord geniuses enjoying a sort of underground success at the time.

The two films could not have been more thematically different, yet for some reason "Did We Meet Somewhere Before" was viewed as musical tofu, blending in wherever it was put (it didn't). Moreover, possibly owing to the fact that the arrangement employed a clarinet (which Beatty's character in the first film played), the song was not even included on *Rock 'n' Roll High School's* soundtrack album.

Such an above average McCartney composition deserved a better fate.

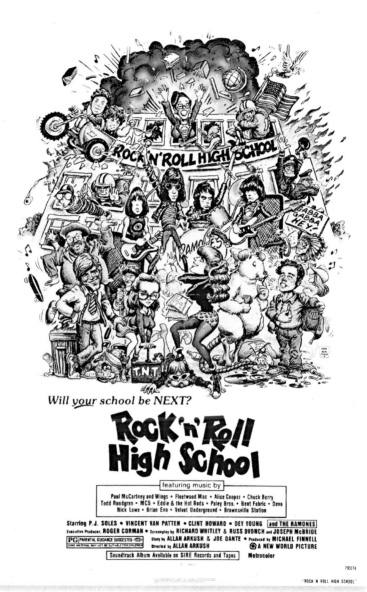

It's hard to imagine what the producers of Rock 'n' Roll High School (which included Roger Corman) heard in Paul's mellow "Did We Meet Somewhere Before?" that screamed suitability for their picture.

Neil Innes, director of the "Blow Away" promo, cemented his friendship with George by composing an array of spot-on Beatle pastiches for The Rutles project. Less remarked on was his acerbic take on John Lennon as "Ron Nasty"—something that George must've gotten many a laugh out of.

CHAPTER 14

OFF TO THE FLICKS WITH THE PIDDLE IN HER NICKS: A SELECTION OF PROMO FILMS – PART TWO

"HEY BABY," "YOU DON'T KNOW ME AT ALL" and "I'LL STILL LOVE YOU" (1976)

Given the promotional efforts from Atlantic/Polydor to make *Ringo's Rotogravure* a hit, it's not surprising that high-quality videos were a part of the plan: three in all. What *is* surprising is that none of them accompanied "A Dose of Rock 'n' Roll," the lead-off single. Instead, they were used for the second US single; a European-only release, and a song not issued as a single at all.

In addition to whatever musical value they contain, these promos are also notable for being a pretty good document of Ringo's shaved head period. It was reported in the foreign media on July 20 that Ringo—in Monte Carlo—had shorn away his locks, ostensibly due to the heat. The cue ball look was particularly newsworthy on a Beatle—a group virtually defined by their hair. But Ringo being Ringo, he seemed to delight in shocking people with his unusual appearance, which extended to shaving his eyebrows as well. (While being interviewed a week later regarding the bestowing of his green card, John asked reporters, "Why'd Ringo cut his hair?")

The setting for "Hey Baby" consisted of a rather palatial looking entry hall, complete with twin staircases and chandeliers (being in fact a set rather than an actual mansion). Ringo, in top hat and tux, is seen as a suave playboy, surrounded by a flock of beauties of every description—ten clad in white; ten in black—whom he serenades individually as he works the stairs. (Ringo's outfit miraculously turns from black to white when he moves from one set of color-coordinated ladies to the next.) That's pretty much the gist of it.

Slightly more visually interesting was the "You Don't Know Me At All" clip, which was filmed in Hamburg and Monte Carlo. A true sentimental journey, the shoot veered back and forth between his new Mediterranean tax exile digs and Hamburg's Große Freiheit, the main drag intersecting with the Reeperbahn, which served as The Beatles' incubator for greatness beginning in 1960. (Though Ringo would not

263

Ringo's post-shaved head period, as documented in this foreign "Hey Baby" picture sleeve (as well as all the promo films accompanying Ringo's Rotogravure).

become a Beatle for another two years, he too apprenticed here in Hamburg's Red Light district with Rory Storm and the Hurricanes.)

Judging by the condition of Ringo's scalp, it's evident that the Monaco sequences were shot before the Hamburg ones, given the greater growth of hair and beard in the latter. While the overall effect of the film is no less silly than much of the efforts that preceded it, it is clear that the production values were quite high. While it is doubtful that these two *Rotogravure* clips were ever shown on US TV in time to promote the album, stateside Beatle fans became acquainted with them through frequent 70s-era screenings at Beatlefest for many years.

The promo for "I'll Still Love You" is perhaps the least familiar of the three, being that the Harrisong in question never saw issue as a single (though it did stir legal matters; see chapter 2). It is also less overtly comic than the other two, being more of a romantically themed one, matching the song's mood. It does feature a brunette model as Ringo's dance partner throughout: it is not Nancy Andrews (though she *would* appear in a 1978 Ringo promo). It also appears to have been shot in Hamburg at the same time as the "You Don't Know Me" video, with a matching park backdrop common to both.

The failure of *Ringo's Rotogravure* to click with the masses meant that such a hefty promotional expenditure would not be tolerated the next time around unless justified; sadly, it was not. (NOTE: The promotional film created for *Ringo the 4th*'s "Drowning in the Sea of Love" is described in detail on page 283-4 of *Fab Four FAQ 2.0*; no need to repeat it here.)

"THIS SONG," "CRACKERBOX PALACE" and "TRUE LOVE" (1976)

For his Dark Horse/Warner Brothers debut, George pulled out all the promotional stops. *Thirty-Three & 1/3*'s marketing plan encompassed interviews, TV and radio appearances, as well as print ads and these three promo films. Whatever toll the whole "My Sweet Lord"/"He's So Fine" episode exacted on him personally, at least he managed to get past it with a sense of humor intact. His musical response to the very public black eye, "This Song," proved to be the perfect vehicle to underscore his own redemption, through levity.

Though George took a pass on any promotional films for 1975's *Extra Texture* release, he showed a year later that he'd mastered the form (or least knew how to pick capable hands for fulfilling his vision). It was scripted by Alan Metter, who would one day direct the Rodney Dangerfield vehicle, *Back To School* (as well as some Olivia Newton-John videos) and co-directed by George and one Michael Collins (presumably not the Apollo 11 astronaut).

The casting of the courtroom farce included some familiar faces, including Jim Keltner (behind the bench sporting the British judicial full-bottom wig; it was *not* Phil Spector, as some have supposed); Ronnie Wood as one of two courtroom "pepperpots" (Python-speak for matronly middle-aged women, usually behaving badly and always played by a men); sax player Tom Scott more or less as himself (standing up to take the solo; he's flanked on his left by engineer Hank Cicalo) and, as the cop manhandling George into and out of the proceedings, Dark Horse Records General Manager, Dennis Morgan.

Filmed on location at (what's now) Los Angeles' Stanley Mosk courthouse, the promo depicted George on trial, mounting a defense that *this* song (in "E") came to him unknowingly, and—what's more—his experts (played by three Dark Horse staffers) assured him it was okay. As the song unspools, things in the courtroom begin to increasingly spin out of control: the stenographer's keyboard becomes a Fender Rhodes; the bailiff begins jamming on bass, a masked juggler appears and by the end, as George, despite his pleadings, gets roughly whisked out of the courtroom, a comely young woman in hot pants begins dancing on the lawyer's table.

Olivia (not yet Olivia *Harrison*) was documented in stills taken on the set for the "This Song" film, but she is not seen in the final cut. She *is* seen briefly—and uncharacteristically—as one of two lingerie-clad ladies sharing George's bed in the next *Thirty-Three & 1/3* promo:

"Crackerbox Palace" ("...some times are good..."). Like the one for "True Love," it was shot at Friar Park and directed by Eric Idle (who himself makes a cameo impersonating Eric Clapton, during the chair sequence where a succession of people change while George remains constant).

Just as the public has for decades elected to believe that Boris Karloff played the title character in 1931's *Frankenstein* (no, he played "The Monster"; Colin Clive played Dr. Henry Frankenstein), Beatle fans persist in believing that George's sprawling Henley-on-

Though replete when any number of Pythonisms, the promo for "Crackerbox Palace"—directed by Eric Idle—did not feature a cameo from Graham Chapman, though his "Colonel" character was represented, as seen here.

Thames estate was called "Crackerbox Palace," or that the song was *about* his home. Wrong and wrong: George's was called Friar Park; "Crackerbox Palace" was the name of the late beatnik comedian Lord Buckley's Los Angeles home.

The song was prompted when George happened to run into Buckley's former manager, who apparently bore a resemblance to his charge. George Greif mentioned in the ensuing conversation that Buckley's home was called "Crackerbox Palace": George wrote the phrase down on a cigarette pack and this tune was the result (hence the line, "I met a Mr. Greif..."). But so vivid was the song's visual association with Friar Park, courtesy of this video, that the connection has become indelible. (The signs seen throughout the film certainly reinforced the misconception.)

If it was George's intent to display his home to good effect, he certainly succeeded: the sheer greenery of the grounds and majesty of

the interior come through in every shot. But the effect is subsumed by the succession of primary focal points, beginning with the pram-pushing matron seen at the start just before George springs forth to mime the words. "She" was played by Neil Innes, who also appeared as one of the "Church Police" straight out of Monty Python, as well as other costumed figures throughout. (Innes' "Stoop Solo" costume, first seen on *Rutland Weekend Television*, also makes an appearance, though not on Neil, as does the Union Jack pajamas). Indeed, Python served as a sort of subtext throughout, via visual cues, including Graham Chapman's Colonel (albeit not played by Graham).

"True Love" began with George, costumed as an Edwardian-era would-be suitor (complete with straw boater and handlebar mustache) serenading an indifferent love interest, aboard a gondola first seen emerging from a grotto, "tunnel of love"-style. They quickly lose the gondolier, and George soon finds himself competing for the lady's attention with the "guardian angel" (played by—you guessed it—Neil Innes). The whole couple-on-a-boat motif may have been an effort to echo where the Cole Porter song was first seen/heard: sung on a yacht (named "True Love") by Bing Crosby and Grace Kelly in the 1956 musical, *High Society*. In absurdist fashion, it's Innes' angel that wins the girl by the song's end.

By every account of all who knew him well, George's sense of humor—sharp, dry and (mostly) high-level—was manifest; in complete contrast to much of his musical work, which tended more toward the serious, ponderous and—it must be said—preachy. But with the 1976 roll-out for *Thirty-Three & 1/3*, his lighthearted side was on full public display in a way it never had been before (nor would it ever be again). These three videos provided ample evidence of it, as did the album's packaging and his appearance on *Saturday Night*. Though the two Friar Park/Eric Idle ones were demonstrably Pythonesque, they were equaled in comedic appeal by the non-Python "This Song" courtroom film. This last one and "Crackerbox Palace" aired on *Saturday Night Live* in November 1976.

"MULL OF KINTYRE," "WITH A LITTLE LUCK," "LONDON TOWN" and "I'VE HAD ENOUGH" (1977-8)

Scotland's rather suggestively-shaped Kintyre Peninsula projects into the Atlantic from the west side; practically due east across the

WINGS DOUBLE A

Graham Hughes

MULL OF KINTYRE

The biggest money-spinner of Wings' career, "Mull of Kintyre" was a McCartney-Laine co-write. Falling on financial hardship in the 1980s, Laine sold his share of the publishing to Paul (for a sum in the low six figures), though he still receives royalties from it—just not a portion from MPL's publishing.

country's breadth lies the city of Edinburgh. The Mull of Kintyre— its southwesternmost point—lies little more than 20 kilometers across the sea from Northern Ireland. To most non-Brits, this bit of geographical information means nothing, beyond it being a place Paul was so smitten with that he wrote a song about it. One might have the impression that it was something much closer to where his farm actually is, but in fact, Paul's spread is on the *east* side of Kintyre, well north of the Mull and close to Campbeltown.

Still, it is a lovely place, full of natural beauty: the kind one might be inspired to sing about, even if one didn't live on it. Clearly, Paul knew his countrymen well, and had a pretty good idea that this song, replete with a sing-along chorus and bagpipe embellishment would go over well, so much so that he kept it separate from the *London Town* album and issued it as a stand-alone single just in time for the holidays. The strategy paid off in spades by rewarding him with the biggest single of his career—in every market but the states. Predictably.

To launch the mega-hit properly, *three* different promos were prepared, though only two aired. The first could've been commissioned by the Mull of Kintyre tourism board, had one existed: the scenery is shown to great effect (though in fact it was shot north of Paul's farm on Kintyre's east side at Saddell Bay), while the engaging nature of the song makes it sound like a place you'd *want* to visit. The film unfolds following the arrangement: first, just Paul with his guitar (with Linda seen in the distant background, cradling baby James—born one month earlier), joined by Denny (playing an unplugged *electric* guitar) for the second chorus and Linda (sans James) for the third. Before her arrival, the two, atop a bluff overlooking the beach, gaze down where the Campbeltown Pipe Band approach, adding their contribution. As the song reaches its climax, the film centers around a roaring bonfire, surrounded by what presumably are the local folk, singing along in a manner recalling the "Hey Jude" promo film, shot nearly a decade earlier. (It should therefore be no surprise, since this clip was directed by Michael Lindsay-Hogg.)

The second promo was directed by another *Ready Steady Go* alumnus: Nicholas Ferguson, who likewise directed the Beatles' Intertel Studio promos from November 1965. (See my *Revolver* book for a detailed discussion.) While it does the job of selling a song that needed little selling, it is less aesthetically pleasing, being wholly set-bound—and every inch looking it—as though staged *on* a TV show rather than to *be broadcast* on a TV show. Of course, that may have been the point: the "Hey Jude" / "Revolution" clips were designed to look as though the Beatles had shown up on David Frost's stage (or the Smothers Brothers'), rather than Twickenham, where they were actually filmed.

This second clip, filmed at Elstree Film Studio, *does* feature Paul, Linda and Denny on an elaborately-dressed set, replete with rocks, trees and much "mist" rolling in from the fog generators (rather than the back screen "sea" seen behind them). Also, the Campbeltown Pipers make an appearance, giving the overall setting a rather cramped look. Both clips aired on *Top of the Pops*, while the third version, produced at EMI's Abbey Road facility in December, never aired anywhere at all. Wings appeared on *The Mike Yarwood Christmas Show* (singing live over the backing track) on December 25, 1977. This appearance staged the three sitting on chairs, on a set decorated with Christmas trees and a large illuminated cross on the back wall. Again, they are surrounded by smoke, and the bagpipers appear. While not an actual promo as such, this performance is on YouTube and has been bootlegged.

When *London Town* was ready to launch, promos for each of the three singles were prepared. Two were directed by Michael Lindsay-Hogg: those for "With a Little Luck" and the album's title track. The first was very much in the style of TV appearances of the time: a simple stage; unadorned, but for a tree at the rear of the set as a backdrop for Paul, who's shown singing and playing bass. Linda—to his left, and Denny—to his right, are on keyboards; close enough to Paul to lean in and share a mic. The clip marked the video debut of drummer Steve Holley with Wings, miming along on his kit to a part played on record by Joe English. As the recording features no conspicuous guitar, Laurence Juber is nowhere to be seen.

Drawing visual interest beyond the four musicians are children seen around them at the onset; dancing around as kids do. Lindsay-Hogg's penchant for filling his productions with people—especially of multiple ethnicities—eventually comes through, with more grown-up dancers eventually drawing the focus as the song goes on. (At the song's end, Denny boosts the little boy seen at the beginning to reach his keyboard and play the keys.) The "With a Little Luck" clip runs at the shortened single version of the track: 3:13 rather than the full-length 5:45.

With "London Town," the visual ante was upped: though thoroughly crafted for the small screen, it featured a visually evocative, yet simple set, illustrating the song's lyrics quite literally: a street for Wings' core trio to walk down; a "barker" playing a flute; "ordinary people" brushing past; a "rozzer" (a cop actually) with a pink balloon tied to his foot. Drawing our attention is old friend Victor Spinetti, as the song's out-of-work actor (though he's made up as a mime). Paul being Paul, he could not be upstaged by the cameo: during the song's guitar break near the end (where he and Denny break out their instruments: Denny, playing slide and Paul, his classic Beatle-era Epiphone), he flashes the camera, revealing garters and lingerie beneath his trench coat.

"I've Had Enough" was directed by Keith McMillan (also known as "Marcus Keef" or simply "Keef"), as the start of a frequent collaboration between Paul and him that would extend through the *Back to the Egg* videos and into the 80s, as far as 1984's "No More Lonely Nights." "Keefco," as McMillan's company was called, produced videos by artists ranging from Queen to Pat Benatar; prior to that, he was an album cover art designer (Black Sabbath, Rod Stewart). He therefore arrived with a strong visual sense, evident in this, his first Wings film.

Though the clip was a straightforward mimed performance (that introduced Laurence Juber as a band member), the moody lighting, arranged by Director of Photography John Henshall, draws our attention most: in stark contrast to the typically cheery McCartney fare, this one looks as though it was lit through Venetian blinds. Dark and cramped, the bandmates appear to be sharing a jail cell—or a padded one. Paul is unshaved and sweaty—a look never heretofore seen in one of their music videos. Even more striking, he never makes eye contact with the camera (a posture adopted by son James while performing decades later).

Though this was the pre-MTV era, more reliable video outlets had begun popping up on late night television in the states. *Don Kirshner's Rock Concert*, *Midnight Special* and various local/cable shows were all in the mix for airing the steady stream of music videos coming out of Britain (and America) by this time. Paul's offerings were no exception, though his band never appeared on either of these shows to perform live, unlike the bulk of their guests.

"TONIGHT" (1978)

Despite the fact that by mid-summer *Bad Boy* was showing itself to be a commercial stiff—notwithstanding the promotional efforts exerted via seemingly endless TV interviews and the *Ringo* special upon its release—and with little to show but anemic sales and no hits, Portrait Records sprang at last for a promotional video: shot on the French Riviera, no less. In a parallel universe, where Ringo wasn't burdened with a goofy but lovable uncle image, and where radio playlists didn't set the bar high for an ex-Beatle, his offerings might have had a chance. "Tonight" was a pleasant piece of period pop; as inoffensive as anything else gracing the Top Forty. There was no reason for it to be shut out on its musical merits (or so Portrait optimistically thought).

To stoke the promotional fires, they produced this romantic little film, shot at a "haunted" chateau and co-starring Nancy Andrews as Ringo's phantom dream woman. (She appears and disappears into thin air throughout, echoing the song's lyrics of disbelief that such a lovely apparition could exist.) She twirls; they dance; Ringo mimes. Completely devoid of any of the usual comedic contrivances seen in his videos, the "Tonight" clip fully supports the song. Interestingly, though the single was only issued overseas (where it did not chart), "Tonight" *was* played on Los Angeles-area radio at the time, before running its course.

"BLOW AWAY" and "FASTER" (1979)

"Silly and cute" is not the same thing as "clever and witty." Therein lies the difference between the promos produced for George's self-titled 1979 release, as contrasted with those that accompanied *Thirty-Three & 1/3* more than two years earlier. Though "Blow Away" marked a musical return to form, with George's gifts for crossover appeal and melodicism intact, the promo he promoted it with ranks as one of those things that fans tend to either love or hate. (Well, perhaps "hate" is too strong a term—maybe "roll their eyes and sigh at" might be a better description.)

"Blow Away" was directed by Seventh Python, Neil Innes: a man that knew a thing or two about musical comedy. In this instance, he deceptively began the film as a pretty straightforward offering,

Tanned, rested and ready: George's return in 1979 with an upbeat self-titled album showed his willingness to make music, stopping short of playing full time rock star.

replete with shots of stormy skies (thereby enforcing the song's theme and implicitly marking it as an update of "All Things Must Pass": "a mind can blow those clouds away) and George singing and playing guitar. But by the first chorus, a subversive element has crept in: George offers an overtly forced smile at the "be happy" line, and is shown taking a few simple dance steps and—for him—getting a little over the top with the guitar poses. By the time the refrain comes around again, the video's theme is established: placing George alongside oversized animal toys, beginning with a small red bird (with moving eyes and wings).

It escalates to placing George inside a white duck by the next chorus and atop a bobbing head dog for the guitar solo. All of this is done as he wears his typically earnest expression, while the stormy cloud shots keep resurfacing before giving way to sunshine by song's end. All in all, not exactly high concept stuff, but it did show that George was still willing to play the game, if on his own terms. As judged by his actions (or inactions), this would wax and wane with each release going forward. (Contrast this with Paul, who was guaranteed to deliver the video goods with each release.)

"Faster" wasn't issued as a single in the US market, perhaps in recognizing the American public's interest in George's Formula One obsession or lack thereof. Whatever the song's merits (which included a chorus that practically invited listeners to mentally sing, "he's a *bastard* at going faster..."), George dedicated the proceeds from its release to the Gunnar Nilsson Cancer Fund. (No relation to Harry, the Swedish racer died at 29 in 1978.) However well-aimed, the single failed to chart, despite being issued in the collectible picture disc format.

In any event, a promo was produced: it depicted much racing

footage—including crashes—intercut with shots of George in the back of his Daimler, singing and playing guitar. The whole thing is played straight, with no laughs offered, save perhaps for the shot of George's driver: Scottish racing legend Jackie Stewart, replete with his trademark tartan cap. The two had developed a close friendship, and one day Jackie would relate the story of how, in Switzerland, George took the time to offer his son a private guitar lesson, showing him how to play "Here Comes The Sun" properly.

The "Blow Away" video was shown in the UK in March 1979 on a program called (fittingly, for George) *Pop Gospel*, directed by former Monkee Micky Dolenz. In the US, it was screened a month later on Burt Sugarman's *Midnight Special*. The "Faster" clip first aired in France, at around roughly the same time.

"GOODNIGHT TONIGHT" and BACK TO THE EGG (1979)

Paul had a lot of high hopes for his deal with CBS, much of them centering on their using their promotional muscle to get him back into the charts where he once belonged. The recent failure of both the "Mull of Kintyre" single *and* the *Wings Greatest* collection (both EMI issues) to set the US charts alight seemed particularly galling to him. It therefore should come as no surprise that an all-out effort was made to produce visual representation of not only the lead-off "Goodnight Tonight" single, but also the ensuing CBS long-player, *Back to the Egg.*

In being set as a period piece, "Goodnight Tonight" deliberately sidestepped any current day dance club associations; Paul may have been self-conscious about so flagrantly boarding the disco bandwagon. Director Keith McMillan suitably attired the band as Prohibition-era sheiks (though a proper flapper look would've required Linda's natural landscape be flattened out; so daunting would the task have been that it probably wasn't even attempted), complete with 1920s crooner-style microphone, though having Paul sing through a megaphone would've been the icing on the cake. The only concession to modernity was the intercutting of Wings in contemporary dress coming two-thirds of the way in—and only briefly. It was a thoroughly stylish presentation that suited the song's eclectic production well.

Back to the Egg spawned some four tracks issued as singles in various markets ("Getting Closer," "Spin It On," "Old Siam, Sir," "Arrow Through Me"); each had its own video. But non-singles "Winter Rose/ Love Awake," "Baby's Request" and Denny Laine's "Again and Again and Again" were all accorded the video treatment as well. (Furthermore, the recording sessions for the Rockestra tracks, "Rockestra Theme" and

"So Glad To See You Here" were filmed, though not necessarily intended as promos unto themselves.)

The aforementioned single releases were served via straight up performance clips in a variety of settings, while "Baby's Request"—a song originally intended as an offering to the Mills Brothers—sounded like something from another era entirely. It therefore required something of a "concept treatment," in this case, setting it during World War II, apparently in North Africa. The khaki-clad ensemble appear on a make-shift stage (in the desert), while Paul steps up to sing, not unlike a USO crooner, simply entertaining the troops. Amidst armored vehicles and a handful of uniformed soldiers, Wings does its usual thing, excepting Linda: looking like a lost Andrews sister, she "plays" the stand-up bass. ("Baby's Request," said to be a favorite tune of George Harrison's, was later re-recorded for the more fitting setting of 2012's *Kisses on the Bottom* pop standard album.)

Keeping with Paul's habit of finding exotic or colorful locales at which to record, Kent's Lympne Castle—said to be haunted—was where a portion of *Back to the Egg* was recorded. Its picturesque setting made it ideal to return to for the visual accompaniment: "Old Siam, Sir" was filmed in the hall, while the "Winter Rose" segment of the two-song medley was shot outside. It depicted Linda on her Appaloosa, after the neat trick of showing summer change to winter at the castle. (The promos were filmed in May/June 1979, so it was a particularly convincing effect that changed the scene from green to a snowscape.) "Love Awake," the medley's second half, had actually been recorded at Lympne, so filming the video inside made sense. It began with Paul gazing outside a window before moving inside, where Linda and the rest of Wings played around a fireplace.

Rather than be unimaginative or lazy by simply filming everything in or outside of the castle, Keefco elected to move things around for subsequent shoots. "Again and Again and Again," for instance, was filmed in a field of yellow flowers located nearby. The band was depicted "playing," Denny and Laurence on acoustics, Paul on acoustic bass, and Steve on his kit, albeit standing and not seated; he might not have been visible otherwise.

"Spin It On" and "Getting Closer" were shot at an aircraft hangar located near Lympne. In true Macca fashion, the "spinning" theme was depicted quite literally: a spinning biplane prop seen at the start let no one mistake the locale, though once inside, all trappings of a hangar were ditched for a proper concert set-up with colored lighting racks, a parachute ceiling and crowd noise. The band members are all wearing leather bomber jackets, and shown to spin on their own axis from time to time. "Getting Closer" was shot on the same set, sans bomber jackets and intercut with again, some literal evocations of the lyrics: the band "getting closer" to the venue in their truck, with the "windscreen wipers" utilized on cue. (Thankfully, no salamanders were apparently at hand; otherwise, they would have made a cameo, too.)

The videos were bundled up into a half-hour long TV special, along with an opening segment that brought to life the album's cover (see chapter 12 for a discussion of the design). The *Back to the Egg* television special was syndicated throughout the US in 1979 at different times (screenings in some cities around the 4th of July, others around Thanksgiving weekend). Inexplicably, it did not air in Britain until 1981, after Wings had officially called it a day.

"COMING UP" and "WATERFALLS" (1980)

Just as many fans believe that Paul played "kazoo" on Ringo's recording of "You're Sixteen" (he didn't—it's his singing a sax imitation), many fans persist in believing Paul was imper-sonating Buddy Holly in the "Coming Up" promo, though this is understandable, given how little known Hank Marvin is in this country. (Courtesy of the Vincent Vigil collection)

McCartney II represented that periodic Macca approach to making an album: doing it all himself, as he'd more or less done at the onset of his post-Beatles career. Promoting the first single from his second one-man-band project with a promo adopting that same idea—more or less by himself—was, by 1980, an idea whose time had come. Once again, Keith McMillan was at the helm of what would be a technically arduous undertaking, for its time at least. (Nowadays, anyone with a computer could whip it together in minutes; in 1980, it took about a week.)

In the "Coming Up" vehicle, Paul introduced the "Plastic Macs"—his play on John's "Plastic Ono Band"—comprised of some twelve personas (real and unreal): all played by himself (and Linda). One would be a 1963 version of himself; another would be Sparks' visually distinctive keyboardist, Ron Mael. His hirsute drummer was *inspired* by Led Zeppelin's John Bonham (without actually resembling him); one of the four brass players Paul played was thought to have been modeled after Roxy Music's Andy Mackay. A generic long-haired guitarist stood beside one commonly (and mistakenly) believed to be Buddy Holly: it was actually The Shadows' Hank Marvin, who had, in recent years, played with Paul as a member of the Rockestra. The remainder of the ensemble, including Linda's female and male back-up singers, were all completely fictitious creations.

For "Waterfalls," Paul is alone, rocking a sweater vest and seen initially in that clichéd songwriter mode: in this case, working on a composition, pausing to change something on the paper in front of him before proceeding. But McMillan was no by-the-numbers artist: with a burst of water and color, he places Paul up and out, suddenly in front of the polar bear he's singing about. More literal evocations follow, sad to say: a castle with a tower; a garden with a flower; a motorcar. But there's something compelling about Paul's uncharacteristic melancholy in this video; it almost seems petty to nitpick every detail.

One last observation: there's an aspect to the film that seems vaguely unsettling or "wrong"; as though Paul is being presented with a mirror image of himself. The note-taking is being done left-handed, so that's not it; but upon closer observation, one can place one's finger on it: he's switched the part in his hair.

The "Waterfalls" promo aired in America on *The John Davidson Show* on September 22, 1980. "Coming Up" was broadcast in the states as part of a hilarious *Saturday Night Live* set-up on "Weekend Update," airing on May 17.

"WOMAN" (1981)

In laying the groundwork for the full-tilt promotional push to be given to *Double Fantasy*, the Lennons were a little tardy. Maybe they were a little out of practice, having been on the recording business sidelines for several years; maybe it was in attempting to run everything themselves, they just didn't have time to (micro) manage every aspect. But though they'd long decided that "(Just Like) Starting Over" would be the first single, its October release had come and gone without a promotional film being created.

Video representation hadn't been *completely* off their radar: on August 19, 1980, in the midst of the sessions, John had hired a camera crew to come to the Hit Factory and document the musicians at work.

276

On November 2, 1980, John and Yoko were photographed by Jack Mitchell (who shot 8 rolls of film). One image (seen here) graced the posthumous "Woman" single sleeve; another, the cover of the issue of People magazine commemorating his death.

The results of the shoot remain one of the few genuine Holy Grails in all of Beatledom: footage of John Lennon running through the remake of "I'm Losing You" (a week after the "Cheap Trick" original take). While audio still exists (recorded by producer Jack Douglas' hidden microphones), the video captured by director Jay Dubin has officially been declared to no longer exist, said to have been destroyed by John Lennon personally (by immersing it in water), on the grounds that he didn't like the way he looked.

There have been amateur investigations into the fate of this footage, assuming that water alone would not have destroyed it. The consensus is that the particularly "wired" John caught on video was simply unfit for public consumption: rather than the returning rocker who'd taken time off to bake bread and raise his son, this John was the embodiment of what the "Lost Weekend" Lennon was supposed to have been: coked up and practically anorexic. So goes the current thinking, though whether it was in fact destroyed or simply suppressed is harder to know. (According to at least one knowledgeable report, some twenty minutes of the footage *still* exists, in the hands of a private collector.)

277

In any event, by late November, the Lennons had started getting their ducks in a row with regard to producing a belated "Starting Over" promo. To that end, they hired a crew to film themselves walking through Central Park, with the intent of incorporating the footage into additional material filmed at Sperone Westwater Gallery in Soho, where a set had been prepared to simulate their bedroom. (Also simulated was the daylight, courtesy of lights set up for the purpose; this was a November evening in New York, after all.) Both shoots that day were directed by old friend Ethan Russell, that renowned rock photographer that had shot not only images for the *Let It Be* project, but also the Beatles' final group photo session, at Tittenhurst Park on August 22, 1969. To capture stills, *Soho News* stringer Allan Tannenbaum tagged along—to *both* locales.

The Central Park footage proved to be poignant unto itself, especially in light of the impending tragedy. John, wearing his silver Gap coat (with the fur collar) strides confidently through the autumn afternoon with Yoko on his arm. They are shown from a variety of angles and distances, but the overall mood is of relaxed devotion; whatever else they may have *really* been going through that year, the two were old pros at projecting whatever message thcy wanted to get across. Lest this footage not fully deliver their message of love renewed, the Sperone sequence left no doubts.

Herewith, the couple, clad in kimonos, calmly disrobed and began simulating marital lovemaking. Nothing terribly graphic was captured (or at least, was publicly revealed); suffice to say, far more was delivered (and with less reason) on the cover of *Unfinished Music No. 1*. But taken together, both sets of film would've made an interesting promo for *Double Fantasy*'s lead-off single. Unfortunately for everybody, events forced by an outside hand made certain that nothing filmed on November 26 would be used for its originally intended purpose, in its originally intended context. (For a further layer of poignancy, the shoot was followed by a get-together at The Plaza with Ringo; it was to be their last meeting.)

Instead, December 8 would leave in its wake no need for additional promotional efforts. "(Just Like) Starting Over" sailed to the top of the charts, and the focus now shifted to the follow-up. "I'm Losing You" had once been considered a clear contender for the next single; this was now completely out of the question. "Woman," however, as *Double Fantasy*'s most Beatlesque track, was a natural to put out before a public still deeply in mourning. Framing it delicately was of utmost concern: one couldn't ignore the tragedy, but one didn't want to immerse the release in it either.

Astutely, Yoko gauged the public mood and recognized the cathartic value some strong visuals could have when accompanying one of John's final musical statements. (His "for the other half of the sky" pronouncement at the beginning of the recording was brought *way up* in the video mix.) The promo she assembled combined the November Central Park footage, along with *new* film starkly depicting her in bereavement. Also included were visuals from the couple's life together: their early collaborations (all three "Unfinished Music" projects are represented); their peace activism; the "househusband" years with Sean. But John's end is evoked throughout with a directness that chilled viewers then as now: before thirty seconds have passed, the *New York Times* announcing John's assassination is shown, while later, in a gut wrenching juxtaposition, his dreamy back cover image from *Imagine* dissolves to reveal his death repose: the slab shot infamously published on the front cover of the *National Enquirer*.

To some, such a graphic reminder of his murder was a shocking exploitation, one-upping the cruel stunt first pulled to increase newsstand sales. That would be one interpretation (doubtless informed by one's disposition toward Yoko). Another would be this: Yoko showing the world that *this really happened.* In 1963, Jacqueline Kennedy ignored repeated entreaties to change from her blood-and-brain stained outfit she'd worn in Dallas upon her return to Washington, knowing the full media glare would be upon her and how unseemly the display would look. The First Lady was well aware of this, but in her shock and devastation, one thought was clear: "I want them to see what they've done." In her own way, Yoko's sharing the reality of what happened is fully understandable, given Mrs. Kennedy's precedent.

Lest the quick visual contrast not quite get the point across, four months later, Yoko released *Season of Glass*, her first solo album in seven years. Her use of John's bloody glasses on the cover struck some as going too far, but she has remained unrepentant about this, tweeting the image again in recent years as a statement against gun violence after the 2012 Sandy Hook schoolhouse shootings. Where she *did* draw the line was in using the bedroom footage shot in Soho: that would first surface in the promo film for "Walking On Thin Ice," the track John had spent his final studio hours working on.

Yoko's "Woman" video—featuring a dedication to John—was first screened (as an "exclusive") on ABC's *20/20* on Thursday, February 12, 1981; introduced by Barbara Walters.

Badfinger on the Top of the Pops set, January 26, 1972.

CHAPTER 15

NO LONGER RIDING ON THE MERRY-GO-ROUND: DEATHS

A s young men in their thirties during the 1970s, one might've expected that any deaths occurring within the ex-Beatles' collective orbit would have befallen their elderly grandparents, or perhaps their parents. Instead, the decade following their heyday saw inordinate contact with mortality, encompassing friends, peers, and at last—unthinkably—one of their own.

This roll call of the fallen includes death from old age and drug abuse, and by suicide and murder. Just as the Beatles' story demonstrates considerable good fortune, acclaim, and joy, so it also felt its share of sudden, tragic loss. Here is a listing of folks that touched the lives of the group in ways great and small; by affecting *their* collective or individual trajectory, they likewise touched us all.

LOUISE HARRISON – JULY 7, 1970

Virtually alone out of all the adults within the nascent Beatles' inner circle, George's mother gave the youths unconditional support. While John's Aunt Mimi famously derided the attention he gave to his guitar at the expense of studies, and Paul's father Jim, though a musician himself, insisted that his son put aside his hobby in order to concentrate on becoming a teacher, it was Louise that attended gigs, provided a rehearsal space when needed and, once Beatlemania hit full force, took the time to personally answer thousands of fan letters. Long after they'd become famous, she'd welcome visitors into her home and tirelessly regale them with stories.

This down-to-earth charm and affability made her a fan favorite around the world. (In the home George bought for his parents was a plaque presented by the United Beatles Fans of Pomona, California "to Harold and Louise Harrison for the time and effort they have shown to Beatle People everywhere," as well as many other gifts.) When not carrying on long-term correspondence with certain fans she especially hit it off with, she found herself invited to fan weddings and, as a local celebrity, judging beauty contests and opening summer fetes.

In the summer of 1969, as her son's band was at work on their final release, Louise began seeking treatment for chronic headaches. A tumor

Written while he watched his mother battle her fatal illness, George's "Deep Blue" graced the flipside of a song that likewise commemorated death.

was growing in her brain, but the attending physician claimed that her troubles were purely "psychological." George rushed to her bedside, offering prayers and readings from holy texts. (Louise supported his spiritual explorations: "As long as no one is hurt.") For a time, she went into remission: George and his brothers were able to enjoy her moments of lucidity, sharing laughs over old reminiscences.

By the time the symptoms had returned, the Beatles were split and George was just getting down to business on *All Things Must Pass*. As the by-now inoperable growth began stealing her very identity from her, George began spending more time at her side, though her ability to recognize him was gone. His father Harry, having cared for her during the illness, developed ulcers and had to himself be hospitalized, compelling George to shuttle between their respective rooms, assuring each that the other was doing fine. One early morning, exhausted, he stumbled home and poured his feelings of helplessness out on paper, expressing the despair and frustration of his inability to take the sickness from his loved ones. ("Deep Blue," as discussed in chapter 9.)

On July 7, 1970—Ringo's thirtieth birthday—Louise slipped away, with George by her side. Three days later, her cremated remains were buried privately. She never lived to see her son release his magnum opus and all the worldwide acclaim that it received. (Given what George had been going through, the album's somber packaging is entirely understandable.)

In a regrettable footnote, the George Harrison Fan Club, run by one of Louise's pen pals, was accused by George one year later of violating the family's privacy by revealing her final resting place. Though no such thing had happened—in fact, the fan club had taken up a collection in honor of Louise and, with Harold's blessing, donated it to the hospital where she'd been treated—an irreparable falling out had occurred. Within a year, the fan club shut down.

KING CURTIS – AUGUST 13, 1971

As students of American rock and roll records, the Beatles were well aware of the work of saxophonist King Curtis (born Curtis Ousley) even before they knew who he was. The gifted studio pro performed on The Coasters' "Yakety Yak," wrote and played on Buddy Holly's "Reminiscing"—a staple of their 1962 Hamburg set, sung by George— as well as "Boys" by The Shirelles. He also scored a few instrumental hits under his own name, among "Soul Twist" and "Memphis Soul Stew."

Curtis' services were very much in demand throughout the sixties, playing in sessions with everyone from Aretha Franklin (that's his sax solo on "Respect," as well as on her version of "Bridge Over Troubled Water") to Jimi Hendrix (when the latter backed up Little Richard). Guitar legend Duane Allman and The Band's Robbie Robertson were huge fans, as was Eric Clapton, who played on Curtis' *Teasin'* album in 1970.

For the Fabs themselves, up close

In his final years, King Curtis was in the habit of re-cording re-imaginings of current chart hits. But his versions were no embarrassments: his 1970 take on Led Zeppelin's (or Willie Dixon's, depending on your point of view) "Whole Lotta Love" featured a funked up arrangement no less powerful than the hit version. A live recording was issued a year later on his Live at the Fillmore West album (which featured Bil-ly Preston in support), one week before his death.

acquaintance came during their 1965 North American tour, when the King Curtis Band appeared as one of the opening acts. (In addition to their own set, the ensemble backed up the other performers on everything from the opening "Star Spangled Banner" to the medley of contemporary hits playing behind "The Discotech Dancers.") Though acting as warm-up to the hottest rock band on earth was a decidedly thankless job, their sheer musicianship carried the day, especially with their incendiary performance of Ray Charles' "What'd I Say." (A portion of their set can be seen in the Shea Stadium concert film.)

Naturally, when John wanted to add a touch of authentic R&B sax to his gritty "It's So Hard," he knew who to turn to. Curtis and Lennon met up at New York City's Record Plant in July 1971, where—as the tapes rolled—the two reminisced about Shea as well as the 1966 tour, where the infamous cherry bomb incident occurred. (Coming off the heels of John's "Bigger than Jesus" controversy, a small explosive during the Memphis show prompted the Fabs to look around to see which one of them had been shot. John confessed to Curtis that he expected it to be Ringo.)

Following the pleasantries, John directed Curtis to deliver a bluesy solo, mouthing the parts he heard in his head. Ever the professional, Curtis quickly nailed it, as he also then did with the raucous "I Don't Want To Be A Soldier." Having captured exactly what Lennon was looking for ("great stuff"), the two parted ways.

Curtis had other sessions booked in the weeks ahead, including one with Sam Moore (formerly of Sam & Dave), as well as some road work with Aretha Franklin, for whom he had been acting as musical director. In February of that year, his set as her opening act had been recorded at the Fillmore West. It was a spectacular showcase, featuring Billy Preston on keys and the infamous Bernard Purdie on drums. They performed an eclectic set for the west coast crowd, ranging from his own "Memphis Soul Stew" to Led Zeppelin's (by way of Willie Dixon) "Whole Lotta Love," to Billy's take on "My Sweet Lord." An album containing portions of the three-day gig was released in August that year. (The complete set has recently been issued on CD.)

The following week (on Friday the 13th), during a typical midsummer New York heat wave, Curtis arranged to meet with Moore and Franklin at his apartment on west 86th Street in Manhattan. While awaiting their arrival, Curtis went out and purchased an air conditioning unit. As he returned and made his way to his building's entrance, his path was blocked by a couple of addicts. A scuffle ensued, and just as Moore and Franklin were arriving, one of the junkies, identified as Juan Montanez, pulled a knife and stabbed Curtis in the heart. Mortally wounded, Curtis died hours later at Roosevelt Hospital. He was thirty-seven. On the day of his funeral, Atlantic Records closed their offices in honor of their "sensitive virtuoso."

Less than a month later, *Imagine*, featuring Curtis' stellar work on two tracks, was released to universal acclaim. It undoubtedly would have pleased him to have his performance exposed to a broader audience; possibly, given John's love of his horn, the two would've worked together again. But the streets of New York proved to be a place of deadly violence, a lesson that remained largely lost on the expatriate ex-Beatle.

RORY STORM – SEPTEMBER 28, 1972

Though the Beatles were considered *the* top Merseyside beat group of the early sixties, rivals Rory Storm and The Hurricanes were equally well regarded as top-drawer *entertainers*. Fronted by the charismatic and athletic Rory Storm (born Alan Caldwell), the group was known as The Raving Texans in 1959 when they hired on a scruffy, bearded drummer named Ritchie Starkey, who soon began calling himself Ringo Starr in order to better fit the Western motif. The band was Allan Williams' first choice to send to Hamburg, but their contractual commitment to play Butlin's Holiday Camp forced Williams to send Derry and The Seniors instead. Eventually Storm and company made the trip, striking up a friendship with fellow Liverpudlians, The Beatles. Though at first put off by Ringo's gray streak, of all things, George Harrison soon grew to become the best of mates with the deadpan percussionist.

Ringo became a featured soloist in Storm's group, given a vocal turn with "Ringo Starrtime," but he soon grew restless with the Hurricanes 'endless cycle of summer camp dates. By the summer of 1962, he was weighing an offer from Kingsize Taylor and The Dominoes when the Beatles came calling and bested it. Interest in Liverpool acts exploded in the wake of the Fabs' success; Rory's group was wooed by Oriole Records, inking a deal with them in 1963 that yielded the single, "Dr. Feel Good." Neither that release, nor the Brian Epstein-produced follow-up (issued on Parlophone) "America" was successful. Ultimately, Rory seemed content to stay where he was.

The Hurricanes eventually broke up in 1967, following the death of lead guitarist Ty O'Brien from appendicitis complications. Storm soon found work as a disc jockey in Benidorm, Spain and Amsterdam. This career path struck many who knew him as odd, considering that Storm was afflicted with a terrible stutter that did not manifest himself when he sang. (Word was that his friends would never allow him to order a round of drinks, since it took too long to string the appropriate words together; also, he had the habit of *singing* simple phrases like "Would you like a cup of tea?" when at home.)

Things came crashing down in September 1972 when word reached him in Amsterdam that his father Ernie had unexpectedly died. Rushing to the family home in Liverpool, Stormsville (so called by the fans), Rory developed a serious chest infection that impacted his breathing and made sleep difficult. To medicate himself, he had taken to having a "drop" of scotch and sleeping pills before bed, knocking himself out cold. In his weakened condition, however, the combination proved fatal. On September 28, Rory went to sleep and did not wake up.

It was speculated in the press following the tragedy that he and his mother, grief stricken over the death of his father, had enacted some sort of suicide pact, after *her* body was found alongside her son's. But an autopsy seemed to support Rory's death as accidental, as the dose of pills he had taken was too low to kill a healthy man. What is probable, though, is that Mrs. Caldwell, already devastated by her husband's death, simply could not cope with the shock of finding her son dead and impulsively took her own life.

Rory Storm was mourned in Liverpool by thousands who remembered the tall, vigorous local hero as—though not quite a star outside of the community—a lively, engaging performer who, in his small way, made the Beatles what they were by launching Ringo as a personality in his own right. For reasons best known to himself, the drummer did not come out to pay his respects, rationalizing "I wasn't there when he was born, either."

PETE HAM – APRIL 24, 1975

The chronicle of Badfinger's hard luck mismanagement and victimhood at the hands of business manager Stan Polley defies belief. Suffice to say, despite charting four hit singles plus penning a money spinner ("Without You"), by the fall of 1974 the band was in serious trouble. Upon the expiration of their Apple contract the year before, they signed with Warner Brothers but this proved not to be the panacea they anticipated. Pigeons coming home to roost, in the form of shady Polley dealings that included the apparent embezzlement of the band's six-figure advance, rebounded onto the group.

With pressures mounting on the group from external forces and internal turmoil, the "classic" line-up—Mike Gibbins, Tommy Evans, Joey Molland, and Pete Ham—pulled together one last time and produced their tour de force, *Wish You Were Here*. Informed by their struggles, the album unleashed a power and passion only hinted at in their previous five releases. Possessing their trademark ringing guitars, pounding drums, and soaring harmonies, songs like "Got To Get Out Of Here" and "Just A Chance" contained a subtext of their struggles while delivering the power pop goods.

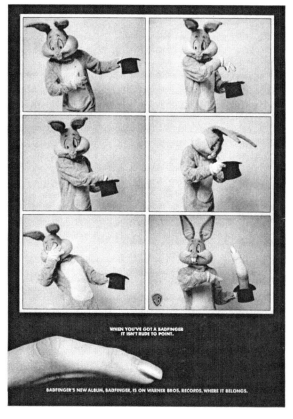

WHEN YOU'VE GOT A BADFINGER
IT ISN'T RUDE TO POINT.

BADFINGER'S NEW ALBUM, BADFINGER, IS ON WARNER BROS. RECORDS, WHERE IT BELONGS.

True: Apple had long since stopped their hands-on, caring support of Badfinger, leading them to take their leave and sign with Warner Brothers. But without a change in management, better results could hardly be expected.

Despite their last two albums stiffing in the marketplace, this new LP, issued in October, showed some promise right out of the gate. Four weeks after first charting, it had risen to one hundred forty-eight: all without the benefit of a single or any coordinated promotion. This steady rise was giving hope for a return to their hit-making form when Warner Brothers, nervous at the pattern of financial irregularities emerging in Badfinger's books, pulled the plug: all copies were recalled from stores and radio stations until the whole mess could be sorted out.

Both the band and their producer, Chris Thomas, were devastated. What had been the one shot they had left at regaining their status after several years of setbacks had been snatched away. In the fall-out, guitarist Joey Molland, long at odds with the others over their inability to recognize their manager's chicanery for what it was, turned in his notice following a U.K. tour. This came after founding member Pete Ham had left briefly, still unshaken in his trust in Polley and chafing at

287

the fact that Molland's wife Kathie had first been the one to look into their tangled affairs and like a Cassandra of ancient myth, tried to alert the naïve ensemble.

Ham returned to the band, but not before keyboardist/singer/ songwriter Bob Jackson had been brought aboard. In the wake of Molland's departure, Polley assured the cash-strapped band that they would receive an advance from Warner if they simply went back into the studio and cranked out another album—just like that. Feeling they had little choice, they pulled together some material—including two biting commentaries from Evans ("Hey, Mr. Manager" and "Rock 'N' Roll Contract") as well as a bittersweet fare-thee-well to Joey from Pete ("Keep Believing")—and laid down ten tracks in two weeks at Apple Studios. Predictably, Warners refused the album, entitled *Head First*. As the New Year dawned, Badfinger was left effectively locked in a box.

With matters at a standstill, Badfinger were left with little more to do than ponder their next move. Meanwhile, for Pete Ham, the walls were closing in. His girlfriend Anne, who with her young son Blair represented the one spot of happiness in his life, was expecting the couple's first child in May. A frugal man (who never owned a new car, despite his command of the hit single), he found himself overdrawn on his bank account and unable to have a phone call from the band's management returned.

On the evening of April 23, he met up with bassist Tommy Evans to discuss yet again their desperate situation. Long the lone hold-out in going after Polley with everything they had (having heretofore given him the benefit of the doubt), Ham at last conceded the point and announced to Evans further that he knew a way out. Remaining inscrutable, he did not reveal what this way was, but as the two men drank, a sort of tranquility seemed to envelop him. Sometime past midnight Evans dropped Ham off; the guitarist told him "goodbye" instead of "see ya," while otherwise giving no clue as to his thoughts.

The answer came early the next morning. Anne awoke to find him absent; knowing that he sometimes worked on music late at night in his garage studio, she ventured in. What she found shattered her world forevermore. Pete was suspended by the neck with a rope tied to an overhead beam. A note recovered later, in handwriting that looked strange ("spidery," according to Mike) read in part: "I will not be allowed to love and trust everybody. This is better. P.S. Stan Polley is a soulless bastard. I will take him with me." It was Thursday morning when Anne found him; on Sunday, he would have turned twenty-eight.

(His daughter was born on May 31; Anne named her Petera.)

When it became clear by late summer that the band was finished, their collective gear was dispersed and their London rehearsal space on Denmark Street was rented out to a new act managed by Malcolm McLaren (one that, in a little more than a year, would turn the country on its ear: the Sex Pistols). Pete's death shattered what was left of the group, especially Tommy Evans. He was never quite able to escape the tragic shadow of Pete's final act, and in 1983, he followed Pete's lead by ending his own life.

If the rock media's coverage of the tragedy was sparse, then the reaction from their former label bosses was even more meager. Of the four ex-Fabs, each one had some interaction with Badfinger through the years, yet all four were notably at a loss for words, as though grappling with an unspoken guilt at the turn of events. Though John never worked with Pete Ham directly, he did share the intimacy of an ex-flame in the form of May Pang. Officially, they were no longer an item in the spring of 1975; nonetheless, May has reported that John was shocked by the news, confiding to her his regrets that he hadn't treated the group better when he was able to.

Paul was the most public in his remarks. With characteristic arch-browed praise, he complimented Pete's abilities while wondering aloud if he had called him a week before if it would've made a difference. Ringo, whom Pete had supported on at least a couple of recordings, called the death "sad" but backed away from any meaningful commentary on the circumstances of his death. George was, of the four, the one who'd worked closest with him, both at Bangladesh and on *Straight Up*, as well as *Living In The Material World*. Furthermore, given the spiritual/philosophical beliefs he was steeped in, might've been expected to offer comfort in *exactly* this circumstance. Instead, though he praised Pete's musicianship if prompted, more often he simply changed the subject.

MAL EVANS – JANUARY 5, 1976

Unlike Neil Aspinall, who also began his career with the Fabs driving their van and moving gear, Mal Evans didn't have an executive role at Apple to keep him busy (briefly he had been deemed a "managing director," though this appeared to be little more than an empty title). Instead, he functioned as a top-tier gofer once the touring ended: procuring on demand ("Socks, Mal" per Lennon's wishes); supplying the odd lyric (for "Fixing A Hole," his contribution earned him a cash payment from Paul, but no credit); and doing whatever was needed

Born in Liverpool, Mal Evans was the Beatles road manager for 11 years, 1963-1974. He appeared as the swimmer in "Help", the 5th magician in "Tour", and in "Let It Be". Mal discovered Badfinger and got them signed to Apple. He produced their Number One song, 'No Matter What', as well as Jackie Lomax, and recently, Keith Moon's first solo album. Mal co-wrote "You and Me Babe" with George and it appears on the "Ringo" LP. His next discovery was Splinter, getting them a part in the Apple Film, "Little Malcolm". George later signed them to his Dark Horse label. Mal recently took time off from writing his autobiography to appear on ABC's Wide World Special, 'Salute to the Beatles', and is current-living in Los Angeles and working on his book.

During his final year, Mal Evans was a guest at Beatlefest. He also appeared on the David Frost-hosted TV special, A Salute to the Beatles in May, talking up his upcoming memoirs.

at any given moment (banging on an anvil during countless takes of "Maxwell's Silver Hammer," for instance, or shutting down their amps just before their Apple rooftop session ended).

As the four individuals segued into solo careers, at least three of them tapped his services in the studio ("Tea, sympathy, and tambourine" as George noted on *All Things Must Pass*), whether out of habit or actual need. Meanwhile, Evans did what he could for Apple's other acts, producing Badfinger—briefly (he scored with the hit "No Matter What" before being elbowed aside by their personal manager, Bill Collins)—as well as talent scouting for the label (Bill Elliott). But in 1974, any official role at Apple ended when he decided to leave his wife and family in England to try his luck in Los Angeles as a producer.

Acting on his midlife crisis proved, as in so many cases, disastrous. Though soon settled in America with his girlfriend, Fran Hughes, and virtually joined at the hip with John and Ringo throughout 1974, he missed his estranged wife and children terribly. The loss of the Beatles as a collective left him rudderless, while an ensuing depression led him to abuse drugs and drink (in considerable quantities, given a man of his size). The non-stop party atmosphere on the west coast alongside Keith Moon and other "Hollywood Vampires" carried with it the accompanying mornings after; Mal found, as small recompense, that for the first time in their professional association, that John actually treated him with something approaching respect as the two lost men bonded as equals.

Professionally, things were going less swimmingly. He undertook the production of Keith Moon's solo debut album but the bloated budget (to accommodate partying costs) sent MCA into shock and resulted in his dismissal from the project. Despite the amount of wealth generated by the Fabs in their day, the largesse did not extend to the most loyal of their inner circle. (Had Paul agreed to pay Mal a small royalty for the *Pepper* track in 1967, it's possible that he might not have found himself in such dire straits years later.)

As 1975 rolled on, prospects for earning a steady living proved elusive. With money an ongoing concern, he tried shaking the Apple tree one last time while at the same time seeking a suitable act to nurture within L.A.'s club scene. As it happened, ex-Badfinger Joey Molland was attempting to launch a new project called Natural Gas, featuring himself and some veteran rockers. Evans produced some demos for the group, but overplayed his hand when it came to negotiating a label deal for the group. (Eventually, their debut album was produced by former Cream/Mountain producer Felix Pappalardi; echoing his predecessor's end, he too was shot to death: by his wife in 1983.)

Just before Christmas, his wife Lil in England filed to end the marriage. Losing the option of returning home had a chilling effect on the increasingly desperate man, for whom this new life hadn't worked out as he expected. Still, he believed he still had a card to play: his memoir. Very early on in his employment with the Fabs, Mal began keeping a diary, recording admittedly mostly mundane entries but nonetheless a lot of up-close history. With a ghost writer named John Hoernie, he began transforming the notes into a workable manuscript entitled *Living With The Beatles Legend*. If ever anyone outside the Beatles themselves was qualified to relate their story from the inside, it was Mal.

In his final weeks, Mal intimated to those around him that a monetary breakthrough had been made with John and Paul, and that he was expecting a payment in five figures. One insider not fooled by the talk was former U.S. Apple president Ken Mansfield. The two men had shared a close friendship during the seventies; only hours before Mal's departure from the material world, Mansfield took a phone call from him. The gentle giant rambled from one subject to another on all the great things coming to fruition: his book; credit from Paul on songs he contributed to; a production deal with Atlantic.

Beneath the bluster, Mansfield recognized that something was seriously amiss. Twice he interrupted the soliloquy to ask what was wrong, only to get chilling silence in response. Mansfield was due that very Sunday evening to attend the *Billboard* Music Awards show, collecting an award on behalf of one of his clients, singer Jessi Colter. He asked Mal if they could meet that evening afterward to talk, but was told "not tonight." Before signing off, the two agreed to meet the next day for lunch.

Within the next several hours, their plans would be undone. Many accounts have been given about what happened, most of them wildly erroneous. Stories asserting that Evans was either drunk or drugged out of his mind are dispelled by both Mansfield's recollections and Mal's autopsy, which later revealed nothing more than a prescriptive amount of valium in his system and no more alcohol then a recreational beer. What *is* known is that at some point after the phone call, Mal fell into a downward spiral of despair, unable to maintain whatever fragile façade of functionability he had left.

Fran Hughes sent for Mal's co-author. Hoernie found him crying and irrational, telling him to make sure that the book was finished. (The draft was due in to his publisher, Grosset and Dunlap, on January 12, 1976—a week later.) To this day, the accounts of what weapon Mal possessed are at variance; some say that he had a pistol, but Natural Gas' Mark Clarke says that Evans, a collector of Western paraphernalia, owned a replica Winchester rifle that shot pellets. Hoernie, perhaps not knowing the difference, apparently tried to relieve Mal of his weapon, without success. Mal then barricaded himself in the bedroom of the duplex, announcing that he was going to kill himself.

It was then that Fran called the police, telling them that her "old man has a gun and has taken Valium and is totally screwed up." If, as seems obvious, her concern was for the potential harm to himself or others, then summoning his eventual executioners was possibly not the right move. Mal himself, given his mental state, may very well have had "suicide-by-cop" in mind, and the Los Angeles police did not disappoint. Responders to the domestic call turned out in force, including among their number one Lt. Charles Higbie, who had been neck deep in the investigation into the murder of Robert Kennedy eight years earlier. They broke into his room: according to the official report,

Evans' final act in response to an order to lay down his weapon was to point it at them. Four of the six shots fired in his direction found their mark—Mal Evans was forty.

Apple chanteuse Mary Hopkin, in a rare interview, described her feelings at the news: "I was horrified…couldn't the police just shot him in the knees or something? They didn't have to kill him…he was the gentlest person I've ever known." No verifiable record exists of how the other ex-Fabs reacted to the report of their first true confidant to fall since Brian Epstein. (Both John and George are reported to have wept at the news but this was not corroborated.) Paul asserted years later that he or any other of their circle could have talked Mal down from his tree, had they been there, since "he was not a nutter." But as with Pete Ham, concern came too late.

It is believed that some sort of financial pay-out was made to Evans' family by the ex-Fabs, either by George or Paul or both. (Lil Evans nonetheless had to sell off Beatle memorabilia through the years to sustain her family.) The biggest mystery of the whole sordid ending was what became of his manuscript. It's hard to imagine a publisher *not* going ahead with plans to market a book already on their schedule, *especially* with all the attendant publicity of a death attached to it. In the chaos that ensued following the shooting and the investigation, the pages went missing. A suitcase full of what was purported to be Mal's possessions turned up in an Australian flea market but upon further investigation was revealed to be a hoax. Today, Mal's memoir of his life with the Fabs is considered to be a Holy Grail of historic Beatle artifacts, assuming it still exists.

JIM MCCARTNEY – MARCH 18, 1976

Without a doubt, much of Paul's innate musicality came straight from his father, a multi-instrumentalist and former bandleader. Jim McCartney, though never a big earner, never skimped on providing entertainment at family gatherings (which were numerous), playing piano and singing standards. While never given formal lessons, it was clear that Paul picked up an awful lot from his Dad, including musical taste, a capacity for plucking melodies out of the air, and the ability to work an audience.

That his father's example stayed with him well past the Beatle years is evidenced by a one-off single, cut by Wings in 1974. Jim had written a tune that he called "Eloise" back in the day (well, perhaps not according to him: "I didn't write it—I made it up"). While recording in Nashville

293

The Country Hams

Never intended for chart success per se, Wings' take on a Jim McCartney tune was intended for nothing more or less than to please its composer.

and meeting local legends Chet Atkins and Floyd Cramer, Paul mentioned his father's composition. At Atkins' suggestion, Macca and company laid down the song—now re-titled "Walking In The Park With Eloise"—and released it under the name, The Country Hams. Though the jaunty little Dixieland piece (something along the lines of "Sweet Georgia Brown") did not chart, it must've warmed the old man's heart enormously. (Both "Eloise" and its flip, "Bridge Over The River Suite" can be found as bonus tracks on the *Speed Of Sound* CD.)

Paul stayed as close with his father as someone based in London could, frequently going up north for visits. He'd bought his father a home (called Rembrandt) in Heswell, Cheshire, as well as a race horse named Drake's Drum. Jim got re-married in 1964 to a widow named Angela, By some accounts though, Paul never fully warmed to either his step-mother or step-sister Ruth (whom Jim adopted), eyeing them warily even as he kept tabs on Jim from afar.

Jim lived long enough to see his son's success in the wake of the Beatles' dissolution, though not quite to the triumph of the *Wings Over The World* tour. In his final years, he became crippled by arthritis; also, his mind seldom seemed focused on the immediate. When his medical bills began to mount, Paul bought Rembrandt back from Jim, moving his father to a bungalow. Though no one doubted that Paul loved Jim, his brand of treatment could be hard to take. Ruth recalled that, to ease the pain, the elder McCartney kept the fireplace burning, making the dwelling quite hot. When Paul would visit, he'd throw open the windows in winter and, according to his step-sister, demand that his father get up and walk, asserting that the illness was in his mind. Whether true or not, Macca did eventually cut off his step-relations financially after his father passed, forcing them to move to London to find work.

Jim at last succumbed at the age of seventy-three. (According to Ruth, his final words were, "I'll be with Mary soon.") Paul was in Denmark, two days away from kicking off the European leg of his world tour, and is said to have received word of his father's passing from none other than John Lennon, who was among the first to know. Whatever his feelings, Paul internalized the loss, not even telling his fellow band members. (Sometime after Jim's death, Denny Laine was stunned to hear Paul tell an interviewer in response to a question that *both* his parents were dead; news he hadn't shared with his bandmates.)

The tour went on as scheduled as the head Wing skipped the funeral. Said brother Michael: "Paul would never face that sort of thing."

FREDDIE LENNON – APRIL 1, 1976

The relationship between John and his father could accurately be described as the polar opposite of Paul and Jim's. Alfred "Freddie" (or "Alf" to his family) Lennon existed to the young boy largely as a conspicuous absence. The interactions that the two shared after John entered adulthood hardly constituted the warm bond enjoyed by Paul, George, and Ringo with their respective father figures. But like so

much else in Lennon's life, their saga seemed to cover every extreme that the human experience offers.

After Freddie and Julia split in 1946, John grew up knowing little of the man. Any gaps in his knowledge were readily filled by his Aunt Mimi, whose antipathy toward "that Lennon" was formidable, to say the least.

Seen here in Amsterdam in 1966 after getting his teeth repaired, Freddie Lennon never enjoyed the closeness to his firstborn that he craved.

By the time John laid on eyes on his father again, after Beatlemania's full force hit and he was "blackmailed" by the press into a meeting, he'd been well-conditioned to greet his long-lost elder with little more than contempt. Freddie showed up at Brian Epstein's NEMS office while *A Hard Day's Night* was filming at the Scala Theatre; a mortified Brian Epstein summoned John over to meet the rather shabby looking, diminutive (he was 5'4") stranger who claimed he was John's father. Unmoved, John ordered Freddie (and the journalist accompanying him) out.

Still, a tenuous attempt at reconciliation was offered after Freddie showed up at John's home in Kenwood. It evaporated at the first whiff John got of Freddie attempting to "cash in" on his son's fame by issuing a single on Pye in England in late 1965 entitled "That's My Life (My Love, My Home)." The song, allegedly a response to John's own recently released "In My Life," was a mostly spoken word biography that in no way addressed John directly but rather seemed a preemptive defense gesture against the inevitable demonization he'd already endured from his son and his biographers. (At John's request, Brian Epstein is alleged to have pulled some strings to kill the record dead.)

Things might have stayed estranged if not for the efforts of Alfred's brother Charlie. On his own accord, in 1967 he wrote John a twenty-page letter, lambasting his nephew for literally slamming the door in his father's face and demanding that he get in touch to hear Freddie's side of the story. In the year of *Sgt. Pepper's* and "All You Need Is Love," John proved astonishingly receptive to the idea. The two then shared an uneasy rapprochement for the next few years, during which time John put the old man on an allowance while the fifty-six year-old became engaged to a nineteen year-old student (not a "Beatle fan," as John later characterized her in interviews).

With Pauline Smith's mother objecting violently to the union, the couple eloped in 1968. John eventually bought a home in Brighton for the newlyweds, who produced their first child the following year. David Henry Lennon was born on February 26, 1969; his brother, Robin Francis Lennon, was born on October 22, 1973. John met his first half brother only once, briefly, on the occasion of his own thirtieth birthday on October 9, 1970. (This was the same day that George visited John and Ringo at work on *POB*'s "Remember.")

Responding to an apparent invitation to a birthday celebration at Tittenhurst Park, the family arrived all dressed up and bearing a gift to honor Freddie's firstborn. What they faced instead was John's full-blown wrath. Having undergone the "primal scream" therapy that summer, the scabs on John's psychic wounds had all been torn off; now in touch with his raw emotions, he laid into his father with all the fury that years of neglect had fueled. As Pauline related years later, John finished his tirade (frightening his toddler step-sibling in the process, who clung to his mother's legs) with an order to "get out of my life!" All financial support was withdrawn, along with the home in Brighton.

In early 1976, Freddie was diagnosed with stomach cancer. Pauline, believing that some sort of healing between father and son was in order, got in touch with John through Apple to give him fair warning. John reached Freddie at the hospital by phone and the two reconciled, with John expressing regret at the way he'd treated him (as well as "primal therapy" generally). He also expressed the desire that Freddie should come and visit his newest grandson, Sean, as soon as he was feeling better. To seal the deal, John arranged for a massive floral display to be sent to his room.

Freddie spent his final hours enjoying the peace of mind that came from being back in John's good graces. He was aware that visitors to his room would know from the flowers that his son was someone important, and that he cared. With closure arriving nearly too late, John's father succumbed. Upon hearing the news, John immediately offered to pay all the funeral expenses. Far less forgiving than her husband, Pauline refused his money. Instead, she sent John a manuscript that Freddie had been working on for years, telling his story and explaining his apparent neglect. John devoured his father's revelatory words and at last began to understand the heart-rending events that had haunted him his entire life. Pauline would later publish the memoir as part of her book, *Daddy Come Home*, in 1990.

As some readers may have noted, John and Paul lost their fathers a fortnight apart. (Apparently, Freddie Lennon and Jim McCartney had never met.) As macabre coincidence would have it, both John *and* Paul were mourning their recently passed fathers when they met up in New York City just three weeks later—for the last time.

MARC BOLAN – SEPTEMBER 16, 1977

By 1977, the golden age of "T. Rextasy" was over for the former Mark Feld. Only five years before, seemingly anything that Marc Bolan touched turned to platinum or gold, but his brand of "glam" had fallen from favor within a couple of years of his peak, superseded by the more compelling sounds of David Bowie and others. Ringo's 1972 documentary *Born To Boogie* documented his act at the height of his powers: while lesser charting hits still came, he was no longer considered a top draw.

Addicted to cocaine, Bolan's weight began to curiously balloon. This fact that did not escape John Lennon: ever alert to someone else's weaknesses, he advised WNEW listeners in 1974, "Buy a few of his records, folks. He's getting fat with worry." Though it isn't clear if the two ever hung out, it was John whom Bolan idolized in the Beatles, citing him as the inspiration to take lyric writing seriously. (In his song "Ballrooms of Mars," Bolan asserted "John Lennon knows your name / And I've seen his.")

In 1973, Bolan left his wife June and took up with American soul singer Gloria Jones. (As a teenager, Jones had worked with Billy Preston in a gospel group called The Cogics. In 1964, she scored a hit with the original recording of "Tainted Love," later a number one in 1981 for Soft Cell.) The couple became the parents of a son they named Rolan (as in "Rolan Bolan," though technically, since his parents were not married, he was "Rolan Jones" while his birth certificate read "Rolan Seymour Feld.")

Despite numerous attempts at reinventing himself after T. Rex, nothing really clicked with the public on the same level as his earlier successes. In his final summer, Granada Television signed him for a six part series directed at teens entitled simply *Marc*. The show afforded him the opportunity to showcase up-and-comers (such as the Boomtown Rats) alongside established acts (like friend and rival Bowie) as well as take the stage himself.

The series began in August 1977; the same month that Elvis died, an event that shook the rock world, Bolan especially. Though not exactly unexpected, given the trajectory of his health, the passing of the King, idolized by nearly everyone who was anyone in rock, served as a reminder of the genre's transitory nature. Punk and New Wave acts were exploding in England while members of the old guard faded away or revamped their approach in order to compete. For Bolan, watching younger acts in ascension as his star was in decline was surely a jarring reminder of his own mortality.

He'd long been sensitive to symbols and signs. A vision he'd had when he was young held that he would die in an automobile accident; as a preventive measure, he never learned to drive. Perhaps because of this, cars fascinated him, and his songs were filled with references to them ("I'll call you 'Jaguar' if I may be so bold," he sang in "Jeepster"). Elvis' death aside, another portent came on his final show. Three days before his death, the taping included a duet with Bowie on a joint composition. Unfortunately, the too-small television stage couldn't contain both men and Bolan fell off. What should have been nothing more than fodder for a blooper reel filled him with unease.

On September 15, Marc and Gloria spent the evening out clubbing in London. In the wee morning hours, the couple decided to pack it in, with Gloria at the wheel of their Mini. (Bolan owned a far more durable Rolls-Royce, but he'd loaned it out to Hawkwind.)

The cumulative effects of early morning mist, fatigue, and an under-inflated front tire all combined to doom the couple; less than a mile from home, the speeding car left the road, slamming into a reinforced fence post on Marc's side of the car, killing him instantly as he was driven into the back seat. The car came to a rest against a tree: contrary to widely believed myth, it was not the tree that caused the fatality. Gloria sustained numerous serious injuries, including a broken jaw and internal injuries; she was not told of Marc's fate until after his funeral.

Once the stunning news was announced, the British pop world went into mourning. Some of the biggest stars in the U.K. turned out for Bolan's funeral service, 'cepting the ex-Beatles, who weren't exactly renowned for showing up at such events. Mourners attending included Elton John, Bowie (who had been told years before by a psychic that Bolan, Hendrix, and himself comprised a trio doomed to early death; erroneously, as it happened), and Mary Hopkin, married to producer Tony Visconti at the time. (She was appalled to see fans at the service hitting up attendees for autographs.) Meanwhile, as Gloria languished in the hospital, the deceased's unoccupied house was looted of nearly every instrument and bit of memorabilia that could be carried off.

Despite their close working friendship of a few years earlier, Ringo had long since moved on professionally and personally. He had been equally close to June Bolan and when the couple split, his relationship cooled somewhat toward the erratic Marc. (June said that Ringo was like an uncle to Marc, often warning him to lay off the nose candy.) Though both men had essentially relocated to America around the same time, the two were now in separate orbits. Still, a Beatley tie remained: in 2006, Sean Lennon covered Bolan's "Would I Be The One" on his *Friendly Fire* album.

HAROLD HARRISON – MAY 1978

In the years following his mother's death, George did all he could to ensure his father's good health and well-being. Like his late wife, Harold Harrison was well liked by the fans, with who he had a reputation as being entirely accommodating and approachable—unlike his famous son. George had bought his parents a home as soon as he was able to and also demanded that his father retire from his thirty-year career of driving a bus, which he did in 1965.

As George predicted, freedom from the daily grind did wonders for his father's vitality. The elder Harrison grew his hair long and, though stopping short of actually moving in at Friar Park (preferring to maintain some independence), Harold was a frequent visitor. (He is shown there in a photograph inside the *Thirty-Three & 1/3* gatefold.) Though as he grew older, his health became shakier, he did accompany George on the road in 1974 as the Dark Horse tour criss-crossed America. (Harold was on hand in December when the entourage was invited to meet President Gerald Ford in the Oval Office.)

Like George, Harold was a heavy smoker and by the age of sixty-three, he was diagnosed with emphysema. There was little to be done with someone so sentenced, but he fought the disease as well as anyone could have, staying active and, like his son, tending to his gardening. After Olivia discovered that she was pregnant in early 1978, Harold was doubtless looking forward to playing grandfather to his youngest son's firstborn. In May—the same month that George and Olivia planned to be married—Harold died at home in Appleton, Cheshire. The exact day remains a mystery; given the Harrison's mania about privacy, it was never formally made public. (Some sources assert that Harold appeared in material form to George at the moment of his death to say "farewell.")

George and Olivia decided to delay their nuptials until well after Harold had been properly laid to rest. In August, their son Dhani was born; they tied the knot one month later.

KEITH MOON – SEPTEMBER 7, 1978

The Harrison wedding, on September 2, was deliberately held in private, outside the world's prying gaze. No press; no superstar guests; only the bride's parents in fact were present at the civil ceremony at the Henley Registry office. Only on the eve of their Tunisian honeymoon a week later did George announce their marriage.

Two days before (on Wednesday the 6th), George's former bandmate and sometime nemesis Paul McCartney was in the middle of celebrating "Buddy Holly Week," an annual event he'd initiated in 1976 (pre-dating his purchase of the Holly music publishing from Norman Petty). Timed to coincide with the week of what would have been Buddy's forty-second birthday (on the 7th), that evening's events included a party and a special premier screening of the soon-to-be released biopic, *The Buddy Holly Story*. The film, starring actor Gary Busey, was largely a work of fiction, though this did not dampen the acclaim it received.

Many of rock's brightest luminaries were invited, but one who was

One of the buttons issued for Paul's Buddy Holly Week celebration, this one bearing the date of attendee Keith Moon's death.

reluctant to attend was, ironically, perhaps rock's most renowned partier, Keith Moon. Two weeks after the release of their *Who Are You* album, seen as a powerful rejoinder to punk's challenge, the band's future was nonetheless in doubt, owing largely to the question mark occupying the drummer's chair. Moon's years of self-inflicted abuse had taken their toll on the recently turned thirty two-year old. Overweight, sluggish, and distinctly lacking the energy that had been his hallmark during the fourteen years since he stepped into the band, the prospect of ever appearing again on stage seemed dismal at best.

There was no mistaking his potential liability to their future. During the *Who Are You* sessions, his erratic, out-of-shape efforts seriously burned up studio time, forcing the band to consider hiring a session player to finish the album. (One song, the aptly titled "Music Must Change," was finished without a drum track, due to Moon's inability to get a handle on the tricky time changes, while the LP's title tune featured drumming cobbled together from multiple takes, given his failure to lay down a *single* usable performance.)

Moon's troubles began years earlier but accelerated rapidly during the Who's downtime. Hyperactive and a pathological attention-seeker, the non-stop activity that defined the band's career for most of their existence created a major vacuum when it stopped, leaving the drummer to seek an outlet—*any* outlet—into which to channel his larger-than-life energies. It so happened that this opening coincided with John and Ringo's marital break-ups and subsequent drunken escapades in Los Angeles circa 1974. Though—typically—it was John whose behavior grabbed the headlines, this is easily explained by the fact that, in contrast, there was nothing especially newsworthy about Keith Moon's brand of debauchery and merrymaking.

By the time John and Ringo recognized the abyss their lifestyle was leading to, they managed to pull back, getting their acts together long enough to produce *Walls and Bridges* and *Goodnight Vienna,* respectively. But Keith had no experience in managing a musical project outside his group before and, possessing even less of the skills and discipline necessary to produce a solid piece of work than say, Ringo did in 1970, predictably floundered. *Two Sides Of The Moon* stirred reactions ranging from curiosity to major embarrassment, depending on one's point of view. Thankfully for Keith, The Who reconvened in 1975 for another album (*The Who By Numbers*) and a world tour that managed to keep him busy and relatively out of trouble for a couple of years.

Keith Moon played his last concert on American soil in San Diego on October 17, 1976. Given The Who's collective inactivity the following year, his descent into unreachable depths was as inevitable as it was tragic. While Roger and Pete worked on solo albums and John produced other acts (The Fabulous Poodles, The Newport Male Voice Choir), Keith spent most of the year just hanging out, blowing through money, drugs, and alcohol as if he could produce more on demand. He shot a cameo, playing a caricature of himself for a *Rolling Stone* television special in May; in August, he was filmed—with and without Ringo—in Malibu for the upcoming Who documentary, *The Kids Are Alright.*

In October, The Who began recording the *Who Are You* album, and it soon became clear that a year's worth of dissipation had completely wrecked Keith's abilities. Bloated from alcohol and seemingly unable to function at all without absorbing the momentary adrenalin rush of cocaine, the project was worked on in fits and starts, punctuated by Keith's struggle for relevancy within a band that was quickly becoming unamused by his antics. (At one point, Townshend pulled him aside and told him to his face, "Get your shit together—otherwise, you're out of the group!") Moon's rejoinder when pushed into a corner was always "But I'm the best Keith Moon-style drummer in the world!"

Oddly, his last moment of glory came in December, at a gig filmed for *The Kids Are Alright* at Kilburn. With Townshend and Entwistle the worse for their apparent brandy consumption that afternoon (the guitarist can be seen lashing out at a roadie at the conclusion of "My Wife"), Keith managed somehow to rise to the occasion for one last time, flaying away at his kit like the Moon of old. Unfortunately, the overall performance was judged lacking. By the time of the re-shoot in May 1978, Keith had reverted back to his lethargic form; though used in the film, his lackluster performance was augmented by overdubs to simulate the firepower he was no longer capable of delivering live.

Townshend had already told the group that there would be no tour to support *Who Are You*, a decision that had much to do with Keith's condition. The drummer had already experienced several dry-out attempts, relapsing just as quickly as he was discharged. By summer, he was being treated as an outpatient, perhaps in an effort to give him the latitude to carry on with life while not penning him up and thereby guaranteeing failure.

In retrospect, it's ironic that a man well-chronicled for his exploits with John and Ringo should end up spending his final day in the company of Paul, the living antithesis of the lifestyle Keith had pursued with a vengeance for much his life. Even more ironic was the fact that he had to be cajoled by his girlfriend Annette Walter-Lax into attending the party; perhaps recognizing the perils of placing himself amidst temptation when he was struggling to maintain his sobriety fueled his resistance. In any event, the couple showed up at Peppermint Park in Upper St. Martin's Lane, where they were seated at the McCartneys table for dinner. (Keith was wearing a Wings t-shirt beneath his leather jacket; later, he was photographed with his Who successor, Kenney Jones.)

In a stunning reversal of established practice though, Keith decided to go home *before* the festivities came to an end. (Usually, he was the *last* to leave.) The couple returned to the Mayfair flat loaned out to them by Harry Nilsson—the same one occupied by singer Cass Elliot when she died of a heart attack four years earlier. Keith was hungry and so Annette fixed him some lamb cutlets. Afterward, she turned in, but he wasn't ready to retire just yet. Instead, he began watching *The Abominable Dr. Phibes*, after downing some water and a handful of a prescription medication called Heminevrin.

The drug, used to treat symptoms of alcohol withdrawal, had been ordered by his doctor. (Ironically, when taken to excess, patients exhibit the behavior associated with being drunk.) Keith's orders had been to take the drug whenever he was feeling the craving, though he had earlier consumed some red wine during the evening—perhaps not a medically sound move, but virtually the same as water by Keith Moon standards.

Only a few hours after drifting off—around 7:30am—Keith awoke, declared that he was still hungry, and demanded that Annette get up and cook him a steak. Her less than speedy response prompted a curt insult—she prepared the food anyway, but then went back to sleep. Keith devoured the meal in bed, resuming *Dr. Phibes* until he finished eating, whereupon he too fell back asleep. His subsequent snoring roused Annette, who then moved to the living room couch. By the time she awoke in the mid-afternoon, his snoring had ceased.

Normally, Heminevrin is only prescribed at treatment centers, not for patients to self medicate at will. When autopsied, Keith was discovered to have *twenty-six* undigested pills in his stomach, in addition to six digested ones. Furthermore, the heavy food he'd ingested had the effect of retarding the break-down of the medication, in effect acting as a time release that kept the drug in his system much longer than desired. In such massive quantities, Heminevrin proved a strong sedative that suppressed his respiratory and circulatory systems, leading inevitably to death. In the days that followed, other medical practitioners weighed in, asserting that Keith's attending physician must have been borderline incompetent for not ordering hospitalization for his patient.

The ex-Fabs all sent floral displays to Keith's funeral. (Perhaps the most memorable one, though, was Roger Daltrey's: it consisted of a champagne bottle sticking out of a TV screen.) Ringo later spoke of how much he missed his two lately departed friends, Keith and Marc Bolan. "But I'm a fatalist, you see…That's the only way I get through most of my friends dying."

JIMMY MCCULLOCH – SEPTEMBER 27, 1979

The Scottish guitarist's departure from Wings in 1977 marked the end of a gig of a lifetime. While describing his resignation as stemming from the desire to play live rather than stay on call as a studio pro, the truth was more complex. His frustration at being ill-used (rarely was he ever again tapped to perform the kind of blistering leads that were his specialty after his debut on "Junior's Farm") was understandable, but McCulloch's drug use, coupled with his persona as a wise-guy with much maturing to do made his presence increasingly insufferable, as drummer Geoff Britton was the first to recognize.

Though he carefully spun his tenure as a fond apprenticeship ("We had some very good times together"), nothing he did after leaving McCartney's employ lived up to the promise of those breathtakingly eventful years. He moved from one project (Small Faces reunion) to another (The Dukes, comprised of highly-regarded sidemen and put together by outsiders) without really jelling anywhere. But he was able to indulge a taste for the high life, supported by royalties from "Medicine Jar" and "Wino Junko." He bought a place in West London's tony Maida Vale district while continuing to indulge in the partying lifestyle he'd grown accustomed to.

Friends say that he never really got over the attention and first class regard he'd been accustomed to in Wings. Though uncomfortable with what the situation had become and not regretting the decision to leave, he still thought of himself as "Jimmy from Wings." But removed from Macca's star power, he became just another journeyman guitarist, unable to find a gig with someone on that same level; furthermore, his drug habit made him one of many other dime-a-dozen users populating rock's shadows.

On paper, The Dukes should have provided a good chance to re-grab the spotlight. Their sound was edgy but with unmistakable pop elements, theoretically fitting well alongside other pop/punk outfits dominating the charts. (Judged critically, it really was an unremarkable project, though Jimmy's one vocal spotlight—"Heartbreaker"—truly was the best thing on the self-titled release.) But McCulloch's increasing unreliability did nothing to boost their reputation, and despite a major label (Warner Brothers) backing them, the album failed to catch fire.

In September 1979, McCulloch kept his options open. He called up current Wings drummer, Steve Holley, and invited him to do some recording in Wales. Holley agreed and then waited for a follow-up phone call to provide further details. Instead, two days later, he saw in the paper that Jimmy had been found dead in his flat by his brother Jack. After failing to show up for a scheduled rehearsal in London at the Dingwall Club in Camden, Jack McCulloch, The Dukes' road manager, decided to check up on his erratic brother. When hard pounding on Jimmy's door failed to yield a response, Jack was about to leave when he began to notice a smell emanating from the locked premises. Breaking the lock, he entered and quickly discovered his brother's body in a chair, the remains of a joint between his fingers. He'd been dead for some time.

Marijuana, alcohol, and morphine were all found in his system, but none in levels high enough to cause a lethal overdose per se (contrary to myth). Instead, death came in the form of heart failure for the twenty-six year old—a fate warned about in his lyrics to "Medicine Jar." Though not altogether unexpected, given the duration and intensity of his habit, it was no less a tragically shabby end for the gifted musician who never quite found a suitable vehicle for his talents.

Predictably, Paul—at work on what became *McCartney II* and gearing up for a fall tour, skipped the services, instead issuing a perfunctory "he will be missed" statement through his fan club mag, *Club Sandwich*. Equally magnanimous was Denny Laine, who at the last minute skipped out on any public mourning. He explained his decision thusly: "…when somebody dies, you can still be angry with them…Besides, I didn't want to upset Paul."

THE BEATLES · HEY JUDE

HEY JUDE · REVOLUTION · PAPERBACK WRITER
I SHOULD HAVE KNOWN BETTER · LADY MADONNA · CAN'T BUY ME LOVE
DON'T LET ME DOWN · BALLAD OF JOHN AND YOKO · RAIN · OLD BROWN SHOE

STEREO

CHAPTER 16

NONE OF LIFE'S DREAMS CAN LAST: A TIMELINE 1970 – 1980

All release dates given are for US issues. (dnc = "did not chart")

January 1970

Topping the US singles chart:
"Raindrops Keep Fallin' On My Head" by B.J. Thomas
"I Want You Back" by the Jackson 5

On the airwaves:
"Whole Lotta Love" by Led Zeppelin
"No Time" by the Guess Who
"Midnight Cowboy" by Ferrante and Teicher

Topping the US album chart:
Abbey Road

Albums released this month include:
Bridge Over Troubled Water by Simon & Garfunkel
The Madcap Laughs by Syd Barrett
Back in the USA by the MC5
Chicago (aka *Chicago II*)

Thursday 1 – *The Primal Scream* by Dr. Arthur Janov is published; a copy sent to John and Yoko prompts their reaching out to the California doctor for therapy

Saturday 3 – *Abbey Road* is in its ninth of eleven total weeks at number one

Saturday 3 – Paul, George and Ringo gather at EMI to record "I Me Mine" – the final "group" recording session of the Beatles in John Lennon's lifetime; though invited, John remains in Denmark on vacation

Sunday 4 – (Early morning hours) Neil Boland, Keith Moon's chauffeur, is killed beneath the wheels of Moon's car, in much-disputed incident outside a pub in Hertfordshire

Sunday 4 – George Martin supervises brass overdubs onto "Let It Be"; George lays down the guitar solo heard on the album version, with Paul in attendance

Thursday 8 – George records the final lead vocal to "For You Blue," marking George Martin's last contribution to a "new" Beatle record

Monday 12 – "Come and Get It" by Badfinger (Apple 1815; peaks at #7)

Wednesday 14 – Ringo cuts the vocals for the title track to his *Sentimental Journey* album and "Love Is A Many Splendoured Thing" at Olympic Studios

Thursday 15 – John's "Bag One" collection of erotic lithographs goes on exhibit at London's Arts Gallery; is declared obscene and shut down the next day

Saturday 17 – Scat singer Billy Stewart, 32 (1966's "Summertime"), dies along with three band members when their car crashes into a river

Tuesday 20 – John and Yoko, vacationing in Denmark, get their long hair cut down to a close crop

Wednesday 21 – In *Rolling Stone*, John is quoted speaking candidly in an article titled "Beatles Splitting? Maybe, Says John"

Saturday 24 – Singer James Sheppard, 35 (The Heartbeats' "A Thousand Miles Away," Shep and the Limelight's "Daddy's Home"), is found shot to death on the Long Island expressway

Tuesday 27 – "Instant Karma" is recorded with help from George, Billy Preston Klaus Voormann and drummer Alan White, production by Phil Spector

Tuesday 27 – In Los Angeles to attend the premier of *The Magic Christian* in two days, Ringo tapes an appearance for *Rowan and Martin's Laugh-In*

Thursday 29 – Badfinger and Mary Hopkin appear on *Top of the Pops*, lip-synching "Come and Get It" and "Temma Harbour" respectively

Saturday 31 – Bluesman Slim Harpo ("I'm A King Bee") dies at 46

February 1970

Topping the US singles chart:
"Venus" by Shocking Blue
"Thank You (Falettinme Be Mice Elf Agin)" by Sly and the Family Stone

On the airwaves:
"The Rapper" by
The Jaggerz
"Who'll Stop The Rain" by CCR
"Arizona" by Mark Lindsay

The Magic Christian is: antiestablishmentarian, antibellum, antitrust, antiseptic, antibiotic, antisocial, & antipasto.

Peter Sellers & Ringo Starr in The Magic Christian

Topping the US album chart:
Led Zeppelin II

Albums released this month include:
Moondance by Van Morrison
Leon Russell's self-titled debut
Morrison Hotel by The Doors
Sweet Baby James by James Taylor
12 Songs by Randy Newman
Nilsson Sings Newman by Harry Nilsson

Tuesday 3 – Ringo's *Sentimental Journey* sessions resume at EMI's Abbey Road Studios, continuing through the next ten days

Wednesday 4 – On the

Savile Row office rooftop, John and Yoko trade their bag of shorn locks for a pair of Muhammad Ali's bloodied boxing trunks to be auctioned off to benefit Michael X's Black House commune

Thursday 5 – John's (non-performance) promo film for "Instant Karma" airs on *Top of the Pops*; Billy Preston lip-synchs "All That I've Got" on the same episode

Saturday 7 – John and Yoko appear on the cover of *Rolling Stone*; John is "Man of the Year"

Saturday 7 – John and Yoko, along with Michael X, tape a TV interview with Simon Dee; it airs the following day

Sunday 8 – Beginning on this day and through the next three, John and Yoko are videotaped by the latter's ex, Tony Cox, at Tittenhurst and in London for use in a possible documentary

Monday 9 – "Temma Harbour" by Mary Hopkin (Apple 1816; peaks at #4 on the Adult Contemporary chart)

Wednesday 11 – John tapes two performances of "Instant Karma" for *Top of the Pops*, featuring live vocals atop the studio backing

Wednesday 11 – *The Magic Christian* premieres in New York.

Thursday 12 – John's first "Instant Karma" performance airs on *Top of the Pops*

Friday 13 – Black Sabbath's self-titled debut LP released on Friday the 13th

Saturday 14 – The Who record their concert at Leeds University

Monday 16 – "All That I've Got" by Billy Preston (Apple 1817)

Monday 16 – *Magic Christian Music* by Badfinger (peaks at number fifty-five)

Tuesday 17 – The "Fatal Vision" murders; Jeffrey McDonald is later convicted

Wednesday 18 – George and Ringo, working with George Martin, lay down early takes of "It Don't Come Easy."

Thursday 19 – John's second "Instant Karma" performance airs on *Top of the Pops*

Friday 20 – "Instant Karma"/"Who Has Seen The Wind?" (Apple 1818; peaks at #3)

Monday 23 – Ringo's appearance on *Rowan and Martin's Laugh-In* airs

Thursday 26 – *Hey Jude* album (peaks at number two)

Saturday 28 – Badfinger appears on West Germany's *Beat-Club*, performing "Come and Get It" and "Rock of All Ages"

March 1970

Topping the US singles chart:
"Bridge Over Troubled Water" by Simon & Garfunkel

On the airwaves:
"Love Grows (Where My Rosemary Goes)" by
Edison Lighthouse
"Spirit In The Sky" by Norman Greenbaum
"Kentucky Rain" by
Elvis Presley

Topping the US album chart:
Bridge Over Troubled Water by Simon & Garfunkel

Albums released this month include:
Déjà Vu by Crosby, Stills, Nash and Young
Band of Gypsies by Jimi Hendrix
Ladies of the Canyon by Joni Mitchell
On Tour with Eric Clapton by Delaney and Bonnie (originally planned as an Apple release)

March – Paul is interviewed by David Wigg at the Apple office; the audio will emerge in 1976 as part of *The Beatles Tapes* double-album

March – Dr. Arthur Janov begins treating John and Yoko at Tittenhurst Park

Sunday 1 – *The Ed Sullivan Show* presents a *Salute to the Beatles*: "Two of Us" and "Let It Be" clips are shown, plus Duke Ellington, Steve and Edie, The Muppets, Peggy Lee and Dionne Warwick all perform Beatle material

Thursday 5 – Final sessions for Ringo's *Sentimental Journey* album (requiring his presence) take place at London's Morgan Studios

Thursday 5 – John and Yoko begin a Primal Scream therapy course at the London Clinic with Dr. Janov, who keeps them in separate hotels

Sunday 8 – The backing track to "It Don't Come Easy" is recorded at Trident Studios

Monday 9 – "How The Web Was Woven" by Jackie Lomax (Apple 1819)

Wednesday 11 – "Let It Be"/"You Know My Name" (Apple 2764; peaks at #1 for two weeks in April)

Thursday 12 – The Harrisons begin moving into Friar Park in Henley-on-Thames

Sunday 15 – Ringo films a promo for "Sentimental Journey" at London's *Talk of the Town*

Monday 16 – Singer Tammi Terrell ("Ain't No Mountain High Enough" and other duets with Marvin Gaye) dies of brain cancer at 24

Monday 16 – "Ain't That Cute" by Doris Troy (Apple 1820)

Monday 23 – Phil Spector begins work on the *Let It Be* tapes

Tuesday 24 – "Govinda" by Radha Krishna Temple (Apple 1821)

Sunday 29 – Ringo appears on *Frost on Sunday* in England

Tuesday 31 – Ringo brings a letter signed by John and George dated this day to Paul's house on Cavendish, requesting that Paul consider delaying the release of *McCartney* to June in order to give *Sentimental Journey* and *Let It Be* a fair shot in the marketplace; enraged, Paul throws Ringo out

April 1970

Topping the US singles chart:
"Let It Be" by The Beatles
"ABC by the Jackson 5

On the airwaves:
"Vehicle" by Ides of March
"Hitching A Ride" by Vanity Fair
"Woodstock" by Crosby, Stills, Nash and Young

Topping the US album chart:
Bridge Over Troubled Water by Simon & Garfunkel

Albums released this month include:
Elton John's self-titled debut
Brinsley Schwarz's self-titled debut
Bitches Brew by Miles Davis
Eric Burdon Declares "War"
McLemore Avenue by Booker T and the MGs (a track by track cover of Abbey Road)

Wednesday 1 – Ringo adds final percussion overdubs to "Across The Universe," "I Me Mine," and "The Long and Winding Road," completing work (before mixing) on the last new Beatles album

Wednesday 1 – John and Yoko announce their presence at the London Clinic as fulfilling their intention to undergo a dual sex-change operation

Thursday 9 – Paul phones John at the clinic: "I'm now doing what you and Yoko were doing last year"

Friday 10 – The Beatles' break-up is announced; Apple's Savile Row office is besieged by reporters and disbelieving fans

an intimate bioscopic experience with

THE BEATLES

APPLE
An abkco managed company
presents

"Let it be"

Produced by NEIL ASPINALL Directed by MICHAEL LINDSAY-HOGG
TECHNICOLOR® United Artists

ORIGINAL MOTION PICTURE SCORE
AVAILABLE ON APPLE RECORDS

Friday 10 – George is interviewed at his Savile Row office by a BBC TV crew for the religious-themed show, *Fact or Fantasy?*

Monday 13 – An oxygen tank aboard Apollo 13 explodes; the crew arrives home safely on Friday the 17th

Sunday 19 – Paul's "Maybe I'm Amazed" promo airs on *The Ed Sullivan Show*

Monday 20 – *McCartney* (peaks at number one for three weeks in late May)

Wednesday 22 – The first Earth Day is celebrated

Thursday 23 – John (and Yoko) and George (and Pattie) travel to the US on the same TWA flight, meeting with Capitol execs in Los Angeles; afterward, John stays in LA for Primal Therapy with Dr. Janov while George heads to New York to see Allen Klein and visit friends

Friday 24 – *Sentimental Journey* (peaks at number twenty-two)

Sunday 26 – George's *Fact or Fantasy?* TV interview airs

Thursday 30 – George tapes a performance of "I'd Have You Anytime" and the still-unreleased "When Everybody Comes To Town" with Bob Dylan at the latter's New York City townhouse

Thursday 30 – Paul appears on the cover of *Rolling Stone*

Thursday 30 – Actress Inger Stevens, 35, takes her own life

May 1970

Topping the US singles chart:
"American Woman" by the Guess Who

On the airwaves:
"Little Green Bag" by George Baker Selection
"Up Around The Bend" by CCR
"Reflections of My Life" by Marmalade

Topping the US album chart:
Bridge Over Troubled Water by Simon & Garfunkel

Albums released this month include:
Live at Leeds by The Who
ABC by the Jackson 5
Woodstock: Music from the Original Soundtrack and More

May – The Beatles appear on the cover of this month's *Hit Parader*

Friday 1 – George jams at Columbia Recording Studio in NYC with Bob Dylan; none of the recordings from the initial informal session are considered fit for release

Saturday 2 – *Melody Maker* publishes a tongue-in-cheek letter titled "Who Does Paul McCartney Think He Is," signed – Paul McCartney

Saturday 2 – In recording beginning this day and running through the following Thursday, Ringo contributes to the *London Howlin' Wolf Sessions* album

Monday 4 – Yet another edition of the Tony Sheridan tapes is issued, this time on Polydor as *In The Beginning (Circa 1960)*

Monday 4 – Four students shot dead at Kent State University

Tuesday 5 – George returns to England

Monday 11 – "The Long and Winding Road"/"For You Blue" (Apple 2832; peaks at #1 for two weeks in June)

Sunday 17 – Ringo's "Sentimental Journey" promo airs on *The Ed Sullivan Show*

Monday 18 – *Let It Be* (peaks at number one for four weeks in June)

Wednesday 20 – *Let It Be* film premiers in London; no Beatles attend

Wednesday 20 – George and Phil Spector get together for pre-production work at Abbey Road studios; the run-throughs were later bootlegged as *Beware of ABKCO!*

Tuesday 26 – *All Things Must Pass* sessions begin at Abbey Road and will run until mid-August; afterward resuming throughout September at Trident Studios

Tuesday 26 – Final original episode of *I Dream of Jeannie* airs on NBC

June 1970

Topping the US singles chart:
"Everything Is Beautiful" by Ray Stevens
"The Long and Winding Road" by The Beatles

On the airwaves:
"Daughter of Darkness" by Tom Jones
"Make Me Smile" by Chicago
"Get Ready" by Rare Earth

Topping the US album chart:
McCartney

Albums released this month include:
Workingman's Dead by the Grateful Dead
Gasoline Alley by Rod Stewart
Alone Together by Dave Mason
Self-Portrait by Bob Dylan
Changes by The Monkees

Monday 15 – "Que Sera, Sera" by Mary Hopkin (Apple 1823; peaks at #7 on the Adult Contemporary chart)

Tuesday 16 – Badfinger records "No Matter What," produced by Mal Evans

Monday 22 – Ringo, taking time off from *All Things Must Pass*, flies to Nashville to record the *Beaucoups of Blues* album

Thursday 25 – Ringo begins laying down vocals, completing the entire *Beaucoups of Blues* album by Saturday the 27th

July 1970

Topping the US singles chart:
"The Love You Save" by the Jackson 5
"Mama Told Me (Not To Come)" by Three Dog Night

On the airwaves:
"Ride Captain Ride" by Blues Image
"My Baby Loves Lovin'" by White Plains
"O-o-h Child" by the Five Stairsteps

Topping the US album chart:
Let It Be

Albums released this month include:
John Barleycorn Must Die by Traffic
Closer To Home by Grand Funk Railroad
Absolutely Live by The Doors
Cosmo's Factory by Creedence Clearwater Revival
Magnetic South by Michael Nesmith and the First National Band
Supertramp's self-titled debut

Wednesday 1 – Ringo returns to England

Saturday 4 – Casey Kasem's *American Top 40* debuts on radio

Tuesday 7 – George's mother Louise passes away; Ringo turns 30
Friday 31 – *The Huntley-Brinkley Report* ends with Chet Huntley's retirement

August 1970

Topping the US singles chart:
"(They Long To Be) Close To You" by The Carpenters
"Make It With You" by Bread
On the airwaves:

"Spill The Wine" by Eric Burdon and War
"In The Summertime" by Mungo Jerry
"Tighter and Tighter" by Alive and Kicking

Topping the US album chart:
Woodstock: Music from the Original Soundtrack and More

Albums released this month include:
After the Gold Rush by Neil Young
Stage Fright by The Band
Sunflower by the Beach Boys
Close To You by The Carpenters
Eric Clapton's self-titled solo debut

August – John and Yoko appear on the cover of this month's *Hit Parader*

Saturday 1 – Cynthia Lennon marries Italian hotelier Roberto Bassanini

Saturday 1 – Yoko miscarries

Wednesday 5 – "Tell The Truth," the first recording by Derek and The Dominos, is laid down at Trident Studios, produced by Phil Spector and featuring George and Dave Mason; it is later re-cut without the involvement of the latter three

Wednesday 19 – Phil Spector composes a letter detailing his suggestions for the mixing of *All Things Must Pass*, in particular bringing up George's vocals

Saturday 29 – *Melody Maker* runs a letter from Paul saying that the Beatles will not play together again ("…this limping dog of a story…")

September 1970

Topping the US singles chart:
"War" by Edwin Starr
"Ain't No Mountain High Enough" by Diana Ross

On the airwaves:
"Candida" by Dawn

"Patches" by Clarence Carter
"Lookin' Out My Back Door" by CCR

Topping the US album chart:
Cosmo's Factory by Creedence Clearwater Revival

Albums released this month include:
Abraxas by Santana
Share The Land by the Guess Who
(Untitled) by The Byrds
Paranoid by Black Sabbath
Kiln House by Fleetwood Mac
Get Yer Ya-Yas Out! by the Rolling Stones

Tuesday 1 – Ringo tapes an appearance for Cilla Black's TV show, dueting with her on "Act Naturally"

Thursday 3 – Ringo records "Early 1970" with help from George

Thursday 3 – Canned Heat's Alan "Blind Owl" Wilson fatally overdoses at 27

Thursday 3 – Football coach Vince Lombardi dies of cancer at 57

Friday 18 – Jimi Hendrix asphyxiates at 27

Monday 21 – "Jacob's Ladder" by Doris Troy (Apple 1824)

Friday 25 – *The Partridge Family* debuts on ABC

Saturday 26 – *John Lennon/Plastic Ono Band* sessions begin, continuing for one month

Monday 28 – *Beaucoups of Blues* (peaks at number sixty-five)

October 1970

Topping the US singles chart:
"Cracklin' Rosie" by Neil Diamond
"I'll Be There" by the Jackson 5

On the airwaves:
"Lola" by the Kinks
"Green Eyed Lady" by Sugarloaf

"Fire and Rain" by James Taylor

Topping the US album chart:
Cosmo's Factory by Creedence Clearwater Revival

Albums released this month include:
Layla and Other Assorted Love Songs by Derek and the Dominos
Tumbleweed Connection by Elton John
New Morning by Bob Dylan
Led Zeppelin III
Jesus Christ Superstar (Original London Cast)
The Partridge Family Album

October – Paul appears on the cover of this month's *Hit Parader*

Thursday 1 – Janis Joplin tapes a birthday greeting for John's upcoming 30th birthday

Sunday 4 – (Early morning hours) Janis Joplin overdoses at 27

Monday 5 – "Beaucoups of Blues"/"Coochy Coochy" (Apple 2969; peaks at #87)

Friday 9 – On his 30th birthday, John sees his father for the last time at Tittenhurst Park; later, while recording "Remember" at Abbey Road studios, John receives birthday greetings in person from George and Ringo

Monday 12 – "No Matter What" by Badfinger (Apple 1822; peaks at #8))

Monday 19 – "Think About Your Children" by Mary Hopkin (Apple 1825; peaks at #27 on the Adult Contemporary chart)

Friday 23 – *Plastic Ono Band* sessions end

Monday 26 – "Carolina In My Mind" by James Taylor (Apple 1805 reissue)

Monday 26 – "Golden Slumbers"/"Carry That Weight" by Trash (Apple 1811 reissue)

Monday 26 – Gary Trudeau's comic strip *Doonesbury* debuts

Wednesday 28 – George and Pattie arrive in New York with Phil Spector

November 1970

Topping the US singles chart:
"I Think I Love You" by the Partridge Family

On the airwaves:
Montego Bay" by Bobby Bloom
"Cry Me A River" by Joe Cocker
"Share The Land" by the Guess Who

Topping the US album chart:
Led Zeppelin III

Albums released this month include:
Twelve Dreams of Dr. Sardonicus by Spirit
His Band and Street Choir by Van Morrison
Tea For The Tillerman by Cat Stevens
American Beauty by the Grateful Dead
Lola Versus Powerman and the Moneygoround by The Kinks
Loose Salute by Michael Nesmith and the First National Band

November – John begins demoing material for future releases, including "I'm The Greatest" and "Mind Games," initially taped as "Make Love Not War"

Monday 9 – *No Dice* by Badfinger (peaks at number twenty-eight)

Monday 9 – *The Whale* by John Tavener

Monday 9 – *Encouraging Words* by Billy Preston
Monday 9 – *Doris Troy*

Wednesday 11 – Maureen Starkey gives birth to daughter Lee

Monday 23 – "My Sweet Lord"/"Isn't It A Pity" (Apple 2995; peaks at #1 for 4 weeks beginning in December)

Tuesday 24 – George introduces Badfinger's set at Ungano's in New York

Friday 27 – *All Things Must Pass* (peaks at number one for seven weeks beginning in January 1971)

December 1970

Topping the US singles chart:
"Tears of a Clown" by Smokey Robinson and
the Miracles
"My Sweet Lord" by
George Harrison

On the airwaves:
"After Midnight" by
Eric Clapton
"One Less Bell To Answer" by the Fifth Dimension
"Domino" by Van Morrison

Topping the US album chart:
Abraxas by Santana

Albums released this month include:
Pendulum by Creedence Clearwater Revival
False Start by Love
Ry Cooder's self-titled debut

December – While the two are in New York, George and Paul meet up but the encounter goes badly

December – Without quite announcing a break-up of Simon & Garfunkel, Paul Simon signs a solo contract with Columbia Records

Tuesday 8 – John and Yoko are interviewed by Jann Wenner for *Rolling Stone*

Friday 11 – *John Lennon/Plastic Ono Band* (peaks at number six)

Friday 11 – *Yoko Ono/Plastic Ono Band* (peaks at number one hundred eighty-two

Monday 14 – "My Sweet Lord" by Billy Preston (Apple 1826; peaks at #23 on the R&B chart))

Monday 14 – John and Yoko begin filming *Up Your Legs Forever*

Wednesday 16 – *Love Story* opens in theaters

Friday 18 – *The Beatles Christmas Album* mailed to US fan club members

Saturday 19 – John and Yoko begin filming *Fly*

Monday 21 – Elvis Presley visits President Richard Nixon at the White House

Monday 28 – "Mother"/"Why" (Apple 1827; peaks at #43)

Thursday 31 – Paul sues the other three Beatles to rid himself of Allen Klein and Apple

1971

Published this year:
We Love You Beatles by Margaret Sutton

January
Topping the US singles chart:
"My Sweet Lord" by George Harrison
"Knock Three Times" by Dawn

On the airwaves:
"Your Song" by Elton John
"Stoney End" by Barbra Streisand
"Love The One You're With" by Stephen Stills

Topping the US album chart:
All Things Must Pass

Albums released this month include:
Chicago III
Nantucket Sleighride by Mountain

Love It To Death by Alice Cooper
Little Feat's self-titled debut
ZZ Top's self-titled debut

January – After Michael X is arrested and charged with extortion, John pays his bail; X then jumps bail and flees to Trinidad

Friday 1 – Cigarette advertising ban goes into effect on US television

Sunday 3 – The McCartneys fly to New York to audition musicians for *Ram*

Sunday 10 – Designer Coco Chanel dies at 87

Monday 11 – *Ram* sessions begin in New York at Columbia Studios

Tuesday 12 – *All in the Family* debuts on CBS

Wednesday 13 – John and Yoko fly to Japan from Toronto; John meets Yoko's family for the first time

Thursday 14 – Badfinger appears on *Top of the Pops*, performing "Believe Me," "Better Days," and "No Matter What"

Tuesday 19 – Court action resumes in London in Paul's case against Apple

Wednesday 20 – The Lennons stay in Japan is cut short by the resumption of litigation in London

Thursday 21- Part one of John's *Rolling Stone* interview, "The Working Class Hero," appears as a cover story

Friday 22 – John records "Power To The People" at his home studio in Tittenhurst Park, one day after giving a political interview to Tariq Ali for *Red Mole* magazine

Monday 25 – Rehearsals begin for Frank Zappa's *200 Motels*, starring Ringo

Topping the US singles chart:
"One Bad Apple" by Osmond Brothers

On the airwaves:
"I Hear You Knocking" by Dave Edmunds
"Doesn't Somebody Want To Be Wanted" by the Partridge Family
"If You Could Read My Mind" by Gordon Lightfoot
Topping the US album chart:
All Things Must Pass

Albums released this month include:

The Yes Album
Stoney End by Barbra Streisand
The Cry of Love by Jimi Hendrix
Carly Simon's self-titled debut
Earth, Wind and Fire's self-titled debut

Monday 1 – Ringo begins shooting *200 Motels*; lasts through the end of the week

Tuesday 2 – On this day, George and Phil Spector produce sessions for Ronnie Spector, assisted by Leon Russell, Jim Gordon, Carl Radle and Badfinger's Pete Ham; their work concludes on the 21st

Tuesday 2 – Harry Nilsson's animated fable, *The Point*, airs on ABC; Dustin Hoffman narrates the original broadcast but is replaced by Ringo for the home video release

Thursday 4 – Part two of John's *Rolling Stone* interview, "Life with the Lions," appears as a cover story

Saturday 6 – Apollo 14 astronaut Alan Shepard hits two golf balls on the moon

Wednesday 10 – Bright Tunes, publishers of "He's So Fine," file suit against George, charging plagiarism over "My Sweet Lord"

Saturday 13 – Ringo's "Act Naturally" performance with Cilla Black airs

Monday 15 – "What Is Life"/"Apple Scruffs" (Apple 1828; peaks at #10)

Monday 22 – "Another Day"/"Oh Woman Oh Why" (Apple 1829; peaks at #5)

March 1971

Topping the US singles chart:
"Me and Bobby McGee" by Janis Joplin

On the airwaves:
"She's A Lady" by Tom Jones
"Proud Mary" by Ike & Tina Turner
"One Toke Over The Line" by Brewer & Shipley

Topping the US album chart:
Pearl by Janis Joplin

Albums released this month include:
Tapestry by Carole King
Aqualung by Jethro Tull
Songs of Love and Hate by Leonard Cohen

Monday 8 – Silent era film comedian Harold Lloyd dies at 77

Friday 12 – Litigation between the former Beatles is momentarily resolved with the appointment of a receiver to collect all monies earned jointly

Tuesday 16 – Paul and Linda accept The Beatles' Grammy for *Let It Be* as winner in the "Best Original Score" category

Monday 22 – "Power To The People"/"Touch Me" (Apple 1830; peaks at #11)

April 1971

Topping the US singles chart:
"Just My Imagination (Running Away With Me)" by the Temptations
On the airwaves:
"Love Her Madly" by The Doors
"Me and You and a Dog Named Boo" by Lobo
"I Am…I Said" by Neil Diamond

Topping the US album chart:
Pearl by Janis Joplin

Albums released this month include:
Sticky Fingers by the Rolling Stones
LA Woman by The Doors
Mud Slide Slim and the Blue Horizon by James Taylor
4 Way Street by Crosby, Stills, Nash and Young
The Doobie Brothers' self-titled debut

Friday 2 – Final episode of TV daytime soap *Dark Shadows* airs

Friday 9 – Charles Manson and three followers are sentenced to death for the Tate-LaBianca murders

Tuesday 13 – John records a demo of "God Save Oz"

Thursday 15 – Quincy Jones accepts an Oscar on behalf of The Beatles for *Let It Be* as winner in the "Best Original Film Score" category; the Best Actor awarded to George C. Scott for *Patton* that night is later refused

Friday 16 – "It Don't Come Easy"/"Early 1970" (Apple 1831; peaks at #4)

Friday 16 – Paul and Linda appear on the cover of *Life*; inside, Paul offers his reasons for taking the other Beatles to court

Monday 19 – "Try Some, Buy Some" by Ronnie Spector (Apple 1832)

Thursday 22 – Ringo's "Sunny Heights" video for "It Don't Come Easy" airs on *Top of the Pops*

Saturday 24 – John and Yoko detained in Mallorca, Spain for alleged "kidnapping" of Yoko's daughter Kyoko

Tuesday 27 – Ringo, filming a TV appearance with Cilla Black in Norway, shoots footage for a second "It Don't Come Easy" promo

Thursday 29 – Ringo's "snow" video for "It Don't Come Easy" is screened on *Top of the Pops*

May 1971

Topping the US singles chart:
"Joy To The World" by Three Dog Night
"Brown Sugar" by the Rolling Stones

On the airwaves:
"Superstar" by Murray Head
"Here Comes The Sun" by Ritchie Havens
"Treat Her Like A Lady" by Cornelius Brothers and Sister Rose

Topping the US album chart:
Jesus Christ Superstar (Original London Cast)

Albums released this month include:
Nevada Fighter by Michael Nesmith and the First National Band
Smash Your Head Against The Wall by John Entwistle
What's Going On by Marvin Gaye
Every Picture Tells A Story by Rod Stewart
Leon Russell and the Shelter People

Wednesday 12 – Mick Jagger weds Bianca de Macias in Saint-Tropez with Paul and Ringo in attendance

Friday 14 – John and Yoko arrive in France, missing Mick Jagger's wedding by days; instead they head to Cannes for the premier of *Fly* and *Apotheosis* on the 15th at the film festival

Saturday 15 – Still in France, Ringo and Maureen are joined by George and Pattie; partying with Cilla Black aboard the yacht *SS Marala*, George and Ringo begin writing "Photograph"

Monday 17 – *Ram* (peaks at number two)

Friday 21 – *The Radha Krsna Temple*

Friday 21 – The *Imagine* sessions begin at Tittenhurst's Ascot Sound Studio; George contributes, playing on "Gimme Some Truth," "How Do You Sleep," "Crippled Inside," "Oh My Love," and "I Don't Want To Be A Soldier, Mama, I Don't Want To Die"

Saturday 22 – John is roused from bed when a stranger is found on the grounds at Tittenhurst Park, explaining that he felt John was sending him messages through his music; after feeding him, John sends him on his way

Saturday 22 – "God Save Us" and "Do The Oz" are recorded at Ascot Sound Studios at Tittenhurst Park

Monday 31 – George begins production work on Badfinger's *Straight Up* album at Abbey Road

June 1971

Topping the US singles chart:
"Want Ads" by the Honey Cone
"It's Too Late" by Carole King

On the airwaves:
"If Not For You" by Olivia Newton-John
"Rainy Days and Mondays" by The Carpenters
"That's The Way I've Always Heard It Should Be" by Carly Simon

Topping the US album chart:
Sticky Fingers by the Rolling Stones

Albums released this month include:
Blue by Joni Mitchell
Tarkus by Emerson, Lake and Palmer
Byrdmaniax by The Byrds
I Wrote A Simple Song by Billy Preston
The Donny Osmond Album

Tuesday 1 – John and Yoko fly to New York

Friday 4 – Work begins at Abbey Road on Badfinger's "Day After Day," George producing

Saturday 5 – On this day and the next, Paul and Linda are filmed at their Scottish farm; video is later used for *Ram* promos

Sunday 6 – (Early morning hours) John and Yoko jam with Frank Zappa and the Mothers at the Fillmore East

Sunday 6 – Final episode of *The Ed Sullivan Show* airs, though no new episodes have run since the end of March

Wednesday 9 – A week of recording sessions begins in London for B.B. King; Ringo is among the contributing musicians

Sunday 13 – *The New York Times* begins publishing the Pentagon Papers

Wednesday 16 – Beginning this day and continuing through Friday, the *Thrillington* sessions take place at EMI's Abbey Road facility
Thursday 17 – Ringo begins shooting *Blindman* in Rome and later, Almeria, Spain

Monday 21 – "Sour Milk Sea" by Jackie Lomax (Apple 1834) is reissued

Thursday 24 – Paul's footage accompanying "Three Legs" and "Heart of the Country" airs on *Top of the Pops*

Wednesday 30 – Three members of the Soviet Soyuz 11 space crew are killed upon re-entry in Earth's atmosphere

July 1971

Topping the US singles chart:
"Indian Reservation (The Lament of the Cherokee Reservation Indian)" by The Raiders
"You've Got A Friend" by James Taylor

On the airwaves:
"Don't Pull Your Love" by Hamilton, Joe Frank and Reynolds

"Get It On" by Chase
"Never Ending Song Of Love" by Delaney and Bonnie

Topping the US album chart:
Tapestry by Carole King

Albums released this month include:
Who's Next by The Who
The Allman Brothers at Fillmore East
Every Good Boy Deserves Favour by the Moody Blues
Fireball by Deep Purple
Masters of Reality by Black Sabbath

July – George flies out to Los Angeles to work on the *Raga* soundtrack with Ravi Shankar

Saturday 3 – (Early morning hours) Jim Morrison dies of apparent heart failure in Paris at 27

Saturday 3 – John and Yoko fly to New York to complete work on *Imagine* and *Fly*

Sunday 4 – King Curtis records sax overdubs for "It's So Hard" and "I Don't Want To be A Soldier Mama"

Monday 5 – George records "Bangla Desh" in Los Angeles

Tuesday 6 – John and Yoko host a wrap party for *Imagine* at Allen Klein's house in Riverdale, New York; attendees include Miles Davis and Andy Warhol

Tuesday 6 – Louis Armstrong suffers a fatal heart attack at 69

Wednesday 7 – "God Save Us" by Bill Elliott and the Elastic Oz Band (Apple 1835; dnc)

Friday 9 – Grand Funk Railroad play Shea Stadium, breaking The Beatles' record for a sell-out

Monday 12 – Back in England, George informs Badfinger that he must bow out of the *Straight Up* project due to the Bangladesh event but agrees to set them up with another producer; he also invites them to perform at the benefit

Saturday 17 – John and Yoko appear on *Parkinson* in the UK

Monday 19 – On this day and the next, John and Yoko meet the press in England to promote the reprint of Yoko's *Grapefruit*

Thursday 22 – John's "Imagine" promo film shot at Tittenhurst Park

Saturday 24 – Paul phones Denny Laine with an invitation to work together

Monday 26 – Rehearsals for the Bangladesh benefit begin in New York

Tuesday 27 – George and Ravi, with Allen Klein, hold a press conference in New York announcing the Bangladesh event

Wednesday 28 – "Bangla Desh"/"Deep Blue" (Apple 1836; peaks at #23)

Saturday 31 – Original scheduled date for the first Bangladesh benefit show; though tickets circulate bearing this date, the show was instead moved to the following day as a matinee

August 1971

Topping the US singles chart:
"How Can You Mend A Broken Heart" by the Bee Gees

On the airwaves:
"Riders On The Storm" by The Doors
"Take Me Home, Country Roads" by John Denver
"Signs" by Five Man Electrical Band

Topping the US album chart:
Tapestry by Carole King

Albums released this month include:
The London Howlin' Wolf Sessions
Surf's Up by the Beach Boys
Al Green Gets Next To You
Barbra Joan Streisand

BIG 10 ALBUMS

1. Carpenters—Carpenters—A & M
2. Every Picture Tells A Story—Rod Stewart—Mercury
3. Tapestry—Carole King—Ode 70
4. Ram—Paul & Linda McCartney—Apple
5. Every Good Boy Deserves Favour—Moody Blues—London
6. Who's Next—The Who—Decca
7. Mud Slide Slim—James Taylor—WB
8. B, S & T #4—Blood, Sweat & Tears—Columbia
9. Stephen Stills #2—Stephen Stills—Atlantic
10. Blue—Joni Mitchell—Reprise

COMING NEXT WEEK:
A look inside the BIG TEN Plaything!

SMALL PRINT DEPARTMENT: The WCFL "ALL HIT MUSIC" represents the relative popularity of records in the Midwest based on industry tabulations, local record sales and requests. WCFL The Voice of Labor, is owned and operated by The Chicago Federation of Labor and Industrial Union Council.

BIG 10 REQUEST GOLD

* In The Summertime—Mungo Jerry—(1970)
* I Can't Get No Satisfaction—Rolling Stones—(1965)
* Love Grows Where My Rosemary Goes—Edison Lighthouse—(1970)
* Aquarius—5th Dimension—(1969)
* Sunshine of Your Love—Cream—(1968)
* Superstar—Murray Head—(1970)
* Yellow Submarine—Beatles—(1968)
* I Started A Joke—Bee Gees—(1969)
* Goin' Up The Country—Canned Heat—(1969)
  Deep Purple—Nino Temple/April Stevens—(1963)

*denotes currently available as gold single or on an album.

Week Ending August 26, 1971

WAS	IS	Title
(10)	1.	Uncle Albert/Admiral Halsey—Paul McCartney—Apple
(3)	2.	Maybe Tomorrow—Jackson 5—Motown
(4)	3.	Rings—Cymarron—Entrance
(7)	4.	Wedding Song (There Is Love)—Paul Stookey—WB
(1)	5.	Smiling Faces Sometimes—Undisputed Truth—Gordy
(9)	6.	Won't Get Fooled Again—The Who—Decca
(15)	*7.	Spanish Harlem—Aretha Franklin—Atlantic
(19)	*8.	Ain't No Sunshine—Bill Withers—Sussex
(2)	9.	Take Me Home, Country Roads—John Denver—RCA
(12)	10.	Resurrection Shuffle—Ashton, Gardner & Dyke—Cap.
(14)	11.	Liar—Three Dog Night—Dunhill
(17)	12.	Mother Freedom—Bread—Elektra
(6)	13.	Mercy Mercy Me—Marvin Gaye—Tamla
(22)	*14.	Go Away Little Girl—Donny Osmond—MGM
(23)	*15.	I Just Want to Celebrate—Rare Earth—Rare Earth
(5)	16.	Never Ending Song of Love—Delaney & Bonnie—Atco
(18)	17.	Whatcha See Is Whatcha Get—Dramatics—Volt
(26)	*18.	Night They Drove Old Dixie—Joan Baez—Vanguard
(28)	*19.	Woke Up In Love This Morning—Partridge Family—Bell
(24)	20.	Roll On—The New Colony Six—Sunlight
(8)	21.	Riders on the Storm—The Doors—Elektra
(13)	22.	Moon Shadow—Cat Stevens—A & M
(16)	23.	Sweet Hitch-Hiker—C. C. Revival—Fantasy
(11)	24.	Mr. Big Stuff—Jean Knight—Stax
(30)	25.	Bangla-Desh—George Harrison—Apple
(20)	26.	Indian Reservation—The Raiders—Columbia
(33)	*27.	I Ain't Got Time Anymore—The Glass Bottle—Avco
(32)	28.	Stagger Lee—Tommy Roe—ABC
(21)	29.	How Can You Mend a Broken Heart—Bee Gees—Atco
(38)	*30.	Marianne—Stephen Stills—Atlantic
(25)	31.	Don't Pull Your Love—H., J. F. & Reynolds—Dunhill
(40)	32.	Take Me Girl, I'm Ready—Jr. Walker/All Stars—Soul
(27)	33.	Beginnings—Chicago—Columbia
(39)	34.	I've Found Someone of My Own—The Free Movement—Decca
(29)	35.	Funky Nassau—Beginning of the End—Alston
(31)	36.	Draggin' the Line—Tommy James—Roulette
(HB)	37.	The Story in Your Eyes—The Moody Blues—Threshold
(HB)	38.	If You Really Love Me—Stevie Wonder—Tamla
(HB)	39.	He'd Rather Have the Rain—Heaven Bound—MGM
(HB)	40.	Sweet City Woman—Stampeders—Bell

*Denotes Big 10 Climbers

August – Sessions for Wings' LP debut, *Wild Life*, begin mid-month and are completed in less than two weeks

Sunday 1 – A quarter-million dollars are raised between two shows as the Concert for Bangladesh is held at Madison Square Garden

Monday 2 – "Uncle Albert/Admiral Halsey"/"Too Many People" (Apple 1837; peaks at #1 in September)

Tuesday 3 – Paul's still-unnamed new band begins rehearsing in Scotland

Tuesday 3 – John's portrait for the Apple label of *Imagine* is taken at Tittenhurst Park

Monday 9 – "Joi Bangla" by Ravi Shankar (Apple 1838)

Wednesday 11 – Back in London, John and Yoko march in support of *Oz* magazine

Wednesday 11 – Lead guitarist Lefty Baker (Spanky and Our Gang) dies at 27

Friday 13 – Sax legend King Curtis, 37, is stabbed to death in New York City

Thursday 19 – On this day and the next, Ringo records "Blindman" at Apple Studios with help from Klaus Voormann and Pete Ham

Saturday 21 – Convicted offender and murder suspect George Jackson is killed during an escape attempt at San Quentin prison

Wednesday 25 – George attends a Carly Simon performance at the Schaefer Music Festival in Central Park

September 1971

Topping the US singles chart:
"Uncle Albert/Admiral Halsey" by Paul and Linda McCartney
"Go Away Little Girl" by Donny Osmond

On the airwaves:
"All Day Music" by War
"The Night They Drove Old Dixie Down" by Joan Baez
"Spanish Harlem" by Aretha Franklin
Topping the US album chart:
Tapestry by Carole King

Albums released this month include:
Future Games by Fleetwood Mac
Electric Warrior by T. Rex
Harmony by Three Dog Night
Goin' Back To Indiana by the Jackson 5

Thursday 2 – George appears on the cover of *Rolling Stone*; full coverage of the Bangladesh event

Friday 3 – John and Yoko leave England for good; initially staying at the St. Regis Hotel on 5th Avenue and East 55th Street in New York City

Friday 3 – Ringo announces the formation of *Ringo or Robin Ltd.*, a company specializing in pricey, rather droll furniture designs

Monday 6 – John and Yoko shoot footage at the St. Regis for their *Imagine* film, including cameos from actors Jack Palance and Fred Astaire, plus talk show host Dick Cavett and George Harrison

Wednesday 8 – John and Yoko tape an appearance on the *Dick Cavett Show*; the interview runs long and so is broadcast on two separate nights

Thursday 9 – *Imagine* (peaks at number one in October)

Thursday 9 – Five days of rioting begins at Attica Correctional Facility in New York, leaving at least 39 dead, including prison employees and civilians

Saturday 11 – The first portion of the Lennons interview runs on the *Dick Cavett Show*

Monday 13 – Stella McCartney born; Paul decides on "Wings" as the name of his new band

Tuesday 14 – John pens a letter to the *New York Times*, defending the Beatles' covers of black artists

Friday 17 – *Come Together* (original motion picture soundtrack)

Monday 20 – *Fly* by Yoko Ono (peaks at number one hundred ninety-nine)

Friday 24 – The second half of the Lennons interview runs on the *Dick Cavett Show*

Wednesday 29 – "Mrs. Lennon" by Yoko Ono (Apple 1839)

Thursday 30 – George, along with Badfinger, the Van Eaton brothers, Klaus Voormann and others, attends the opening of Apple Studios at Savile Row in London

October 1971

Topping the US singles chart:
"Maggie May" by Rod Stewart

On the airwaves:
"Do You Know What I Mean" by Lee Michaels
"Sweet City Woman" by Stampeders
"One Fine Morning" by Lighthouse

Topping the US album chart:
Every Picture Tells A Story by Rod Stewart

Albums released this month include:
Teaser and the Firecat by Cat Stevens
American Pie by Don McLean
Other Voices by The Doors
Tupelo Honey by Van Morrison
Meddle by Pink Floyd
REO Speedwagon's self-titled debut

October – Ringo appears on the cover of this month's *Circus*

October – John is interviewed by David Wigg at the St. Regis Hotel; the audio will emerge in 1976 as part of *The Beatles Tapes* double-album

Friday 1 – Walt Disney World opens in Orlando, Florida

Saturday 2 – *Soul Train* debuts on US television

Saturday 9 – Yoko's *This Is Not Here* exhibition opens in Syracuse, running through the 27th

Saturday 9 – John's 31st birthday celebration at his Syracuse hotel room includes Ringo, Mal Evans, Klaus Voormann, Jim Keltner, Phil Spector and many others; the party is filmed and recorded, while John begins writing "Attica State"

Monday 11 – "Imagine"/"It's So Hard" (Apple 1840; peaks at #3)

Tuesday 12 – Gene Vincent ("Be Bop A-Lula") dies at 37

Thursday 14 – John and Yoko appear on the PBS show *Free Time*

Friday 15 – John and George attend the *Rock and Roll Revival* concert at Madison Square Garden, featuring Chuck Berry, Bobby Rydell and Rick Nelson, among others; (Nelson's misreading of the crowd's behavior during his set prompts him to write "Garden Party")

Saturday 16 – The Lennons move to 105 Bank Street, Greenwich Village

Thursday 28 – John and Yoko begin work on "Happy Xmas (War Is Over)" at the Record Plant

Friday 29 – Duane Allman dies in a motorcycle accident at 24

Sunday 31 – On Halloween, the Harlem Community Choir lay down backing vocals on "Happy Xmas (War Is Over)"

November 1971

Topping the US singles chart:
"Gypsies, Tramps and Thieves" by Cher
"Theme from Shaft" by Isaac Hayes

On the airwaves:
"Peace Train" by Cat Stevens
"Everybody's Everything" by Santana
"Tired Of Being Alone" by Al Green

Topping the US album chart:
Shaft by Isaac Hayes

Albums released this month include:
Led Zeppelin IV (aka "Runes," "Zoso," etc.)
Madman Across The Water by Elton John
Fragile by Yes
There's a Riot Goin' On by Sly and the Family Stone
Anticipation by Carly Simon
The Low Spark of High-Heeled Boys by Traffic
Nilsson Schmilsson by Harry Nilsson

November – Paul appears on the cover of this month's *Hit Parader*

November – George appears on the cover of this month's *Circus*

Wednesday 3 – *Earth Song – Ocean Song* by Mary Hopkin

Monday 8 – The Wings launch party is held at the Empress Ballroom, Leicester Square

Thursday 10 – "Day After Day" by Badfinger (Apple 1841; peaks at #4)

Thursday 10 – *200 Motels* opens in theaters

Saturday 20 – In an interview published in *Melody Maker* under the provocative title 'Why Lennon is Uncool,' Paul holds forth on the business differences between the ex-Beatles, "How Do You Sleep," and Allen Klein

Monday 22 – John and George are together at the press screening of the Ravi Shankar documentary, *Raga*, an Apple film

Tuesday 23 – George appears alongside Ravi Shankar on the *Dick Cavett Show*; sits in with Gary Wright's Wonderwheel

Wednesday 24 – George tapes an appearance with Ravi Shankar for the *David Frost Show*

Wednesday 24 – On this Thanksgiving Eve, skyjacker Dan (not "DB") Cooper vanishes over Washington with $200,000 in cash

Saturday 27 – Ringo appears on *Cilla in Scandinavia*, performing comedy and singing "The Snowman Song"; shooting occurred in Norway months earlier

December 1971

Topping the US singles chart:
"Family Affair" by Sly and the Family Stone
"Brand New Key" by Melanie

On the airwaves:
"Old Fashioned Love Song" by Three Dog Night
"Sunshine" by Jonathan Edwards
"Got To Be There" by Michael Jackson

Topping the US album chart:
Santana III

Albums released this month include:
Hunky Dory by David Bowie
Electric Light Orchestra's self-titled debut
America's self-titled debut
Hot Rocks 1964-1971 by the Rolling Stones

Wednesday 1 – "Happy Xmas (War Is Over)"/"Listen The Snow Is Falling" (Apple 1842; dnc)

Wednesday 1 – "Water, Paper and Clay" by Mary Hopkin (Apple 1843; peaks at #113)

Friday 3 – George appearance with Ravi Shankar airs on the *David Frost Show*

Saturday 4 – John responds to Paul's recent interview with a letter published in *Melody Maker*

Saturday 4 – The Montreux Casino in Switzerland burns down during a Frank Zappa concert; later immortalized in Deep Purple's "Smoke On The Water"

Tuesday 7 – *Wild Life* (peaks at number ten)

Tuesday 7 – *Raga/Original Soundtrack*

Friday 10 – Frank Zappa is attacked and seriously injured onstage at London's Rainbow

Saturday 11 – (Early morning hours) John and Yoko perform at the Free John Sinclair rally in Ann Arbor

Monday 13 – *Straight Up* by Badfinger (peaks at number thirty-one)

Thursday 16 – John and Yoko tape an appearance for *The David Frost Show*

Friday 17 – John and Yoko appear at the Apollo Theatre in Harlem

Saturday 18 – Harry Nilsson's "Without You," written by Badfinger's Pete Ham and Tom Evans, is released as a single

Monday 20 – *The Concert for Bangla Desh* (peaks at number two)

Wednesday 22 – Tony Cox disappears with the eight year-old Kyoko

Saturday 25 – Another letter from John and Yoko (dated December 13) is published in *Melody Maker* this Christmas day, explaining Apple and defending "How Do You Sleep"

Monday 27 – *El Topo/Original Soundtrack*

Wednesday 29 – Ringo is interviewed discussing comics on the BBC show, *Man Alive*

Friday 31 – TV actor Peter Duel (*Alias Smith and Jones*) commits suicide at 31

1972

Published this year:
Body Count by Francie Schwartz
The Longest Cocktail Party by Richard DiLello
Apple To The Core by Peter McCabe and Robert D. Schonfeld
January
Topping the US singles chart:
"Brand New Key" by Melanie
"American Pie" by Don McLean

On the airwaves:
"Day After Day" by Badfinger
"I'd Like To Teach The World To Sing" by the New Seekers
"Never Been To Spain" by Three Dog Night

Topping the US album chart:
Music by Carole King

Albums released this month include:
Let's Stay Together by Al Green
Weird Scenes Inside The Gold Mine by The Doors

Baby I'm-a Want You by Bread
Paul Simon's self-titled debut
Jackson Browne's self-titled debut
Rockpile by Dave Edmunds

January – Bob Dylan's non-album single "George Jackson" peaks at 33

Saturday 1 – French entertainer Maurice Chevalier dies at 83

Friday 7 – Billionaire recluse Howard Hughes denounces fraudulent biographer Clifford Irving in a conference call

Wednesday 12 – *Blindman* opens in theaters
Thursday 13 – John and Yoko's appearance on *The David Frost Show* airs

Friday 14 – John and Yoko tape the first day of their weeklong guest hosting of the *Mike Douglas Show* in Philadelphia, to air one month later

Sunday 16 – Chipmunks creator David Seville dies at 52

Tuesday 18 – John and Yoko tape day two of their *Mike Douglas Show* appearance

Thursday 20 – John and Yoko tape day three of their *Mike Douglas Show* appearance, this time with guest Chuck Berry

Monday 24 – Henry McCullough is invited to join Wings

Thursday/Friday 27/28 – John and Yoko tape the last two days of their weeklong guest hosting appearance on the *Mike Douglas Show*
Thursday 27 – Gospel legend Mahalia Jackson dies at 60

Friday 28 – Ringo tapes a segment with Lulu for *Monty Python's Flying Circus*

Sunday 30 – "Bloody Sunday" in Derry, Northern Ireland, when thirteen unarmed civilians are slain by British troops, prompting both John and Paul to write songs

February 1972

Topping the US singles chart:
"Let's Stay Together" by Al Green
"Without You" by Harry Nilsson

On the airwaves:
"Joy" by Apollo 100
"Precious and Few" by Climax
"Everything I Own" by Bread

Topping the US album chart:
American Pie by Don McLean
Albums released this month include:
Harvest by Neil Young
Eat A Peach by the Allman Brothers Band
Tantamount to Treason Vol. 1 by Michael Nesmith and the Second National Band
Hendrix In The West

February – John and Yoko appear on the cover of this month's *Hit Parader*

February – Early this month, Wings are filmed rehearsing material for their upcoming live dates

February – Jesse Ed Davis releases his second solo album, *Ululu*, featuring George's "Sue Me Sue You Blues"

February – *Some Time in New York City* sessions begin at Record Plant East

Friday 4 – Secret memo from Sen. Strom Thurmond to attorney general John Mitchell asserts the need to eliminate the "threat" of John's presence in the US to President Nixon's reelection chances

Tuesday 8 – The Beatles Official Fan Club shuts down

Wednesday 9 – Wings debut live at the University of Nottingham; their hit-and-run tour would take them to eleven cities through the 23rd

Monday-Friday 14-18 – John and Yoko's co-hosting of *The Mike Douglas Show* is broadcast

Sunday 27 – On this day and the next, Ringo and Maureen attend a 40th birthday gala for Elizabeth Taylor in Budapest

Monday 28 – "Give Ireland Back To The Irish"/"(version)" (Apple 1847; peaks at #21)

Monday 28 – Days after receiving his driver's license back for previous offenses, George crashes his car during a power outage, severely injuring Pattie and himself

March 1972

Topping the US singles chart:
"Heart of Gold" by Neil Young
"A Horse With No Name" by America

On the airwaves:
"Down By The Lazy River" by the Osmond Brothers
"Mother and Child Reunion" by Paul Simon
"Bang A Gong (Get It On)" by T. Rex

Topping the US album chart:
Harvest by Neil Young

Albums released this month include:
Smokin' by Humble Pie
Music of My Mind by Stevie Wonder
Thick As A Brick by Jethro Tull
Just Another Band From L.A. by Frank Zappa and the Mothers
Machine Head by Deep Purple

March – George and Ringo contribute to the *Son of Schmilsson* sessions at Trident Studios, the making of which is filmed for an unreleased documentary entitled *Did Somebody Drop His Mouse?*

Monday 6 – "Baby Blue" by Badfinger (Apple 1844; peaks at #14)

Monday 6 – "Sweet Music" by Lon and Derrek Van Eaton (Apple 1845)

Give Ireland back to the Irish

By
Wings

🍀🍀🍀🍀🍀

New McCartney single

BANNED EVERYWHERE

BBC Radio and Television
Radio Luxembourg
ITV and GPO

Hear the uncensored version
at your
local record shop

KEEP ON TRUCKING

Monday 6 – Scheduled release date for John's "Luck of the Irish"/"Attica State" (Apple 1846); the single is canceled

Tuesday 7 – Wings are filmed by an ABC news rehearsing "Give Ireland Back To The Irish"

Thursday 16 – John and Yoko are served with deportation notices

Saturday 18 – Ringo films T. Rex at London's Wembley Pool for the documentary, *Born To Boogie*

Monday 20 – "Back Off Boogaloo"/"Blindman" (Apple 1849; peaks at #9)

Monday 20 – A promo film for "Back Off Boogaloo" is shot at Tittenhurst with Ringo and a Frankenstein monster

Monday 20 – The *Some Time in New York City* sessions end
Tuesday 21 – The T. Rex jam sequence for *Born To Boogie* is filmed at Apple Studios with Elton John and Ringo

Wednesday 22 – John attends a preview of *The Concert for Bangladesh* film at the DeMille Theater

Friday 24 – *The Godfather* opens

Saturday 25 – Final original episode of *Bewitched* airs on ABC

Spring – George travels to India with Gary Wright

April 1972

Topping the US singles chart:
"The First Time Ever I Saw Your Face" by Roberta Flack

On the airwaves:
"Doctor My Eyes" by Jackson Browne
"Rockin' Robin" by Michael Jackson
"Baby Blue" by Badfinger

Topping the US album chart:
America's self-titled debut

Albums released this month include:
Mardi Gras by Creedence Clearwater Revival
Bare Trees by Fleetwood Mac
#1 Record by Big Star
Manassas' self-titled debut
Woman by Mike McGear

Thursday 6 – Ringo's "Back Off Boogaloo" promo airs on *Top of the Pops*

Monday 17 – *The Pope Smokes Dope* by David Peel and the Lower East Side

Tuesday 18 – Following their first deportation hearing, John and Yoko are interviewed at the INS office by Geraldo Rivera

Saturday 22 – John and Yoko appear at the Duffy Square Peace Rally in New York, alongside Vietnam veteran/anti-war spokesman John Kerry

Sunday 23 – Actor George Sanders (*All About Eve*), 65, commits suicide

Monday 24 – "Woman Is The Nigger of the World"/"Sisters, O Sisters" (Apple 1848; peaks at #57)

Friday 28 – John and Yoko hold a press conference, detailing the Kyoko custody case

May 1972

Topping the US singles chart:
"Oh Girl" by The Chi-Lites

On the airwaves:
"Morning Has Broken" by Cat Stevens
"Sylvia's Mother" by Dr. Hook and the Medicine Show
"Betcha By Golly Wow" by The Stylistics

Topping the US album chart:
First Take by Roberta Flack

Albums released this month include:
You Don't Mess Around with Jim by Jim Croce
Whistle Rymes by John Entwistle
Carl and the Passions – "So Tough" by the Beach Boys
Honky Chateau by Elton John
Raspberries' self-titled debut
Exile on Main Street by the Rolling Stones

Wednesday 3 – "We're On Our Way" by Chris Hodge (Apple 1850)

Wednesday 3 – Stone the Crows guitarist Les Harvey, 27, is electrocuted onstage

Wednesday 3 – FBI director J. Edgar Hoover dies at 77

Wednesday 3 – John and Yoko tape their second appearance on the *Dick Cavett Show*

Thursday 11 – The Lennons interview is broadcast on the *Dick Cavett Show*; they also perform "Woman Is The Nigger Of The World" with Elephants Memory

Saturday 13 – In Chicago, John and Yoko appear on Irv Kupcinet's local talk show; it is one of several media appearances the couple makes around this time, publicizing their custody case

Monday 15 – Former Alabama governor George Wallace is shot and seriously wounded

Wednesday 17 – John is interviewed by reporters outside the INS office

Monday 22 – Wings reheare in London for their upcoming tour

Wednesday 24 – Badfinger appears on Granada's *Set of Six*, showcasing five tracks from *Straight Up*, plus "No Matter What"

Monday 29 – "Mary Had A Little Lamb"/"Little Woman Love" (Apple 1851; peaks at #28)

June 1972

Topping the US singles chart:
"I'll Take You There" by The Staple Singers
"The Candy Man" by Sammy Davis Jr.

On the airwaves:
"Outa-Space" by Billy Preston
"Nice To be With You" by Gallery
"Tumbling Dice" by the Rolling Stones

Topping the US album chart:
Thick As A Brick by Jethro Tull

Albums released this month include:
The Rise and Fall of Ziggy Stardust and the Spiders from Mars by David Bowie
School's Out by Alice Cooper
Obscured by Clouds by Pink Floyd
Living in The Past by Jethro Tull
Eagles' self-titled debut

Tuesday 6 – Wings films a promo for "Mary Had A Little Lamb" at the BBC's Shepherds Bush studio

Monday 12 – *Some Time in New York City* (peaks at number forty-eight)

Tuesday 13 – Singer Clyde McPhatter of The Drifters dies at 39

Saturday 17 – (Early morning hours) Five burglars arrested after breaking into the DNC Headquarters at the Watergate Hotel in Washington

Saturday 24 – One of three versions of the Wings promo for "Mary Had A Little Lamb" airs in the UK on *The Basil Brush Show*, a children's program

Monday 26 – Responding to interest stirred by Billy Preston's recent releases and his performance as seen in the *Concert for Bangladesh* film, Apple reissues the single "That's The Way God Planned It" (Apple 1808; dnc)

Thursday 29 – A second version of Wings' "Mary Had A Little Lamb" promo airs on *Top Of The Pops*

July 1972

Topping the US singles chart:
"Song Sung Blue" by Neil Diamond
"Lean On Me" by Bill Withers

On the airwaves:
"Take It Easy" by Eagles
"Daddy Don't You Walk So Fast" by Wayne Newton
"Too Late To Turn Back Now" by Cornelius Brothers and Sister Rose

Topping the US album chart:
Exile On Main Street by the Rolling Stones

Albums released this month include:
Son of Schmilsson by Harry Nilsson
The Harder They Come by Jimmy Cliff
Saint Dominic's Preview by Van Morrison
Never A Dull Moment by Rod Stewart
National Lampoon's Radio Dinner

Wednesday 5 – George and Ravi Shankar are awarded "Child is Father to the Man" Award by UNICEF

Thursday 6 – Actor Brandon De Wilde, 30, is killed in a car accident

Sunday 9 – Wings begin a two-week jaunt across Europe, performing in France, West Germany and Switzerland

Wednesday 26 – Paul and Linda, taking a break from Wings' European tour, fly to New York and attend the Rolling Stones' concert at Madison Square Garden

August 1972

Topping the US singles chart:
"Alone Again (Naturally)" by Gilbert O'Sullivan
"Brandy (You're A Fine Girl)" by Looking Glass

On the airwaves:
"If Loving You Is Wrong" by Luther Ingram
"Long Cool Woman" by The Hollies
"Where is the Love" by Roberta Flack and Donny Hathaway

Topping the US album chart:
Honky Chateau by Elton John

Albums released this month include:
Summer Breeze by Seals and Crofts
Full Circle by The Doors
Ben by Michael Jackson
And the Hits Just Keep on Comin' by Michael Nesmith

Tuesday 1 – The Wings tour resumes, with the band playing seventeen cities throughout the continent until the 24th

Tuesday 1 – Democratic Vice-Presidential nominee Thomas Eagleton is dropped from the ticket after his treatment for depression is made public

Thursday 3 – John and Yoko set out by car to San Francisco, in part to see the country but also to seek addiction treatment from an acupuncturist

Thursday 10 – While on tour in Sweden, Paul, Linda and Denny are arrested for marijuana possession

Saturday 12 – John and Yoko are interviewed by Geraldo Rivera for TV in San Francisco

Tuesday 15 – Ringo leads an all-star cast of musicians, including Harry Nilsson, Keith Moon, Peter Frampton and John Bonham, in shooting musical sequences for *Count Downe*, later re-titled *Son of Dracula*

Friday 18 – Rehearsals for the One-to-One shows begin at New York's Butterfly Studios, resuming on the 21st and 22nd before moving to the Fillmore East on the 25th and 26th; John and Yoko's numerous run-throughs of originals and a few oldies with Elephants Memory are taped and later bootlegged

Monday 21 – Wings' concert at the Congresgebouw in The Hague, Holland, is recorded; one song, "The Mess," is released in 1973 as the B-side of "My Love"

Wednesday 30 – The One-to-One Concert: John and Yoko, backed by Elephants Memory, headline two shows at Madison Square Garden

Thursday 31 – American Bobby Fischer defeats Soviet Boris Spassky to win the World Chess Championship

September 1972

Topping the US singles chart:
"Alone Again (Naturally)" by Gilbert O'Sullivan
"Black and White" by Three Dog Night
"Baby Don't Get Hooked On Me" by Mac Davis

On the airwaves:
"Rock and Roll Part 2" by Gary Glitter
"Saturday In The Park" by Chicago
"Hold Your Head Up" by Argent

Topping the US album chart:
Chicago V

Albums released this month include:
Catch Bull at Four by Cat Stevens
Close To The Edge by Yes
Styx's self-titled debut
Live Full House by J. Geils Band

Rocky Mountain High by John Denver
All The Young Dudes by Mott The Hoople

September – George appears on the cover of this month's *Hit Parader*

Tuesday 5 – On this day and the next, eleven Israeli athletes and coaches are slain by terrorists in Munich at the Olympic Games

Wednesday 6 – John and Yoko appear on the *Jerry Lewis Muscular Dystrophy* telethon, performing "Imagine," Yoko's "Now or Never" and "Give Peace A Chance

Sunday 17 – *M*A*S*H* debuts on CBS

Monday 18 – *Elephants Memory*

Wednesday 20 – The McCartneys farm in Scotland is raided by police on a tip that they're growing marijuana

Friday 22 – *Brother* by Lon and Derrek Van Eaton

Monday 25 – *Those Were The Days* by Mary Hopkin

Tuesday 26 – "Saturday Night Special" by the Sundown Playboys (Apple 1852)

Thursday 28 – Rory Storm dies at 33

October 1972

Topping the US singles chart:
"Ben" by Michael Jackson
"My Ding-a-Ling" by Chuck Berry

On the airwaves:
"Burnin' Love" by Elvis Presley
"Go All The Way" by The Raspberries
"Tightrope" by Leon Russell

Topping the US album chart:
Chicago V

Albums released this month include:
Can't Buy A Thrill by Steely Dan
Music Is My Life by Billy Preston
Talking Book by Stevie Wonder
Fresh Raspberries by the Raspberries
Loggins and Messina's self-titled debut
Who Came First by Pete Townshend

October – John and Yoko appear on the cover of this month's *Jet*

October – Sessions for *Living in the Material World* begin at Apple Studios

Monday 2 – Badfinger appears on Kenny Rogers' syndicated *Rollin' On The River* variety show, performing "Baby Blue"

Thursday 12 – Wings' third promo for "Mary Had A Little Lamb" (the "psychedelic" one) airs on the *Flip Wilson Show* in the US

Monday 16 – The break-up of Creedence Clearwater Revival is announced

Monday 16 – A plane carrying Congressman Hale Boggs and three others vanishes in Alaska

Monday 23 – Ringo begins shooting *That'll Be The Day*

Sunday 26 – Ringo's appearance with Lulu airs on *Monty Python's Flying Circus*

November 1972

Topping the US singles chart:
"I Can See Clearly Now" by Johnny Nash

On the airwaves:
"Listen To The Music" by the Doobie Brothers
"Garden Party" by Rick Nelson
"I'll Be Around" by The Spinners

Topping the US album chart:
Super Fly by Curtis Mayfield

Albums released this month include:
They Only Come Out At Night by the Edgar Winter Group
No Secrets by Carly Simon
Journey Through The Past by Neil Young
Seventh Sojourn by the Moody Blues
The World Is A Ghetto by War

Friday 3 – James Taylor and Carly Simon marry

Tuesday 7 – President Richard Nixon re-elected; John reacts by committing open adultery at a gathering hosted by Jerry Rubin

Wednesday 8 – "Knock Knock, Who's There?" by Mary Hopkin (Apple 1855; peaks at #11 on the Adult Contemporary chart))

Wednesday 8 – UK Detective Sergeant Norman Pilcher, who arrested John in October 1968 and George in March 1969 on drug charges, is extradited from Australia and returned to Britain, facing perjury charges

Saturday 11 – Allman Brothers Band bassist Berry Oakley dies in a motorcycle accident at 24

Monday 13 – "Now or Never" by Yoko Ono (Apple 1853)

Friday 24 – *In Concert* premieres on ABC

Saturday 25 – Wings films promos for "Hi Hi Hi" and "C Moon" at ITV Studios

Monday 27 – An orchestrated version of The Who's *Tommy*, featuring an all-star cast (with Ringo as "Uncle Ernie") is released by Ode as a deluxe box set

Thursday 30 – "Liberation Special" by Elephants Memory (Apple 1854)

December 1972

Topping the US singles chart:
"Papa Was A Rollin' Stone" by The Temptations

THE CRYSTALS·THE RONETTES·DARLENE LOVE ···· XX & THE BLUE JEANS

"I Am Woman" by Helen Reddy
"Me and Mrs. Jones" by Billy Paul

On the airwaves:
"It Never Rains In Southern California" by Albert Hammond
"Ventura Highway" by America
"Operator (That's Not The Way It Feels)" by Jim Croce

Topping the US album chart:
Catch Bull At Four by Cat Stevens

Albums released this month include:
Hot August Night by Neil Diamond
Transformer by Lou Reed

December – The North Tower of the World Trade Center is completed

Monday 4 – "Hi Hi Hi" /"C Moon" (Apple 1857; peaks at #10)

Thursday 7 – Apollo XVII, the final NASA manned lunar mission, is launched

Monday 11 – Phil Spector's 1963 *Christmas Album* is reissued on Apple

Tuesday 12 – On *The Old Grey Whistle Test*, clips of "Gimme Some Truth" from the *Imagine* film and "Children of the Revolution" from *Born to Boogie* air

Thursday 14 – A promo clip for "Happy Xmas (War Is Over)" airs on *Top of the Pops*; the single's UK release had been delayed for a year

Friday 15 – Excerpts from the One-to-One show air on ABC's *In Concert*

Saturday 16 – Wings' promo for "Hi Hi Hi" airs in the UK on *Russell Harty Plus*

Monday 18 – *Born To Boogie* opens in the UK

Saturday 23 – Over a year after the album depicted was released, John and Yoko's *Imagine* film is shown on ABC

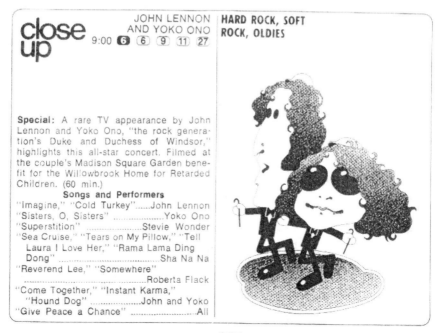

close up

JOHN LENNON AND YOKO ONO
9:00 **6** ⑤ ⑨ ⑪ ㉗

HARD ROCK, SOFT ROCK, OLDIES

Special: A rare TV appearance by John Lennon and Yoko Ono, "the rock generation's Duke and Duchess of Windsor," highlights this all-star concert. Filmed at the couple's Madison Square Garden benefit for the Willowbrook Home for Retarded Children. (60 min.)

Songs and Performers
"Imagine," "Cold Turkey".....John Lennon
"Sisters, O, Sisters" ....Yoko Ono
"Superstition" ....Stevie Wonder
"Sea Cruise," "Tears on My Pillow," "Tell Laura I Love Her," "Rama Lama Ding Dong" ....Sha Na Na
"Reverend Lee," "Somewhere"
.........................Roberta Flack
"Come Together," "Instant Karma," "Hound Dog" ....John and Yoko
"Give Peace a Chance" ....All

355

Sunday 24 – Two days after being arrested for violating the terms of custody, Tony Cox goes into hiding with wife Melinda and daughter Kyoko

Tuesday 26 – Former President Harry Truman dies at 88

Thursday 28 – Ringo's "Back Off Boogaloo" is played on the year-end edition of *Top of the Pops*, accompanied by studio dancers

1973

Published this year:
As Time Goes By by Derek Taylor

January
Topping the US singles chart:
"You're So Vain" by Carly Simon
"Superstition" by Stevie Wonder

On the airwaves:
"Rockin' Pneumonia and the Boogie Woogie Flu" by Johnny Rivers
"Your Mama Don't Dance" by Loggins and Messina
"I Wanna Be With You" by The Raspberries

Topping the US album chart:
Seventh Sojourn by the Moody Blues

Albums released this month include:
Holland by the Beach Boys
Don't Shoot Me I'm Only The Piano Player by Elton John
Life in a Tin Can by the Bee Gees
Greetings from Asbury Park, NJ by Bruce Springsteen and the E Street Band

January – *The Beatles Alpha-Omega* pirate album sets begin to be advertised on TV and radio

Monday 8 – *Approximately Infinite Universe* by Yoko Ono (peaks at one hundred ninety-three)

Saturday 13 – Eric Clapton's comeback concert at London's Rainbow; George and Ringo attend

Sunday 14 – Elvis Presley's *Aloha From Hawaii* concert is broadcast live worldwide

Monday 22 – "Goodbye Sweet Lorraine" by Chris Hodge (Apple 1858)

Monday 22 – Former President Lyndon Johnson suffers a fatal heart attack at 64

Tuesday 23 – Nixon's "Peace With Honor" speech signals the coming end of the Vietnam War

February 1973

Topping the US singles chart:
"Crocodile Rock" by Elton John

On the airwaves:
"Oh Babe, What Would You Say" by Hurricane Smith
"The World Is A Ghetto" by War
"Do It Again" by Steely Dan

Topping the US album chart:
No Secrets by Carly Simon

Albums released this month include:
Billion Dollar Babies by Alice Cooper
Raw Power by The Stooges
In The Right Place by Dr. John

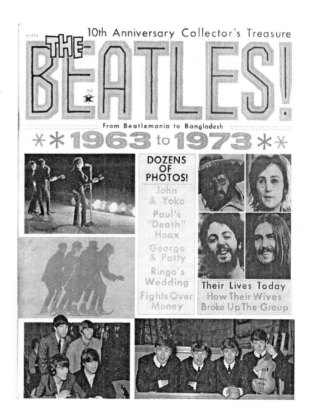

357

Friday 2 – *Midnight Special* debuts on NBC

Thursday 8 – Dairy farmer Max Yasgur, host of the Woodstock concert, suffers a fatal heart attack at 53

Thursday 15 – Actor Wally Cox (*Hollywood Squares*) suffers a fatal heart attack at 46

Monday 26 – "Death of Samantha" by Yoko Ono (Apple 1859)

March 1973

Topping the US singles chart:
"Killing Me Softly With His Song" by Roberta Flack
"Love Train" by The O'Jays

On the airwaves:
"Rocky Mountain High" by John Denver
"Last Song" by Edward Bare
"I'm Just A Singer In A Rock and Roll Band" by the Moody Blues

Topping the US album chart:
Don't Shoot Me I'm Only The Piano Player by Elton John

Albums released this month include:
A Wizard, A True Star by Todd Rundgren
Houses of the Holy by Led Zeppelin
Penguin by Fleetwood Mac
The Dark Side of the Moon by Pink Floyd

Friday 2 – Badfinger performs "No Matter What" and "Suitcase" on *Midnight Special*

Saturday 3 – Ringo appears alongside Harry Nilsson as a presenter at the Grammy Awards, held in Nashville

Monday 5 – Sessions for the *Ringo* album begin in Los Angeles

Monday 5 – Michael Jeffery (Jimi Hendrix's co-manager) is killed in a plane crash

Tuesday 6 – Paul is interviewed outside the courthouse after facing cannabis charges

Thursday 8 – Grateful Dead keyboardist Ron "Pigpen" McKernan dies from a gastrointestinal hemorrhage at 27

Tuesday 13 – Recording session for "I'm The Greatest" brings John, George and Ringo together in Los Angeles

Thursday 15 – Paul and Linda are filmed at ATV Elstree studios, as Paul performs his acoustic medley and Linda takes photos

Sunday 18 – The concert segment of the *James Paul McCartney* special is taped at ATV Elstree studios

Friday 23 – John ordered to leave US within sixty days or face deportation

Monday 26 – English playwright/actor Noel Coward dies at 73

Tuesday 27 – *Ringo* sessions end in Los Angeles

Tuesday 27 – At the *45th Annual Academy Awards* held this evening, Marlon Brando sends Native American actress Sacheen Littlefeather to collect his Oscar

Saturday 31 – Ringo appears on *Russell Harty Plus* to plug *That'll Be The Day*

Saturday 31 – Allen Klein's contract with John, George and Ringo ends

JOHN AND YOKO, MOVE OVER.

Here come Archie and Edith, with their first single,
"Oh, Babe, What Would You Say?"
and it's from their brand new album "Side by Side."

With their hit show "All in the Family" and important guest shots like the ones below, Carroll O'Connor and Jean Stapleton are already Number One on the tube.

They're looking to be Number One on the charts.

JEAN STAPLETON, co-hosting The Mike Douglas Show, week of May 14 (primary markets) week of May 21 (secondary markets.)
CARROLL O'CONNOR, special 90-minute guest, singing his songs on The Dick Cavett Show, May 15.

RCA Records and Tapes

359

April 1973

Topping the US singles chart:
"The Night The Lights Went Out In Georgia" by Vicki Lawrence
"Tie A Yellow Ribbon Round The Old Oak tree" by Dawn featuring Tony Orlando

On the airwaves:
"Danny's Song" by Anne Murray
"Little Willie" by The Sweet
"Stir It Up" by Johnny Nash

Topping the US album chart:
Lady Sings The Blues (original soundtrack)

Albums released this month include:
Made In Japan by Deep Purple
Desperado by Eagles
Diamond Girl by Seals and Crofts
Ooh La La by Faces
The Blue Ridge Rangers by John Fogerty
Daltrey by Roger Daltrey

Sunday 1 – John and Yoko hold press conference to announce the formation of the country, Nutopia

Sunday 1 – The final shoot of the *James Paul McCartney* special: "Live and Let Die," ending with an exploding piano

Monday 2 – *1962-1966* (The Red Album) and *1967-1970* (The Blue Album)

Wednesday 4 – Wings lipsynch "My Love" for *Top of the Pops*, which airs the clip the next day

Friday 6 – John and Yoko are interviewed for the *Weekend World* TV show in Los Angeles; it airs two days later

Sunday 8 – Pablo Picasso dies at 91, prompting a song from Paul

Sunday 8 – John and Yoko appear on *Weekend World*, discussing Allen Klein and Apple

Monday 9 – "My Love"/"The Mess" (Apple 1861; peaks at #1 in June)

Thursday 12 – London premiere of *That'll Be The Day*

Friday 13 – *In Concert 1972* by Ravi Shankar and Ali Akbar Khan

Monday 16 – Paul and Linda record "Six O'Clock" with Ringo at Apple Studios on Savile Row

Monday 16 – *James Paul McCartney* special airs on ABC television

Saturday 21 – *King Kong* director Merian C. Cooper dies at 79; one day after *King Kong*'s lead actor, Robert Armstrong, 82

Friday 27 – Sessions for the *Ringo* album are finished

Monday 30 – *Red Rose Speedway* (peaks at number one for three weeks in June)

May 1973

Topping the US singles chart:
"You Are The Sunshine Of My Life" by Stevie Wonder
"Frankenstein" by the Edgar Winter Group

On the airwaves:
"Stuck In The Middle With You" by Stealers Wheel
"Sing" by The Carpenters
"Wildflower" by Skylark

Topping the US album chart:
Aloha from Hawaii: Via Satellite by Elvis Presley

Albums released this month include:
There Goes Rhymin' Simon by Paul Simon
Tubular Bells by Mike Oldfield
Rigor Mortis Sets In by John Entwistle
Bachman-Turner Overdrive's self-titled debut

Tuesday 1 – John and Yoko sublet apartments in the Dakota from actor Robert Ryan

Monday 7 – "Give Me Love"/"Miss O'Dell" (Apple 1862; peaks at #1 in June)

Friday 11 – Wings begins a month of live theatre dates in Britain, supported by Brinsley Schwarz; this first leg of their tour concludes with three nights at London's Hammersmith Odeon on May 25-27

Saturday 12 – At a news conference, Paul, when asked about "Six O'Clock," which he'd written for Ringo, answered flippantly that he'd write a song for anyone who asked, Rod Stewart included; shortly thereafter, Stewart takes him up on the offer and "Mine For Me" is the result

Saturday 12 – John and Yoko are filmed at Record Plant East, where Yoko runs down songs from *Approximately Infinite Universe* with Elephants Memory; it's broadcast on *Flipside* in late June

Thursday 17 – Televised Senate Watergate hearings begin

Wednesday 30 – *Living In The Material World* (peaks at number one for five weeks)

Thursday 31 – Attending a birthday party in Los Angeles for Led Zeppelin drummer Jon Bonham's 25th birthday celebration, George and Pattie are tossed into the swimming pool – fully dressed – after George throws cake at Bonham

June 1973

Topping the US singles chart:
"My Love" by Paul McCartney and Wings

"Give Me Love (Give Me Peace On Earth)" by George Harrison

On the airwaves:
"Right Place, Wrong Time" by Dr. John
"Hocus Pocus" by Focus
"Playground In My Mind" by Clint Holmes

Topping the US album chart:
Red Rose Speedway by Paul McCartney & Wings

Albums released this month include:
Touch Me In The Morning by Diana Ross
A Little Touch of Schmilsson in the Night by Harry Nilsson
Chicago VI
Farewell Andromeda by John Denver

June – The Beatles appear on the cover of this month's *Crawdaddy*

June – Nicky Hopkins releases *The Tin Man Was A Dreamer*, featuring instrumental contributions from George

Monday 18 – "Live and Let Die"/"I Lie Around" (Apple 1863; peaks at #2)

Thursday 28 – Allen Klein files suit against John for un-repaid loans

Friday 29 – John and Yoko attend the Watergate hearings; having recently shaved his head, John's hair is just beginning to re-grow

July 1973

Topping the US singles chart:
"Will It Go Around In Circles" by Billy Preston
"Bad, Bad Leroy Brown" by Jim Croce

On the airwaves:
"Kodachrome" by Paul Simon
"Long Train Runnin'" by the Doobie Brothers
"Boogie Woogie Bugle Boy" by Bette Midler

Topping the US album chart:
Living In The Material World by George Harrison

Albums released this month include:
Foreigner by Cat Stevens
Countdown To Ecstasy by Steely Dan
Tres Hombres by ZZ Top
Moontan by Golden Earring
We're An American Band by Grand Funk

July – The South Tower of the World Trade Center is completed

Monday 2 – Actress/pin-up Betty Grable dies of cancer at 56

Tuesday 3 – Ringo attends David Bowie's farewell performance as Ziggy Stardust at the Hammersmith-Odeon

Wednesday 4 – Wings begin their last round of live dates with Henry McCullough and Denny Seiwell, playing four cities in Britain beginning with Sheffield and concluding in Newcastle-upon-Tyne on the 10th

Wednesday 4 – *Mind Games* sessions begin at Record Plant East

Friday 13 – The Everly Brothers split up after an onstage argument at Knots Berry farm

Saturday 14 – Ex-Byrds guitarist Clarence White struck by a car and killed at 29

Wednesday 25 – George is forced to pony up £1 million to Britain's Inland Revenue in taxes for the Bangladesh benefit

Saturday 28 – Over 600,000 fans turn out to see the Allman Brothers, Grateful Dead and The Band at the Summer Jam, Watkins Glen, New York

August 1973

Topping the US singles chart:
"The Morning After" by Maureen McGovern
"Touch Me In The Morning" by Diana Ross
"Brother Louie" by Stories

On the airwaves:
"Diamond Girl" by Seals and Crofts
"Shambala" by Three Dog Night
"Feeling Stronger Every Day" by Chicago

Topping the US album chart:
Chicago VI

Albums released this month include:
Goats Head Soup by the Rolling Stones
Let's Get It On by Marvin Gaye
Innervisions by Stevie Wonder

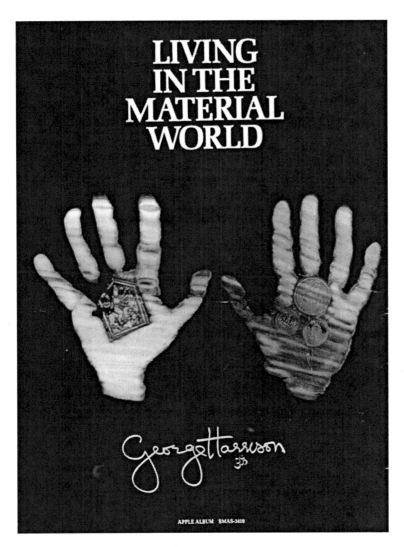

APPLE ALBUM SMA5-3410

Killing Me Softly by Roberta Flack
41 Original Hits from the Soundtrack of American Graffiti

August – Ringo begins filming the non-musical sequences of *Son of Dracula* (original title: *Count Downe*) in London with Harry Nilsson
Saturday 4 – John records "Rock 'N' Roll People," issued years later on *Menlove Avenue*

Monday 6 – Stevie Wonder seriously injured in a car accident

Saturday 11 – *American Graffiti* opens in theaters

Wednesday 15 – Allan Williams visits George and Ringo at Apple's office, attempting to interest them in the Star-Club tapes; George passes, but gives Williams 16 uncut rubies as payment for any services owed from years back

Friday 17 – Paul Williams, 34, of the Temptations is found shot to death

Friday 24 – A Yoko essay, *Feeling The Space*, appears in the *New York Times*; it is later reproduced on the rear cover of the album of the same name

Saturday 25 – Henry McCullough quits Wings

Monday 27 – Cheech and Chong's "Basketball Jones" single, featuring George on guitar

Thursday 30 – Denny Seiwell quits Wings

September 1973

Topping the US singles chart:
"Let's Get It On" by Marvin Gaye
"Delta Dawn" by Helen Reddy
"We're An American Band" by Grand Funk Railroad

On the airwaves:
"Loves Me Like A Rock" by Paul Simon
"Ramblin' Man" by the Allman Brothers band
"Roll Over Beethoven" by Electric Light Orchestra

Topping the US album chart:
Chicago VI

Albums released this month include:
Don't Call Me Mama Anymore by Cass Elliott
Angel Clare by Art Garfunkel
Everybody Likes Some Kind of Music by Billy Preston
Over-Nite Sensation by Frank Zappa
The Wild, the Innocent & the E-Street Shuffle by Bruce Springsteen and the E Street Band

Saturday 1 – Wings leaves London for Lagos, Nigeria; sessions for *Band on the Run* begin soon after their arrival

Tuesday 18 – John moves out of the Dakota

Tuesday 18 – Ringo purchases Tittenhurst Park from John

Wednesday 19 – Gram Parsons fatally overdoses at 26

Thursday 20 – Jim Croce dies in a plane crash at 30

Thursday 20 – Billie Jean King defeats Bobby Riggs in tennis "Battle of the Sexes"

Saturday 22 – Lagos sessions for *Band on the Run* end

Sunday 23 – Wings arrives back in London

Monday 24 – "Photograph"/"Down and Out" (Apple 1865; peaks at #1 in November)

Monday 24 - Scheduled release date for George's "Don't Let Me Wait Too Long"/"Sue Me Sue You Blues" (Apple 1866); the single is canceled

Monday 24 – "Woman Power"/"Men Men Men" by Yoko Ono (Apple 1867)

Thursday 27 – *Don Kirshner's Rock Concert* debuts

October 1973

Topping the US singles chart:
"Half-Breed" by Cher
"Angie" by the Rolling Stones
"Midnight Train To Georgia" by Gladys Knight and the Pips

On the airwaves:
"The Hurt" by Cat Stevens
"Heartbeat, It's A Lovebeat" by the DeFranco Family
"China Grove" by the Doobie Brothers

Topping the US album chart:
Brothers and Sisters by the Allman Brothers Band

Albums released this month include:
Quadrophenia by The Who
Selling England By The Pound by Genesis
Mystery To Me by Fleetwood Mac
Moondog Matinee by The Band
Goodbye Yellow Brick Road by Elton John

October – John heads to California with May Pang

October – Wings finishes work on *Band on the Run* at George Martin's AIR Studios, London

Wednesday 10 – US Vice-President Spiro Agnew resigns

Tuesday 16 – Drummer Gene Krupa dies at 64

Wednesday 17 – The first session for John's *Rock 'N' Roll* album (originally titled *Back To Mono*, then *Oldies...but Mouldies*) takes place in Los Angeles at A&M Studios

Monday 22 – Robin Francis Lennon, Freddie Lennon's last child (and John's half-brother) is born

Tuesday/Sunday 23/28 – Yoko plays a series of dates at Kenny's Castaways in Greenwich Village

Wednesday 24 – On May Pang's 23rd birthday, John films a TV promo for *Mind Games* in Los Angeles with Apple's Tony King dressed as Queen Elizabeth II; around this time, King introduces John to Elton John

Sunday 28 – Clive Arrowsmith shoots the *Band on the Run* album cover in Osterley Park, Hounslow

Monday 29 – "Mind Games"/"Meat City" (Apple 1868; peaks at 18)

Monday 29 – Los Angeles premiere of *That'll Be The Day*

November 1973

Topping the US singles chart:
"Keep On Truckin' (Part 1)" by Eddie Kendricks
"Photograph" by Ringo Starr

On the airwaves:
"All I Know" by Art Garfunkel
"Leave Me Alone" by Helen Reddy
"Free Ride" by Edgar Winter Group

Topping the US album chart:
Goats Head Soup by the Rolling Stones

Albums released this month include:
On The Third Day by Electric Light Orchestra
Brain Salad Surgery by Emerson, Lake and Palmer
Piano Man by Billy Joel
Abandoned Luncheonette by Hall & Oates
Jonathan Livingston Seagull by Neil Diamond

Thursday 1 – Ringo's promo film for "Photograph," shot at Tittenhurst Park, airs on *Top of the Pops*

Thursday 1 – John is interviewed on a California beach for ABC by Elliot Mintz

Friday 2 – *Ringo* (peaks at number two)

Friday 2 – *Mind Games* (peaks at number nine)

Friday 2 – *Feeling The Space* by Yoko Ono (dnc)

Friday 2 – John, George and Ringo file suit against Allen Klein

Saturday 3 – *Melody Maker* runs a lengthy interview with John

Saturday 10 – *Hee Haw*'s David "Stringbean" Akeman and his wife are shot dead during a robbery at their home

Monday 12 – "Helen Wheels"/"Country Dreamer" (Apple 1869; peaks at #10)

Thursday 15 – Paul, Linda and Denny record with Jimmy McCulloch for the first time in Paris, laying down some Suzy and the Red Stripes tracks, including "Wide Prairie"

Tuesday 20 – Keith Moon collapses at Cow Palace; Scott Halpin fills in

Friday 23 – Backed by Elephants Memory, Yoko appears as a solo act on the *Mike Douglas Show*

Monday 26 – Ronnie Wood incurs George's wrath by telling the press that he and Pattie are an item

Monday 26 – *Ass* by Badfinger (peaks at number one hundred sixty-one)

Wednesday 28 – The last *Rock 'N' Roll* session at A&M Studios occurs on this night

December 1973

Topping the US singles chart:
"Top of the World" by The Carpenters
"The Most Beautiful Girl" by Charlie Rich
"Time In A Bottle" by Jim Croce

On the airwaves:
"Hello It's Me" by Todd Rundgren
"Be" by Neil Diamond
"Just You 'n Me" by Chicago

Topping the US album chart:
Goodbye Yellow Brick Road by Elton John

Albums released this month include:
I Got A Name by Jim Croce
Tales From Topographic Oceans by Yes
Wild Tales by Graham Nash

December – Ringo is interviewed by David Wigg at the Apple office; the audio will emerge in 1976 as part of *The Beatles Tapes* double-album

December – Cynthia Lennon's marriage to Roberto Bassanini ends

Monday 3 – John's *Rock 'N' Roll* sessions resume at Record Plant West

Monday 3 – "You're Sixteen"/"Devil Woman" (Apple 1870; peaks at #1 in January 1974)

Wednesday 5 – *Band on the Run* (peaks at number one for four weeks in spring/summer 1974)

Monday 10 – "Apple of My Eye" by Badfinger (Apple 1864; peaks at #102)

Friday 14 – Final Phil Spector-produced *Rock 'N' Roll* session takes place at Record Plant West

Thursday 20 – Singer/actor Bobby Darin dies after heart surgery at 37

Wednesday 26 – *The Exorcist* opens in theaters

Wednesday 26 – Paul and Linda host *Disneytime*, an hour-long BBC TV special serving up clips from Disney films

January 1974

Topping the US singles chart:
"Time In A Bottle" by Jim Croce
"The Joker" by Steve Miller
"Show and Tell" by Al Wilson
"You're Sixteen" by Ringo Starr

On the airwaves:
"One Tin Soldier" by Coven
"Sister Mary Elephant" by Cheech and Chong
"Smokin' In The Boys Room" by Brownsville Station

Topping the US album chart:
The Singles: 1969-1973 by The Carpenters

Albums released this month include:
Court and Spark by Joni Mitchell
Sundown by Gordon Lightfoot
Hotcakes by Carly Simon
The Way We Were by Barbra Streisand

January – Beginning this month and running through till February, Paul and Wings work on Mike McGear's album at 10cc's Strawberry Studios

Tuesday 8 – *The Early Beatles*, Capitol's abridgment of *Please Please Me*, is finally certified gold nearly eleven years after its issue

Monday 28 – "Jet"/"Mamunia" (Apple 1871; peaks at #7)

Thursday 31 – Paul and Linda appear on the cover of *Rolling Stone*

Thursday 31 – Film producer Samuel Goldwyn dies at 94

February 1974

Topping the US singles chart:
"The Way We Were" by Barbra Streisand
"Love's Theme" by Love Unlimited Orchestra

On the airwaves:
"Doo Doo Doo Doo Doo (Heartbreaker)" by the Rolling Stones
"Americans" by Byron MacGregor
"Let Me Be There" by Olivia Newton-John

Topping the US album chart:
You Don't Mess Around With Jim by Jim Croce

Albums released this month include:
Radio City by Big Star
Can't Get Enough by Barry White
Rock 'n' Roll Animal by Lou Reed
What Were Once Vices Are Now Habits by the Doobie Brothers

Monday 4 – Newspaper heiress Patricia Hearst is kidnapped by the Symbionese Liberation Army

Monday 11 – Badfinger's self-titled Warner Brothers debut

Friday 15 – *Happy Days* debuts on ABC

Monday 18 – "Oh My My"/"Step Lightly" (Apple 1872; peaks at #5)

Tuesday 19 – "Let Me Roll It" replaces "Mamunia" on new pressings of "Jet"

Wednesday 20 – Cher files for divorce from Sonny Bono

Thursday 28 – Bobby Bloom ("Montego Bay") dies from a gunshot wound at 28

March 1974

Topping the US singles chart:
"Seasons In The Sun" by Terry Jacks

"Dark Lady" by Cher
"Sunshine On My Shoulders" by John Denver

On the airwaves:
"Rock On" by David Essex
"Jim Dandy" by Black Oak Arkansas
"Last Kiss" by Wednesday

Topping the US album chart:
Planet Waves by Bob Dylan

Albums released this month include:
Pretzel Logic by Steely Dan
On The Border by Eagles
Bridge of Sighs by Robin Trower
Get Your Wings by Aerosmith
Apostrophe by Frank Zappa

March – John appears on the cover of this month's *Crawdaddy*

March – George produces *Shankar Family and Friends* sessions in Los Angeles at A&M Studios

Monday 4 – A Badfinger show at Cleveland's Agora is recorded for possible release

Monday 4 – *People* magazine begins publishing

Friday 8 – Paul and Linda are interviewed at the Soho MPL office for NBC's *Today*; it airs in two parts on March 12 and 13

Friday 8 – Final new episode of *The Brady Bunch* airs, co-starring future wife of future Wings guitarist Laurence Juber, Hope Schwartz

Tuesday 12 – The Troubadour incident in Los Angeles, wherein John and Harry Nilsson are tossed out for heckling the Smothers Brothers and being drunk and disorderly

Wednesday 13 – John and May Pang attend the *American Film Institute Salute to James Cagney* with Mick Jagger, held at the Century Plaza Hotel in Los Angeles

Friday 22 – John and May move into attorney Harold Seider's Santa Monica beach home

Thursday 28 – John and Paul jam at Burbank studios; a recording is later bootlegged as *A Toot and A Snore*

Thursday 28 – Arthur "Big Boy" Crudup ("That's All Right") dies at 68

Friday 29 – Ringo is filmed at the Aquarius Theatre in Los Angeles with Keith Moon for *In Concert*, to air in November that year

April 1974

Topping the US singles chart:
"Hooked On A Feeling" by Blue Swede
"Bennie and The Jets" by Elton John
"TSOP (The Sound of Philadelphia)" by MFSB and the Three Degrees

On the airwaves:
"Mockingbird" by James Taylor and Carly Simon
"Sunshine On My Shoulders" by John Denver
"Eres Tu" by Mocedades

Topping the US album chart:
John Denver's Greatest Hits

Albums released this month include:
Diamond Dogs by David Bowie
Second Helping by Lynyrd Skynyrd
Meet The Residents by The Residents

Monday 1 – The last publicly seen photos of John and Paul together are taken in Santa Monica

Tuesday 2 – Paul and Linda attend the *46th Annual Academy Awards*, where Wings is nominated for "Live and Let Die" (they do not win); this was the night of the famous "streaker" incident

Saturday 6 – 200,000 fans attend the California Jam festival in Ontario, California; acts include Eagles, Seals and Crofts, Deep Purple and Emerson, Lake and Palmer

Monday 8 – "Band on the Run"/ "Nineteen Hundred and Eighty-Five" (Apple 1873; peaks at #1 in June)

Monday 8 – In a game against the Los Angeles Dodgers, Atlanta Braves outfielder Henry Aaron hits home run number 715, breaking Babe Ruth's record

Tuesday 9 – For the next month, Badfinger records their *Wish You Were Here* album at Caribou studios in Colorado

Monday 15 – (Just past midnight) Ringo's drunken, expletive-laden appearance on Pasadena's KROQ (alongside Keith Moon) gets radio hosts Howard Kaylan and Mark Vollman fired

Friday 19 – Yoko again performs (with Elephants Memory) on the *Mike Douglas Show*

Friday 19 – Ringo and Harry Nilsson attend the premier of *Son of Dracula* in Atlanta

Thursday 25 – Jim Morrison's "widow," Pamela Courson, overdoses at 27

Friday 26 – Geoff Britton is among the 52 drummers to audition for Wings at the Albery Theatre in London

Saturday 27 – John and May return to New York, taking up residence at the Pierre Hotel on Fifth Avenue (while maintaining rental on the Santa Monica home)

Sunday 28 – John and Harry Nilsson attend the March of Dimes walk-a-thon event in Central Park

Sunday 28 – Sam Goody store manager Mark Lapidos secures John's permission to host the first *Beatlefest* later that year

Monday 29 – Possible recording date of "Too Many Cooks" (as both John and Mick Jagger were known to be at New York's Record Plant), sung by Mick and produced by John

May 1974

Topping the US singles chart:
"The Locomotion" by Grand Funk
"The Streak" by Ray Stevens

On the airwaves:
"Star Baby" by the Guess Who
"Best Thing That Ever Happened To Me" by Gladys Knight and the Pips
"Come And Get Your Love" by Redbone

Topping the US album chart:
The Sting (original soundtrack)

Albums released this month include:
Too Much Too Soon by New York Dolls
If You Love Me, Let Me Know by Olivia Newton-John
Monkey Grip by Bill Wyman

May – Willy Russell's *John, Paul, George, Ringo…and Bert* begins an eight-week run at Liverpool's Everyman Theater

Wednesday 15 – George inks a deal with A&M for distribution of the Dark Horse label roster
Thursday 16 – Geoff Britton is selected as Wings' new drummer

Friday 17 – Members of the SLA are killed in a shoot-out with a SWAT team in Inglewood, CA

Thursday 23 – Dark Horse Records is launched, with a public announcement coming in June

Friday 24 – Bandleader/composer Duke Ellington dies from lung cancer at 75

Monday 27 – *Goodnight Vienna* sessions begin this week at Sunset Sound in Los Angeles, though work would stop after a few days, resuming in July

Monday 27 – Nancy Andrews meets Ringo at the Santa Monica beach home rented by John; they become an item two months later

An Academy Award for acting for Ringo Starr? You've got to be kidding!

June 1974

Topping the US singles chart:
"Band on the Run" by Paul McCartney and Wings
"Billy Don't Be A Hero" by "Bo Donaldson and the Heywoods
"Sundown" by Gordon Lightfoot

On the airwaves:
"The Entertainer" by Marvin Hamlisch
"The Show Must Go On" by Three Dog Night
"Midnight At The Oasis" Maria Muldaur

Topping the US album chart:
Band on the Run by Paul McCartney & Wings

Albums released this month include:
Caribou by Elton John
Endless Summer by the Beach Boys
Holiday by America
Walking Man by James Taylor
Bad Company's self-titled debut

Thursday 13 – While The Who are in town for a series of dates at Madison Square Garden, John and May visit Keith Moon at his hotel

Monday 17 – *Walls and Bridges* sessions begin at New York's Record Plant

Friday 28 – John records a demo of "Goodnight Vienna" for Ringo

July 1974

Topping the US singles chart:
"Rock The Boat" by Hues Corporation
"Rock Your Baby" by George McCrae
"Annie's Song" by John Denver

On the airwaves:
"Help Me" by Joni Mitchell
"La Grange" by ZZ Top
"Dancing Machine" by the Jackson 5

Topping the US album chart:
Band on the Run by Paul McCartney & Wings
Albums released this month include:
Fulfillingness' First Finale by Stevie Wonder
461 Ocean Boulevard by Eric Clapton
On The Beach by Neil Young

Saturday 6 – Wings arrives in Nashville, Tennessee for six weeks
of rehearsing and recording at Sound Shop studios; their residence
during the stay is the home of songwriter Curly "Junior" Putnam
("Green, Green Grass of Home")

Tuesday 9 – Wings records the non-LP B-side "Sally G" in Nashville

Monday 15 – Florida TV news anchor Christine Chubbock fatally
shoots herself on the air

Tuesday 16 – John and May take up residence at a penthouse located
at 434 E. 52nd Street

Tuesday 16 – In Nashville, Wings records (as the Country Hams)
"Walking In The Park With Eloise," written by Paul's father, and
"Bridge Over The River Suite"; guest musicians include Floyd
Cramer and Chet Atkins

Tuesday 16 – John records the non-LP B-side, "Move Over Ms. L"

Thursday 18 – Wings departs Nashville and head to New York

Monday 22 – The McCartneys depart New York for England but not before visiting John and May at their new place

Friday 26 – *Goodnight Vienna* sessions resume at Richard Perry's Producers Workshop in Los Angeles

Friday/Sunday 26/28 – Joe Pope's *Magical Mystery Tour* Beatle convention held in Boston at the Bradford Hotel

Monday 29 – Cass Elliott suffers a fatal heart attack in London at 32

August 1974

Topping the US singles chart:
"Feel Like Makin' Love" by Roberta Flack
"The Night Chicago Died" by Paper Lace
"(You're) Having My Baby" by Paul Anka and Odia Coates

On the airwaves:
"Radar Love" by Golden Earring
"Waterloo" by ABBA
"You Won't See Me" by Anne Murray

Topping the US album chart:
Caribou by Elton John

Albums released this month include:
Not Fragile by Bachman-Turner Overdrive
AWB by Average White Band
I'm Leaving It All Up To You by Donny and Marie Osmond

August – *Little Malcolm*, the final Apple film (produced by George) is shown at the Atlanta Film Festival

Tuesday 6 – With John's help, Ringo records "Only You" and "Goodnight Vienna"

Thursday 8 – President Richard Nixon gives his resignation speech; Vice-President Gerald Ford sworn in the following day

Friday 9 – Yoko Ono arrives in Japan to play a series of concerts

Thursday 15 – *John, Paul, George, Ringo…and Bert* opens at the Lyric Theatre in London's West End

Monday 19 – Harry Nilsson's *Pussy Cats*, produced by John

Friday 23 – John spots a UFO from the rooftop of his 52nd Street apartment, above the East River

Saturday 24/Friday 30 – Wings films their rehearsals at Abbey Road Studios for a proposed television special, *One Hand Clapping*

Monday 26 – Aviator Charles Lindbergh dies at 72

Friday 30 – John is interviewed outside a New York federal courthouse following an immigration hearing

September 1974

Topping the US singles chart:
"I Shot The Sheriff" by Eric Clapton
"Can't Get Enough of Your Love, Babe" by Barry White
"Rock Me Gently" by Andy Kim

On the airwaves:
"The Air That I Breathe" by The Hollies
"Don't Let The Sun Go Down On Me" by Elton John
"Tell Me Something Good" by Rufus

Topping the US album chart:
461 Ocean Boulevard by Eric Clapton

Albums released this month include:
Wrap Around Joy by Carole King
Crime of the Century by Supertramp
Eldorado by Electric Light Orchestra
Heroes Are Hard To Find by Fleetwood Mac
Sneakin' Sally Through the Alley by Robert Palmer

Thursday 5 – Dark Horse Records' first releases: Splinter (*The Place I Love*) and Ravi Shankar (*Shankar Family and Friends*)

Saturday 7/ Sunday 8 – The first *Beatlefest* is held at New York's Commodore Hotel

Sunday 8 – President Gerald Ford grants former President Nixon a full pardon

Sunday 8 – Stuntman Evel Knievel fails to jump the Snake River canyon with a rocket-powered motorcycle

Wednesday 11 – *Little House on the Prairie* debuts on NBC

Friday 13 – Ronnie Wood's *I've Got My Own Album To Do* is released, featuring the collaboration with George, "Far East Man"

Saturday 14 – In the course of a *Melody Maker* interview, Todd Rundgren launches a gratuitous attack on John

Monday 16 – George holds a London press conference announcing the Dark Horse tour with Ravi Shankar

Monday 23 – George introduces Ravi Shankar at the Royal Albert Hall for the Music Festival from India
Monday 23 – "Whatever Gets You Thru the Night"/"Beef Jerky" (Apple 1874; peaks at #1 in November)

Thursday 26 – *Walls and Bridges* (peaks at number one in November)

Friday 27 – John guest deejays (by phone) on Los Angeles's KJH-AM radio

Saturday 28 – John sits in with WNEW deejay Denis Elsas and spins records between radio chores and chat

Monday 30 – In a letter dated this day, John addresses accusations made against him by Todd Rundgren; it runs in *Melody Maker* under the title, "An Opened Lettuce to Sodd Runtlestuntle"

October 1974

Topping the US singles chart:
"I Honestly Love You" by Olivia Newton-John
"Nothing From Nothing" by Billy Preston
"Then Came You" by Dionne Warwick with The Spinners

On the airwaves:
"Who Do You Think You Are" by Bo Donaldson and the Heywoods
"Beach Baby" by First Class
"Sweet Home Alabama" by Lynyrd Skynyrd

Topping the US album chart:
Endless Summer by the Beach Boys

Albums released this month include:
Having Fun With Elvis On Stage by Elvis Presley
It's Only Rock 'n Roll by the Rolling Stones
Hotter Than Hell by Kiss
Odds and Sods by The Who

Sunday 13 – Ed Sullivan dies of cancer at 72

Monday 14 – *McGear*, an album by Paul's brother, featuring contributions from Paul, Linda, Denny Laine and Jimmy McCulloch

Monday 14 – *Wish You Were Here*, the last Badfinger album by the "classic" line-up

Monday 21 – After two days' rehearsal at Morris Levy's upstate New York farm, Sunnyview, sessions resume for John's *Rock 'N' Roll* album at Record Plant East; work is completed in five days

Wednesday 23 – George holds another news conference for his upcoming tour, this time at the Beverly Wilshire Hotel

Thursday 24 – The Beatles appear on the cover of *Rolling Stone*

Wednesday 30 – John is photographed in front of the Statue of Liberty by Bob Gruen

Wednesday 30 – The *Rumble In The Jungle*: Muhammad Ali defeats George Foreman in Zaire

Wednesday 30 – In a burst of activity on this day and the next, George records five songs for the upcoming *Dark Horse* album at A&M Studios in Los Angeles; he also films a promo for the title track

November 1974

Topping the US singles chart:
"You Haven't Done Nothing" by Stevie Wonder
"You Ain't Seen Nothing Yet" by Bachman-Turner Overdrive
"Whatever Gets You Thru The Night" by John Lennon and the Plastic Ono Nuclear Band
"I Can Help" by Billy Swan

On the airwaves:
"The Bitch Is Back" by Elton John
"Another Saturday Night" by Cat Stevens
"Jazzman" by Carole King

Topping the US album chart:
So Far by Crosby, Stills and Nash

Albums released this month include:
The Lamb Lies Down On Broadway by Genesis
Desolation Boulevard by Sweet
Autobahn by Kraftwerk
Heart Like A Wheel by Linda Ronstadt
November – Ringo and Harry Nilsson begin shooting *Ringo and Harry's Night Out* but the film is never completed

November – In London studio sessions this month, Wings begins work on *Venus and Mars*

Saturday 2 – Dark Horse tour begins in Vancouver (John and May send flowers); it will entail forty-five shows in twenty-six cities

Monday 4 – "Junior's Farm"/"Sally G" (Apple 1875; peaks at #3)

Monday 4 – Rod Stewart's "Mine For Me," written by Paul and featuring Paul and Linda on backing vocals

Wednesday 6 – Paul and Linda take part in a taping of *This Is Your Life*, setting up boxer John Conteh for a surprise at Abbey Road studios

Friday 8 – Ringo appears alongside Keith Moon on *In Concert's 2nd Anniversary* special, broadcast on ABC

Saturday 9 – *Melody Maker* runs an apology from Todd Rundgren to John for his earlier remarks

Monday 11 – "Only You"/"Call Me" Apple 1876; peaks at #6)

Wednesday 13 – Paul and Linda's appearance on *This Is Your Life* with John Conteh airs in Britain

Wednesday 13 – Nuclear power plant worker Karen Silkwood is killed in a car accident under suspicious circumstances

Thursday 14 – Ringo (with Harry Nilsson) is filmed atop and around the Capitol Tower in Los Angeles for the "Only You" video

Friday 15 – John is filmed out and about in New York (in Central Park and by the Beacon Street Theatre where the *Sgt. Pepper* musical is about to open) for use in the "Whatever Gets You Through The Night" promo

Sunday 17 – John attends the opening performance of *Sgt. Pepper's Lonely Hearts Club Band On The Road* at New York's Beacon Street Theatre; attendees at the party afterward include Ronnie Spector and Bianca Jagger

Monday 18 – *Goodnight Vienna* (peaks at number eight)

Monday 18 – "Dark Horse"/"I Don't Care Anymore" (Apple 1877; peaks at #15)

Monday 18 – "Lucy In The Sky With Diamonds," recorded by Elton John, featuring John on guitars and backing vocals

Wednesday 20 – Wings is taped lip-synching "Junior's Farm," which airs the next day on *Top of the Pops*

Thursday 21 – At the Tulsa stop of the Dark Horse tour, Leon Russell joins George onstage for "My Sweet Lord"

Saturday 23 – *Melody Maker* runs an interview with Ringo, who opines that the Beatles will never get back together so long as George won't play with Paul

Sunday 24 – John rehearses with Elton John and his band

Monday 25 – George appears on Houston radio station KLOL, promoting the tour and the upcoming *Dark Horse* album

Wednesday 27 – Paul and Linda appear onstage in England with Rod Stewart

Thursday 28 – John appears onstage at Madison Square Garden with Elton John

Saturday 30 – In England, Paul announces plans for Wings' upcoming world tour, which will take them across Europe, Australia, Japan, and North America over the next two years

Saturday 30 – Wings drummer Geoff Britton is filmed in London by MPL Productions at a karate tournament; the unreleased short film, *Empty Hand*, features an original soundtrack by Paul

Saturday 30 – While the Dark Horse tour is in Chicago, Ravi Shankar takes ill and will not perform again until the penultimate show on December 19

December 1974

Topping the US singles chart:
"Kung Fu Fighting" by Carl Douglas
"Cat's In The Cradle" by Harry Chapin
"Angie Baby" by Helen Reddy

On the airwaves:
"My Melody of Love" by Bobby Vinton
"Tin Man" by America
"Life Is A Rock (But The Radio Rolled Me)" by Reunion

Topping the US album chart:
Elton John's Greatest Hits

Albums released this month include:
Stormbringer by Deep Purple
All The Girls in the World Beware!!! by Grand Funk Railroad

Monday 2 – The Country Hams' "Walking In The Park With Eloise"/"Bridge Over The River Suite" (dnc)

Monday 9 – *Dark Horse* (peaks at number four)

Monday 9 – John is interviewed by Howard Cosell during *Monday Night Football*

Thursday 12 – "#9 Dream"/"What You Got" (Apple 1878; peaks at #9)

Thursday 12 – Mick Taylor quits the Rolling Stones

Friday 13 – George and entourage visit President Gerald Ford at the White House

Friday 13 – Two songs taped at this evening's show in Largo, Maryland would see limited-edition issue years later: "For You Blue" with the Genesis book, Songs by George, and "Hari's On Tour (Express)," with Songs by George 2

Saturday 14 – George arrives in New York and meets up with John and May at the Plaza Hotel

Sunday 15 – John and May attend George's concert at the Nassau Coliseum

Monday 16 – John is interviewed on NBC's *Today* show

Thursday 19 – Ringo's "Only You" promo airs on *Top of the Pops*

Thursday 19 – George appears on the cover of *Rolling Stone*

Thursday 19 – After becoming angered over business matters, George un-invites John from joining him onstage. He and Paul are filmed signing the dissolution papers at The Plaza

Thursday 19 – Paul and Linda, heavily but comically disguised, attend George's Madison Square Garden Concert, as does Julian and Ringo's manager Hilary Gerard

Friday 20 – The Dark Horse Tour ends at Madison Square Garden; afterward, George parties with John and Paul at *Club Hippopotamus* (it marks George's last documented meeting with John)

Sunday 22 – *That'll Be The Day* opens in US theaters

Monday 23 – "Ding Dong Ding Dong"/"Hari's On Tour (Express)" (Apple 1879; peaks at #36)

Monday 23 – George films a promo for "Ding Dong, Ding Dong" at Friar Park

Tuesday 24 – Vacationing at Disney World, John on this day adds the final signature to the document dissolving the Beatles

Thursday 26 – Comedian Jack Benny dies at 80

1975

Published this year:
All Together Now by Harry Castleman and Wally Podrazik

January
Topping the US singles chart:
"Lucy In The Sky With Diamonds" by Elton John
"Mandy" by Barry Manilow
"Please Mr. Postman" by The Carpenters

On the airwaves:
"When Will I See You Again" by the Three Degrees
"You Got The Love" by Rufus
"Please Mr. Postman" by The Carpenters

Topping the US album chart:
Elton John's Greatest Hits

Albums released this month include:
Blood On The Tracks by Bob Dylan

January – John records "Across the Universe" and "Fame" with David Bowie at New York's Electric Lady Studios
Thursday 2 – John and his lawyers are given access to his INS files

Thursday 9 – The Beatles' partnership is officially dissolved in a London court

Thursday 16 – The McCartney family and band members arrive in New Orleans to resume work on *Venus and Mars*; during the sessions, drummer Geoff Britton is replaced by Joe English

Monday 27 – "No No Song"/"Snookeroo" (Apple 1880; peaks at #3)

February 1975

Topping the US singles chart:
"Laughter In The Rain" by Neil Sedaka
"Fire" by the Ohio Players
"You're No Good" by Linda Ronstadt
"Pick Up The Pieces" by Average White Band

On the airwaves:
"Never Can Say Goodbye" by Gloria Gaynor
"Bungle In The Jungle" by Jethro Tull
"Lady" by Styx

Topping the US album chart:
Elton John's Greatest Hits

Albums released this month include:
Physical Graffiti by Led Zeppelin

Fly By Night by Rush
Modern Times by Al Stewart
Have You Never Been Mellow by Olivia Newton-John

February – John reconciles with Yoko and moves back to the Dakota

February – *Little Malcolm* debuts in London's West End

Monday 3 – Ringo begins shooting *Lisztomania* with Roger Daltrey, directed by Ken Russell

Tuesday 4 – Rock and roll pioneer Louis Jordan ("Caldonia") dies at 66

Wednesday 12 – Wings records "My Carnival" in New Orleans

Thursday 13 – Paul and Linda hold a press conference aboard a riverboat; they are later filmed wearing top hats and celebrating Mardi Gras in the streets

Monday 17 – *Rock 'N' Roll* (peaks at number six)

Monday 17 – David Hentschel's *Startling Music*, an album-length synthesizer-based re-imagining of the *Ringo* album, issued on Ring O'Records

Friday 21 – In a chaotic conference call with numerous radio stations all at once, John publicly reiterates what he'd already privately mentioned to others about his plans to travel to New Orleans to meet up with Paul

Monday 24 – Elton John's "Philadelphia Freedom" single, featuring the live recording of "I Saw Her Standing There" performed with John on the B-side

Monday 24 – Wings completes work on the New Orleans phase of *Venus and Mars*

Wednesday 26 – The final stretch of *Venus and Mars* recordings begin in Los Angeles at Wally Heider Studio

March 1975

Topping the US singles chart:
"Best Of My Love" by Eagles
"Have You Never Been Mellow" by Olivia Newton-John
"Black Water" by the Doobie Brothers
"My Eyes Adored You" by Frankie Valli
"Lady Marmalade" by LaBelle

On the airwaves:
"Roll On Down The Highway" by Bachman-Turner Overdrive
"Lonely People" by America
"Up In A Puff Of Smoke" by Polly Brown

Topping the US album chart:
Blood On The Tracks by Bob Dylan

Albums released this month include:
That's The Way Of The World by Earth Wind And Fire
Katy Lied by Steely Dan
The Original Soundtrack by 10cc
Young Americans by David Bowie

March – John appears on the cover of this month's *Hit Parader*

Saturday 1 – John and Yoko attend the Grammys; John acts as presenter with Paul Simon, while Wings – who are not present – win two Grammys for *Band on the Run*

Monday 3 – Linda McCartney is arrested for marijuana possession in Los Angeles

Thursday 6 – Abraham Zapruder's home movie of President Kennedy's assassination is broadcast for the first time on late night television

Friday 7 – *Young Americans* by David Bowie, featuring John on "Fame" and "Across The Universe"

Friday 7 – Lon and Derrek Van Eaton release their first post-Apple album, *Who Do You Out Do*, on A&M; produced by Richard Perry, it features Klaus Voormann and Gary Wright

Saturday 8 – *Melody Maker* runs an interview with John

Sunday 16 – Electric blues innovator T-Bone Walker dies at 64

Monday 17 – Keith Moon's *Two Sides of the Moon*, featuring instrumental and vocal contributions from Ringo (and John's "Move Over Ms. L")

Monday 17 – Not long before sitting for an interview on this day to air the following month on *Old Grey Whistle Test*, John learns that Yoko is pregnant

Tuesday 18 – John is filmed at The Dakota for French TV

Tuesday 18 – John films promos at Record Plant East for "Stand By Me" and "Slippin' and Slidin'"

Wednesday 19 – "Stand By Me"/"Move Over Ms. L" (Apple 1881; peaks at #20)

Monday 24 – George and Olivia attend a party thrown for Wings aboard the *Queen Mary* in Long Beach, California; other guests include Mal Evans, Derek Taylor and Michael Jackson

Wednesday 26 – Ken Russell's film version of The Who's *Tommy* premiers in London

Saturday 29 – Jeff Beck's *Blow by Blow*, produced by George Martin

Monday 31 – After twenty years, the final episode of *Gunsmoke* airs on CBS

April 1975

Topping the US singles chart:
"Lovin' You" by Minnie Riperton
"Philadelphia Freedom" by Elton John
"(Hey Won't You Play) Another Somebody Done Somebody Wrong Song" by B.J. Thomas

On the airwaves:
"Fire" by Ohio Players
"Emma" by Hot Chocolate
"Don't Call Us, We'll Call You" by Sugarloaf

Topping the US album chart:
Physical Graffiti by Led Zeppelin

Albums released this month include:
Hair Of The Dog by Nazareth
Diamonds and Rust by Joan Baez
Fandango! By ZZ Top
Beautiful Loser by Bob Seger
Toys In The Attic by Aerosmith

Wednesday 2 – The McCartneys and fellow band members return to the UK

Friday 4 – Ringo officially announces Ring O'Records, though the label has been active for some time

Monday 7 – John is interviewed at the Dakota for a French TV show, *Un Jour Futur*

Tuesday 8 – John, along with attorney Leon Wildes, tape their appearance on Tom Snyder's *Tomorrow* show

Thursday 10 – Five years since the Beatles broke up

Friday 18 – John's *Rock 'N' Roll* clips, plus his interview with Bob Harris, air on *Old Grey Whistle Test*

Friday 18 – John tapes performances of "Slippin' and Slidin'," "Stand By Me" and "Imagine" for the *Salute to Sir Lew Grade* special

Monday 21 – Paul and Linda appear on the cover of *People*

Monday 21 – *Extra Texture* sessions begin in Los Angeles at A&M Studios; recording is finished on May 7, with overdubs and tweaking occurring after

Thursday 24 – (Early morning hours) Pete Ham commits suicide at 27

Friday 25 – A film clip showing Paul and Linda singing onstage with Rod Stewart the previous November is shown on *Midnight Special*

Monday 28 – Ringo guests on *The Smothers Brothers Show*

Monday 28 – John's interview with Tom Snyder airs on *Tomorrow*

Wednesday 30 – Personnel evacuated by helicopter from the US embassy in Saigon

April – Some time this month, John is interviewed for Tony Palmer's sprawling documentary on popular music, *All You Need Is Love* (exactly when is difficult to determine, since John is wearing the exact same apparel he's seen wearing in other interviews around this time); sometime this year, Paul also submits to an interview

May 1975

BADFINGER'S HAM DIES

PETE HAM, founder member of Badfinger, died last Thursday morning. He apparently took his own life, and was found hanging in his garage by his girl friend. It is understood that Pete (27) was in a very depressed state of mind, because Badfinger's recent American tour was not very successful. The funeral was taking place this week in Swansea. Besides writing much of Badfinger's material, Pete was the composer of many songs for other artists, his best-known being "Without You" which was a million seller for Nilsson. At presstime, it was still not clear whether Badfinger are to continue as a group.

Topping the US singles chart:
"He Don't Love You (Like I Love You)" by Tony Orlando and Dawn
"Shining Star" by Earth, Wind and Fire
"Before The Next Teardrop Falls" by Freddie Fender

On the airwaves:
"Jackie Blue" by Ozark Mountain Daredevils
"How Long" by Ace
"Chevy Van" by Sammy Johns

Topping the US album chart:
Chicago VIII

Albums released this month include:
Love Will Keep Us Together by The Captain and Tennille
Captain Fantastic and the Brown Dirt Cowboy by Elton John

May – Paul and Linda appear on the cover of this month's *Hit Parader*

Thursday 1 – The Rolling Stones publicize their North American tour by performing "Brown Sugar" from a flatbed truck rolling down 5th Avenue in New York

Saturday 10 – Neil Sedaka's "The Immigrant," written for John, tops the Billboard Adult Contemporary chart

Tuesday 13 – Western swing pioneer Bob Wills dies at 70

Friday 16 – Apple Studios is closed

Friday 16 – Beginning this day through Sunday, John attends the *WFIL Helping Hand Marathon* in Philadelphia, guesting on radio and on the station's sister TV news

Friday 16 – Michael X is hanged in Trinidad

Wednesday 21 – *A Salute To The Beatles*, hosted by David Frost, airs on ABC's late night *Wide World of Entertainment*

Thursday 22 – Ringo performs "No No Song" with its writer, Hoyt Axton, on the latter's syndicated *Boogie Woogie Gospel Rock and Roll Show*

Friday 23 – "Listen To What The Man Said"/"Love In Song" (Capitol 4091; peaks at #1 in July)

Monday 27 – *Venus and Mars* (peaks at number one in July)

June 1975

Topping the US singles chart:
"Thank God I'm A Country Boy" by John Denver
"Sister Golden Hair" by America

On the airwaves:
"Killer Queen" by Queen
"Bad Time" by Grand Funk
"Long Tall Glasses" by Leo Sayer

Topping the US album chart:
Captain Fantastic and the Brown Dirt Cowboy by Elton John

Albums released this month include:
Made In The Shade by the Rolling Stones

Main Course by the Bee Gees
Tonight's The Night by Neil Young
Red Octopus by Jefferson Starship

June – *The Beatles: An Illustrated Record* by Roy Carr and Tony Tyler is published

June – John writes a letter to Robert Weinstein of *Modern Hi-Fi and Music* magazine, informing him that a man named Hal Fein claiming to have discovered the Beatles (in an issue published that year) is full of it

Monday 2 – "It's All Down To Goodnight Vienna"/"Oo-Wee" (Apple 1882; peaks at #31)

Monday 2 – Scheduled release date for John's "Slippin' and Slidin'"/"Ain't That A Shame" (Apple 1883); the single is canceled

Tuesday 3 – Bandleader/actor Ozzie Nelson dies at 69

Thursday 5 – John Lennon interview with Pete Hamill runs in *Rolling Stone*

Friday 13 – *A Salute To Sir Lew Grade* airs on ABC; John's last live performance

Saturday 28 – John interview taped in April at the Dakota airs on French TV

Saturday 28 – *Twilight Zone* and *Night Gallery* creator Rod Serling dies during heart surgery at 50

Sunday 29 – Tim Buckley overdoses on heroin at 28

Monday 30 – Cher marries Greg Allman

July 1975

Topping the US singles chart:
"Love Will Keep Us Together" by the Captain and Tennille
"Listen To What The Man Said" by Paul McCartney and Wings
"The Hustle" by Van McCoy

On the airwaves:
"Wildfire" by Michael Murphy
"When Will I Be Loved" by Linda Ronstadt
"Magic" by Pilot

Topping the US album chart:
Captain Fantastic and the Brown Dirt Cowboy by Elton John

Albums released this month include:
Fleetwood Mac's self-titled album debuting Buckingham and Nicks
Metal Machine Music by Lou Reed
Thursday 17 – Ringo and Maureen's marriage officially dissolved

Thursday 31 – Teamsters President Jimmy Hoffa goes missing

August 1975

Topping the US singles chart:
"One Of These Night" by Eagles
"Jive Talkin'" by the Bee Gees
"Fallin' In Love" by Hamilton, Joe Frank and Reynolds
"Get Down Tonight" by KC and the Sunshine Band

On the airwaves:
"Someone Saved My Life Tonight" by Elton John
"I'm Not In Love" by 10CC
"Midnight Blue" by Melissa Manchester

Topping the US album chart:
One Of These Nights by Eagles

Albums released this month include:
Atlantic Crossing by Rod Stewart
Love To Love You Baby by Donna Summer
Born To Run by Bruce Springsteen

WLS MUSICRADIO 89
WLS MUSICRADIO 89

JOHN LANDECKER
PLAYS
THE BEST MUSIC
IN CHICAGO
6PM — 10PM

LW	TW	WEEK ENDING AUGUST 16, 1975	VOL. 15, NO. 49
1	1	Listen To What The Man Said	Wings
3	2	Love Will Keep Us Together	Captain And Tennille
4	3	Someone Saved My Life Tonight	Elton John
8	4	Jive Talkin	Bee Gees
2	5	I'm Not In Love	10 cc
9	6	Why Can't We Be Friends	War
10	7	Midnight Blue	Melissa Manchester
6	8	Please Mr. Please	Olivia Newton-John
7	9	One Of These Nights	Eagles
5	10	Hustle	Van McCoy
14	11	Dynamite	Bazuka
13	12	Rockin Chair	Gwen McCrae
11	13	Magic	Pilot
xx	14	Rockford Files	Mike Post
xx	15	Rhinestone Cowboy	Glen Campbell
		Pinball Wizard (Not Available As A 45)	Elton John
		Wildfire	Michael Murphey
		Sister Golden Hair	America
		Mornin Beautiful	Tony Orlando & Dawn
		Could It Be Magic	Barry Manilow
		When Will I Be Loved	Linda Ronstadt
		Take Me In Your Arms (Rock Me)	Doobie Brothers
		Killer Queen	Queen
		Only Yesterday	Carpenters
		Thank God I'm A Country Boy	John Denver

MUSICRADIO LP'S & TAPES

1	1	Capt. Fantastic & The Brown Dirt Cowboy	Elton John
2	2	Venus And Mars	Wings
3	3	Love Will Keep Us Together	Captain And Tennille
5	4	One Of These Nights	Eagles
4	5	Four Wheel Drive	Bachman-Turner Overdrive
6	6	Chicago VIII	Chicago
7	7	Spirit Of America	Beach Boys
xx	8	Greatest Hits	Cat Stevens
xx	9	Gorilla	James Taylor
9	10	Horizon	Carpenters

The WLS Musicradio Surveys represent the station's estimate of current and potential music popularity as reflected in such measures as record sales, juke box play, audience interviews, listener requests, and national charts. Last week's and this week's positions are listed under LW and TW respectively.

Saturday 16 – The Ramones debut at CBGB's

Monday 18 – David Bowie's "Fame," featuring and co-written by John, is released

Saturday 23 – Peter Gabriel leaves Genesis

Monday 25 – Bobby Keys' "Gimme the Key" issued on Ring O'Records

September 1975

Topping the US singles chart:
"Rhinestone Cowboy" by Glen Campbell
"Fame" by David Bowie
"I'm Sorry" by John Denver

On the airwaves:
"Why Can't We Be Friends" by War
"Tush" by ZZ Top
"Could It Be Magic" by Barry Manilow

Topping the US album chart:
Red Octopus by Jefferson Starship

Albums released this month include:
Wish You Were Here by Pink Floyd
John Fogerty's self-titled Asylum debut
Face The Music by Electric Light Orchestra
Wind on The Water by Crosby & Nash
Fool For The City by Foghat

Friday 5 – Lynette Fromme, 26, is arrested for threatening President Ford with a loaded gun in Sacramento

Saturday 6 – Wings begins a tour of Britain, performing in England as well as Wales and Scotland, where the tour ends on the 23rd

Saturday 6 – It's reported in England that George attended *John, Paul, George, Ringo...and Bert* the week before with Derek Taylor; finding the experience excruciating, he pulls permission for the use of "Here Comes The Sun"

Friday 12 – Paul is interviewed by Granada TV backstage at a Wings gig in Manchester

Monday 15 – "You"/"World of Stone" (Apple 1884; peaks at #20)
Thursday 18 – Kidnapped heiress/SLA member Patricia Hearst captured

Sunday 21 – Wings' Glasgow gig is filmed, with performances of "Letting Go" and "Venus and Mars/Rock Show" culled for use as promo clips

Monday 22 – *Extra Texture (Read All About It)*; the last original Apple album (peaks at number eight)

Monday 22 – Sara Jane Moore, 45, is arrested and charged with attempted assassination after squeezing off a round at President Ford in San Francisco

Monday 29 – "Letting Go"/"You Gave Me The Answer" (Capitol 4195; peaks at #39)

Monday 29 – Jackie Wilson suffers a massive heart attack onstage that leaves him in a coma until his death in January 1984

October 1975

Topping the US singles chart:
"Fame" by David Bowie
"Bad Blood" by Neil Sedaka with Elton John

On the airwaves:
"At Seventeen" by Janis Ian
"Miracles" by Jefferson Starship
"Ballroom Blitz" by Sweet

Topping the US album chart:
Wish You Were Here by Pink Floyd

Albums released this month include:
The Who By Numbers
Siren by Roxy Music

Trying To Get The Feeling Again by Barry Manilow
Still Crazy After All These Years by Paul Simon

Saturday 4 – Lengthy interview with Paul runs in *Melody Maker*

Sunday 5 – George appears on the syndicated radio program, *Rock Around The World*

Monday 6 – *Harder to Live* by Splinter, featuring Mal Evans' "Lonely Man"

Monday 6 – Jiva's self-titled debut, also on Dark Horse

Tuesday 7 – John Lennon wins his court case against the INS

Thursday 9 – Sean Taro Ono Lennon is born

Friday 10 – *Lisztomania* opens in theaters

Saturday 11 – NBC's *Saturday Night* premiers; Billy Preston is a guest

Monday 20 – Dark Horse issues *Mind Your Own Business* by ex-Wings guitarist Henry McCullough

Friday 24 – *Shaved Fish* (peaks at number twelve)

Monday 27 – "Venus and Mars/Rock Show"/"Magneto and Titanium Man" (Capitol 4175; peaks at #12)

Monday 27 – Bruce Springsteen simultaneously appears on the covers of *Time* and *Newsweek*

Tuesday 28 – Wings arrives in Australia for a series of live dates

Thursday 30 – *New York Daily News* runs headline, "Ford to City: Drop Dead"

November 1975

Topping the US singles chart:
"Island Girl" by Elton John
"That's The Way (I Like It)" by KC and the Sunshine Band

On the airwaves:
"Lyin' Eyes" by Eagles
"Dance With Me" by Orleans
"My Little Town" by Simon & Garfunkel

Topping the US album chart:
Red Octopus by Jefferson Starship

Albums released this month include:
A Night At The Opera by Queen
Horses by Patti Smith
Pressure Drop by Robert Palmer

Saturday 1 – Wings' Australian tour begins in Perth; the band will perform in nine cities before finishing in Melbourne on the 14th

Monday 10 – The ore carrier *SS Edmund Fitzgerald* vanishes during a storm on Lake Superior with the loss of all 29 hands

Tuesday 11 – Wings is denied entrance to Japan on the grounds of prior drug arrests, forcing the cancellation of three dates that had already sold out

Thursday 13 – Wings' Melbourne concert is filmed, later broadcast in Japan

Monday 17 – David Bowie's "Golden Years," featuring an apparent cameo from John

Wednesday/Friday 19/21 – These were the dates that Wings was to have performed in Japan

Thursday 20 – Generalissimo Francisco Franco, 82, dies in Spain

Tuesday 25 – *Blast From Your Past*; the last album of Apple's original run (peaks at number thirty)

Thursday 27 – Ross McWhirter of the *Guinness Book of World Records* is assassinated by the IRA

December 1975

Topping the US singles chart:
"Fly Robin Fly" by Silver Convention
"That's The Way (I Like It)" by KC and the Sunshine Band
"Let's Do It Again" by Staple Singers

On the airwaves:
"Who Loves You" by the Four Seasons
"The Way That I Want To Touch You" by Captain & Tennille
"S.O.S. by ABBA

Topping the US album chart:
Still Crazy After All These Years by Paul Simon

Albums released this month include:
Equinox by Styx

December – Mal Evans produces demos for Natural Gas, Joey Molland's post Badfinger band, in Los Angeles; he is later fired from the project

Monday 8 – "This Guitar (Can't Keep From Crying)"/"Maya Love" (Apple 1885; dnc)

Thursday 25 – Paul and Linda visit John and Yoko at the Dakota on Christmas Day

Friday 26 – George appears on *Rutland Weekend Television* in England, parodies the "My Sweet Lord" lawsuit with "The Pirate Song"

1976

Published this Year:
Growing Up with the Beatles by Ron Schaumburg
John Lennon: One Day At A Time by Anthony Fawcett

January
Topping the US singles chart:
"Saturday Night" by Bay City Rollers

"Convoy" by C.W. McCall
"I Write The Songs" by Barry Manilow
"Theme from Mahogany (Do You Know Where You're Goin' To?)" by Diana Ross
"Love Rollercoaster" by Ohio Players

On the airwaves:
"Feelings" by Morris Albert
"Sky High" by Jigsaw
"Heat Wave" by Linda Ronstadt

Topping the US album chart:
Chicago IX (Chicago's Greatest Hits)
Albums released this month include:
Frampton Comes Alive!
Run With The Pack by Bad Company
Desire by Bob Dylan
Station To Station by David Bowie

January – Beginning this month and running through into February, recording sessions for *Wings at the Speed of Sound* at Abbey Road

Thursday 1- John is interviewed by Elliot Mintz at the Dakota

Monday 5 – (Early morning hours) Mal Evans is shot and killed by Los Angeles police; he was 40

Saturday 10 – Blues legend Howlin' Wolf (Chester Burnett) dies at 65

Monday 12 – Harry Nilsson's *Sandman*, featuring cover photography by the recently departed Mal Evans, is released

Monday 19 – Promoter Bill Sargent offers the four ex-Beatles $30 million to reunite

Friday 23 – New York Judge Thomas Grisea declares a mistrial in the Lennon vs. Levy case

Friday 23 – Actor/singer/activist Paul Robeson dies at 77

Sunday 25 – Ringo sits in with Bob Dylan at a benefit concert for former boxer Rubin "Hurricane" Carter in Houston

Sunday 25 – Chris Kenner ("I Like It Like That") suffers a fatal heart attack at 46

Monday 26 – The Beatles' contract with EMI, signed in 1967, expires, freeing the company to issue releases as they see fit

February 1976

Topping the US singles chart:
"50 Ways To Leave Your Lover" by Paul Simon
"Theme From SWAT" by Rhythm Heritage

On the airwaves:
"Rock and Roll All Night" by Kiss
"Love To Love You Baby" by Donna Summer
"Nights On Broadway" by the Bee Gees

Topping the US album chart:
Desire by Bob Dylan
Albums released this month include:
Dreamboat Annie by Heart
A Trick of the Tail by Genesis
Come On Over by Olivia Newton-John
Their Greatest Hits (1971-1975) by Eagles

Friday 6 – Jazz pianist Vince Guaraldi suffers a fatal heart attack at 47

Thursday 12 – Actor Sal Mineo (*Rebel without a Cause*), 37, is stabbed to death

Friday 13 – Stairsteps' *2nd Resurrection*, co-produced by Billy Preston, issued on Dark Horse

Friday 13 – Attitudes' self-titled Dark Horse debut; group features Jim Keltner, Danny Kortchmar, Paul Stallworth and David Foster

Friday 13 – Ravi Shankar's *Music Festival From India* on Dark Horse

Friday 20 – Court rules in John's favor against Morris Levy in the *Roots* case

Sunday 22 – Former Supremes singer Florence Ballard dies from a blood clot at 32

Monday/Wednesday 23/25 – George appears in a New York court in the "My Sweet Lord"/"He's So Fine" case

March 1976

Topping the US singles chart:
"Love Machine (Part 1)" by The Miracles
"December 1963 (Oh What A Night)" by the Four Seasons

On the airwaves:
"Lonely Night (Angel Face)" by Captain & Tennille
"Breaking Up Is Hard to Do" by Neil Sedaka
"Evil Woman" by Electric Light Orchestra

Topping the US album chart:
Their Greatest Hits (1971-1975) by Eagles

Albums released this month include:
Presence by Led Zeppelin
2112 by Rush
Takin' It To The Streets by the Doobie Brothers
Silk Degrees by Boz Scaggs

Wednesday 10 – Ringo inks a record deal with Polydor outside the US; Atlantic within

Sunday 14 – Hollywood musical director Busby Berkeley dies at 80

Thursday 18 – Jim McCartney, Paul's father, dies of pneumonia at 73

Friday 19 – Ex Free guitarist Paul Kossoff ("All Right Now") dies from drug-related heart failure at 25

Saturday 20 – Wings begins another European tour, this one taking them to Denmark, West Germany, The Netherlands and France; it ends in Paris on the 26th

Thursday 25 – *Wings At The Speed Of Sound* (peaks at number one for seven weeks in spring/summer 1976)
Friday 26 – Jimmy McCulloch breaks a finger in Paris, forcing the delay of the Wings Over America tour

April 1976

Topping the US singles chart:
"Disco Lady" by Johnnie Taylor

On the airwaves:
"Bohemian Rhapsody" by Queen
"All By Myself" by Eric Carmen
"Dream Weaver" by Gary Wright

Topping the US album chart:
Their Greatest Hits (1971-1975) by Eagles

Albums released this month include:
Faithful by Todd Rundgren
Live Bullet by Bob Seger
The Ramones' self-titled debut
Black And Blue by the Rolling Stones

April – The Beatles appear on the cover of this month's *Creem*

April – Paul appears on the cover of this month's *Crawdaddy*

Thursday 1 – "Silly Love Songs"/"Cook Of The House" (Capitol 4256; peaks at #1 in May)

Thursday 1 – Freddie Lennon, John's father, dies of stomach cancer at 63

Thursday 1 – On this night and the next, CBS airs *Helter Skelter*, a made-for-TV film on the Tate-LaBianca murders; Beatles music featured throughout

Thursday 1 – Apple Computer Company is founded in California; the Apple I home computer goes on sale in June

Monday 5 – The Beatles appear on the cover of *People*

Monday 5 – Billionaire recluse Howard Hughes dies at 70

Thursday 8 – Original date of the Wings US tour; postponed due to Jimmy McCulloch's broken finger

Friday 9 – Folk singer/activist Phil Ochs, 35, commits suicide

Tuesday 20 – George appears onstage with the Monty Python troupe to perform "The Lumberjack Song" at City Center on West 55th in New York

Saturday 24 – John and Paul enjoy an evening together at the Dakota

Saturday 24 – *Saturday Night* producer Lorne Michaels offers The Beatles $3,000 to reunite on their show

Sunday 25 – Paul is turned away at John's door; the two never meet again

May 1976

Topping the US singles chart:
"Let Your Love Flow" by the Bellamy Brothers
"Welcome Back" by John Sebastian
"Boogie Fever" by The Sylvers

"Silly Love Songs" by Wings
"Love Hangover" by Diana Ross

On the airwaves:
"Right Back Where We Started From" by Maxine Nightingale
"Only Sixteen" by Dr. Hook
"Rhiannon" by Fleetwood Mac

Topping the US album chart:
Presence by Led Zeppelin

Albums released this month include:
Fly Like An Eagle by Steve Miller Band
Rocks by Aerosmith
Warren Zevon's self-titled debut
Agents of Fortune by Blue Oyster Cult
Tales of Mystery and Imagination by the Alan Parsons Project

Saturday 1 – Cynthia Lennon marries John Twist

Monday 3 – Wings Over America tour begins in Fort Worth, Texas; the band will perform thirty-one shows in twenty-one cities

Friday 14 – Former Yardbirds singer Keith Relf, 33, electrocutes himself

Saturday 22 – Lorne Michaels raises his reunion offer to $3,200 on *Saturday Night*

Monday 24 – Sessions for George's *Thirty-Three & 1/3* begin at his home studio

Saturday 29 – Natural Gas' self-titled debut

Sunday 30 – George is stricken with hepatitis; it will keep him bedridden until mid-July, delaying the completion of his Dark Horse label debut

Monday 31 – "Got To Get You Into My Life"/"Helter Skelter" (Capitol 4274; peaks at #7)

Monday 31 – Paul appears on the cover of *Time* (artwork by Peter Max)

June 1976

Topping the US singles chart:
"Silly Love Songs" by Wings

On the airwaves:
"Shannon" by Henry Gross
"Show Me The Way" by Peter Frampton
"Get Up and Boogie" by Silver Convention

Topping the US album chart:
Black and Blue by the Rolling Stones

Albums released this month include:
15 Big Ones by the Beach Boys
A Night On The Town by Rod Stewart
Are You Ready For The Country by Waylon Jennings
The Runaways' self-titled debut

Sunday 6 – Tara Richards, son of Keith and Anita Pallenberg, dies of respiratory failure at ten-weeks old

Monday 7 – *Rock 'N' Roll Music* (peaks at number two)

Monday 7 – Paul appears on the cover of *People*

Thursday 10 – Wings' set at Seattle's Kingdome is filmed for *Rockshow*

Saturday 12 – John records "Cookin' (In the Kitchen of Love)" with Ringo at Cherokee Studios in Los Angeles

Thursday 17 – Paul and Linda appear on the cover of *Rolling Stone*

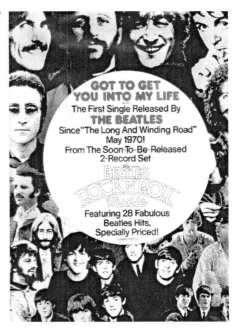

Saturday 19 – Paul and Linda record "Pure Gold" with Ringo at Cherokee Studios in Los Angeles

Saturday June 19 – Ringo is filmed being interviewed at length for Australian TV

Sunday 20 – Paul and Linda attend a birthday party for Brian Wilson

Monday 21 – Ringo attends the Wings concert at LA's Forum, presenting flowers onstage at the show's end

Monday 28 – Paul and Linda interviewed by Geraldo Rivera for ABC's late night *Goodnight America*

July 1976

Topping the US singles chart:
"Afternoon Delight" by Starland Vocal band
"Kiss and Say Goodbye" by The Manhattans

On the airwaves:
"The Boys Are Back In Town" by Thin Lizzie
"Sara Smile" by Hall and Oates
"Crazy On You" by Heart

Topping the US album chart:
Wings At The Speed Of Sound

Albums released this month include:
Year of the Cat by Al Stewart
Beautiful Noise by Neil Diamond
Howlin' Wind by Graham Parker
Boston's self-titled debut

July – Ringo shaves his head in Monte Carlo

July – In three week's time, Denny Laine's *Holly Days* album is recorded at Rude Studio in Scotland with help from Paul and Linda

Friday 2 – Brian Wilson joins the Beach Boys onstage for the first time in over a decade in Oakland, CA

Sunday 4 – America celebrates the Bicentennial

Thursday 15 – The Beatles appear on the cover of *Rolling Stone*

Tuesday 20 – In Monte Carlo, Ringo films segments for the promo films "Hey Baby" and "You Don't Know Me At All"

Tuesday 20 – Viking I lands on the surface of Mars

Wednesday 21 – Career criminal Gary Gilmore arrested in Provo, Utah for two homicides

Monday 26 – Master tapes to George's Dark Horse debut are due on this date to A&M records; behind schedule due to his illness, he does not comply

Monday 26 – A lengthy conversation between George and guru Srila Prabhupada takes place in London

Tuesday 27 – After John receives his "Green Card," he is interviewed outside the INS building

Wednesday 28 – "Let 'Em In"/"Beware My Love" (Capitol 4293; peaks at #3)

Thursday 29 – The "Son of Sam" serial killings begin in Pelham Bay, New York

Friday 30 – *The Beatles Tapes*, a double album comprised of interviews with all four Beatles conducted by journalist David Wigg, is released in Britain

August 1976

Topping the US singles chart:
"Don't Go Breaking My Heart" by Elton John and Kiki Dee

On the airwaves:
"Takin' It To The Streets" by the Doobie Brothers
"Rock and Roll Music" by the Beach Boys
"More More More" by the Andrea True Connection

Topping the US album chart:
Breezin' by George Benson

Albums released this month include:
The Roaring Silence by Manfred Mann's Earth Band
The Modern Lovers' self-titled debut
Hasten Down The Wind by Linda Ronstadt

August – Paul appears on the cover of this month's *Creem*

August – As of this month, the Beatles have officially been apart for as long as the four of them worked together

Wednesday 4 – On this day and the next two, Ringo shoots segments in Hamburg, West Germany for "Hey Baby," "You Don't Know Me At All," and "I'll Still Love You" promo films

Wednesday 11 – Klaatu's debut album released

Saturday 28 – Former child actress Anissa Jones (*Family Affair*) dies of a drug overdose at 18

Tuesday 31 – George is found guilty of "subconscious plagiarism" with "My Sweet Lord" in U.S. district court

September 1976

Topping the US singles chart:
"You Should Be Dancing" by the Bee Gees
"(Shake, Shake, Shake) Shake Your Booty" by KC and the Sunshine Band
"Play That Funky Music" by Wild Cherry

On the airwaves:
"You're My Best Friend" by Queen
"Get Closer" by Seals and Crofts
"Love Is Alive" by Gary Wright

Topping the US album chart:
Fleetwood Mac's eponymous release
Albums released this month include:
Children of the World by the Bee Gees
Hard Rain by Bob Dylan

One More From The Road by Lynyrd Skynyrd
Songs In The Key Of Life by Stevie Wonder

Friday 17 – *Ringo's Rotogravure* (peaks at number twenty-eight)

Friday 17 – Sid Bernstein places a full-page ad in the *New York Herald Tribune*, requesting that the Beatles get together for a one-off charitable concert

Saturday 18 – Dark Horse begin to vacate A&M offices

Sunday 19 – Wings returns to the European stage, with shows in Austria, Yugoslavia and West Germany (again) before finishing up in Britain

Monday 20 – "A Dose of Rock 'N' Roll"/"Cryin'" (Atlantic 3361; peaks at #26)

Wednesday 22 – *Charlie's Angels* debuts on ABC

Friday 24 – John and Yoko are captured by Ugly George's roving camera at a Manhattan restaurant

Tuesday 28 – George is sued by A&M Records for non-delivery of his first Dark Horse album for the label

Wednesday 29 – Ringo flies to Copenhagen, where he runs into Cat Stevens

Thursday 30 – Ringo jams with Cat Stevens in the studio, playing on "Blue Monday" and "I Just Want To Make Love To You," among other songs

October 1976

Topping the US singles chart:
"A Fifth of Beethoven" by Walter Murphy and the Big Apple Band
"Disco Duck (Part 1)" by
Rick Dees and his Cast of Idiots
"If You Leave Me Now" by Chicago

On the airwaves:
"Baby I Love Your Way" by Peter Frampton
"I'm Easy" by Keith Carradine
"Devil Woman" by Cliff Richard

Topping the US album chart:
Frampton Comes Alive!

Albums released this month include:
Leftoverture by Kansas
Night Moves by Bob Seger
Crystal Ball by Styx
A New World Record by Electric Light Orchestra

October – At some point this month, George produces videos for "Crackerbox Palace" and "True Love" at Friar Park, directed by Eric Idle

Saturday 2 – Eric Idle hosts *Saturday Night*; airs "I Must Be In Love" Rutles clip

Monday 4 – US agriculture secretary Earl Butz resigns after flack stirred by telling a racist joke

Tuesday 5 – Ringo sits in with the studio band on the Dutch TV show, *Voor de Vuist Weg* ("Offhand")

Tuesday 19 – Wings wraps up a year of touring with three sold-out shows at London's Wembley Pool beginning this night

November 1976

Topping the US singles chart:
"Rock'n Me" by Steve Miller Band
"Tonight's The Night (Gonna Be Alright)" by Rod Stewart

On the airwaves:
"Muskrat Love" by Captain & Tennille
"Wreck of the Edmund Fitzgerald" by Gordon Lightfoot
"I Only Want To Be With You" by Bay City Rollers

Topping the US album chart:
Songs In The Key Of Life by Stevie Wonder

Albums released this month include:
Endless Flight by Leo Sayer
The Pretender by Jackson Browne
Tom Petty and the Heartbreakers' self-titled debut

Friday 5 – *All This and World War II* original soundtrack

Monday 8 – *The Best of George Harrison* (peaks at number thirty-one)

Monday 8 – "Ob-La-Di Ob-La-Da"/"Julia" (Capitol 4347; peaks at #49)

Monday 15 – "This Song"/"Learning How To Love You" (Dark Horse 8294; peaks at #25)

Friday 12 - *All This and World War II* opens in theaters
Wednesday 17 – George is interviewed at Chasen's in Los Angeles for local TV

Thursday 18 – An interview with George by Joel Siegel is broadcast on New York's WABC *Eyewitness News*

Thursday 18 – George tapes a performance with Paul Simon for NBC's *Saturday Night*

Saturday 20 – George on *Saturday Night*: he opens the show and duets with Paul Simon as musical guest; promos for "This Song" and "Crackerbox Palace" also air

Monday 22 – "Hey Baby"/"Lady Gaye" (Atlantic 3371; peaks at #74)

Wednesday 24 – *Thirty-Three & 1/3* (peaks at number eleven)

Thursday 25 – On this Thanksgiving evening, Ringo sits in on "I Shall Be Released" with The Band as part of *The Last Waltz* at San Francisco's Winterland Ballroom

Tuesday 30 – George is interviewed on *Old Grey Whistle Test*; promos for "This Song" and "True Love" air

December 1976

Topping the US singles chart:
"Tonight's the Night (Gonna Be Alright)" by Rod Stewart

On the airwaves:
"Beth" by Kiss
"More Than A Feeling" by Boston
"Nights Are Forever" by England Dan and John Ford Coley

Topping the US album chart:
Songs In The Key Of Life by Stevie Wonder

Albums released this month include:
A Day At The Races by Queen
Wind & Wuthering by Genesis
Blondie's self-titled debut
Hotel California by Eagles

Wednesday 1 – Sex Pistols' "Filth and Fury" appearance on Bill Grundy show in UK

Friday 3 – George is interviewed in the UK by Granada TV; is filmed watching a 1963 clip of The Beatles performing "This Boy" and "Twist and Shout"

Friday 3 – *Rocky* opens in theaters

Sunday 5 – George and Olivia are in India to attend the wedding of Ravi Shankar's niece

Friday 10 – *Wings Over America* (peaks at number one in January 1977)

Saturday 25 – John and Yoko spend Christmas Day with Mick and Bianca Jagger

Friday 31 – John and Yoko see the New Year in at Manhattan's Shun Lee Dynasty restaurant with Mrs. And Mrs. James Taylor and ten others

1977

Published this year:
Nicholas Schaffner's *The Beatles Forever*

January
Topping the US singles chart:
 "You Don't Have To Be A Star (To Be In My Show)" by Marilyn McCoo and Billy Davis Jr.
"You Make Me Feel Like Dancing" by Leo Sayer
"I Wish" by Stevie Wonder
"Car Wash" by Rose Royce

On the airwaves:
"Stand Tall" by Burton Cummings
"Nadia's Theme" by De Vorzon and Botkin
"Livin' Thing" by Electric Light Orchestra

Topping the US album chart:
Songs In The Key Of Life by Stevie Wonder

Albums released this month include:
Animals by Pink Floyd
Hard Again by Muddy Waters
Low by David Bowie
Changes in Latitudes, Changes in Attitudes by Jimmy Buffet
Monday 10 – A settlement of the litigation between Allen Klein and the Beatles is announced

Monday 10 – *Ringo the 4th* sessions begin in New York

Monday 17 – Ringo appears on the cover of *People*

Monday 17 – Convicted murderer Gary Gilmore, 36, is put to death by the state of Utah

Tuesday 18 – John and Yoko attend the opening night of Merce Cunningham's modern dance troupe at New York's Minskoff Theatre with James Taylor and Carly Simon

Wednesday 19 – In Washington DC, John and Yoko attend an inaugural ball for Jimmy Carter, who takes the oath of office the following day; they are also photographed with boxer Muhammad Ali

Sunday 23/30 – Alex Haley's *Roots* mini-series airs

Monday 24 – "Crackerbox Palace"/"Learning How To Love You" (Dark Horse 8313; peaks at #19)

Saturday 29 – (Early morning hours) TV actor Freddie Prinze commits suicide at 22

February 1977

Topping the US singles chart:
"Torn Between Two Lovers" by Mary MacGregor
"Blinded By The Light" by Manfred Mann's Earth Band
"New Kid In Town" by Eagles

On the airwaves:
"Walk This Way" by Aerosmith
"Dazz" by Brick
"After The Loving" by Engelbert Humperdinck

Topping the US album chart:
Hotel California by Eagles

Albums released this month include:
Peter Gabriel's self-titled debut
Cheap Trick's self-titled debut
Marquee Moon by Television
Sleepwalker by The Kinks
Rumours by Fleetwood Mac

February – George appears on the cover of this month's *Crawdaddy*

Thursday 3 – George, in Amsterdam, is interviewed for Dutch TV

Friday 4 – George, in Hamburg, West Germany promoting *Thirty-Three & 1/3*, meets Tony Sheridan for the first time in years

Saturday 5 – George appears on the German TV show *Disco 1977* to lip-synch "This Song"

Saturday 5 – BBC radio airs a conversation between George and journalist Anne Nightingale taped days earlier

Monday 7 – "Maybe I'm Amazed"/"Soily" (Capitol 4385; peaks at #10)

Monday 7 – Sessions for *London Town* begin at Abbey Road studio; work will continue here until March 31 and then resume in the Virgin Islands in May

Sunday 13 – Article appearing in the *Providence Journal* suggests that Klaatu is really the Beatles

Tuesday 15 – Sid Vicious replaces Glen Matlock on bass in the Sex Pistols

Saturday 19 – Ringo is a presenter at the Grammys alongside Paul Williams

Sunday 27 – Keith Richards is busted in Toronto for possession of cocaine and heroin, with the intent to traffic the latter

March 1977

Topping the US singles chart:
"Evergreen (Love Theme From *A Star is born*)" by Barbra Streisand
"Rich Girl" by Hall & Oates

On the airwaves:
"The Year of the Cat" by Al Stewart
"Carry On Wayward Son" by Kansas
"Go Your Own Way" by Fleetwood Mac

Topping the US album chart:
A Star Is Born by Barbra Streisand

Albums released this month include:
Foreigner's self-titled debut
The Idiot by Iggy pop
Anytime...Anywhere by Rita Coolidge
Welcome To My World by Elvis Presley

March – The Lennons travel to Singapore, Hong Kong and Canada

Tuesday 15 –*Three's Company* debuts on ABC

Wednesday 16 – "B-side to Seaside" is recorded by Paul and Linda at Abbey Road

Tuesday 22 – World's worst air disaster occurs in the Canary Islands when two 747 aircraft collide, taking 583 lives

Tuesday 29 – John, Yoko and Sean are caught (with Mick Jagger) by a TV news crew at the circus in Madison Square Garden

April 1977

Topping the US singles chart:
"Dancing Queen" by ABBA
"Don't Give Up On Us" by David Soul
"Don't Leave Me This Way" by Thelma Houston
"Southern Nights" by Glen Campbell

On the airwaves:
"So Into You" by the Atlanta Rhythm Section
"Night Moves" by Bob Seger
"The Things We Do For Love" by 10cc

Topping the US album chart:
Rumours by Fleetwood Mac

Albums released this month include:
Caught Live + 5 by the Moody Blues
Deceptive Bends by 10cc
Get It by Dave Edmunds
Even In the Quietest Moments by Supertramp

Sunday 3 – George attends the Long Beach Grand Prix

Sunday 3 – Sid Vicious plays first gig with the Sex Pistols

Wednesday 6 – Beatles lose their court bid to stop the release of the Star Club tapes

Saturday 23 – Eric Idle again hosts *Saturday Night*; screens the Rutles' "Cheese and Onions" clip, performed ala Lennon by Neil Innes

Tuesday 26 – New York's *Studio 54* disco opens

May 1977

Topping the US singles chart:
"Hotel California" by Eagles
"When I Need You" by
Leo Sayer
"Sir Duke" by Stevie Wonder

On the airwaves:
"I Like Dreaming" by Kenny Nolan
"Feels Like The First Time" by Foreigner
"Couldn't Get It Right" by Climax Blues Band

Topping the US album chart:
Hotel California by Eagles

Albums released this month include:
I'm In You by Peter Frampton
One Of The Boys by Roger Daltrey
Book Of Dreams by Steve Miller Band
Trans-Europe Express by Kraftwerk
Little Queen by Heart

Sunday 1 – *London Town* sessions resume aboard the Fair Carol, anchored in the US Virgin Islands; they will finish up on the 31st

Monday 2 – *The Beatles at the Hollywood Bowl* (peaks at number two)

Friday 6 – *Holly Days* by Denny Laine

Friday 13 – *Good News* by Attitudes

Tuesday 17 – *Thrillington* (dnc)

Wednesday 25 – *Star Wars* (now called "Episode IV: A New Hope") opens

Thursday 26 – Elvis Presley performs his final concert at Indianapolis' Market Square Arena

Tuesday 31 – "Seaside Woman" by Suzy and the Red Stripes (Epic 50403; peaks at #59)

Tuesday 31 – *Beatlemania* opens on Broadway at the Winter Garden Theatre

June 1977

Topping the US singles chart:
"I'm Your Boogie Man" by KC and the Sunshine Band
"Dreams" by Fleetwood Mac
"Got To Give It Up (Part 1)" by Marvin Gaye

On the airwaves:
"Lido Shuffle" by Boz Scaggs
"Lonely Boy" by Andrew Gold
"Lucille" by Kenny Rogers

Topping the US album chart:
Rumours by Fleetwood Mac

Albums released this month include:
JT by James Taylor

Love Gun by Kiss
CSN by Crosby, Stills and Nash
American Stars and Bars by Neil Young
Exodus by Bob Marley and the Wailers

Thursday 9 – George and Pattie's marriage officially dissolved

Monday 13 – *Live! At the Star-Club* in Hamburg, Germany; 1962 (peaks at one hundred eleven)

Monday 20 – Linda records a pair of oldies in Jamaica: "Mr. Sandman" and "Sugartime"; both were eventually released posthumously

Saturday 25 – The body of film director Mike Todd, killed in 1958, is stolen from its grave by thieves looking for valuable jewelry; it is recovered days later

Tuesday 28 – George attends a "Farewell from Britain" salute to Derek Taylor; Ringo appears via satellite

Summer – Ringo cuts at least two jingles – "I Love My Suit" – for the Japanese leisure suit company, Simple Life (they feature backing vocals from ex-Monkee Davy Jones and Harry Nilsson); he also appears in their TV ads

July 1977

Topping the US singles chart:
"Gonna Fly Now (Theme From Rocky)" by Bill Conti
"Undercover Angel" by Alan O'Day
"Da Doo Ron Ron" by Shaun Cassidy
"Looks Like We Made It" by Barry Manilow

On the airwaves:
"Margaritaville" by Jimmy Buffet
"Life In The Fast Lane" by Eagles
"Peace Of Mind" by Boston

Topping the US album chart:
Rumours by Fleetwood Mac

Albums released this month include:
My Aim Is True by Elvis Costello

It's A Game by Bay City Rollers
Going For The One by Yes
The Grand Illusion by Styx
Moody Blue by Elvis Presley

Wednesday 13 – On this day and the next, the New York City blackout leaves most of the city in darkness, prompting widespread looting

Friday 15 – George attends practice for the upcoming British Grand Prix

Wednesday 20 – Gary Kellgren, co-founder of the Record Plant, dies at 38

Tuesday 26 – Robert Plant's 6 year-old son Karac dies from a virus; Led Zeppelin cancels the remaining dates on their US tour and returns home

August 1977

Topping the US singles chart:
"I Just Want To Be Your Everything" by Andy Gibb
"Best of My Love" by The Emotions

On the airwaves:
"You Made Me Believe In Magic" by Bay City Rollers
"I'm In You" by Peter Frampton
"Barracuda" by Heart

Topping the US album chart:
Rumours by Fleetwood Mac

Albums released this month include:
In Color by Cheap Trick
Pacific Ocean Blue by Dennis Wilson
Beauty On A Back Street by Hall & Oates
Before We Were So Rudely Interrupted by The Animals
August – *London Town* sessions resume in Scotland, where "Mull of Kintyre" would be among the songs laid down

Tuesday 2 – George films his cameo for *The Rutles: All You Need Is Cash*

Wednesday 10 – David Berkowitz is arrested for the "Son of Sam" murders in New York

Friday 12 – Ringo films interview segments at Keith Moon's Malibu home for The Who documentary, *The Kids Are Alright*

Tuesday 16 – Elvis Presley dies at 42

Friday 19 – Keni Burke (former bassist with the Stairsteps) self-titled Dark Horse debut

Friday 19 – Groucho Marx dies at 86

Tuesday 23 – The RCA VBT200 becomes the first VHS recorder to go on sale in the US

Thursday 25 – "Wings"/"Just A Dream" (Atlantic 3429; dnc)

September 1977

Topping the US singles chart:
"I Just Want To Be Your Everything" by Andy Gibb
"Best of My Love" by The Emotions

On the airwaves:
"Whatcha Gonna Do" by Pablo Cruise
"Black Betty" by Ram Jam
"Higher and Higher" by Rita Coolidge

Topping the US album chart:
Rumours by Fleetwood Mac

Albums released this month include:
Talking Heads '77
Bad Reputation by Thin Lizzie
The Stranger by Billy Joel
Rough Mix by Pete Townshend and Ronnie Lane
Aja by Steely Dan

Thursday 8 – Jimmy McCulloch leaves Wings to join the reformed Small Faces

Monday 12 – James Louis McCartney is born in London

Monday 12 – Allan Williams' memoir, *The Man Who Gave The Beatles Away*, is published in paperback in the US

Tuesday 13 – Conductor Leopold Stokowski (*Fantasia*) dies at 95

Friday 16 – Marc Bolan, 29, is killed in an auto accident

Tuesday 20 – On this evening's episode of *Happy Days*, Fonzie ski-jumps the shark tank
Monday 26 – *Ringo the 4th* (peaks at number one hundred sixty-two)

Wednesday 28 – Bing Crosby and David Bowie tape "Little Drummer Boy"/"Peace on Earth" for Crosby's upcoming Christmas special

October 1977

Topping the US singles chart:
"Star Wars Theme" by Meco
"You Light Up My Life" by Debbie Boone

On the airwaves:
"Just Remember I Love You" by Firefall
"Nobody Does It Better" by Carly Simon
"Swayin' To The Music" by Johnny Rivers

Topping the US album chart:
Rumours by Fleetwood Mac

Albums released this month include:
Street Survivors by

LINDA'S PICTURES
113 photographs by Linda McCartney

The best of her camera work from The Beatles to Jimi Hendrix The Rolling Stones Dylan and McCartney

Size:
9½ x 12½
80 pages
in color
41 pages
in black and white

LINDA'S PICTURES
a collection of photographs by Linda McCartney

A unique look at a fascinating world
$25 at all bookstores · Published by Knopf

Lynyrd Skynyrd
News of the World by Queen
Out of the Blue by Electric Light Orchestra
Bat Out Of Hell by Meatloaf
Little Criminals by Randy Newman

October – The Beatles appear on the cover of this month's *Hit Parader*

October – The Beatles are satirized in this month's issue of *National Lampoon*

Monday 3 – Splinter's *Two Man Band*, on Dark Horse

Tuesday 4 – At the end of a four-month visit to Japan, John takes questions from the press; it was here that he delivered his "Elvis died when he went into the army" comment

Tuesday 11 – Allen Klein is indicted in a New York court for tax evasion

Thursday 13 – Wings films a promo clip for "Mull of Kintyre" in Scotland, directed by Michael Lindsay-Hogg
Thursday 13 – Advance copies of "Girl"/"You're Going To Lose That Girl" (Capitol 4506) are issued in the US; the release is later canceled.

Friday 14 – Actor/singer Bing Crosby dies at 74

Tuesday 18 – "Drowning In The Sea Of Love"/"Just A Dream" (Atlantic 3412; dnc)

Thursday 20 – Three members of Lynyrd Skynyrd are killed in a Mississippi plane crash

Friday 21 – *Love Songs* (peaks at number twenty-four)

Friday 21 – John serves as Best Man at the wedding of actor Peter Boyle to journalist Lorraine Altman

Tuesday 25 – Six weeks after the birth of their son James, the McCartneys (plus Denny Laine and Joe English) resume work on *London Town* at Abbey Road

November 1977

Topping the US singles chart:
"You Light Up My Life" by Debbie Boone

On the airwaves:
"I Feel Love" by Donna Summer
"Don't It Make My Brown Eyes Blue" by Crystal Gayle
"Boogie Nights" by Heat Wave

Topping the US album chart:
Rumours by Fleetwood Mac
Albums released this month include:
Slowhand by Eric Clapton
Rocket To Russia by The Ramones
Chic's self-titled debut
Greatest Hits, Etc. by Paul Simon
Never Mind the Bollocks, Here's the Sex Pistols

November – Sessions for Ringo's *Bad Boy* begin in Canada

November – Joe English quits Wings

Thursday 3 – *Rolling Stone* publishes "An Open Letter To John Lennon" by critic Dave Marsh, beseeching him to begin recording again; John responds with a caustic "I don't owe anybody anything"

Friday 4 – "Girls School"/"Mull of Kintyre" (Capitol 4504; peaks at #33)

Wednesday 16 – *Close Encounters of the Third Kind* opens

Sunday 20 – George writes "Faster"

December 1977

Topping the US singles chart:
"You Light Up My Life" by Debbie Boone
"How Deep Is Your Love" by the Bee Gees

On the airwaves:
"Come Sail Away" by Styx
"We're All Alone" by Rita Coolidge

"It's So Easy" by Linda Ronstadt

Topping the US album chart:
Simple Dreams by Linda Ronstadt

Albums released this month include:
Running On Empty by Jackson Browne
Don Juan's Reckless Daughter by Joni Mitchell
Draw The Line by Aerosmith

December – *Linda's Pictures* is published

Friday 9 – Ringo's *Scouse The Mouse* album is issued in Britain

Friday 9 – Wings' "Mull of Kintyre" video airs on *Midnight Special* in the US

Saturday 10 – Wings tapes a live performance of "Mull of Kintyre" to air on the *Mike Yarwood In Persons* show

Wednesday 14 – *Saturday Night Fever* opens in theaters
Thursday 15 – The Who are filmed performing at Gaumont State Cinema in Kilburn for the documentary, *The Kids Are Alright*

Saturday 17 – One millionth copy of "Mull of Kintyre" is sold in Britain

Saturday 17 – Elvis Costello is banned from *Saturday Night Live* after going musically off-script

Sunday 25 – Wings appears on *Mike Yarwood In Persons* show before an estimated audience of 21.4 million viewers

Sunday 25 – Film legend Charlie Chaplin dies at 88

January 1978

Topping the US singles chart:
"How Deep Is Your Love" by the Bee Gees
"Baby Come Back" by Player

On the airwaves:

"We Will Rock You"/"We Are The Champions" by Queen
"Here You Come Again" by Dolly Parton
"Isn't It Time" by The Babys

Topping the US album chart:
Rumours by Fleetwood Mac

Albums released this month include:
City To City by Gerry Rafferty

Weekend in L.A. by George Benson
Excitable Boy by Warren Zevon
Infinity by Journey

Saturday 14 – Wings studio footage shot in October showing them at work on *London Town* airs in the UK on *The South Bank Show*

Saturday 14 – The Sex Pistols implode at a gig in San Francisco

Monday 23 – Sessions for *London Town* come to an end; it is the longest in-the-making project of Wings' career

Monday 23 – Chicago guitarist Terry Kath dies from an accidental shooting at 31

Wednesday 25 – George appears on an episode of *This Is Your Life* honoring Formula One driver Barry Sheene

February 1978

Topping the US singles chart:
"Stayin' Alive" by the Bee Gees

On the airwaves:
"Short People" by Randy Newman
"Slip Slidin' Away" by Paul Simon
"Just The Way You Are" by Billy Joel

Topping the US album chart:
Saturday Night Fever (original soundtrack)

Albums released this month include:
Earth by Jefferson Starship
Van Halen's self-titled debut

Wednesday 1 – Film director Roman Polanski skips bail and flees to France to avoid sentencing for statutory rape

Saturday 11 – Shooting begins in Hollywood on Ringo's upcoming television special

Sunday 19 – An installment of Tony Palmer's 17-part documentary on popular music, *All You Need Is Love*, focusing on The Beatles ("Mighty Good") airs on US PBS stations

Wednesday 22 – Shooting wraps on Ringo's television special

March 1978

Topping the US singles chart:
"(Love Is) Thicker Than Water" by Andy Gibb
"Night Fever" by the Bee Gees

On the airwaves:
"Baby Come Back" by Player
"Sometimes When We Touch" by Dan Hill
"Emotion" by Samantha Sang
Topping the US album chart:
Saturday Night Fever (original soundtrack)

Albums released this month include:
Waiting For Columbus by Little Feat
You Can Tune A Piano But You Can't Tuna Fish by REO Speedwagon
Champagne Jam by Atlanta Rhythm Section
Easter by Patti Smith Group

March – Sessions begin for the *George Harrison* album at F.P.S.H.O.T.

March – Drummer Steve Holley is asked to join Wings

Wednesday 1 – Charlie Chaplin's corpse is stolen and held for ransom

Friday 3 – *Sextette*, starring Mae West and featuring Ringo and Keith Moon, opens in theaters

Monday 6 – *Hustler* publisher Larry Flynt shot and left paralyzed

Tuesday 21 – Paul and Linda appear on the cover of *Us*

Tuesday 21 – Wings films a video for "London Town," featuring a cameo by actor Victor Spinetti

Wednesday 22 – Wings hosts members of the press on a boat sailing on the Thames in London to promote the upcoming *London Town* release

Wednesday 22 – *The Rutles: All You Need Is Cash* airs on NBC

Wednesday 22 – High-wire aerialist Karl Wallenda dies after a fall in Puerto Rico

Friday 24 – "With A Little Luck"/"Backwards Traveler-Cuff Link" (Capitol 4559; peaks at #1 for two weeks in May)
Wednesday 29 – Ringo tapes an appearance on the *Phil Donahue Show*

Friday 31 – *London Town* (peaks at number two)

April 1978

Topping the US singles chart:
"Night Fever" by the Bee Gees

On the airwaves:
"Lay Down Sally" by Eric Clapton
"Thunder Island" by Jay Ferguson
"Jack and Jill" by Raydio

Topping the US album chart:
Saturday Night Fever (original soundtrack)

Albums released this month include:
The Kick Inside by Kate Bush
Pure Pop For Now People by Nick Lowe
Shadow Dancing by Andy Gibb
...And Then There Were Three by Genesis
Grease (original motion picture soundtrack)

Monday 3 – British Big Band-era composer/bandleader Ray Noble dies at 74

Tuesday 11 – Back home after much traveling, George begins recording "Flying Hour," a song that would go unreleased on a

George Harrison album

Monday 17 – Ringo's appearance on the *Phil Donahue Show* airs

Monday 17 – Ringo guests on *The Mike Douglas Show*

Monday 17 – "Lipstick Traces (On A Cigarette)"/"Old Time Relovin'" (Portrait 6-70015; dnc)

Monday 17 – *Bad Boy* (peaks at one hundred twenty-nine)

Thursday 20 – *FM* opens in theaters

Friday 21 – *I Wanna Hold Your Hand* opens in theaters

Friday 21 – Singer Sandy Denny ("Who Knows Where The Time Goes") dies at 31 from injuries sustained in a fall

Saturday 22 – The Blues Brothers debut on *Saturday Night Live*

Tuesday 25 – Ringo is interviewed in New York by Connie Collins for WNBC

Wednesday 26 – The *Ringo* television special airs

May 1978

Topping the US singles chart:
"If I Can't Have You" by Yvonne Elliman
"With A Little Luck" by Wings

On the airwaves:
"Dust In the Wind" by
Kansas
"Running On Empty" by Jackson Browne
"Closer I Get To You" by Roberta Flack and Donny Hathaway

Topping the US album chart:
Saturday Night Fever (original soundtrack)

Albums released this month include:

Heaven Tonight by Cheap Trick
This Year's Model by Elvis Costello
Stranger In Town by Bob Seger
David Gilmour's self-titled solo debut
Misfits by The Kinks

May – Harold Harrison, George's father, dies

Friday 5 – Laurence Juber's first session with Wings, on the "Same Time Next Year" recording date

Sunday 7 – George attends the Monaco Grand Prix in Monte Carlo

Wednesday 17 – Charlie Chaplin's stolen body is recovered

Thursday 25 – Paul and Linda appear on the cover of *Circus*

Thursday 25 – The Who play their final gig with Keith Moon at Shepperton Film Studios for the documentary, *The Kids Are Alright*

June 1978

Topping the US singles chart:
"Too Much, Too Little Too Late" by Johnny Mathis and Deniece Williams
"You're The One The One That I Want" by John Travolta and Olivia Newton-John

On the airwaves:
"Imaginary Lover" by Atlanta Rhythm Section
"Feels So Good" by Chuck Mangione

"On Broadway" by George Benson

Topping the US album chart:
Saturday Night Fever (original soundtrack)

Albums released this month include:
The Cars' self-titled debut
Peter Gabriel's self-titled second album
Darkness on the Edge of Town by Bruce Springsteen and the E Street Band
Some Girls by the Rolling Stones

June – Mark Shipper's *Paperback Writer: The Life and Times of the Beatles*, is published

Sunday 11 – Cynthia Lennon's upcoming memoir is serialized in *The News of the World* in Britain, prompting John to file an injunction against its publication

Monday 12 – "I've Had Enough"/"Deliver Your Children" (Capitol 4594; peaks at #25)

Friday 16 – A London court finds John's action is without merit

Friday 16 – *Grease* opens in theaters

Thursday 29 – *Back to the Egg* sessions begin this day at Paul's Spirit of Ranachan studio in Scotland; this phase concludes a month later

Thursday 29 – Cynthia Lennon's memoir, *A Twist of Lennon*, is published in the UK

Thursday 29 – TV actor Bob Crane, 49, is murdered

July 1978

Topping the US singles chart:
"Shadow Dancing" by Andy Gibb
On the airwaves:
"Baker Street" by Gerry Rafferty
"Just What I Needed" by The Cars
"It's A Heartache" by Bonnie Tyler

Topping the US album chart:
Saturday Night Fever (original soundtrack)

Albums released this month include:
More Songs About Buildings and Food by Talking Heads
Nightwatch by Kenny Loggins
Sgt. Pepper's Lonely Hearts Club Band (original motion picture soundtrack)

July – Ringo films a promo film in France with Nancy Andrews for "Tonight"

Monday 3 – "Heart On My Sleeve"/"Who Needs A Heart" (Portrait 6-70018; dnc)

Sunday 16 – Racing sounds taped on this day's British Grand Prix are later used on George's "Faster"

Friday 21 – *Sgt. Pepper's Lonely Hearts Club Band* opens in theaters

Saturday 22 – On this day and the next, Ringo begins laying down tracks at a Copenhagen studio for a follow-up to *Bad Boy*; the four songs cut go unreleased

August 1978

Topping the US singles chart:
"Miss You" by the Rolling Stones
"Three Times A Lady" by The Commodores

On the airwaves:
"Last Dance" by Donna Summer
"Take A Chance On Me" by ABBA
"Copacabana" by Barry Manilow

Topping the US album chart:
Grease (original motion picture soundtrack)

Albums released this month include:
Who Are You by The Who
Q: Are We Not Men? A: We Are Devo!
C'est Chic
Don't Look Back by Boston

Tuesday 1 – Dhani Harrison born

Wednesday 2 – State of Emergency declared in New York's Love
Canal neighborhood, prompting the evacuation of residents
Monday 14 – "London Town"/"I'm Carrying" (Capitol 4625; peaks at
#39)

Monday 14 – "Sgt. Pepper's Lonely Hearts Club Band/With A Little
Help"/"A Day In The Life" (Capitol 4612; peaks at #71)

Tuesday 15 – *Sgt. Pepper* picture disc plus colored vinyl editions of
1962-1966 (the Red album), *1967-1970* (the Blue Album) and *The
Beatles* (the White Album)

September 1978

Topping the US singles chart:
"Grease" by Frankie Valli
"Boogie Oogie Oogie" by A Taste of Honey

On the airwaves:
"Love Will Find A Way" by Pablo Cruise
"Hot Blooded" by Foreigner
"Hopelessly Devoted To You" by Olivia Newton-John

Topping the US album chart:
Grease (original motion picture soundtrack)

Albums released this month include:
Parallel Lines
by Blondie
Pieces of Eight by Styx
Dog and Butterfly by Heart

The Bride Stripped Bare by Bryan Ferry
Bloody Tourists by 10cc
September – Wings appears on the cover of this month's *Song Hits*

Saturday 2 – George marries Olivia Arias

Wednesday 6 – Paul and Linda host their annual Buddy Holly party at Peppermint Park in London; attendees include David Frost, Micky Dolenz, and Keith Moon

Thursday 7 – Keith Moon, 32, dies from an accidental overdose of prescription medication

Monday 11 – Beginning this day and running through the end of the month, Wings resumes *Back to the Egg* sessions at Lympne Castle in Kent

Saturday 16 – *Life of Brian* begins filming in Tunisia

Sunday 17 – The Camp David Accords are signed between Israeli President Menachem Begin and Egyptian President Anwar El Sadat at the White House

Friday 29 – Wings' "With a Little Luck" and "I've Had Enough" videos air on *Midnight Special*

October 1978

Topping the US singles chart:
"Kiss You All Over" by Exile
"Hot Child In The City" by Nick Gilder

On the airwaves:
"Magnet and Steel" by Walter Egan
"Macho Man" by the Village People
"Life's Been Good" by Joe Walsh

Topping the US album chart:
Don't Look Back by Boston

Albums released this month include:
52ⁿᵈ Street by Billy Joel
Comes A Time by Neil Young
Toto's self-titled debut
Dire Straits' self-titled debut

Tuesday 3 – The Beatles appear on the cover of *Circus*

Tuesday 3 – The "Rockestra" session for *Back to the Egg* takes place at EMI's Abbey Road studio

Friday 6 – Ringo is interviewed in Hollywood for the short-lived *Everyday* TV show

Thursday 12 – Sid Vicious' girlfriend Nancy Spungen, 20, is stabbed to death at New York's Chelsea Hotel; Vicious is charged

Friday 20 – In Tunisia to visit the set of *Life of Brian*, George is pulled into the production for a bit part as "Mr. Papadopoulos"

Tuesday 24 – The animated promo clip for Linda's "Oriental Nightfish" airs in Britain on the *Old Grey Whistle Test*

Friday 27 – Wings' "London Town" video shown on *Midnight Special*

November 1978

Topping the US singles chart:
"You Needed Me" by Anne Murray
"MacArthur Park" by Donna Summer

On the airwaves:
"Who Are You" by The Who
"Summer Nights" by Cast of Grease
"Reminiscing" by Little River Band

Topping the US album chart:
Living In The USA by Linda Ronstadt
Albums released this month include:
Bush Doctor by Peter Tosh
Move It On Over by George Thorogood and The Destroyers

Blondes Have More Fun by Rod Stewart
The Gambler by Kenny Rogers
Outlandos d'Amour by the Police

Friday 17 – The *Star Wars Holiday Special* airs on CBS

Saturday 18 – The Jonestown Massacre in Guyana leaves 918 dead by coerced suicide

Wednesday 22 – *Wings Greatest* (peaks at twenty-nine)

December 1978

Topping the US singles chart:
"You Don't Bring Me Flowers" by Barbra Streisand and Neil Diamond
"Le Freak" by Chic

On the airwaves:
"How Much I Feel" by Ambrosia
"Whenever I Call You Friend" by Kenny Loggins
"Double Vision" by Foreigner

Topping the US album chart:
52nd Street by Billy Joel

Albums released this month include:
Minute By Minute by the Doobie Brothers
Destiny by The Jacksons

Friday 1 – *The Beatles Collection* box set

Thursday 7 – George performs "Further On Up The Road" with Eric Clapton and Elton John at Civic Hall in Guilford, England

Friday 22 – Serial killer John Wayne Gacy arrested

Wednesday 27 – (Early morning hours) Chris Bell of Big Star dies in a car accident at 27

January 1979

Topping the US singles chart:
"Too Much Heaven" by the Bee Gees
"Le Freak" by Chic

On the airwaves:
"Time Passages" by Al Stewart
"YMCA" by the Village People
"My Life" by Billy Joel

Topping the US album chart:
Barbra Streisand's Greatest Hits Volume 2

Albums released this month include:
Armed Forces by Elvis Costello
Spirits Having Flown by the Bee Gees
Strangers In The Night by UFO

January – The Lennons travel to Egypt

Friday 5 – Jazz bassist/composer Charles Mingus dies at 56

Saturday 6 – George attends Formula One race at Donington Park Racetrack

Saturday 13 – Singer Donny Hathaway ("Where is The Love?") ends his life at 33

Wednesday 24 – The 1962 Star-Club tapes are re-issued in two separate volumes by Pickwick as *1st Live Recordings*

Monday 29 – School shooting in San Diego kills two and prompts the song "I Don't Like Mondays" by the Boomtown Rats

Wednesday 31 – The Harrison's fly with Gary Wright to Rio de Janeiro to attend the Brazilian Grand Prix

February 1979

Topping the US singles chart:
"Shadow Dancing" by Andy Gibb
"Do Ya Think I'm Sexy" by Rod Stewart

On the airwaves:
"Hold The Line" by Toto
"A Little More Love" by Olivia Newton-John
"September" by Earth, Wind and Fire

Topping the US album chart:
Briefcase Full of Blues by the Blues Brothers

Albums released this month include:
Alive On Arrival by Steve Forbert
Three Hearts by Bob Welch
Mirror Stars by the Fabulous Poodles
Cheap Trick at Budokan

Friday 2 – Sid Vicious, freed on bail, overdoses on heroin at 21

Wednesday 7 – George is interviewed on Brazilian TV, plays a few bars of "Something" on guitar

Sunday 11 – The made-for-TV biopic, *Elvis!*, airs on ABC

Monday 19 – After returning home following a radio interview to promote his upcoming album, George is injured when the brakes fail on his tractor, tossing him to the ground and running over his foot

Monday 19 – "Blow Away"/"Soft-Hearted Hana" (Dark Horse 8763; peaks at #16)

Monday 19 – Fred Seaman begins working for the Lennons

Tuesday 20 – *George Harrison* (peaks at number fourteen)

February – George films a video for "Blow Away," directed by Neil Innes

March 1979

Topping the US singles chart:
"I Will Survive" by Gloria Gaynor
"Tragedy" by the Bee Gees

On the airwaves:

"Fire" by Pointer Sisters
"Shake Your Groove Thing" by Peaches and Herb
"Lotta Love" by Nicolette Larson

Topping the US album chart:
Spirits Having Flown by the Bee Gees

Albums released this month include:
Breakfast In America by Supertramp
Manifesto by Roxy Music
Squeezing Out Sparks by Graham Parker and The Rumour
Rickie Lee Jones' self-titled debut
Airwaves by Badfinger

Friday 9 – *Heroes of Rock and Roll* TV special, hosted by Jeff Bridges, airs on ABC

Friday 16 – "Goodnight Tonight"/"Daytime Nighttime Suffering" (Columbia 10939; peaks at #5)

Friday 16 – *Wings Over The World* TV special airs on CBS

Tuesday 27 – Eric Clapton marries Pattie Boyd in Tucson, AZ

Wednesday 28 – An accident occurs at the Three Mile Island nuclear power plant near Harrisburg, Pennsylvania

Friday 30 – Ravi Shankar's daughter Norah Jones born

April 1979

Topping the US singles chart:
"What A Fool Believes" by the Doobie Brothers
"Knock On Wood" by Amii Stewart
"Heart of Glass" by Blondie

On the airwaves:
"Music Box Dancer" by Frank Mills
"Heaven Knows" by Donna Summer
"Sultans of Swing" by Dire Straits

Topping the US album chart:

Minute by Minute by the Doobie Brothers

Albums released this month include:
Look Sharp! By Joe Jackson
Evolution by Journey
Black Rose by Thin Lizzie

Sunday 1 – Julian joins John, Yoko, Sean and three of Yoko's nieces for a week-long vacation in Palm Beach. It will be the last time Julian sees his father

Tuesday 3 – Wings films "Goodnight Tonight" video(s)

Friday 6 – George's promo for "Blow Away" is shown on *Midnight Special*

Thursday 19 – *Top of the Pops* airs one of the "Goodnight Tonight" clips

Sunday 22 – The New Barbarians, featuring Keith Richards and Ronnie Wood, perform along with the Rolling Stones at a benefit for the blind in Canada to fulfill Keith's sentence for drug offenses

Friday 27 – Allen Klein is found guilty of tax evasion

Saturday 28 – Ringo is rushed to a Monte Carlo hospital for emergency surgery, following an attack of peritonitis

May 1979

Topping the US singles chart:
"Reunited" by Peaches and Herb

On the airwaves:
"Shake Your Body" by The Jacksons
"Stumblin' In" by Suzi Quatro and Chris Norman
"Lady" by the Little River Band

Topping the US album chart:
Minute by Minute by the Doobie Brothers

Albums released this month include:
Mick Taylor's self-titled solo debut
Lodger by David Bowie
Wave by Patti Smith Group
Minnie by Minnie Riperton
Discovery by Electric Light Orchestra

Friday 4 – The re-formed Badfinger appear on *Midnight Special*, performing "Look Out California," "The Winner," and "Love Is Gonna Come At Last"

Monday 14 – "Love Comes To Everyone"/"Soft Touch" (Dark Horse 8844; dnc)

Saturday 19 – Paul, Ringo and George perform together at the wedding celebration for Eric Clapton and Pattie Boyd at Hurtwood Edge, Surrey

Saturday 19 – Badfinger appears on *American Bandstand*, performing "Look Out California" and "Love Is Gonna Come At Last"

Friday 25 – American Airlines flight 191 crashes at Chicago's O'Hare airport, killing all 271 onboard plus 2 on the ground

Saturday 26 – George and Ringo, attending the Grand Prix in Monaco, are interviewed on ABC's *Wide World of Sports*

Sunday 27 – "A Love Letter From John And Yoko To People Who Ask Us What, When And Why" is published in the *New York Times*

Monday 28 – Wings films the "Old Siam, Sir" video at Lympne Castle

Monday 28 – In Monte Carlo to attend the Monaco Grand Prix, George persuades racer Jackie Stewart to make a cameo in his video for "Faster"

Tuesday 29 – Wings films the "Getting Closer" and "Again and Again and Again" videos in Lympne

Tuesday 29 – Ringo visits John at the Dakota; the two are

photographed together by Fred Seaman

Tuesday 29 – Federal Judge John H. Wood Jr. is assassinated outside his San Antonio home by the father of actor Woody Harrelson

Wednesday 30 – Wings films the "Winter Rose/Love Awake" video at Lympne Castle

June 1979

Topping the US singles chart:
"Hot Stuff" by Donna Summer
"Love You Inside Out" by the Bee Gees

On the airwaves:
"Renegade" by Styx
"Makin' It" by David Naughton
"The Logical Song" by Supertramp

Topping the US album chart:
Breakfast In America by Supertramp

Albums released this month include:
Candy-O by The Cars
First Under The Wire by Little River Band
Labour of Lust by Nick Lowe
Repeat When Necessary by Dave Edmunds
Get The Knack

Friday 1 – Wings films the "Baby's Request" video at Camber Sands, Kent

Saturday 2 – George is filmed giving a Formula One car a spin at Donington

Monday 4 – "Getting Closer"/"Spin It On" (Columbia 11020; peaks at # 20)

Wednesday 6 – Wings films the "Arrow Through Me" video

Friday 8 – On *Midnight Special*, Ringo drums behind Ron Wood on

"Buried Alive"

Monday 11 – Wings launches *Back to the Egg* with an elaborate press event held at EMI's Abbey Road facilities in Studio Two

Monday 11 – *Back to the Egg* (peaks at number eight)

Monday 11 – Actor John Wayne dies of cancer at 72

Friday 29 – Little Feat's Lowell George dies from drug-induced heart failure at 34

July 1979

Topping the US singles chart:
"Ring My Bell" by Amii Stewart
"Bad Girls" by Donna Summer

On the airwaves:
"You Take My Breath Away" by Rex Smith
"I Want You To Want Me" by Cheap Trick
"Chuck E's In Love" by Rickie Lee Jones

Topping the US album chart:
Bad Girls by Donna Summer

Albums released this month include:
Highway to Hell by AC/DC
The B-52s' self-titled debut
Rust Never Sleeps by Neil Young
July – The Sony *Walkman* is introduced

Friday 6 – Producer/songwriter Van McCoy dies at 39

Thursday 12 – Paul appears on the cover of *Rolling Stone*

Thursday 12 – "Disco Demolition" at Chicago's White Sox Park

Thursday 12 – Minnie Riperton ("Loving You") dies of cancer at 31

Friday 13 – George is filmed at the racetrack in Silverstone for ABC's

August 1979

Topping the US singles chart:
"Bad Girls" by Donna Summer
"Good Times" by Chic
On the airwaves:
"She Believes In Me" by Kenny Rogers
"Rock & Roll Fantasy" by Bad Company
"Gold" by John Stewart

Topping the US album chart:
Bad Girls by Donna Summer

Albums released this month include:
Off The Wall by Michael Jackson
Fear Of Music by Talking Heads
In Through The Out Door by Led Zeppelin
Degüello by ZZ Top
Slow Train Coming by Bob Dylan

August – George appears on the cover of this month's *Song Hits*

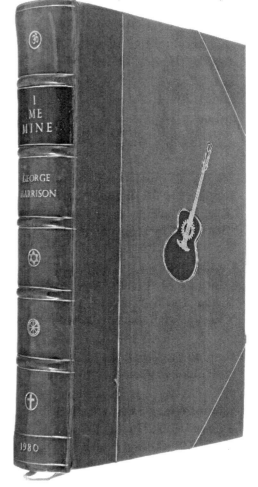

Monday 13 – "Arrow Through Me"/"Old Siam, Sir" (Columbia 11070; peaks at #29)

Wednesday 15 – *Apocalypse Now* opens in theaters

Friday 17 – *Life of Brian* opens in theaters

Sunday 19 – Rockabilly singer Dorsey Burnette ("Train Kept-a Rollin'") dies at 46

Wednesday 22 – George's *I Me Mine* book published in a limited edition by Genesis

Saturday 25 – Big Band-era singer Ray Eberle dies at 60

Monday 27 – British Lord Louis Mountbatten, 79, is assassinated by the IRA

September 1979

Topping the US singles chart:
"My Sharona" by The Knack

On the airwaves:
"The Main Event/Fight" by Barbra Streisand
"Let's Go" by The Cars
"The Devil Went Down To Georgia" by the Charlie Daniels Band

Topping the US album chart:
Get The Knack

Albums released this month include:
Dream Police by Cheap Trick
Low Budget by The Kinks
The Long Run by Eagles
Joe's Garage, Act I by Frank Zappa

Monday 3 – Ringo makes an appearance at the annual *Jerry Lewis Muscular Dystrophy* telethon, participating in an all-star jam with Bill Wyman and Todd Rundgren, among others

Wednesday 5 – John begins recording an oral diary

Friday 7 – ESPN launches

Monday 10 – Paul appears (alongside other stars of the day) on the cover of *People*

Friday 14 – Paul and Denny Laine appear separately onstage at London's Hammersmith Odeon as part of television documentary, *The Music Lives On*, celebrating Buddy Holly

Friday 21 – The four ex-Beatles are asked by UN Secretary-General

Kurt Waldheim to consider reuniting for a benefit to aid Vietnamese boat people

Friday 21 – The No Nukes benefit concert is held in New York, featuring performers including James Taylor, Bonnie Raitt, Gil Scott-Heron and Bruce Springsteen

Thursday 27 – In New York, lawyers representing the Beatles file suit against the producers of *Beatlemania*

Thursday 27 – Jimmy McCulloch dies at 26 of drug-related heart failure

October 1979

Topping the US singles chart:
"Sad Eyes" by Robert John
"Don't Stop 'Til You Get Enough" by Michael Jackson
"Rise" by Herb Alpert

On the airwaves:
"Is She Really Going Out With Him?" by Joe Jackson
"When You're In Love With A Beautiful Woman" by Dr. Hook
"You Can't Change That" by Raydio

Topping the US album chart:
In Through The Out Door by Led Zeppelin

Albums released this month include:
Damn The Torpedoes by Tom Petty and the Heartbreakers
Eat To The Beat by Blondie
Jackrabbit Slim by Steve Forbert
Broken English by Marianne Faithfull
Prince's self-titled debut

October – The Beatles appear on the cover of this month's *High Times*

Wednesday 24 – In an elaborate ceremony, Paul is honored by the publishers of *The Guinness Book of Records* as "the most successful composer and recording artist of all time" and presented with a rhodium-plated disc to commemorate the achievement

November 1979

Topping the US singles chart:
"Pop Muzik" by M
"Heartache Tonight" by Eagles
"Still" by Commodores
"No More Tears (Enough Is Enough)" by Barbra Streisand and Donna Summer

On the airwaves:
"Don't Bring Me Down" by Electric Light Orchestra
"Tusk" by Fleetwood Mac
"Goodbye Stranger" by Supertramp

Topping the US album chart:
The Long Run by Eagles

Albums released this month include:
Drums and Wires by XTC
No Nukes by various artists
Live Rust by Neil Young
Present Tense by Shoes

Thursday 1 – Paul and Linda interviewed by Geraldo Rivera for a segment of *20/20*

Friday 2 – The Who's *Quadrophenia* opens in theaters

Sunday 4 – Iranian radicals seize the US embassy in Tehran and take 53 American hostages

Monday 5 – Cartoonist/conservative commentator Al Capp dies at 70

Friday 9 – *The Rose* opens in theaters

Monday 12 – John signs his will
Friday 16 – Wings films a promo for "Wonderful Christmastime" at a pub, The Fountain, in West Sussex

Friday 23 – *Birth of the Beatles* made-for-TV biopic airs on ABC

Friday 23 – Wings commences what will be their final tour, playing 19 dates throughout the UK

Monday 26 – "Wonderful Christmastime"/"Rudolph the Red-Nosed Reggae" (Columbia 11162; dnc)

Wednesday 28 – Ringo's rented Los Angeles home burns

Late November – 4 year-old Sean Lennon is recorded singing "With A Little Help"

December 1979

Topping the US singles chart:
"Babe" by Styx
"Escape (The Piña Colada Song)" by Rupert Holmes

On the airwaves:
"Babe" by Styx
"Dream Police" by Cheap Trick
"Lovin' Touchin' Squeezin'" by Journey

Topping the US album chart:
The Long Run by Eagles

Albums released this month include:
The Wall by Pink Floyd

Monday 3 – Eleven Who fans die following a stampede at Cincinnati's Riverfront Stadium

Wednesday 5 – Paul and Linda are interviewed by Tom Snyder backstage at the Rainbow Theatre in London

Friday 7 – At a Wembley news conference, Paul and Linda held a news conference announcing the Kampuchea benefit at month's end

Thursday 13 – Paul's "Wonderful Christmastime" promo airs on *Top of the Pops*

Monday 17 – Glasgow, Scotland – last show of the tour: Paul rolls tape for a possible live release; their performance of "Coming Up," an as-yet unreleased song showcased live, will be issued as a single in the US

Thursday 20 – The Tom Snyder interview with Paul and Linda airs on *Tomorrow*

Monday 24 – The Soviet Union invades Afghanistan

Wednesday 26 – Queen kicks off the four-night Concerts for the People of Kampuchea benefit, held at London's Hammersmith Odeon theatre

Thursday 27 – Ian Dury and the Blockheads, Matumbi and The Clash perform on the second night

Friday 28 – *Abbey Road* is issued by Mobile Fidelity Sound Lab as a "half-speed master"

Friday 28 – The Pretenders, The Specials and The Who perform on the third night

Saturday 29 – After opening sets from Elvis Costello and the Attractions and Rockpile, Wings headline the final show, which ends with the "Rockestra"

Monday 31 – John sees in the New Year with Elliot Mintz at "Club Dakota"

January 1980

Topping the US singles chart:
"Please Don't Go" by KC and the Sunshine Band
"Escape (The Piña Colada Song)" by Rupert Holmes

On the airwaves:
"We Don't Talk Anymore" by Cliff Richard
"Bad Case of Lovin' You" by Robert Palmer
"Send One Your Love" by Stevie Wonder

Topping the US album chart:
On The Radio: Greatest Hits Volumes 1&2 by Donna Summer

Albums released this month include:
Love Stinks by J. Geils Band

London Calling by The Clash
Adventures in Utopia
The Romantics' self-titled debut
The Pretenders' self-titled debut

Monday 7 – Larry Williams ("Slow Down," "Bad Boy") dies of a gunshot wound at 44

Sunday 13 – Paul and family arrive in New York en route to Japan

Monday 14 – Paul attempts to reach John but is blocked by Yoko

Wednesday 16 – Paul is arrested in Tokyo upon arrival for possession of a half-pound of marijuana

Friday 25 – Paul is released from an Tokyo jail and escorted out of the country

Wednesday 30 – In the UK, George Martin is honored on *This Is Your Life*; Paul is seen (on tape) after George declined to get involved

Wednesday 30 – New Orleans piano legend Professor Longhair dies at 61

February 1980

Topping the US singles chart:
"Rock With You" by Michael Jackson
"Do That To Me One More Time" by the Captain and Tennille

On the airwaves:
"Coward of the County" by Kenny Rogers
"Yes I'm Ready" by Teri De Sario and KC
"Cruisin'" by Smokey Robinson

Topping the US album chart:
The Wall by Pink Floyd
Albums released this month include:
Mad Love by Linda Ronstadt
The Rose by Bette Midler
Get Happy!! By Elvis Costello
Willie Nile's self-titled debut

Argybargy by Squeeze

Sunday 17 – Upon his arrival in Mexico to begin filming *Caveman*, Ringo is strip-searched

Monday 18 – Shooting begins on *Caveman*, starring Ringo, Dennis Quaid, Shelly Long and Barbara Bach

Tuesday 19 – AC/DC singer Bon Scott dies of alcohol poisoning at 33

Friday 22 – The US Men's Hockey team beats the Soviets in the "Miracle on Ice" at the Winter Olympics

Tuesday 26 – "Another Day," U2's first single, is issued

Wednesday 27 – In London, Paul is awarded the "Outstanding Music Personality of 1979" award   by the *Daily Mirror*

Wednesday 27 – At this year's Grammys, "Rockestra Theme" garners an award for "Best Rock Instrumental Performance"

March 1980

Topping the US singles chart:
"Crazy Little Thing Called Love" by Queen

On the airwaves:
"Longer" by Dan Fogelberg
"Workin' My Way Back To You" by Spinners
"On The Radio" by Donna Summer

Topping the US album chart:
The Wall by Pink Floyd

Albums released this month include:
Sacred Songs by Darryl Hall
Duke by Genesis
Let's Get Serious by Jermaine Jackson
Departure by Journey
Glass House by Billy Joel

Monday 10 – *Scarsdale Diet* doctor Herman Tarnower is shot and killed by Jean Harris

Friday 21 – The character of J.R. Ewing is shot on the TV drama *Dallas*

Monday 24 – *The Beatles Rarities* (peaks at number twenty-one)

Wednesday 26 – On this day and the next, Paul and Linda work on an elaborate video shoot for "Coming Up" that sees the two take on multiple roles

Saturday 29 – Pop symphony conductor Mantovani dies at 74

Monday 31 – An article centering on Ringo runs in London's *Daily Mirror*, accompanied by a recent photo of John sporting an *Abbey Road*-sized beard

April 1980

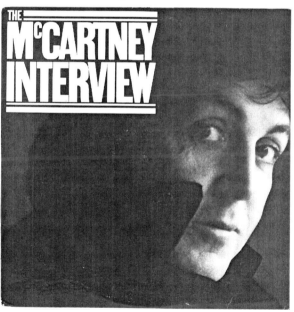

Topping the US singles chart:
"Another Brick In The Wall (Part 2)" by Pink Floyd

On the airwaves:
"With You I'm Born Again" by Billy Preston and Syreeta Wright

"Too Hot" by Kool and the Gang
"Ride Like The Wind" by Christopher Cross
Topping the US album chart:
The Wall by Pink Floyd

Albums released this month include:
Empty Glass by Pete Townshend
Los Angeles by X
British Steel by Judas Priest

April – Paul is interviewed by Vic Garbarini for *Musician* magazine at MPL's Soho office; excerpts would later be issued as a limited edition LP

Friday 4 – Country music singer Red Sovine ("Teddy Bear") dies at 64

Thursday 10 – Ten years after the Beatles split up: George is recording *Somewhere in England*; Ringo is filming *Caveman*; Paul is completing work on the video to his next single, and John is professionally inactive

Friday 11 – Beginning on this day, John, Yoko and Sean are videotaped at their Cold Spring Harbor home; John sings "Dear Yoko" to the camera

Monday 14 – "Coming Up"/"Coming Up (Live in Glasgow)"/"Lunch Box – Odd Sox" (Columbia 11263; the live version peaks at #1 for three weeks in June/July)

Sunday 20 – After extensive home movies were shot on this day at their Cold Spring Harbor home, John begins a ten day vow of silence

Monday 28 – Marshall Tucker band bassist Tommy Caldwell dies in an automobile accident at 30

Tuesday 29 – Director Alfred Hitchcock dies at 80

Wednesday 30 – Upon ending his vow of silence, John shaves off his heavy beard; he will remain more or less clean-shaven for the remainder of his life
Wednesday 30 – Roger Daltrey's film, *McVicar*, opens in London

May 1980

Topping the US singles chart:
"Call Me" by Blondie

On the airwaves:
"Don't Fall In Love With A Dreamer" by Kenny Rogers and Kim Carnes
"Lost In Love" by Air Supply
"Brass In Pocket" by The Pretenders

Topping the US album chart:
Against The Wind by Bob Seger

Albums released this month include:
Peter Gabriel's self-titled third album
The Up Escalator by Graham Parker
Unmasked by Kiss

Friday 2 – Denny Laine's "Japanese Tears" single is issued in the UK

Saturday 17 – Paul and Linda appear on *Saturday Night Live*, interviewed by "Father Guido Sarducci" at dawn before screening the "Coming Up" video

Sunday 18 – Joy Division singer Ian Curtis, 23, commits suicide

Sunday 18 – John, Sean and Fred Seaman leave Cold Spring Harbor and return to The Dakota

Monday 19 – (Early morning hours) Following a party, Ringo rolls his Mercedes with Barbara Bach as his passenger, narrowly escaping serious injury

Monday 19 – Paul schedules a full day of promotional interviews for *McCartney II*, including a Q&A with lyricist Tim Rice

Tuesday 20 – Paul is interviewed by the BBC's Andy Peebles

Tuesday 20 – On a flight to Los Angeles, Ringo proposes to Barbara Bach and she accepts

Wednesday 21 – *The Empire Strikes Back* (Star Wars Episode V) opens

Monday 26 – *McCartney II* (peaks at number three)

Monday 26 – John is in Cape Town, South Africa; while here, he talks to May Pang by phone for the last time and is photographed by a fellow passenger on board the plane taking him back to New York

Friday 30 – Bassist Carl Radle (Delaney and Bonnie, Derek and the Dominos) dies of kidney failure at 37

June 1980

Topping the US singles chart:
"Funky Town" by Lipps Inc

On the airwaves:
"The Rose" by Bette Midler
"Against The Wind" by Bob Seger
"Biggest Part Of Me" by Ambrosia

Topping the US album chart:
Against The Wind by Bob Seger

Albums released this month include:
Flesh + Blood by Roxy Music
Saved by Bob Dylan
One For The Road by The Kinks
The Game by Queen
Emotional Rescue by the Rolling Stones

Sunday 1 – CNN launches

Wednesday 4 – John sets sail from Newport, Rhode Island aboard the Megan Jaye for Bermuda

Thursday 12 – Having endured a three-day storm at sea, during which time John was forced to take the wheel, the Megan Jaye arrives safely in Bermuda

Monday 16 – Sean and Fred Seaman arrive in Bermuda

Monday 16 – Ringo and Barbara Bach tape an appearance on the *John Davidson Show*; Ringo is, by some accounts, drunk

Saturday 21 – Bert Kaempfert, producer of the Beatles' Tony Sheridan sessions, dies at 56

Monday 23 – While John is demoing new material in Bermuda, agents working on behalf of the Lennons sell a Holstein pedigree dairy cow (named Daisy) for a record-breaking $265,000

Friday 27 – John records the "fast" version of "Serve Yourself" in Bermuda

July 1980

Topping the US singles chart:
"Coming Up (Live in Glasgow)" by Paul McCartney
"It's Still Rock and Roll To Me" by Billy Joel

On the airwaves:
"Little Jeannie" by Elton John
"Steal Away" by Robbie Dupree
"Tired of Toein' The Line" by Rocky Burnette

Topping the US album chart:
Glass Houses by Billy Joel

Albums released this month include:
Back In Black by AC/DC
Freedom of Choice by Devo
Full Moon by the Charlie Daniels Band
Voices by Darryl Hall & John Oates
Saturday 5 – Bjorn Borg defeats John McEnroe 8-6 at Wimbledon in the Men's Singles championship

Monday 7 – Ringo turns 40

Monday 7 – An on-set interview of Ringo and Barbara Bach during the filming of Caveman airs on the *John Davidson Show*

Friday 11 – Ringo begins laying down tracks for a new album at a

Paris studio, with help from Paul, Linda and Laurence Juber; sessions finish on the 21st

Wednesday 16 – While in France with Ringo, Wings lays down the backing of Linda's "Love's Full Glory," later released posthumously on *Wide Prairie*

Monday 21 – "Waterfalls"/"Check My Machine" (Columbia 11335; peaks at one hundred and six)

Thursday 24 – Actor Peter Sellers suffers a fatal heart attack at 54

Monday 28 – The Ringo and Barbara Bach interview taped earlier airs on *The John Davidson Show*

Tuesday 29 – John and Sean fly home to New York from Bermuda

Thursday 31 – Yoko contacts producer Jack Douglas, informing him of John's wish that he produce his new album practically immediately; she further confides to Jack that she too will appear on the record

August 1980

Topping the US singles chart:
"Magic" by Olivia Newton-John
"Sailing" by Christopher Cross
On the airwaves:
"Fame" by Irene Cara
"Let My Love Open The Door" by Pete Townshend
"Emotional Rescue" by the Rolling Stones

Topping the US album chart:
Emotional Rescue by the Rolling Stones

Albums released this month include:
Panorama by The Cars
One-Trick Pony by Paul Simon
Wild Planet by The B-52s
Crimes Of Passion by Pat Benatar

August – Paul appears on the cover of this month's *Musician*

August – Wings begins rehearsing material that will appear on Paul's solo *Tug of War* album

Friday 1 – George and partner Denis O'Dell form HandMade Films

Monday 4 – The *Double Fantasy/Milk and Honey* sessions begin at the Hit Factory

Thursday 7 – *Meet Paul McCartney*, a half-hour special promoting *McCartney II*, airs in the UK

Monday 11 – Ringo begins four days of sessions with Stephen Stills in North Hollywood at Devonshire Sound Studios

Tuesday 12 – Drummer Daxx Nielsen, son of Cheap Trick guitarist Rick Nielsen, is born

Tuesday 12 – Rick Nielsen and Cheap Trick drummer Bun E. Carlos record "I'm Losing You" and "Yoko's "I'm Moving On"

Thursday 14 – The basic track for Yoko's "Walking On Thin Ice" is cut

Thursday 14 – *Playboy*

LW	TW	WEEK ENDING JULY 19, 1980	VOL. 20, NO. 40
1	1	Coming Up (4th Week No. 1)	Paul McCartney & Wings
2	2	It's Still Rock & Roll To Me	Billy Joel
3	3	The Rose	Bette Midler
6	4	Steal Away	Robbie Dupree
4	5	Against The Wind	Bob Seger
5	6	Funky Town	Lipps, Inc.
8	7	Misunderstanding	Genesis
11	8	Little Jeannie	Elton John
15	9	Tired Of Toein' The Line	Rocky Burnette
14	10	Gimme Some Lovin'	Blues Brothers
7	11	Lost In Love	Air Supply
12	12	Cars	Gary Numan
10	13	Biggest Part Of Me	Ambrosia
13	14	You May Be Right	Billy Joel
9	15	Brass In Pocket (I'm Special)	The Pretenders
16	16	Call Me	Blondie
20	17	Don't Fall In Love With A Dreamer	Rogers/Carnes
17	18	Love Stinks	J. Geils Band
19	19	Let's Get Serious	Jermaine Jackson
21	20	Let Me Love You Tonight	Pure Prairie League
18	21	Ride Like The Wind	Christopher Cross
24	22	Cupid	Spinners
22	23	Sexy Eyes	Dr. Hook
34	24	Magic	Olivia Newton-John
28	25	It's Hard To Be Humble	Mac Davis
31	26	One Fine Day	Carole King
26	27	Another Brick In The Wall (Part 2)	Pink Floyd
23	28	Train In Vain	Clash
25	29	Hurt So Bad	Linda Ronstadt
32	30	Pilot Of The Airwaves	Charlie Dore
41	31	Take Your Time	S. O. S. Band
35	32	I'm Alive	Electric Light Orchestra
42	33	In America	Charlie Daniels Band
27	34	Rock Lobster	B52's
29	35	Breakdown Dead Ahead	Boz Scaggs
37	36	Stay In Time	Off Broadway
30	37	Fire Lake	Bob Seger
43	38	Landlord	Gladys Knight & The Pips
38	39	Any Way You Want It	Journey
33	40	Two Places At The Same Time	Ray Parker Jr. & Raydio
xx	41	More Love	Kim Carnes
xx	42	All Night Long	Joe Walsh
37	43	Heartbreaker	Pat Benatar
xx	44	Love The World Away	Kenny Rogers
40	45	Heart Hotels	Dan Fogelberg
Extra		Emotional Rescue	Rolling Stones
Extra		Let Me Love Over The Door	Peter Townshend

"Playmate of the Year" Dorothy Stratten, 20, is murdered by her estranged husband

Sunday 17 – Having acquired the rights from United Artists, Capitol reissues *A Hard Day's Night* and *Let It Be*, the latter minus the original gatefold sleeve

Monday 18 – On this night and into the early morning, a film crew shoots the *Double Fantasy* sessions for future promotional use, but the footage later disappears

Sunday 24 – Sean visits the studio to watch the sessions

September 1980

Topping the US singles chart:
"Upside Down" by Diana Ross

On the airwaves:
"Give Me The Night" by George Benson
"More Love" by Kim Carnes
"All Out Of Love" by Air Supply
Topping the US album chart: *Emotional Rescue* by the Rolling Stones

Albums released this month include:
Scary Monsters (and Super Creeps) by David Bowie
Nothing Matters (And What If It Did) by John Cougar
One Step Closer by the Doobie Brothers
Guilty by Barbra Streisand

Thursday 4 – Ringo begins recording with Ronnie Wood through the next four days at Devonshire Sound Studios

Wednesday 10 – John and Yoko begin a lengthy series of interviews with David Sheff for *Playboy*; the sessions wrap up by month's end

Thursday 11 – Yoko meets with label head David Geffen

Wednesday 17 – Quotes from an upcoming *Newsweek* interview with John are released to the press

Wednesday 17 – Following weeks of strikes at a Gdańsk, Poland shipyard, the trade union Solidarity is established

Thursday 18 – Journalist Robert Palmer interviews John for the *New York Times*
Monday 22 – A clip of Paul being interviewed by Tim Rice airs on *The John Davidson Show*, followed by the "Waterfalls" video

Monday 22 – John and Yoko sign a record deal with David Geffen

Tuesday 23 – George completes work on *Somewhere In England*

Tuesday 23 – Ringo resumes recording with Ronnie Wood for the next five days at Cherokee Studios in Los Angeles

Thursday 25 – Led Zeppelin drummer John Bonham dies of alcohol poisoning at 32

Monday 29 – The week's issue of *Newsweek* contains an interview with John, ruining the "exclusive" that David Sheff thought he had for *Playboy*

October 1980

Topping the US singles chart:
"Another One Bites The Dust" by Queen

On the airwaves:
"I'm Alright" by Kenny Loggins
"Real Love" by the Doobie Brothers
"Lookin' For Love" by Johnny Lee

Topping the US album chart:
The Game by Queen

Albums released this month include:
All Shook Up by Cheap Trick
Clues by Robert Palmer
The River by Bruce Springsteen and the E Street Band
Seconds of Pleasure by Rockpile
Making Movies by Dire Straits

October – The original release of George's *Somewhere in England* was slated for late this month, but objections from Warner Brothers push it back to June 1981

Thursday 2 – Paul begins rehearsing Wings on material that will end up on *Tug Of War*, an album that will be recorded without the band

Thursday 9 – John turns 40, Sean 5: Yoko hires a skywriter to post a message to them over New York City

Friday 10 – John is interviewed at the Hit Factory by Los Angeles rock critic Robert Hilburn

Monday 13 – A UK-only single record compilation, *The Beatles' Ballads*, is issued in a sleeve featuring artwork originally conceived for 1968's *The Beatles*

Monday 13 – John and Sean have a belated birthday celebration at Tavern on the Green

Thursday 16 – On this day and the next, EMI auctions off much equipment used by the Beatles and other artists at the Abbey Road Studios

Monday 20 – "(Just Like) Starting Over"/"Kiss Kiss Kiss" (Geffen 49604; peaks at #1 for five weeks in December/January 1981)

Monday 27 – 1976's *Rock 'N' Roll Music* compilation is reissued as a budget pressing (with new artwork) in two separate volumes

Thursday 30 – Wings assembles again to rehearse *Tug of War* material; only Denny Laine will appear on the finished album

Friday 31 – Wings lay down the backing tracks for "We All Stand Together" – a *Rupert the Bear* recording – at George Martin's A.I.R. studios; work will resume on November 4th

November 1980

Topping the US singles chart:
"Woman in Love" by Barbra Streisand
"Lady" by Kenny Rogers

On the airwaves:
"Dreaming" by Cliff Richard
"Drivin' My Life Away" by Eddie Rabbitt
"He's So Shy" by Pointer Sisters

Topping the US album chart:
Guilty by Barbra Streisand

Albums released this month include:
The Jazz Singer by Neil Diamond
Autoamerican by Blondie
Hi-Infidelity by REO Speedwagon
Gaucho by Steely Dan

November – John appears on the cover of this month's *Esquire*

Sunday 2 – John and Yoko are photographed by Jack Mitchell.

Tuesday 4 – Ringo records with Harry Nilsson at Evergreen Recording Studios in Burbank

Tuesday 4 –President Jimmy Carter is defeated for reelection by former California governor Ronald Reagan

Friday 14 – John demos his final new composition: "You Saved My Soul"

Saturday 15 – John and Ringo get together at the Plaza Hotel

Sunday 16 – Don Henley is arrested for possession of Quaaludes, marijuana, and cocaine, following the overdose of a 16 year-old in his hotel room

Monday 17 – *Double Fantasy* (peaks at number one for eight weeks beginning in December)

Wednesday 19 – Ringo begins recording at George's home studio, laying down tracks for his own upcoming album as well as "All Those Years Ago"

Friday 21 – John and Yoko are photographed in Central Park for promotional purposes

Friday 21 – "Who Shot JR?" is revealed on TV's *Dallas*

Saturday 22 – Actress Mae West dies at 87

Tuesday 25 – Ringo's sessions at George's Friar Park Studio Henley-on-Thames (F.P.S.H.O.T.) finish

Wednesday 26 – *Rockshow* premieres in New York, but Paul does not attend

Wednesday 26 – John and Yoko are filmed in Central Park; later, they're filmed/photographed in (and out of) kimonos; the footage ends up used in the videos for "Woman" and "Walking On Thin Ice"

Wednesday 26 – Ringo again meets with John at The Plaza on this Thanksgiving Eve; it's the last time they see each other

Thursday 27 – Thanksgiving Day: Paul and Linda are interviewed on *Good Morning America*

Friday 28 – Under oath, John gives a deposition asserting plans with the other three to reunite for a concert in conjunction with their sanctioned documentary entitled *The Long and Winding Road*

December 1980

Topping the US singles chart:
"Lady" by Kenny Roger
"(Just Like) Starting Over" by John Lennon

On the airwaves:
"Jesse" by Carly Simon
"Late In The Evening" by Paul Simon
"Whip It" by Devo

Topping the US album chart:
Guilty by Barbra Streisand

Albums released this month include:
Arc Of A Diver by Steve Winwood
Black Sea by XTC
Sandanista! by The Clash

Monday 1 – Ringo begins recording with Harry Nilsson in the Bahamas; sessions last through Friday

Wednesday 3 – *Soho News* features a cover story headlined "Yoko Only"

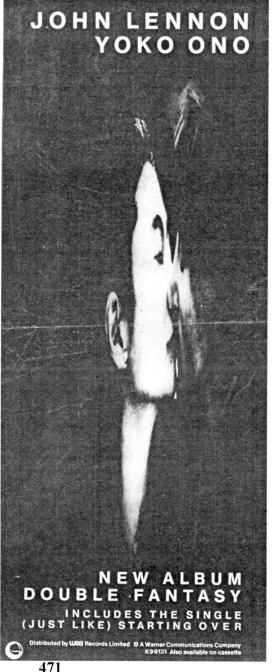

JOHN LENNON
YOKO ONO

NEW ALBUM
DOUBLE FANTASY
INCLUDES THE SINGLE
(JUST LIKE) STARTING OVER

Distributed by WEA Records Limited © A Warner Communications Company
K99131 Also available on cassette

Thursday 4 – The *McCartney Interview* LP is released (peaks at one hundred fifty-eight)

Friday 5 – John is interviewed by Jonathan Cott for *Rolling Stone*

Saturday 6 – John and Yoko are interviewed by the BBC's Andy Peebles

Saturday 6 – The January 1981 issue of *Playboy* containing the lengthy John and Yoko interview hits newsstands; the same issue features a nude pictorial of Barbara Bach

Sunday 7 – Paul's *Tug of War* sessions begin with the recording of "Ballroom Dancing"

Sunday 7 – Darby Crash of punk rock band The Germs fatally overdoses

Monday 8 – John and Yoko are photographed at the Dakota by Annie Leibovitz; later they're interviewed at the Dakota by staff from RKO radio

Monday 8 – John is shot and killed

Tuesday 9 – Paul, with George Martin and Denny Laine, attempts to work on "Rainclouds" before abandoning the effort

Tuesday 9 – George likewise tries to work through his grief in the studio ("Dream Away") but cannot

Tuesday 9 – Ringo and Barbara arrive at the Dakota to express their condolences; Julian arrives from Wales later that day

Tuesday 9 – A shell-shocked Jack Douglas and rock journalist Lisa Robinson appear on Tom Snyder's *Tomorrow* show to discuss the tragedy

Sunday 14 – Around the world, ten minutes of silence is observed as people gather in public places to mourn John; on US radio, some stations go silent while others play an agreed upon sequence of songs (in Chicago: "Imagine," "In My Life and "Come Together")

Saturday 20 – *Billboard* coverage of the tragedy includes a scathing remembrance from former Capitol exec Dave Dexter Jr.

Monday 22 – John appears on the cover of *Time*, *Newsweek*, *People* and *New York* magazine
Monday 29 – Tim Hardin ("Reason To Believe") fatally overdoses at 39

Tuesday 30 – A photo of John's corpse runs on the cover of the *National Enquirer*

ACKNOWLEDGEMENTS

I am grateful for all the support, input and commentary my readers have been offering these past few years, chiefly on Facebook (www. facebook.com/fabfourfaq2) but also in person: at The Fest in Chicago, as well as area library presentations. It is your tremendous enthusiasm, curiosity and devotion to the lives and careers of these four that has in turn stirred my curiosity and renewed energy. I have been writing about the Beatles now for some seven years: I never set out to be the guy that only writes about the group, but I have been fortunate to have a base that keeps me at work. Don't ever underestimate the value of what you give to me by your kind words, encouragement and "likes."

Occupying a more immediate role are the people making this new enterprise possible. First, my partner in literary crime, Richard Buskin. Also Julie Shamon, Gail Bravos, Frank Miranda and Thomas White. Colleagues past, present and future include Doug Brooks, Dave Hogan, Jamie Santoro, Chris Sienko, Dave Aretha, Jacque Day Pallone, Jim Slate. A huge note of thanks to Tom Repetny—an endlessly creative artist; as well as to Radio Hall of Famer and Chicago legend Terri Hemmert, who's been essential in helping get the word out.

Dan Miles and Al Sussman are key allies with something special to bring to the table. My many thanks those whose forums I've had a lot of fun with: the *Fab 4 Free 4 All* gang: Mitch Axelrod – Rob Leonard – Tony Traguardo. Also, Jude Southerland Kessler, Lanea Stagg, Dennis Mitchell, Joe Johnson, Tony Peters at *Icon Fetch*, Bruce Spizer, Jorie Gracen and Mario Novelli, Christie Springer, Casey Piotrowski, Ken Michaels, Jim Richards, Chris Carter, Mitch Michaels, Bart Shore; as well as those at *Beatlefan*: Bill King, Kit O'Toole, Tom Frangione, Howie Edelson, Brad Hundt, Rick Glover. In the local media: Marc Vitali at WTTW, as well as WGN's Dan Sugrue, Bill Leff and Nick Digilio. From *Rock Cellar* magazine: Jeff Cazanov and Greg Feo and from *Beatles Examiner*, Steve Marinucci. Charles Pekow, Barb Szemplinski, Susan Dienes, Karen Stoessel.

Other fellow travelers include (in no particular order): Rick Wey, Pete Pecoraro, Alan Goldsher, Charles Pekow, Barb Szemplinski, Susan Dienes, Karen Stoessel, Pat Korman, Mike Eder, Greg Alexander, Andrew Grant Jackson, Sean Murphy, Georgina Flood, Mark Caro, Mike Segretto, GiGi Monaco, Wally Podrazik, Rick Schlesinger, Jim Cherry,

Ken Sharp, John Niems, Allan and Paula Kozinn, Woody Lifton, Tina Kukla, Winona Patterson, TJ Shanoff, John Luerssen, Adam Phillips, Sandy Ann Perez, Stu Shea, Jeff Paszkiet, Barb Szemplinski, Craig and Terry Locaciato, Mark Clark, Bob Purse, Andy Gore, Jill Rodriguez, Susan Ratisher Ryan, Sarah Schmidt, Tom DeMichael, Verneann Swintek, Craig Cermak, Mike Sekulich. As always, the Lapidos family: Mark, Carol, Michelle, Jessica. In a class unto themselves: Kim Kupisch Brondyke, Sharon Basso-Mayes, Carole Walther, Kevin Wendorf, Mike Tau, Karen Parent, Brian Benac, Ed Walkwitz, Cindi Long, Ken Pieper.

There are those virtual supporters: far too many to call out each and every, but among them include Blaine Bowman, Richard W. Nason, Joseph Buckley, Vincent Vigil, Shirley Tulloch, Steve Petrica, Walzer Carluccio, Chelle Colling, Keith James, Jon Oye, Giuseppe Milella, Pete Nash, Barry Rudolph,James D. Jones, Gary Owen, Ed Rudy, Peggy Barry, Olivia Fuchs, Corey A. Wolf, Glen Boyd, Roger Stormo, Gustavo Machado, Sarah Mourad, Bu Castro, Terry Ott, Bootsy Bass, Kristen Hanlin, Gary Jucha, Eric Banister, Andy Vaughan, Ron Morgan, Aviva Rothschild, Raven Knight, Dorrit Takach, Keith Sluchansky, Robert Barnes, Joe Soccodato, Stephen K. Peeples, Todd Costa Rica, Wayne Cabral and Charlotte Taylor

Finally, the near and the dear ones: there's no escaping that writing and researching is an all-consuming preoccupation. (I'd like to think it isn't necessarily a wholly self-indulgent one but your mileage may vary.) I hope in the end that what the effort produces brings a certain amount of satisfaction to not just the creator, but also those in the orbit of its creation. My everlasting love and thanks to my families: the Rodriguezs and Holcombs, as well as Porters, Holopigians, Beans, Powells, Cervenkas, Antons, Hoopers, Hostetlers, The Butts, the Spedoskes, Frymans, Loks et al.

Mostly though, to those in my immediate proximity: Kati – Zane – Zoe.

A SELECTED BIBLIOGRAPHY

BOOKS

Andrews, Nancy Lee. *A Dose of Rock 'n' Roll*. Deerfield: Dalton Watson, 2008.

Badman, Keith. *The Beatles Off The Record 2: The Dream Is Over.* London: Omnibus, 2002.

Bielen, Ken, and Urish, Ben. *The Words and Music of John Lennon*. Santa Barbara: Praeger, 2007.

Boyd, Pattie and Junor, Penny. *Wonderful Today: The Autobiography*. London: Headline Review, 2007.

DiLello, Richard. *The Longest Cocktail Party: An Insider's Diary of the Beatle, Their Million Dollar "Apple" Empire, and Its Rise and Fall.* Chicago: Playboy Press, 1972.

Editors of *Rolling Stone*. *The Ballad of John and Yoko*. New York: Doubleday, 1982.

Editors of *Rolling Stone*. *Harrison*. New York: Simon and Schuster, 2002.

Greene, Joshua M. *Here Comes the Sun: The Spiritual and Musical Journey of George Harrison.* Hoboken: John Wiley and Sons, 2007.

Huntley, Elliot J. *Mystical One: George Harrison After the Break-up of the Beatles.* Toronto: Guernica Editions, 2004.

Kane, Larry. *Lennon Revealed*. London: Running Press Book Publishers, 2005.

Leng, Simon. *While My Guitar Gently Weeps: The Music of George Harrison.* Milwaukee, WI: Hal Leonard, 2006.

McGee, Garry. *Band on the Run: A History of Paul McCartney and Wings.* Lanham, MD: Taylor Trade, 2003.

Miles, Barry. *Paul McCartney: Many Years From Now.* New York, New York: Henry Holt and Company, 1997.

Norman, Philip. *John Lennon: The Life*. New York: Ecco, 2008.

Pang, May. *Instamatic Karma: Photographs of John Lennon.* New York: St. Martin's Press, 2008.

Pang, May, and Edwards, Henry. *Loving John: The Untold Story.* New York: Warner Books, 1983.

Paytress, Mark. *Bolan: The Rise and Fall of a 20th Century Superstar.* London: Music Sales, 2007.

Piper, Jorg and McCarthy, Ian. *The Solo Beatles Film & TV Chronicle.* Lulu, 2013.

Ribowsky, Mark. *He's A Rebel: Phil Spector, Rock and Roll's Legendary Producer.* New York: Cooper Square press, 1989.

Rodriguez, Robert, and Shea, Stuart. *Fab Four FAQ.* Milwaukee, WI: Hal Leonard, 2007.

Rodriguez, Robert. *Fab Four FAQ 2.0.* Milwaukee, WI: Backbeat, 2010.

Rodriguez, Robert. *Revolver: How the Beatles Re-Imagined Rock 'n' Roll.* Milwaukee, WI: Backbeat, 2012.

Sandford, Christopher. *McCartney.* New York, New York: Carroll and Graf, 2006.

Spizer, Bruce. *The Beatles Solo on Apple Records.* New Orleans: 498 Productions, 2005.

Sulpy, Doug, and Schweighart, Ray. *Get Back: The Unauthorized Chronicle of the Beatles' "Let It Be" Disaster.* New York, New York: St. Martin's Griffin, 1999.

Wiener, Jon. *Come Together: John Lennon In His Time.* New York: Random House, 1984.

PERIODICALS

Beatlefan (1978-present)
Billboard (1968-1981)
Circus (1969-1981)
Crawdaddy (1970-1977)
Creem (1970-1980)
Disc (1971-1973)
Discoveries (1995-2000)
Goldmine (1988-present)
Hit Parader (1970-1980)
Melody Maker (1969-1980)
Modern Drummer (1981-1987)
Mojo (1995-present)
Musician (1980-1984)
National Lampoon (1973-1977)
New Musical Express (1970-1980)
People (1975-1988)
Playboy (January 1981)
Rolling Stone (1969-present)
Song Hits (1977-1981)
Trouser Press (1977-1981)
Uncut (2000-present)

WEBSITES
Too many to list fully; just check out Revolverbook.com and

Listen to the podcast at SomethingabouttheBeatles.com

https://www.facebook.com/fabfourfaq2

Also: Paradingpress.com
TWITTER
@Fabfourfaq2

Index

CPSIA information can be obtained at www.ICGtesting.com
Printed in the USA
BVOW04s1007070514

352841BV00012B/288/P